Southern Biography Series

Bertram Wyatt-Brown, Series Editor

Andrew Jackson Donelson in the mid-1850s.

Courtesy The Hermitage: Home of President Andrew Jackson, Nashville, TN

Mark R. Cheathem

OLD HICKORY'S NEPHEW

THE POLITICAL AND PRIVATE STRUGGLES OF ANDREW JACKSON DONELSON

LOUISIANA STATE UNIVERSITY PRESS
BATON ROUGE

Published by Louisiana State University Press

Manufactured in the United States of America
First printing

Designer: Amanda McDonald Scallon
Typeface: Minion
Typesetter: Newgen
Printer and binder: Edwards Brothers, Inc.

Library of Congress Cataloging-in-Publication Data

Cheathem, Mark Renfred.
Old Hickory's nephew : the political and private struggles of Andrew Jackson Donelson / Mark R. Cheathem.
p. cm. — (Southern biography series)
Includes bibliographical references and index.
ISBN-13: 978-0-8071-3238-8 (cloth : alk. paper)
1. Donelson, Andrew Jackson, 1799–1871. 2. Jackson, Andrew, 1767–1845—Friends and associates. 3. Politicians—United States—Biography. 4. United States—Politics and government—1815–1861. 5. Political parties—United States—History—19th century. 6. Jackson, Andrew, 1767–1845—Family. 7. Nephews—United States—Biography. 8. Plantation owners—Southern States—Biography. I. Title.
E382.1.D57C48 2007
973.5′6092—dc22
[B]

2006024951

The paper in this book meets the guidelines for permanence and durability of the Committee on Production Guidelines for Book Longevity of the Council on Library Resources. ♾

For my teachers, Mrs. Catogge,
Mr. Hamby, and Dr. Farris,
and my mentors, Monty Pope,
Fred Rolater, and John Marszalek

CONTENTS

ACKNOWLEDGMENTS

I first became acquainted with Andrew Jackson Donelson in 1995, when I was working as a docent at the Hermitage. Part of my duties included giving tours of Tulip Grove, Donelson's home; it was telling his story there that sent me down the path resulting in the book presently before you.

Despite my personal interest in Donelson, I could not have recounted his life without the help of numerous colleagues along the way. Any errors or omissions are in spite of, not because of, their assistance. At Louisiana State University Press, Rand Dotson, Bertram Wyatt-Brown, and the anonymous second reader made this process easier than I could have imagined. Karin Kaufman did an extraordinary job as copy editor, for which I am grateful. With their extensive knowledge about Old Hickory, C. Monty Pope and Fred S. Rolater guided me during my very earliest forays into the Jacksonian period. Richard B. Latner was gracious enough to serve on my dissertation committee, and his comments greatly influenced my thinking about Donelson. Connie L. Lester exhibited tremendous patience and thoroughness in reading many early drafts of this book. She is a teacher in every sense of the word. My graduate advisor, John F. Marszalek, made me a better scholar and continues to influence my writing.

In addition to the above, the following people contributed their time by reading pieces of the manuscript in its various stages, listening to me argue for Donelson's importance, and offering their critique of my contentions: Thomas P. Anderson, Jonathan M. Atkins, Tom Boschert, Donald B. Cole, Daniel Feller, Buck T. Foster, Russell Fowler, the late Shannon Mallard, Andrew S. Moore, William E. Parrish, Mark Reeder, William J. Rorabaugh, Clifford Ryan, and Matthew S. Warshauer. Several others gave substantial help with research questions. Dr. Andrew Jackson Donelson Jr. was kind enough to share his knowledge of Donelson family history, while Johnny Summers drove me out to what remains of the old Donelson home in Bolivar County. Marsha Mullin and Tony Guzzi at the Hermitage were prompt, courteous, patient, and thorough in answering my queries about small details. Doug Spence, who is also working on a biography of Donelson, was more generous than I could have expected in sharing his thoughts and even research notes about certain aspects of Donelson's life.

Staff members at the Tennessee State Library and Archives, Vanderbilt University's Heard Library, the Library of Congress, Milwaukee County Historical Society, National Archives II, the State University of New York–Oswego's Penfield Library, the University of Tennessee–Knoxville's Hoskins Library, and the Historical Society of Pennsylvania also made my task easier. Special recognition goes to Brenda Valentine at Mississippi State University's Mitchell Memorial Library and Debbie Wilcox and Barbara Hickok at Southern New Hampshire University's Shapiro Library for their attention to my many interlibrary loan requests and book orders.

This book also benefited from institutional and organizational support. The history department and School of Arts and Sciences at Mississippi State University funded my research through travel grants and a dissertation fellowship. The Vice President for Academic Affairs office at Southern New Hampshire University awarded me a summer research grant to complete revisions to the manuscript. Both the Tennessee Historical Society and the White House Historical Association awarded me research fellowships during the dissertation stage.

I would be remiss if I also did not remember those who influenced my professional and personal lives during this journey. These include Jerry Brookshire, Ren Crowell, James Dressler, Bob Hunt, Janice Leone, Elizabeth Nybakken, and Thad Smith. These families in the Southside and Broadmoor communities were a great encouragement: the Carmans, the Culvers, the Littles, the McReynolds, the Nelsons, the Pearsons, the Sharps, the Smiths, the Taylors, the Thompsons, and the Wrights.

My family has provided stability throughout this process. I could not have asked for better in-laws than Layne and Dot Livingston, who were instrumental in helping me achieve my professional goals. My parents, Danny and Brenda, my sister, Lisa, and my aunt, Wanda, have always believed in and encouraged me; I appreciate them. My wife, Amber, has been very supportive and understanding when I have given my time and energy to the various stages of completing this book. I appreciate her constant reminder that life is about more than books. Our two girls, Laney and Allison, prefer that I spend my time on activities that involve ladybugs, bunnies, and swings. I hope that when they read this one day, they will realize that my time with them was a welcome and pleasant diversion from my professional life.

Finally, the individuals listed on the dedication page influenced me in significant ways. More than just educators, they taught me something about life; words are not adequate to express my gratitude.

ABBREVIATIONS

AJ Andrew Jackson
AJD Andrew Jackson Donelson
AJJr. Andrew Jackson Jr.
BDP Bettie M. Donelson Papers, Tennessee State Library and Archives, Nashville
CAJ *Correspondence of Andrew Jackson*
CJKP *Correspondence of James K. Polk*
DLC Andrew Jackson Donelson Papers, Library of Congress, Washington, D.C.
DPL Prussian Letterbook, Andrew Jackson Donelson Papers, Library of Congress, Washington, D.C.
DSA Department of State Archives, National Archives II, College Park, Md.
DSD Daniel Smith Donelson
DTL Andrew Jackson Donelson Papers, Tennessee State Library and Archives, Nashville
DUT Andrew Jackson Donelson Papers, James D. Hoskins Library, University of Tennessee, Knoxville
ERD Elizabeth Martin Randolph Donelson
ETD Emily Tennessee Donelson
FPB Francis Preston Blair
JAW John A. Wilcox
JB James Buchanan
JBP James Buchanan Papers, Historical Society of Pennsylvania, Philadelphia
JCC John C. Calhoun
JCM John C. McLemore
JDC Andrew Jackson–Jackson Donelson Collection, Joint University Libraries, Nashville

JHE	John Henry Eaton
JKP	James K. Polk
JLC	Andrew Jackson Papers, Library of Congress, Washington, D.C.
JMC	James M. Calhoun
JSR	Andrew Jackson Papers, Scholarly Resources, Wilmington, Del.
MED	Mary Emily Donelson (Wilcox)
MF	Millard Fillmore
MVB	Martin Van Buren
NPT	Nicholas P. Trist
NPTP	Nicholas P. Trist Papers, Library of Congress, Washington, D.C.
PAJ	*The Papers of Andrew Jackson*
PJCC	*The Papers of John C. Calhoun*
PLC	James K. Polk Papers, Library of Congress, Washington, D.C.
RDC	Robert Dyas Collection, Tennessee State Library and Archives, Nashville
SH	Sam Houston
SHL	Samuel H. Laughlin
TDH	Tennessee Documentary Project, James D. Hoskins Library, University of Tennessee, Knoxville
THQ	*Tennessee Historical Quarterly*
VBC	Martin Van Buren Papers (Chadwyck-Healey Collection), Library of Congress, Washington, D.C.
VBL	Martin Van Buren Papers, Library of Congress, Washington, D.C.
WBL	William Berkeley Lewis

OLD HICKORY'S NEPHEW

INTRODUCTION

"Again has death visited our land and taken from us a citizen distinguished for his talent and the high position he has enjoyed before the country," the *Memphis Daily Appeal* announced in June 1871. The editors of the Tennessee newspaper lauded Andrew Jackson Donelson's service to the nation, praising him for having "been prominently before the public, [and] intimately connected with many of the great events" of the past fifty years. They noted, however, that a "long political career of mingled prosperity and adversity, had somewhat soured the impulses of a naturally amiable nature"; nevertheless, "Major Donelson was loved and honored by even those whom he goaded with his biting sarcasm."[1]

The accuracy of the obituary was uncanny. Andrew Jackson's nephew and namesake had indeed lived a life interwoven with nineteenth-century American history. Known primarily as Jackson's protégé, Donelson participated in the construction of the Jacksonian Democrats both before and after his uncle's elevation to the presidency, was considered for cabinet positions under two later presidents, accepted diplomatic appointments in Texas and Europe, obtained political patronage in the form of the editorship of a national Democratic newspaper, and received the vice-presidential nomination of a major political party. At the state and local levels, Donelson was intimately involved in the Tennessee political scene, both in Davidson County, where he maintained residency most of his life, and Shelby County, where he lived out the last years of his life. Donelson's personal life also thrived. He and his two wives, Emily, who died in 1836, and Elizabeth, whom he married in 1841, had twelve children. He owned several plantations during his lifetime, including Tulip Grove, just a short distance from Andrew Jackson's home, the Hermitage, and land in Mississippi and Arkansas. To any observer, Andrew Jackson Donelson was a successful politician,

1. *Memphis Daily Appeal,* 27 June 1871.

husband, father, and planter who had achieved the prosperity attributed to him when he died.

The *Daily Appeal* obituary also hinted at other, less sanguine aspects of Donelson's life, however. His relationship with his famous uncle was tense for years; it appeared that Jackson had little confidence in his nephew's political skills beyond the completion of pedestrian tasks. Other politicians also seemed to look askance at Donelson's abilities. As a diplomat, Donelson successfully helped bring about the annexation of the Republic of Texas, but his mission to Germany was a disappointment. His editorship of the *Washington Union,* a Democratic newspaper, ended disastrously when the party leadership forced him out. Disenchanted with the Democrats, Donelson turned to the Know-Nothing, or American, party, which unsuccessfully attempted to win the 1856 presidential election with him as Millard Fillmore's running mate. Donelson later joined the Constitutional Union party, which ultimately failed to prevent the Civil War.

Donelson witnessed even more misfortune in his personal life. Some of his trials, such as Emily's death at the age of twenty-nine and that of his children, two of whom died in violent circumstances, were beyond his control. In situations that he could manage, particularly regarding finances, however, Donelson frequently made foolish choices. His plantations never turned the profit that he predicted, an outcome he blamed on every conceivable reason except his own financial ineptitude and ignorance of farming. Donelson not only borrowed money from family, friends, and politicians to maintain his plantations but also avoided repaying the loans, repeatedly ignoring requests for payment until he had exhausted the creditors' patience. Donelson's economic problems also affected his public life, as he often absented himself from his diplomatic and political positions to take care of his finances.

Donelson's life, with all of its successes and disappointments, sheds light on several important aspects of nineteenth-century America. It helps us to understand better the expectations placed upon young southern men in prominent families and the complexities and contradictions of southern honor, masculinity, and kinship, which often determined these expectations. Examining Donelson's ideology also reveals what many antebellum southern politicians found normal but what we now find ironic: supporting the enslavement of African Americans while arguing passionately for the preservation of American liberty. Historians have also long debated how much influence Jackson had on those around him, and Donelson's career gives unique insight into that area. Finally, his life demonstrates the turmoil that many antebellum politicians faced in trying to differentiate themselves from previous generations and prove their own worth. For Donelson, the party divisions and sectionalism that preceded the Civil War were symbolic of the internal divisions that he himself felt about Jackson and his place in American political life.

In sum, Donelson experienced a life of struggles, one marked by the highs and lows of the human experience. Having a famous name was often a benefit, but sometimes a detriment, to advancing his political and private fortunes. Fairly or unfairly, contemporaries and historians alike judged Donelson's successes and failures by comparing him to Andrew Jackson. It is my hope that this biography gives Donelson his own identity and serves to awaken interest in the contributions that he made to American history.

Part 1

HONOR, LOYALTY, AND DUTY

Cheers rang from the raucous crowd as Andrew Jackson was introduced. A group of college students, prominent politicians, and local well-wishers had gathered around the steps of Nashville's courthouse on this sunny May afternoon in 1815 to welcome home the Hero of New Orleans. As the crowd quieted, Jackson thanked them for their enthusiastic response. His speech, which emphasized the success of American virtue in the recent victory over the corrupt British empire, also included words of encouragement for the young men at Cumberland College, who had gathered with the jubilant throng. He prompted them to pursue their academic endeavors in order to "[fulfill] the high expectations of [their] relatives and friends." When Jackson finished speaking, he bowed and strode off the stage, the crowd roaring its approval of the man and his words. As Old Hickory basked in the huzzahs, his nephew, fifteen-year-old Andrew Jackson Donelson, glowed with pride. A student at Cumberland College, Donelson had joined with his fellow classmates to salute his uncle's return. As Jackson waved to the crowd one final time, the cheering increased. Donelson enthusiastically added to the volume, his uncle's advice and the people's ovation ringing in his ears.[1]

1. AJ's speech to Cumberland College students, 15 May 1815, in James Parton, *Life of Andrew Jackson*, 3 vols. (New York: Mason Brothers, 1861), 2:329–30; and Pauline Wilcox Burke, *Emily Donelson of Tennessee*, ed. Jonathan M. Atkins (Knoxville: University of Tennessee Press, 2001) (hereafter cited as Atkins, *Emily Donelson*), 47.

1

"Never My Son, Outlive Your Honour"

Born in Sumner County, Tennessee, on 25 August 1799, Andrew Jackson Donelson came from prominent family stock. The Donelson family first came to North America from Scotland in 1716, when Patrick Donelson and his son, John, settled in the colony of Maryland. John married Catherine Davis, the daughter of a local Presbyterian pastor, and their union produced two children, John and Mary. Born at some point between 1718 and 1725, this younger John Donelson (Andrew's paternal grandfather and often referred to by the title colonel) moved to Virginia in 1744, where he became a successful land surveyor and planter. He married Rachel Stockley, the daughter of another successful Virginian; together, they had eleven children, born between approximately 1749 and 1773. Their ninth child, Samuel, was born about 1770; he was Andrew's father.[1]

Colonel John Donelson was noted for his political service in support of the American Revolution and for his desire to help the colony of Virginia expand its western landholdings. The military conflict with Great Britain and its native allies, however, depleted Donelson's finances and led him to accept an offer to help North Carolinian James Robertson survey land and establish permanent settlements in Middle Tennessee, which they did in the winter of 1779–80. Colonel Donelson initially located his family at a home several miles north of present-day Nashville, but Native American attacks

1. Pauline Wilcox Burke, *Emily Donelson of Tennessee*, 2 vols. (Richmond, Va.: Garrett and Massie, 1941) (hereafter cited as Burke, *Emily Donelson*), 1:3–15; and Richard Douglas Spence, "John Donelson and the Opening of the Old Southwest," *THQ* 50 (Fall 1991): 162–9. Unless noted otherwise, genealogical information on AJD and members of his family comes from the various Andrew Jackson Donelson collections and papers; Pauline Wilcox Burke's biography of Emily Tennessee Donelson; Marsha Mullin and Tony Guzzi, curator and former assistant curator at the Hermitage in Nashville, Tennessee; and Andrew Jackson Donelson Jr. of Bowling Green, Kentucky.

convinced him to move to Harrodsburg, Kentucky, in 1780. His death in 1786 while on a surveying trip compelled his widow, Rachel Stockley Donelson, to return the family to the now-safer confines of the Nashville settlement.[2]

Andrew's maternal grandfather, Daniel Smith, was born in Stafford County, Virginia, in 1748. The Smith family probably emigrated to the United States from England sometime before 1715, the year Daniel's father, Henry, was likely born. Daniel's mother, Sarah Crosby, was born sometime around 1718. Her ancestry presumably was English as well; her parents' families seem to have settled in the colony of Virginia by the mid-seventeenth century. As an older teenager, Daniel Smith moved west to Albemarle County to study medicine and, perhaps, law. Neither of those professions suited him, apparently, so he received training in land surveying. In 1773, he married Sarah "Sallie" Michie, whose family probably hailed from Maryland, and moved with her to Fincastle County, Virginia.[3]

During the American Revolution, Smith achieved the rank of brigadier general, having joined the local militia upon locating in the Clinch River region. His battlefield experience was limited; Smith spent most of the war surveying and serving in other public positions. In April 1781, Sallie gave birth to their second child, a daughter they named Mary Ann Michie. Daniel's reputation continued to grow, and as a result, he was one of five men appointed in 1784 to survey and establish the town of Nashville. He moved his family from East Tennessee, where they had been living, to the new settlement in Middle Tennessee that same year.[4]

The flourishing romance between Andrew's parents, Samuel Donelson and Mary Ann Michie Smith, eventually united these two prominent families. Born in 1770, Samuel was the fifth son of John and Rachel Donelson. As an up-and-coming lawyer and politician, he would have made a good match for many young frontier women. Judge Joseph Anderson, who would later serve as a U.S. senator from Tennessee, called Samuel "one of the Cleverest young fellows I ever was acquainted with, and whose principles and Mental Virtues do Honor to human nature." Samuel was also a slave owner

2. Burke, *Emily Donelson* 1:3–15; and Spence, "John Donelson," 162–9.

3. Burke, *Emily Donelson* 1:3–15; and Walter T. Durham, *Daniel Smith: Frontier Statesman* (Gallatin, Tenn.: Sumner County Library Board, 1976), 1–18.

4. Durham, *Daniel Smith,* 19–92.

and large landholder, owning at least four slaves from his deceased father's estate and perhaps as many as 1,174 acres of land in Davidson, Sumner, and Wilson Counties. Mary Ann Michie Smith, or Polly, as she was called, certainly believed that he would make a fine companion. Unfortunately for fifteen-year-old Polly, her father thought otherwise. Daniel Smith planned to send her away to relatives living in Philadelphia who would provide her with access to a good education and, not surprisingly, keep her far away from young Samuel. His plan came to naught, however, when the two young lovers eloped in 1796. Smith was none too pleased and resorted to "pouting," as one Tennessean put it, a posture that disappeared once the couple's first child, John Samuel Donelson, was born the following year.[5]

Samuel and Polly Donelson had found help for their secret elopement in the person of Andrew Jackson. Originally from the Waxhaws region of the Carolinas, Jackson, a lawyer, had moved to Nashville as a member of a law-enforcement delegation intent on protecting the area from Spanish influence. Jackson, along with several other young men, had taken up residence at the widow Donelson's blockhouse, arriving in the midst of a family crisis. The youngest Donelson daughter, Rachel Donelson Robards, and her husband, Lewis Robards, were having marital difficulties. Their marriage suffered from Rachel's flirtatious nature and Lewis's fits of jealousy. They separated, then reconciled. When Jackson moved into the widow Donelson's house, his presence only exacerbated an already deteriorating situation. The emotional and, perhaps, physical chemistry between Jackson and Mrs. Robards seemed obvious from the start. After several heated exchanges with Jackson over the attention the newcomer was paying to his wife, Robards moved back to Kentucky in disgust. He petitioned the Virginia legislature for a divorce in late 1790 but did not receive the final decree until 27 September 1793.[6]

5. Ibid., 201–3; Burke, *Emily Donelson* 1:23–6, 28; and inventory, appraisal, and division of John Donelson's estate, 28 January and 15 April 1791, Elisha Rice to AJ and Samuel Donelson, 15 May 1795 (two land warrants), Joseph Anderson to AJ, 3 December 1795, State of North Carolina to AJ and Samuel Donelson, 7 March 1796 (two land warrants), AJ to Samuel Donelson, [c. June 1796], and Joseph Anderson to AJ, 4 August 1796, in Sam B. Smith and Harriet Chappell Owsley, eds., *The Papers of Andrew Jackson,* vol. 1, *1770–1803* (Knoxville: University of Tennessee Press, 1980), 425–7, 439, 77–8, 441, 92–3, 97–8.

6. Robert V. Remini, *Andrew Jackson and the Course of American Empire, 1767–1821* (New York: Harper and Row, 1977), 41–4, 57–62. Remini suggests that Robards was guilty of adultery and perhaps even violent behavior toward Rachel.

In the meantime, Jackson and Rachel Robards went to the Natchez settlement, located in Spanish territory, ostensibly to protect her from her husband's threats to force a return to Kentucky. What actually happened in Natchez is still debated. Some historians claim that Jackson and Rachel were married in Natchez, while others wonder if they were not already married by the time they made the trip. What is known is that the couple, once they returned to Nashville, presented themselves as married for the next two years and expressed shock when they discovered that Robards's divorce from Rachel had not been granted until late 1793. After first denying the necessity of another wedding ceremony, Jackson eventually relented to the pressure of a good friend, John Overton, and agreed to "remarry" his wife. That ceremony, conducted by Rachel's brother-in-law, Robert Hays, took place in Nashville on 18 January 1794.[7]

Knowing something about the problems of romance, then, Andrew and Rachel Jackson had been happy to assist Samuel, who was Rachel's brother, and Polly in eloping, allowing them to take their wedding vows at their home, Hunter's Hill. Jackson and Samuel Donelson had already struck up a friendship that led them in 1795 to open a trading store along the Cumberland River. They also collaborated on several land deals, and Jackson even supported Donelson's unsuccessful bid for a state attorney general position.[8]

Donelson and Jackson remained close, so much so that when the former died of pneumonia in 1804, Jackson acted as the executor of Samuel's estate and the caretaker of his three sons: John Samuel, Andrew Jackson, and Daniel Smith, born in 1801. General Smith, who reportedly had been angry with Jackson for helping Samuel and Polly elope, expressed his gratitude to Jackson for his "beneficent disposition" and "friendship and benevolence"

7. Ibid., 57–69; and Harriet Chappell Owsley, "The Marriage of Rachel Donelson," *THQ* 36 (Winter 1977): 479–92. Owsley and Remini differ over the plausible date of the marriage. Owsley offers the February 1791 date as the only reasonable time for the marriage, while Remini, after examining several possible scenarios, indicates that the marriage likely occurred between July and October 1790.

8. Burke, *Emily Donelson* 1:23–6, 28; Robert Beeler Satterfield, *Andrew Jackson Donelson: Jackson's Confidant and Political Heir* (Bowling Green, Ky: Hickory Tales, 2000), 2–3; Remini, *Course of American Empire,* 88, 161; and John Overton to AJ, 8 March 1795, account of expenses, May–August 1795, Elisha Rice to AJ and Samuel Donelson, 15 May 1795 (two land warrants), Samuel Donelson to AJ, 29 June 1795, AJ to William Blount, 29 February 1796, State of North Carolina to AJ and Samuel Donelson, 7 March 1796 (two land warrants), AJ to Samuel Donelson, [c. June 1796], in Smith and Owsley, *PAJ* 1:54, 58–9, 439, 62–3, 82–3, 441, 92–3.

in helping his widowed daughter and her three sons. Unfortunately, no descriptions of the lives of Andrew Jackson Donelson and his brothers exist from this period. It seems certain that the Jacksons, who were and remained childless, enjoyed the presence of the Donelson children. Undoubtedly, the three boys liked living with Uncle Andrew and Aunt Rachel and playing with the several other children for whom the Jacksons were also caring.[9]

All was not idyllic for young Andrew Donelson and his brothers, however. Losing their father was a tremendous blow that the boys had difficulty accepting. Not long after Samuel's death, local men began calling on the young widow. With their father only recently in the grave, the Donelson boys resented these amorous advances toward their mother and her complicity in them. Their reaction was likely born out of immaturity and emotional pain, as remarriage was a common occurrence for both widows and widowers alike. Andrew particularly rebelled. According to family legend, he cut the saddle stirrups of one beau, a wealthy planter nicknamed "Jimmy Dry," who had an interest in his mother. Probably at Polly's request, a family friend, James Sanders, whipped Andrew for his mischief, which only served to increase the young boy's resentment.[10]

The situation only worsened when, in 1806, Polly married this same James Sanders. From Polly's viewpoint, Sanders was a good catch. He was a Sumner County planter who had served as a North Carolina land surveyor in Middle Tennessee and, in 1801, had been elected as a senator to the Tennessee legislature. He offered the social status and marital stability that Polly had lacked since Samuel's death. He was also one of Daniel Smith's old friends. When Sanders proposed to Polly, her father urged her to accept, which she did, much to her sons' chagrin.[11]

The marriage between James Sanders and Polly Donelson proved troublesome to Jackson. He and Sanders had been longtime acquaintances, but in 1807, word reached Jackson that Sanders had allegedly accused him of committing treason by supporting Aaron Burr's conspiracy to set up an

9. Burke, *Emily Donelson* 1:23–6, 28; Atkins, *Emily Donelson,* 33–6; Satterfield, *Jackson's Confidant,* 2–3; Durham, *Daniel Smith,* 235; Remini, *Course of American Empire,* 160–1; and account, 28 May–9 July 1804, in Harold D. Moser, Sharon Macpherson, and Charles F. Bryan Jr., eds., *The Papers of Andrew Jackson,* vol. 2, *1804–1813* (Knoxville: University of Tennessee Press, 1984), 24.

10. Atkins, *Emily Donelson,* 75–6.

11. Durham, *Daniel Smith,* 89, 210, 235–6; and Atkins, *Emily Donelson,* 75–6.

independent southwestern empire. Jackson angrily dashed off a letter in which he challenged Sanders "to give testimony to the world, that I am this base charector, or atone for the injury." Jackson warned him to expect violence if his honor was not satisfied. "I have one life to loose," he remarked, "[and] by the gods I never will permit such an attempt to assassinate my reputation go unpunished." Sanders hastily wrote his angry friend back, assuring Jackson that he had been mistaken about Sanders's true words.[12]

The tension between the two men grew over the next few years and seems to have been centered, at least in part, on Sanders's treatment of the oldest Donelson boy, John Samuel. In 1809, Jackson sent a letter to Sanders in which he related John Samuel Donelson's complaint that his stepfather was mistreating him. John had told his mother and stepfather that Jackson had ordered him to disobey his mother. More than likely, he was simply trying to stay out of trouble by pitting the authority figures in his life against one another, as children sometimes do. Sanders, however, had scolded John and told him that his Uncle Andrew "had no wright to give Such Orders." John conveyed the message to Jackson, who threatened to beat Sanders with a cowhide for undermining his authority. Sanders dismissed the warning with one of his own. "I fear not your threats nor cow hide," he wrote Jackson, "and in your weay of giving advice, I causion you to be a ware [*sic*] how you youse you[r] cow hide, or it may fall never to rise."[13]

Apparently, nothing more came of the incident, but the open hostility between Jackson and Sanders only encouraged the Donelson boys' rebelliousness and greatly influenced their conception of paternal authority. Later in life, Andrew and Daniel expressed great resentment toward Sanders, accusing him of marrying their mother solely to increase his landholdings. Their perception of Jackson, on the other hand, was overwhelmingly positive. His charisma, protectiveness, and personal attention to Andrew and his brothers endeared him to them.

Jackson's ability to inspire their confidence and loyalty comes as no surprise. He seemed to have that effect on many young men during his life. Jackson embodied the traits of a successful southern gentleman, although he had not been born into that class. He strove to be a man of republican

12. AJ to James Sanders, [c. 13 January 1807], and James Sanders to AJ, 13 January 1807, in Moser, Macpherson, and Bryan, *PAJ* 2:145–6, 146–7.

13. James Sanders to AJ, 26 March 1809, in ibid.

virtue who held the nation and its Constitution dear and defended it at all costs. Jackson also attempted to uphold a personal code of honor, which was influenced in part by his regional and class identity. That honor sometimes led to violence, which was not unusual in the South, but it also engendered unquestioned loyalty among those who supported him and his reputation with the same fierce devotion. He was, as well, a man of ambition. From humble origins in the Carolinas, where he had lost every member of his immediate family, Jackson had used his extended family and political connections to advance his career in North Carolina. By linking himself with the Donelson clan, arguably the most prominent family in Tennessee, he had enhanced both his political and personal worth. Jackson had secured his position and reputation in elite southern society and, like any good southern father, looked to bestow those benefits on his progeny. Unable to produce his own children, however, he had to look elsewhere for a worthy protégé.[14]

Determined to give his wards, including the Donelson boys, better opportunities than he had possessed, Jackson provided them with access to a proper education. When the Donelson boys were younger, he enlisted the aid of two local tutors, William Ballard and John Caldwell. As they grew older, something more was needed. Young Andrew showed enough promise that Jackson entered him into Nashville's Cumberland College, at that time one of the best schools in the West. Its president, noted classical scholar James Priestley, had been a well-respected educator in Kentucky and Maryland before coming to Tennessee in 1809.[15]

Donelson's specific experiences at Cumberland College are unknown, since none of his correspondence from that period survives. One may surmise from contemporary accounts, however, that he spent his time there in several of the classes that Priestley taught, which included mathematics,

14. Lorman Ratner highlights the importance of reputation to Jackson in his *Andrew Jackson and His Tennessee Lieutenants: A Study in Political Culture* (Westport, Conn.: Greenwood Press, 1997), chap. 2. Other recent works that provide fascinating insight into Jackson's younger years and relationships with those around him include Hendrik Booraem, *Young Hickory: The Making of Andrew Jackson* (Dallas: Taylor, 2001) and Andrew Burstein, *The Passions of Andrew Jackson* (New York: Knopf, 2003).

15. William Ballard to AJ, 24 March 1807, William Ballard's receipts to AJ, 3 January 1808, and AJ's account with John Caldwell, 25 April 1808, in Moser, Macpherson, and Bryan, *PAJ* 2:546, 550, 552; Alfred L. Crabb, "James Priestley, Pioneer School Master," *THQ* 12 (June 1953): 129–34; and John H. Thweatt, "James Priestley, Classical Scholar of the Old South," *THQ* 39 (Winter 1980): 423–39.

moral philosophy, rhetoric, logic, and natural philosophy. Donelson also likely enjoyed the camaraderie of his classmates, some of whom became prominent state and national politicians. Ephraim H. Foster, for example, later served as United States senator from Tennessee and helped found the state's Whig party. Another classmate, John Bell, who also served in the United States Senate, was one of Jackson's early supporters, although he eventually defected to the Whigs and antagonized Jackson and Donelson for many years. (Ironically, in 1860, the Constitutional Union party nominated Bell as its party presidential contender, and Donelson was one of his most vocal Tennessee supporters.) Cave Johnson, who eventually served as postmaster general in James K. Polk's cabinet and with whom Donelson worked closely over the years in state politics, was also at Cumberland College during these years. Donelson, in fact, may have participated in the student body strike in 1813 that began over the dismissal of Johnson and another student, both of whom balked at following the required curriculum. An unfortunate dispute with the state of Tennessee over funding for educational institutions led Priestley to resign his post at Cumberland College in 1816, and without his leadership, the school closed later that year—though not before Donelson had graduated.[16]

With Donelson having finished his studies at Cumberland College, Jackson determined that his nephew should receive a strong military education as well. Therefore, he prepared to secure Donelson's appointment to the United States Military Academy at West Point. Obtaining a military education was very important to Jackson, as evidenced by the attendance at West Point of several of his wards, including Edward G. W. Butler, who was already at the academy when Donelson arrived, and Andrew Donelson's brother, Daniel, who would attend in the early 1820s. The transition from classical studies to military training was not unusual for aspiring southern cadets, and Andrew Donelson's reasons for attending were clear. Jackson, who had made a name for himself as a soldier, wanted his nephew to receive

16. Burke, *Emily Donelson* 1:29–30, 50; Robert Beeler Satterfield, "Andrew Jackson Donelson: A Moderate Nationalist Jacksonian" (Ph.D. diss., Johns Hopkins University, 1961), 5–6; Crabb, "James Priestley," 129–34; Thweatt, "James Priestley," 423–39; John E. Windrow, ed., *Peabody and Alfred Leland Crabb: The Story of Peabody as Reflected in Selected Writings of Alfred Leland Crabb* (Nashville: Williams Press, 1977), 227; and C. L. Grant, "The Public Career of Cave Johnson," *THQ* 10 (September 1951): 196.

a military education that would accomplish several tasks: provide Donelson with a career, develop his moral character and produce virtuous and honorable conduct, acquaint him with young men with whom he would interact at future social and political events, and embed in him a love for the Republic. Not inconsequentially, it would also engender in his nephew a habit of following orders from authority figures, perhaps even encouraging him to be a loyal lieutenant to his uncle.[17]

In January 1817, Donelson set out for West Point, accompanied by John H. Eaton, one of Jackson's favorite aides and trusted friends. With him, Donelson carried a letter of introduction from his uncle to Gen. Joseph G. Swift, the superintendent of the academy. In the letter, Jackson described his nephew as "young & inexperienced, but possessing an amiable disposition." After a "disagreeable jaunt," Donelson and Eaton reached a snow-covered Washington, D.C., on 1 February 1817. A visit to the War Department revealed that Donelson's acceptance at the academy was virtually assured. His entrance examination was scheduled to take place in June 1817. He would have to wait, however, until September to begin classes. Jackson advised his nephew to find housing near, if not at, West Point in order to become better acquainted with the "rules & regulations" of the academy. Capt. Alden Partridge, the senior member of the faculty and acting superintendent in Swift's absence, agreed to allow Donelson to eat and live with the other cadets, as well as use the library. Per Jackson's instructions, Donelson introduced himself to one of his uncle's old acquaintances, Philadelphia merchant Samuel Carswell, whom Jackson directed to provide whatever funds were necessary for his nephew's needs.[18]

Jackson was noticeably concerned about Donelson's first extended separation from him. He warned his nephew to proceed cautiously in his rela-

17. Bertram Wyatt-Brown, *Southern Honor: Ethics and Behavior in the Old South* (New York: Oxford University Press, 1982), 92–3, 190; Rod Andrew Jr., *Long Gray Lines: The Southern Military School Tradition, 1839–1915* (Chapel Hill: University of North Carolina Press, 2001), 8–11; and Remini, *Course of American Empire,* 100.

18. AJ to Joseph G. Swift, 12 January 1817, JHE to AJ, 4 February, 20 March 1817, and AJ to AJD, 24 February 1817, in Harold D. Moser, David R. Hoth, and George H. Hoemann, eds., *The Papers of Andrew Jackson,* vol. 4, *1816–1820* (Knoxville: University of Tennessee Press, 1994), 83–4, 87–9, 103–5, 91–2; and AJ to AJD, 23 February 1817, Andrew Jackson Donelson Papers, Library of Congress, Washington, D.C. (hereafter cited as DLC).

tionships with the people he would meet, not trusting acquaintances until they had proved themselves worthy of confidence. While expressing faith in Donelson's "judgment [and], when ripened with experience . . . your morality & virtue," Jackson counseled him to avoid the "snares" his enemies would place before him. "You should alone intermix, with the better class of society," Jackson reflected, "whose charectors are well established for their virtue, & upright conduct." The General followed the example of many southern fathers when he also advised Donelson to spend time with virtuous females and "shun the intercourse of the others as you would the society of the viper or base character." The company of immoral women, he warned, "engender[ed] corruption, & contaminate[d] the morals, and fit[ted] the young mind for any act of unguarded baseness." Above all, Jackson wanted Donelson to "part with existance, before you will tarnish your honor."[19]

Eaton reassured Jackson that his nephew would conduct himself appropriately. He noted that Donelson was "now at an age tender and dangerous," but his "prudence and correct conduct" would "shield him against the allurements of vice." "I have seen few young men in my life whose reflections conduct & deportment were as correct," Eaton wrote his friend, noting that "if he persevers in his present course of steadiness, he will never want a welcome passport to the confidence and friendship of the good and deserving."[20]

Donelson successfully completed West Point's entrance exam, entering as a cadet on 20 June 1817. News of his older brother's death, however, tempered Donelson's anticipation of starting at the academy. Both Jackson and Daniel Smith informed the young man in May that John, who had been surveying land in the nearby Middle Tennessee wilderness, had died after a four-week bout with a severe cold and cough. (John had frequently been ill while visiting Jackson's army in 1814 and, in fact, may never have fully recovered his health.) Despite their sadness over his brother's death, both Jackson and Smith assured Donelson that they found his own conduct encouraging and had every confidence that he would pursue his upcoming studies with great "industry and application."[21]

19. AJ to AJD, 24 February 1817, in Moser, Hoth, and Hoemann, *PAJ* 4:91–2; and Wyatt-Brown, *Southern Honor,* 195.

20. JHE to AJ, 20 March 1817, in Moser, Hoth, and Hoemann, *PAJ* 4:103–5.

21. AJD to AJ, 5 April 1817, and AJ to AJD, 29 April, 4 August 1817, DLC; Daniel Smith to AJD, 6 May 1817, Robert Dyas Collection, Tennessee State Library and Archives, Nashville (hereafter cited as RDC);

Donelson's official acceptance into West Point placed him in a maelstrom of egos and lax discipline. The United States Military Academy, located in the Hudson River Valley of New York, was in the midst of a power struggle between the War Department and Captain Partridge. General Swift, who preferred not to reside on campus, had allowed Partridge, a vain, bombastic officer, too much leeway, and the captain considered himself the head of the academy. He had interfered in the school's affairs to the point of attempting to teach all of the classes himself and refused to consult the faculty about issues pertinent to their positions. Despite his overbearing demeanor, Partridge endeared himself to the cadets. They viewed him with sympathy when stories of his conflicts with the other faculty members circulated. Complaints lodged by the faculty led President James Monroe to visit the academy personally in June 1817. Those grievances and his own observations convinced Monroe that Partridge needed to be removed as the school's superintendent.[22]

Partridge, however, was not ready to relinquish his power. After Swift conveyed Monroe's sentiments, Partridge took action against the treasonous faculty. He arrested all its members and took over their classes. The arrival of the new acting superintendent (and Partridge's former classmate), Bvt. Maj. Sylvanus Thayer, interrupted his vengeful measures. Thayer carried with him orders from Swift authorizing Partridge to turn over control of the school to him. Partridge departed that day but stubbornly returned six weeks later to resume command. His stay was short-lived, as Swift had him arrested. A subsequent court-martial found Partridge guilty of disobedience of orders and mutiny; given the option of being cashiered or resigning, he chose the latter.[23]

Thayer faced an arduous task. Securing the support of the faculty was of utmost importance. To do that, he began implementing Secretary of State William H. Crawford's regulations, issued in 1816 but ignored by Partridge's regime. These rules established a rigorous and orderly academic regimen.

AJ to Rachel Jackson, 15, 17, 21 November 1814, in Harold D. Moser, David R. Hoth, Sharon Macpherson, and John H. Reinhold, eds., *The Papers of Andrew Jackson,* vol. 3, *1814–1815* (Knoxville: University of Tennessee Press, 1991), 186–8, 190–1, 194–5; and Atkins, *Emily Donelson,* 62.

22. Stephen E. Ambrose, *Duty, Honor, Country: A History of West Point* (Baltimore: Johns Hopkins University Press, 1966), 38–58; and Thomas J. Fleming, *West Point: The Men and Times of the United States Military Academy* (New York: William Morrow, 1969), 26–9.

23. Ambrose, *Duty, Honor, Country,* 58–61; and Fleming, *West Point,* 3–14.

Entering cadets would be admitted only once a year, in September, and all cadets would follow a four-year academic course that emphasized math, engineering, and French. Cadets would also be subject to biennial evaluations and were placed on a merit system, which would grade their conduct in and out of the classroom on a weekly, monthly, and annual basis. When graduation came, the merit system ranked the class members, with those near the top choosing their preferred service branch, usually engineering or cavalry.[24]

Winning over the cadets proved more difficult for Thayer than converting the faculty. His strict implementation of regulations led the faculty to dismiss many cadets for poor grades; other cadets simply chafed under his firm hand. Thayer's choice of an officer charged with instilling discipline into the young cadets only added to their growing resentment. During Donelson's first year at West Point, Thayer appointed Capt. John Bliss as commandant of the cadets. Bliss was a veteran of the recent war with Britain and had impressed Thayer with his disciplined troops. His duty was to train the cadets in tactics, teach them discipline, and distribute demerits as needed. The approach Bliss used with regular troops in warfare, however, fared poorly with young cadets, particularly those used to Partridge's lax regime. Moving artillery pieces in the sweltering summer heat without the assistance of horses and practicing drill instructions longer than normally required caused many cadets to grumble among themselves about both Thayer and Bliss.[25]

The tension between the acting superintendent and the cadets eventually culminated in a physical confrontation. On 22 November 1818, Edward L. Nicholson, a cadet from Maryland, defiantly refused to maintain order during a parade drill. After Nicholson ignored repeated orders to get back in line with the other cadets, Bliss, according to witnesses, "violently seized [him] by the collar; [and] *shook, jerked,* and publicly *damned*" him in front of his comrades. The cadets met that night and wrote a petition to Thayer outlining their grievances against Bliss. Approximately 180 cadets signed the list. That number included Donelson, who told Jackson that he "signed with all my heart," and Donelson's friend and new cadet, Nicholas P. Trist of Virginia. The disgruntled cadets then selected a committee of five cadets,

24. Ambrose, *Duty, Honor, Country,* 67–76.

25. Ibid.; and Fleming, *West Point,* 38–41.

four of whom had been close to Partridge before his dismissal, to present the petition to the superintendent.[26]

The next day, Thomas Ragland, the committee's leader, and the other four cadets approached Thayer with their petition. The acting superintendent calmly told them that they were out of order in submitting their grievances via a petition. Cadets could voice their complaints individually, he said, but not collectively. The committee members went back to their quarters, expanded the list of charges against Bliss, and returned to Thayer's office the next morning. The committee warned him that the cadets were ready to mutiny if he did not dismiss Bliss. In response, Thayer instructed the five to leave the campus. They did so, but not before accumulating 108 cadet signatures on another petition pledging to stand by the five in "common cause."[27]

Donelson expressed disgust with Bliss's conduct and displeasure with Thayer's response. He condemned Bliss as "unfit for a Commandant of Gentlemen, or a company of soldiers" and further wished upon him the "weight of woe" that accompanied a "violation" of honor and duty. As for Thayer, Donelson commented, he "differs from my idea of a good officer." The acting superintendent had not even allowed the five cadets enough time to collect clothes or money. Out of sympathy, Donelson had given them eighty dollars of his own, he told Jackson, to enable them to live off campus until they could secure their possessions.[28]

Despite his iron discipline over his own troops during the War of 1812, Jackson agreed that Bliss's actions were "unpardonable." From Donelson's reports, he could only conclude that the commandant's "conduct" had been "inconsistant with the feelings of a man of honour." Jackson applauded his nephew's behavior throughout the entire affair, calling his aid to the five expelled cadets "the buds of virtue." He encouraged him to "aid injured innocence when & wheresoever you meet with it." The General wisely

26. Ambrose, *Duty, Honor, Country,* 77–9; Fleming, *West Point,* 40–4; Wallace Ohrt, *Defiant Peacemaker: Nicholas Trist in the Mexican War* (College Station: Texas A&M University Press, 1997), 16–22; AJD to AJ, 23 November 1818, and Cadets' Petition, [November 1818], Andrew Jackson Papers, Library of Congress, Washington, D.C. (hereafter cited as JLC); and AJD to AJ, 29 November 1818, in Moser, Hoth, and Hoemann, *PAJ* 4:253–5.

27. Ambrose, *Duty, Honor, Country,* 77–8; and Fleming, *West Point,* 40–3.

28. AJD to AJ, 29 November 1818, in Moser, Hoth, and Hoemann, *PAJ* 4:253–5.

cautioned, however, that "it ought allways to be clearly shewn to you, that the subject of abuse is innocent, and the treatment unjust," particularly when superior authorities, such as military officers, stood accused of misconduct. Jackson especially encouraged Donelson to protect his own honor. "Suffer death before you will dishonour," he advised. "If the superior attempts either to strike or kick you, put him to instant death the moment you receive either—never my son, outlive your honour—never do an act that will tarnish it." As an up-and-coming southern elite, Jackson had learned early on that "redress was most of all a remedy . . . to offset a perceived threat to his as yet undeveloped reputation." He wanted Donelson to remember this advice for future use.[29]

Jackson's correspondence with Donelson reveals much about their relationship. His uncle's letters were full of advice designed to guide the young cadet into leading a virtuous, honorable life. Jackson especially encouraged Donelson's private conduct. He promised his nephew that "so long as you continue in that virtuous path, you have had from your infancy, so long will my thoughts delight to dwell upon you." Jackson prompted the young cadet to pay heed to his counsel, particularly as he saw "how corrupt the world was growing." Should Donelson persist in his virtuous and honorable behavior, his uncle would "feel my ample reward in all advances for your benefit, in your future good conduct, and future greatness." The General had no doubt that Donelson would "become a great, good, and usefull member of society" because he possessed "genius & application." Jackson also advised his ward to avoid friendships with immoral cadets. "Morality is the basis of Virtue," he reminded him. Jackson's letters clearly indicated his desire to see Donelson succeed as a southern gentleman personally and publicly.[30]

Jackson also gave attention to other facets of Donelson's conduct that, on the surface, appeared trivial but that he believed were important to his nephew's development as a sound member of the southern elite. For instance, Jackson incessantly pleaded with Donelson to spend more time on his correspondence, repeating the admonition in nearly every letter. "There is none of your conduct that has ever been condemed by me, or complained

29. AJ to AJD, 20 October 1817, 3 August 1818, DLC; AJ to AJD, 28 December 1818, in Moser, Hoth, and Hoemann, *PAJ* 4:262–3; and Burstein, *Passions*, 19.

30. AJ to AJD, 29 April, 4 August, 4 December 1817, 6 August, 12 October, 3, 30 December 1819, DLC.

of," Jackson chided, "except your not writing oftener." The encouragement to write was not for Jackson's benefit, he insisted, but for Donelson's, for his nephew to become experienced in expressing himself privately in anticipation of one day taking the public stage. Jackson also prompted his nephew to exercise great care in his spending habits. The Panic of 1819 hit the western United States, as well as Jackson's finances, particularly hard. He cautioned Donelson to be prudent and efficient in his use of funds and repeatedly asked him to acknowledge the receipt of bank notes. Jackson's concern, however, was not simply personal. His advice to Donelson to practice "aeconomy" but not "parsimony" was born out of personal experience shaped by southern culture. A southern gentleman needed to look and act the part of an elite, which required spending money and even going into debt. At the same time, one had to avoid placing oneself in a precarious financial situation that could lead to the loss of elite status. Finding the balance, Jackson told his nephew, was the key to financial success.[31]

Donelson's response to his uncle's frequent missives on women, virtue, honor, writing, and money is often difficult to ascertain for this period. He wrote infrequently, apparently ignoring Jackson's advice to practice his correspondence skills. The hardworking cadet was almost certainly too engrossed in his studies to expend the time-consuming effort needed to keep his uncle informed of the minute details of his classwork and social life. Like many well-mannered young adolescents, Donelson probably thought that silence was the best response to unappreciated directives and impossible tasks. He apparently heeded Jackson's guidance on money matters, however, informing his uncle in 1819 that he intended to pay off some debts that he had acquired by the next year, albeit with Jackson's help. Although Donelson rarely responded in writing to his uncle's counsel, Jackson must have assumed that his nephew was absorbing his advice on all of these matters and trying to follow it. Jackson was his patriarch and had been for years; young Donelson had no reason to defy him.[32]

31. AJ to AJD, 4 August 1817, 24 November 1818, 6 August, 12 October, 16 November, 3 December 1819, 29 February, 21 March 1820 (two letters), DLC; and AJ to AJD, 21 November 1819, in John Spencer Bassett and J. Franklin Jameson, eds., *Correspondence of Andrew Jackson,* 7 vols. (Washington, D.C.: Carnegie Institute of Washington, 1926–35), 2:440–2.

32. AJD to AJ, 5 May 1819, in Moser, Hoth, and Hoemann, *PAJ* 4:296–8; and Atkins, *Emily Donelson,* 64.

Jackson was not Donelson's only correspondent during his time at West Point. Daniel, his surviving brother, wrote him several times, sending family news and reports of his own academic progress studying under Priestly, Donelson's former teacher at Cumberland College. His mother, Polly, reminded him to be careful in his choice of friends and "endeavour to deserve the confidence and regard which all of your relations have for you." His grandfather, Daniel Smith, wrote him until his death on 16 June 1818, repeating much of Jackson's advice about the importance of family, writing, education, morality, and temperance. Donelson's aunt, Rachel, also reminded him to avoid life's sorrows by living a God-centered existence. The letters from his grandfather, mother, and aunt only served to reinforce Jackson's own instructions.[33]

Donelson had other things on which to concentrate as well. The stricter regulations imposed upon the cadets required them to exert more effort to complete their studies satisfactorily. Donelson's academic record was exemplary. Even in the middle of the Bliss affair, he notified Jackson that he had been "a little studious" recently, having passed the most difficult examination at the academy, that of "Gregories['] Mechanics." Donelson estimated that the rest of the course work, which included "Enfield's Philosophy, . . . Descriptive Geometry, the Science of War and Fortification, [and] drawings in Topography & Fortification," would be easier. He apparently discovered that it was, as he finished second in the thirty-member class of 1820. Donelson was only one of two cadets admitted in 1817 to complete the required four years of class work in three years, a task that, by his own estimation, he could have finished in just two years. For his hard work, he received the rank of second lieutenant.[34]

Even before the graduation date of 4 July 1820, Donelson knew where his future would be: Florida. Following the victory at New Orleans in 1815, General Jackson had enjoyed a hero's welcome back in Tennessee. His stay there did not last long. Over the next few years, Jackson negotiated and

33. DSD to AJD, 22 March 1818, 12 March 1819, Daniel Smith to AJD, 6 May 1817, 25 March 1818, RDC; Mary Smith Donelson Sanders to AJD, 19 May 1817, and DSD to AJD, 18 December 1819, DLC; and Rachel Jackson to AJD, 19 October 1818, in Moser, Hoth, and Hoemann, *PAJ* 4:244–5.

34. AJD to AJ, 23 November 1818, JLC; AJD to AJ, 5 May 1819, in Moser, Hoth, and Hoemann, *PAJ* 4:296–8; Satterfield, "Moderate Nationalist Jacksonian," 17–8; and *Register of Graduates and Former Cadets of the United States Military Academy* (New York: West Point Alumni Foundation, 1953), 156–7.

signed treaties with the Cherokees and Chickasaws that added millions of acres to the United States. Not satisfied with these land acquisitions, Jackson, in an expedition intended to capture and remove Seminoles along the Georgia-Florida border, knowingly misinterpreted orders from President James Monroe and Secretary of War John C. Calhoun and invaded Spanish Florida in 1818. What Jackson accomplished, in short, was the deliberate military conquest of a foreign territory.[35]

His actions caused the Monroe administration and members of Congress not a little consternation. Secretary of State John Quincy Adams stood by Jackson, however. Adams had been involved in negotiations with the Spanish minister, Don Luis de Onís, even before Jackson's invasion, and his sense was that Spain was already resigned to United States ownership of Florida. Jackson's escapades, while striking a blow at Spanish pride, only seemed to seal its fate. Adams, therefore, urged Monroe not to lose the opportunity, which he did not. The president chose to chastise Jackson privately, while allowing Adams to continue the negotiations with Spain, using the invasion as leverage. Specters of an American Napoleon inspired Henry Clay and several of his congressional colleagues to try passing a censure resolution against Jackson, but their efforts failed.[36]

Anticipating war between the United States and Spain over Florida, Jackson told his ward that he had already asked Secretary of War John C. Calhoun to allow the cadet to take his examination two months early. Although the General expressed his hope that Donelson would pursue another profession if peacetime continued in the nation, he wanted his nephew near him now so that he could "obtain a little experience of active military operations, under my own eye." Since war was not imminent, Calhoun advised

35. Remini, *Course of American Empire,* 321–40, 352–64; and Frank L. Owsley Jr. and Gene A. Smith, *Filibusters and Expansionists: Jeffersonian Manifest Destiny, 1800–1821* (Tuscaloosa: University of Alabama Press, 1997), 141–60. Historians do not agree that Jackson invaded Florida against orders. Remini believes that the Monroe administration purposely sent vague orders, with the assumption that Jackson would understand their true intention. Noble Cunningham Jr. and Harry Ammon argue that the administration never authorized the invasion, explicitly or implicitly. See Remini, *Course of American Empire;* Noble Cunningham Jr., *The Presidency of James Monroe* (Lawrence: University Press of Kansas, 1995), 67–8; and Harry Ammon, *James Monroe: The Quest for National Identity* (New York: McGraw-Hill, 1971), 414–7.

36. John C. Niven, *John C. Calhoun and the Price of Union: A Biography* (Baton Rouge: Louisiana State University Press, 1988), 69–71; Owsley and Smith, *Filibusters and Expansionists,* 161–3; and Ammon, *James Monroe,* 421–5.

Jackson to allow his nephew to finish at the regular time so he would not lose the opportunity to choose his service branch. Jackson agreed, and he recommended that Donelson enter the corps of engineers when he received his commission, which he did.[37]

There was much for the young man to contemplate as he rode up the carriage drive to the Hermitage, his new military commission in hand. His uncle's invasion of Florida had led not to war, as Jackson had expected, but to a treaty making that territory part of the United States. Still, Donelson was going to work at the side of his uncle and mentor. By pursuing his education and military training, he had followed his Uncle Andrew's advice given that May afternoon in 1815 and was confident that by doing so, he was about to reap the rewards of his association with the Hero of New Orleans.

37. AJ to AJD, 30 December 1819, 29 February 1820, DLC; JCC to AJ, 23 January 1820, in W. Edwin Hemphill, ed., *The Papers of John C. Calhoun,* vol. 4, *1819–1820* (Columbia: University of South Carolina Press for the South Caroliniana Society, 1969), 591–2; JCC to AJ, 1 June 1820, in *The Papers of John C. Calhoun,* vol. 5, *1820–1821* (Columbia: University of South Carolina Press for the South Caroliniana Society, 1971), 164–5; AJ to AJD, 9 February 1820, Andrew Jackson Papers, Scholarly Resources, Wilmington, Del. (hereafter cited as JSR); and AJ to AJD, 6 May 1820, in Moser, Hoth, and Hoemann, *PAJ* 4:367–8.

2

“The Great Contrast between Virtue and Vice”

After graduating from West Point in July 1820, Andrew Donelson stayed busy assisting Jackson, replacing Richard Ivy Easter as Jackson’s aide-de-camp in September. That same fall, Donelson accompanied his uncle to Doak’s Stand, located along the Natchez Trace, to aid in the negotiation of a new land cession from the Choctaws. From there, Donelson traveled west, spending the winter of 1820–21 under orders from Jackson to study potential locations for fortifications on the Sabine River, which meandered along the border of present-day Texas and Louisiana. He then traveled to Mobile, Alabama, to examine fortifications there and finally settled in New Orleans and awaited his uncle’s next orders. Jackson’s letters of introduction for his nephew assured recipients that he was “a youth of fine morals [and a] high sense of honor.”[1]

As a reward for his acquisition of Florida, Jackson was offered the governorship of the new American territory in early 1821, and he wanted Donelson to go with him. Jackson received his Florida commission in March of that year and instructed Donelson to remain in New Orleans until he and his traveling party reached him, which they did on 22 April. From there, Donelson accompanied Jackson’s party to Mobile and then Blakely, Alabama, “a sickly town” Donelson found unbearable. After a short stay there, they journeyed to Montpelier, Alabama, where Jackson impatiently waited several weeks for Spain to officially transfer the Florida government. Donelson sent out Jackson’s instructions during this lull, ordering troop and

1. AJ to George Gibson, 10 July 1820, AJ to Rachel Jackson, 30 September 1820, in Moser, Hoth, and Hoemann, *PAJ* 4:374–5, 390–1; AJD to NPT, 30 November 1820, Nicholas P. Trist Papers, Library of Congress (hereafter cited as NPTP); Robert V. Remini, *Andrew Jackson and His Indian Wars* (New York: Viking Penguin, 2001), 194; Satterfield, *Jackson’s Confidant,* 7–8; AJ to AJD, 18 February 1821, AJD to AJ, 8 March 1821, and AJ to Edward Livingston, 15 February 1821, JLC; and AJ to David Corbin Ker, 15 February 1821, DLC.

equipment movements. Although his appointment as aide-de-camp ended on 1 May, Donelson remained with Jackson for the next few months.[2]

Jackson's stint as Florida's governor lasted only from July to November 1821, but Donelson hated his time there, calling the country's "greatness overrated." A disagreement between Jackson and the Spanish governor of Florida, José Maria Callava, initially delayed the transfer of the territory, but when it appeared certain that Jackson would finally take charge of Florida, Donelson accompanied Rachel and other members of the Jackson party to Pensacola on 28 June 1821. (Jackson remained in Manuels, some fifteen miles away, until the official transfer of government on 17 July.) James C. Bronaugh, Jackson's personal doctor, was one member of the party, as were Ephraim A. Blain, the family steward, and family slaves. For an aspiring military officer, Donelson's duties in Pensacola were mundane. He assisted Bronaugh and Blain in supervising the servants; on at least one occasion, Jackson placed him in charge of overseeing the food preparation for a meeting with Spanish officials. His only excitement, it seems, was in accompanying his young relative, Narcissa Hays, to Pensacola's parties.[3]

On 3 July, Donelson received news that Calhoun had ordered him to report to Capt. René Edward DeRussy in Mobile, Alabama. Jackson, however, replied that his nephew would remain with him. He had sent Donelson to New Orleans on quartermaster duty, he told Calhoun, and still needed his services. Donelson apparently never made it to Mobile, and Captain DeRussy eventually granted him an extended leave in September. The return home to Nashville in late 1821 was a welcome relief to Donelson.[4]

2. AJ to AJD, 31 March 1821, and AJ to John Coffee, 11 May 1821, in Harold Moser, David R. Hoth, and George H. Hoemann, eds., *The Papers of Andrew Jackson,* vol. 5, *1821–1824* (Knoxville: University of Tennessee Press, 1996), 24–5, 41–3; AJD to Ralph E. W. Earle, 6 May 1821, Andrew Jackson Donelson Papers, James D. Hoskins Library, University of Tennessee, Knoxville (hereafter cited as DUT); AJD to Chester Root, 12 (two letters), 13 May 1821, AJD to [Joseph] Swiler, 13 May 1821, JLC; and AJD to Alex Macomb, 9 June 1821, Andrew Jackson–Jackson Donelson Collection, Joint University Libraries, Nashville, Tenn. (hereafter cited as JDC).

3. AJD to Ralph E. W. Earle, 6 May 1821, DUT; Remini, *Course of American Empire,* chap. 25; Herbert J. Doherty Jr., "Andrew Jackson vs. the Spanish Governor," *Florida Historical Quarterly* 34 (October 1955): 142–58; AJ to James C. Bronaugh, 3, 15 July 1821, in Moser, Hoth, and Hoemann, *PAJ* 5:66–7, 73–4; Atkins, *Emily Donelson,* 73; and Parton, *Life of AJ* 2:599–600.

4. AJ to Robert Butler, 27 July 1821, AJ to JCC, 29 July 1821, and AJ to James Jackson, 2 August 1821, in Moser, Hoth, and Hoemann, *PAJ* 5:84–6, 86–8, 91–3; JCC to AJ, 3 July 1821, in W. Edwin Hemphill, ed.,

Donelson's dissatisfaction with his time in Florida was not surprising. He expected more benefits from his classical education and military training and from being so near his uncle. This experience was hardly what he had anticipated when he envisioned working side by side with the famed Hero of New Orleans. Jackson, however, had considered it important, so Donelson had acquiesced for the time being. Before leaving Florida, however, Donelson indicated his desire to leave the army, citing the "fluctuating feelings of Congress" in providing enough money for military defense. Jackson, who had concluded that the Monroe administration was inadequately supporting the military, endorsed his nephew's wishes, informing Calhoun of the decision in January 1822. Instead of remaining "idle," Jackson believed that Donelson's "present age is favorable to acquire the knowledge of a profession . . . by which he will be prepared for civil as well as military service life, and in every way capable of rendering services to his country and to himself." The secretary of war expressed his regret that "one of the most promising young officers of his corps" was unhappy with his present situation but agreed to accept his resignation.[5]

Donelson's future course now lay in the study and practice of law, a profession that Jackson and Daniel Smith had previously suggested to him. At Jackson's prompting, Donelson applied to attend Transylvania University, located in Lexington, Kentucky. The university had grown under the presidency of Reverend Horace Holley, a man Jackson admired. Around the time of Donelson's enrollment, the school had nineteen professors and 404 students, 48 of whom were studying law. In addition to Holley, Donelson also expected to study under William T. Barry, former lieutenant governor of Kentucky, and Jesse Bledsoe, former U.S. senator from Kentucky. Jackson thought them "both men of great talents." There was really no other place for Donelson to study law, Jackson concluded, since "there was no legal charector of sufficient standing in morality & law knowledge" in Nashville "who was in the habit of taking legal

---

The Papers of John C. Calhoun, vol. 6, *1821–1822* (Columbia: University of South Carolina Press for the South Caroliniana Society, 1972), 239–41; and René Edward DeRussy to AJ, 5 September 1821, JLC.

5. *Nashville American Banner,* 19 April 1856, 67; AJD to NPT, 19 February 1822, NPTP; JCC to AJ, 28 October 1821, and AJ to JCC, 5 January 1822, in Hemphill, *PJCC* 6:476–9, 607–8; and James Gadsden to AJ, 3 December 1821, JLC.

students, under whom I could have placed you, to have received those benefits I wish."[6]

The benefits to which Jackson referred were crucial to success in southern society. Jackson understood from his own experience, as one historian has noted, "that becoming a lawyer was a promising way for a young man to rise out of the lower classes and become a gentleman." While Donelson's family connections hardly allowed him to be considered part of the lower classes, increasing his reputation by studying and practicing law, just like receiving a military education, was one avenue to solidifying his status as an elite. Southerners wanted educated leaders, and lawyers were crucial in providing social and political guidance. The legal profession, therefore, would give Donelson legitimate claim to being a member of the southern elite. It would also provide him with the stability that military life could not.[7]

Determined to achieve that status, Donelson set out for Lexington in February 1822. Upon his arrival at the university, he presented a letter of introduction from Jackson to Holley. Donelson's interviews with Holley and Barry went well, so he began studying on his own, as lectures would not resume until the fall term. Donelson had a difficult time adjusting to his new surroundings, however, mainly because of a recurring pain in his side. Nevertheless, he assured Jackson that the illness, which he called "the rod of old Blackstone," would not prevent his "progress in the Law." After taking a trip to Blue Licks, a nearby hot springs, to find some relief, Donelson resumed his studies.[8]

Once lectures began in the fall of 1822, Donelson spent much of his time examining Kentucky's economic issues, particularly the Relief War, as the state's banking conflict was called. Originating during the Panic of 1819, the Relief War centered on the bankruptcy of state banks, allegedly triggered by the corrupt practices of the Second Bank of the United States. This widespread bankruptcy led the Kentucky state legislature to pass stay laws,

6. Robert Peter and Johanna Peter, *Transylvania University: Its Origin, Rise, Decline, and Fall* (Louisville: Filson Club Historical Society, 1896), 104, 114–5, 119; AJ to Horace Holley, 27 February 1822, DUT; AJ to AJD, 1 April 1822, in Bassett and Jameson, *CAJ* 3:157; Satterfield, *Jackson's Confidant*, 9; and AJ to AJD, 26 April, 11 October 1822, in Moser, Hoth, and Hoemann, *PAJ* 5:176–7, 220–1.

7. Booraem, *Young Hickory*, 131; and Wyatt-Brown, *Southern Honor*, 89.

8. AJ to Horace Holley, 27 February 1822, AJ to AJD, 26 April 1822, in Moser, Hoth, and Hoemann, *PAJ* 5:154, 176–7; AJ to AJD, 15 March 1822, DLC; and AJD to AJ, 5 June 1822, JLC.

which prohibited foreclosures and put an end to imprisonment for debt. The legislature also chartered a new state bank, authorizing it to produce and distribute paper money in order to alleviate the economic downturn. The state's Republican party divided into the Relief faction, which supported the measures, and the Anti-Relief bloc, which opposed the measures. The Anti-Relief bloc eventually took over the legislature and established a new court system.[9]

The Relief War gave Donelson an opportunity to exercise his growing legal skills. He participated in the debates before the law school's moot court and imaginary legislative assembly. He argued the side of the Relief faction, much to his uncle's disappointment. Jackson, however, expressed pleasure in Donelson's "conclusive, and well founded" argument. Since the scenario simply tested legal acumen and he had taken great care to relate his estimation of the crisis to Donelson, Jackson did not protest too vehemently. If his lectures were not enough to convince the young scholar of the corruption of the "designing Demagogues [and] their wicked purposes," his difficulty in sending Donelson money to cover his expenses conclusively displayed the inadequacy of "ragg" money.[10]

Donelson's participation in the moot court and his understanding of the Relief War did not prevent him from squandering Jackson's financial resources, however. In August 1822, he admitted to his uncle that he would have to request more money than he had anticipated. While in Florida, Donelson had borrowed $240 from Henry M. Rutledge and had authorized Nicholas P. Trist to purchase a number of books for him with the promise of reimbursement. Although Trist had not mentioned Donelson's failure to repay him, Rutledge was pressing the law student for payment. Plagued with guilt, Donelson told Trist, "I feel myself blameable, and there is nothing which I will not forgoe to relieve any inconvenience which this circumstance may have occasioned." Jackson's absence, Donelson explained,

9. Robert V. Remini, *Andrew Jackson and the Bank War* (New York: W. W. Norton, 1967), 28–9; and Richard P. McCormick, *The Second American Party System: Party Formation in the Jacksonian Era* (Chapel Hill: University of North Carolina Press, 1966), 209–14.

10. Satterfield, "Moderate Nationalist Jacksonian," 29–31; AJ to AJD, 5 July 1822, 19 August 1820 [1822], 13 December 1822, and AJD to AJ, 9 November 1822 (draft), DLC; AJ to AJD, 25 July, 6 August, 11, 23 October, and 23 December 1822, in Moser, Hoth, and Hoemann, *PAJ* 5:205–7, 212–5, 220–1, 221–3, 229–31; and AJ to AJD, 8 February 1823, in Bassett and Jameson, *CAJ* 3:186–7.

had left his finances "strained" and him unable to raise enough money to satisfy his accounts. "I hope," he wrote Trist apologetically, "that you still view me your friend."[11]

Jackson's personal experiences, about which he repeatedly reminded his nephew, shaped Donelson's guilt over his Florida debts. As the lives of the southern elite clearly showed, debt was not unusual; it was, in fact, a necessity. Jackson, however, "hated debt," as historian Robert V. Remini has observed, and his actions bore out that statement. He had carefully worked his way up in North Carolina and Tennessee society by accumulating wealth through marriage, community connections, land ownership, and entrepreneurial ventures. Because of some poor financial decisions of his own, he learned to despise debt and did not look kindly upon wasteful extravagance. It was, he believed, dishonorable and immoral. He raised Donelson with these lessons and reinforced them constantly in his correspondence, but Donelson never quite grasped the importance of living free of debt. Like other southern planters, he would live his life under the weight of enormous debt, all the while expressing his remorse for his inability to pay creditors.[12]

Donelson's indebtedness at such an early age also reflected his reliance upon Jackson. "I possess but little property and am dependent for that little upon another," he informed Trist. To preserve Jackson's trust in him, Donelson had to reassure his uncle that, if he were patient with him, he would "redeem the misuse of time & money" once he entered the bar. "My mind has ever been the dupe of my heart," Donelson sadly wrote Jackson. "I feel conscious that the greatest struggles which I have to encounter, will be those which I will inflict upon myself, not for hasty and considerate acts; but for doing, exactly, those things which I would not do."[13]

Donelson's failure to heed Jackson's warning about debt did not keep Jackson from reiterating other lessons he had previously taught Donelson. The doting uncle made sure to remind his nephew how important virtu-

11. AJD to AJ, 19 August 1822, JLC; AJ to AJD, 19 August 1822, JSR; and AJD to NPT, 30 November 1820, 19 February 1822, NPTP.

12. Wyatt-Brown, *Southern Honor,* 23; Remini, *Course of American Empire,* 131; and idem, *Andrew Jackson and the Course of American Freedom, 1822–1832* (New York: Harper and Row, 1981), 33–4. According to Herbert E. Sloan, Thomas Jefferson was another prominent southerner who held similar views about private debt. See Sloan's *Principle and Interest: Thomas Jefferson and the Problem of Debt* (Oxford: Oxford University Press, 1995).

13. AJD to NPT, 30 November 1820, NPTP; and AJD to AJ, 19 August 1822, JLC.

ous and honorable conduct was. On one occasion, he recommended that Donelson read Jane Porter's novel, *The Scottish Chiefs*. In it, Donelson would find the story of Scottish hero William Wallace,

> a virtuous patriott, & warrior [who] was the best model for a young man—In him we find a stubborn virtue, which was never overcome by vice, it was too pure for corruption.—we find in him the truly undaunted courage, allways ready to brave any dangers, for the relief of his country or his friend—In him we find true greatness of soul capable of true friendship, and in his enemies, a lesson from the want of it, necessary for every virtuous high minded youth to be acquainted with, that he may be guarded against that vile hypocrisy, & deceipt, that often lurks beneath a fair exterior which is cloathed with power[.]

In the example of Wallace's life, Jackson judged, "you will See the great contrast between virtue & vice, between the high Minded honourable man, & the base treacherous deceiver."[14]

Jackson had no doubt that Donelson would follow Wallace's virtuous and honorable example. "Believe me when I say to you," Jackson solemnly declared, "I have watched over all your acts, and well understood (or I believe) your disposition and your feelings from your childhood and know how to appreciate them. . . . Your Virtue and moral course, with your talents, if life lasts, will lead you to fill the highest stations in our government." Donelson needed only to avoid "the political vortex of contesting parties" and there would come a day when his "age and experience will Justify your country calling you" to a position of leadership. Jackson echoed those sentiments in a letter advising his protégé to speak carefully on political subjects. "One of my objects in placing you at Lexington was that you might become acquainted with the young gentlemen from various part of the south & west," he wrote, "that when you enter in to professional life, . . . you may then be known—for I will not disguise, I look forward, if you live, to the time when you will be selected to preside over the destinies of america."[15]

14. AJ to AJD, 21 March 1822, in Moser, Hoth and Hoemann, *PAJ* 5:163–4; and Bertram Wyatt-Brown, "Andrew Jackson's Honor," *Journal of the Early Republic* 17 (Spring 1997): 22.

15. AJ to AJD, 12 April, 2 May 1822, DLC; and AJ to AJD, 20 May 1822, in Moser, Hoth, and Hoemann, *PAJ* 5:188–9.

Jackson was convinced that he recognized in Donelson a similar regard for honor and virtue. As one historian observes, Jackson "imagined himself an infallible judge of others" and tended to project onto people his own fears and hopes. This was especially true with Donelson. By following his uncle's advice, which he usually did, Donelson reinforced Jackson's trust in him and fulfilled his obligations as son and client. He was developing "the credentials and potentialities of the client [that] really mattered," including rhetorical and writing skills, financial economy, ambition, honor, virtue, and fealty. As another historian rightly notes, "Patrons like General Jackson did not feel obliged to move any numbskull ahead." Donelson could not count on his kinship with Jackson to make him successful; through his behavior, he had to prove himself worthy of his name and his inclusion in his uncle's elite circle.[16]

Just as Donelson was fulfilling his obligations as son and client, Jackson was also satisfying his responsibilities as patriarch and patron. He bestowed on his nephew every conceivable advantage—education, social and political connections, instruction on proper conduct, financial support—necessary to become a thriving, successful member of the southern elite. By aiding Donelson, however, Jackson was not simply looking out for his nephew's interests; he was protecting his own reputation as well. Recent historians have noted Jackson's propensity for surrounding himself with younger men who were on the rise socially and who were bound to him by ties of kinship, honor, and loyalty. Jackson certainly considered his nephew one of those young men, and as with his other protégés, he had plans for how Donelson could help him continue his own political success.[17]

In addition to his usual advice to Donelson, Jackson's letters increasingly contained news of the political maneuvering leading up to the 1824 presidential election. When the Tennessee legislature nominated him for president in the summer of 1822, Jackson denied playing any role in the decision. "They [*sic*] people have the right to elect whom they think proper," he assured Donelson in August 1822. "I shall leave the people free to adopt such course as they may think proper, & elect whom they choose, to fill the

16. Burstein, *Passions,* 218; and Wyatt-Brown, "AJ's Honor," 18.

17. Burstein, *Passions,* 103; Wyatt-Brown, "AJ's Honor," 16, 33; and Ratner, *Tennessee Lieutenants,* 1–34.

Presidential chair, without any influence of mine exercised by me." His only desire, he declared, was that the people choose an individual who would maintain their prosperity, happiness, and republican institutions. "Believe me my D[ea]r Andrew," Jackson modestly concluded, "I never had a wish to be elevated to that station if I could, my sole ambition is to pass to my grave in retirement." That desire to retire faded, however, as Jackson threw himself into attacking his political opponents and strengthening his image among supporters.[18]

The more of Jackson's esteem-building missives and diatribes against perceived and real enemies that Donelson received, the less interested he was in staying at Transylvania. His uncle was running for the nation's highest political office while he was in Kentucky studying law. The news that Jackson had been nominated for the presidency convinced Donelson that his services might best be used at the Hermitage. While professing his ignorance of political "intrigues," Donelson indicated to Jackson that he was ready to abandon his law studies and take on the task of helping his uncle win the presidency. He had "studied attentively," acquiring the necessary instruction from reading law. The rest of his studies, Donelson judged, "must be supplied by individual & laborious study." While regretting the loss of experience he would face because of his absence from moot court, Donelson reckoned that his time with Jackson would prove more profitable in the end than further schooling. Both he and his uncle realized that the ongoing presidential contest provided Donelson with an opportunity to learn the intricacies of the political world, a prerequisite for someone being groomed for future political office.[19]

Donelson had maintained contact with his uncle's supporters in Kentucky and performed other political duties in the state, but Jackson believed that his talents were better used close by. Jackson, who had previously allowed his nephew to keep his letterbook, especially valued Donelson's skill for research and writing, which the study of law had only benefited. By December, the two men had reached an agreement whereby Donelson would return home once the lectures finished in the spring. After some delay on Jackson's part, in March 1823, he sent one of the Hermitage's male slaves,

18. AJ to AJD, 2 June, 6 August 1822, in Moser, Hoth, and Hoemann, *PAJ* 5:191–2, 212–5.

19. AJD to AJ, 5 June, 19 August 1822, JLC.

George, to accompany Donelson on the trip from Lexington to Middle Tennessee.[20]

Upon returning to Nashville, Donelson obtained his law license, most likely by simply appearing before a panel of Nashville lawyers and responding orally to their questions. Granted on 21 April 1823, Donelson's license listed the simple requirements that he had met: twenty-one years of age, "a man of honesty, probity and good moral character," and sufficient "legal acquirements." It was not until 1824 that the state supreme court required a rigorous bar. No matter, Donelson was well prepared for the task, challenging the "cliché that eloquence and quickness rather than learning and precedents marked the way to success for frontier lawyers," as one historian described it. He opened a law partnership with Thomas A. Duncan in December 1823 in an office located on Deadrick Street in downtown Nashville. Most of the cases Donelson took involved the settlement of personal debts, but even those seemingly drew little of his attention.[21]

Donelson allowed his law practice to languish as the majority of his time was consumed by Jackson's presidential candidacy. The 1824 presidential election had become paramount to those closest to the General. Jackson faced formidable opposition to reaching the nation's highest political office. Three of President James Monroe's cabinet members—John C. Calhoun, William H. Crawford, and John Quincy Adams—were running, as was Henry Clay, who had returned to the House of Representatives in 1823 after a two-year absence. By the summer of 1824, the contest had narrowed to two realistic contenders: Adams and Jackson. Calhoun had dropped out to pursue the vice-presidency. Crawford had suffered a stroke that nearly killed him and left him incapacitated. Clay's campaign, which was predicated on the election going to the House for a final decision, had petered out in the absence of support from eastern states. Adams, meanwhile, had strong backing in New England and was gaining momentum in the middle Atlantic states. Jackson benefited from the decline of Crawford and Clay and

20. Satterfield, "Moderate Nationalist Jacksonian," 31; AJ to AJD, 13 December 1822, 5, 8, 10 March 1823, DLC; AJ to John Coffee, 10 March 1823, in Moser, Hoth, and Hoemann, *PAJ* 5:257–9; and AJD to AJ, 5 June 1822, JLC.

21. AJD's law license, 21 April 1823, DLC; Anita Shafer Goodstein, *Nashville, 1780–1860: From Frontier to City* (Gainesville: University of Florida Press, 1989), 24; and Satterfield, "Moderate Nationalist Jacksonian," 33–42. Chattanooga lawyer Russell Fowler provided the information on the probability of Donelson's oral examination. Russell Fowler, e-mail to author, 29 April 2003.

the rise of national sentiment associated with the fiftieth anniversary of the Revolution and the visit of the Marquis de Lafayette.[22]

Despite his expectations, Donelson played only a minor role in the campaign. Remaining in Tennessee, he practiced the law only infrequently and spent most of his time tending to Jackson's accounts while his uncle served in the Senate. Jackson requested Donelson's assistance in retrieving letters and compiling evidence to counter anticipated attacks upon his character and his service to the nation. Jackson felt certain that "my charector will stand the test of the most exact scrutiny." By April 1824, Jackson was telling Donelson that he wanted him to come to Washington that fall. John Eaton had been assisting Jackson in responding to incoming correspondence and accusations, but his own affairs, including the composition of the pro-Jackson "Wyoming" letters, had left Jackson without his services. "I hold no correspondence with any one but yourself," Jackson informed his nephew. "I am fearfull my business has interrupted your attention to your profession," Jackson admitted to Donelson, but, he said, he had "had no person who I could apply to but you."[23]

While in Florida, Donelson had written Nicholas P. Trist that he wanted to "[better] my condition in the practice of the Law; or perhaps I had better say, in marrying some lovely girl and digging the Earth." With the first goal accomplished, Donelson set out in pursuit of the second. In the middle of the chaos surrounding the presidential race, Donelson found time to marry his seventeen-year-old cousin, Emily Tennessee Donelson, the youngest daughter of Rachel Jackson's brother, John. Her biographer describes Emily as "spoiled [and] petted," which was not far from the truth. Being the youngest of thirteen children and suffering the debilitating effects of tuberculosis from an early age seemingly helped Emily become a young lady who expected to, and usually did, get her way.[24]

22. James F. Hopkins, "Election of 1824," in *History of American Presidential Elections,* 4 vols., ed. Arthur M. Schlesinger and Fred L. Israel (New York: Chelsea House, 1971), 1:350–1; Robert V. Remini, *Henry Clay: Statesman for the Union* (New York: W. W. Norton, 1991), 237–44; and idem, *Course of American Freedom,* 80–3.

23. AJ to AJD, 6 March, 4, 11 April 1824, in Moser, Hoth, and Hoemann, *PAJ* 5:372–3, 388–9, 391–3; AJ to AJD, 16 January 1824, William Carroll to AJD, 4 October 1824, JLC; AJ to AJD, 1 March 1824, DLC; and Robert P. Hay, "The Case for Andrew Jackson in 1824: Eaton's *Wyoming Letters,*" *THQ* 29 (Summer 1970): 139–51.

24. AJD to NPT, 30 November 1820, NPTP; and Atkins, *Emily Donelson,* 39, 321.

According to family legend, the romance between Andrew and Emily began shortly before the young man set out for West Point. One afternoon, the story goes, Andrew escorted ten-year-old Emily home from school, carrying her across a creek in his arms. It was at that moment, one family historian gushed, that Andrew "realized that he loved" Emily. This tale, depicting Andrew as a loving paternal figure and Emily as an adoring innocent child, is surely idealized. Emily may have had a crush on her older cousin at that young age, and Andrew may have enjoyed protecting his young relative, but assuming anything more is highly speculative.[25]

Whatever role physical and emotional attraction eventually played in their relationship, other factors encouraged the marriage between these two first cousins. One was their family history. Of the prominent Tennessee families in the early nineteenth century, the Donelsons almost certainly possessed the most complicated and intertwining family genealogy. First-cousin marriages were seemingly the norm, not the exception, in the family and were intended to strengthen kinship ties, a common goal among many elite southern families. "These intricate marriage patterns," according to one historian of the southern household, "generated extensive kinship networks that provided crucial connections in both economic and political arenas, as well as a sense of social stability." The prospect of strengthening property ties was an important motivation for a young man whose efforts at law were half-hearted at best. The desire to establish his own paternal authority also certainly influenced Andrew's pursuit of Emily. She was young, which undoubtedly led him to believe, like many aspiring southern patriarchs, that she would be acquiescent to his will. Finally, Andrew's interest in Emily probably spawned from one other obvious factor: her availability. For all of these reasons, Andrew Donelson's interest in Emily made sense to the rising southern gentleman.[26]

Despite family legend, the first evidence of interest between Andrew and Emily does not emerge until the fall of 1823, when they were engaged. In

25. Atkins, *Emily Donelson*, 60–1.

26. Wyatt-Brown, *Southern Honor*, 201, 217, 220–1; Peter W. Bardaglio, *Reconstructing the Household: Families, Sex, and the Law in the Nineteenth-Century South* (Chapel Hill: University of North Carolina Press, 1995), 440–4; Jane Turner Censer, *North Carolina Planters and Their Children, 1800–1860* (Baton Rouge: Louisiana State University Press, 1984), 86–7; and Lorri Glover, *All Our Relations: Blood Ties and Emotional Bonds among the Early South Carolina Gentry* (Baltimore: Johns Hopkins University Press, 2000), 9, 48–9, 96–7.

November 1823, Emily's father, Capt. John Donelson III, informed John Coffee, "Tell Polly, her sister Emily will not be long before [she] is married. She has many suitors and among [them] she has chosen one and perhaps she could g[u]ess who he is." As expected, even though he was in Washington, Andrew Jackson knew what had been growing between his nephew and niece, asking Donelson in a December letter to present his regards to "your little girl."[27]

Preparations for the wedding consumed much of the couple's time in 1824. Andrew continued to assist his uncle and practice law, albeit infrequently, while Emily spent her time planning the many details involved in a wedding. This included spending six hundred dollars on her wedding trousseau, not a small sum even for Captain Donelson. The couple's happy day arrived on 16 September. As final preparations were being made on the Hermitage grounds, where the wedding was to take place, bad news arrived from a neighboring plantation. Emily's brother, William Donelson, sent word that his wife, Rachel, had died earlier that day. Despite the sad report, the family agreed that the wedding must take place. Later that afternoon, in front of family and friends, the Reverend William Hume conducted the ceremony that joined Andrew and Emily as husband and wife. It was, however, a tempered celebration.[28]

As his gift to the new couple, Andrew Jackson gave his nephew the deed to 348 1/4 acres of land adjoining the Hermitage, which the Donelsons named Springdale, and a slave, John Fulton, whom he had bought in Florence, Alabama. Since returning to Nashville in 1823, Donelson had worked hard tending to Jackson's accounts and sale of cotton, looking after Rachel and Andrew Jr., and tracking down correspondence that his uncle wanted to use against his political opponents. All of this he had done to the detriment of his own legal career, a sacrifice Jackson could not have failed to recognize. By transferring the land and slave to his nephew, Jackson was rewarding Donelson's loyalty and labor. The land had the added effect of keeping Donelson in close proximity to the Hermitage, where he could be at

27. John Donelson III to John Coffee, 10 November 1823, quoted in Atkins, *Emily Donelson,* 80; and AJ to AJD, 5 December 1823, JLC.

28. Atkins, *Emily Donelson,* 90, 92–3; and AJ to John Coffee, 20 September 1824, AJ to WBL (summary) [c. 13 September 1824], in Moser, Hoth, and Hoemann, *PAJ* 5:440–1, 571.

his uncle's beck and call should Jackson not win the upcoming presidential election.[29]

With the wedding now a happy memory, the election returned to the forefront of Donelson's mind. The newlyweds, along with Andrew and Rachel Jackson, left the Hermitage for Washington on 7 November 1824. Jackson planned to return to his senatorial duties, but considering his entourage, he also appeared ready for news that he had won the presidency. Along the way, the group experienced an accident with their carriage outside Harrodsburg, Kentucky, but they arrived safely in the nation's capital in early December. They received news on their journey that although the votes had been counted, the election had not yet been decided.[30]

Jackson had received a plurality, but not a majority, of the electoral and popular votes. The Tennessean had won 99 electoral and 152,901 popular votes, while Adams had garnered 84 and 114,023, respectively. Clay and Crawford lagged far behind: Clay had 37 electoral and 47,217 popular votes, while Crawford had 41 electoral and 46,979 popular. In Jackson's mind, and those of his supporters, the people had clearly indicated their choice. The Constitution, however, dictated otherwise. The Twelfth Amendment, adopted after the disputed 1800 election between Thomas Jefferson and Aaron Burr, required the names of the top three electoral vote-getters in such a scenario to be submitted to the House for a deciding vote. In this procedure, each state received one vote, with the candidate gaining the most votes winning the presidency.[31]

The names of Jackson, Adams, and Crawford were presented to the House. Despite Clay's absence from this list, his influence proved crucial. With Crawford still debilitated from his stroke, the Kentucky politician had to decide whether he would use his considerable influence in the House to support either Jackson or Adams. Clay allegedly approached both candidates with promises to deliver them the presidency in return for a cabinet post. Jackson supposedly turned down his offer, which apparently sealed his fate. Clay was probably disposed to support Adams anyway. They touted similar political programs, looking to expand government for the benefit of the na-

29. AJ to John Coffee, 24 October 1823 (fn. 4), in Moser, Hoth, and Hoemann, *PAJ* 5:311. For summaries of Donelson's work on behalf of Jackson, see ibid., August 1823–September 1824.

30. John Donelson to John Coffee, 8 December 1824, in Burke, *Emily Donelson* 1:119–20.

31. Remini, *Course of American Freedom*, 83.

tion. Adams was also an easterner; Jackson was a westerner and future competitor for the Kentuckian. With those and other considerations in mind, Clay convinced the delegations from Kentucky, Ohio, Maryland, Louisiana, and Missouri to change their states' votes and give Adams the victory. The final tally was Adams thirteen, Jackson seven, and Crawford, four.[32]

When Adams appointed Clay secretary of state a mere five days after the House election, the Jackson camp reacted riotously. They had heard rumors of a "corrupt bargain" between Adams and Clay before the House vote but had decided that neither man would dare risk the political backlash. Clay, "the *Judas* of the West," had apparently calculated the risks, Jackson fumed, and thought them worth the "thirty pieces of silver." Adams was so bent on securing the presidency, the Tennessean charged, that he willingly participated in the betrayal of American liberty. "What a farce!" Donelson wrote to John Coffee soon after the House's decision. He was "sickened with the result of the election." John Quincy Adams, "his Highness," now possessed "a Power which he has purchased from representatives who betrayed the constitution, and which he must distribute among them as rewards for the majority." Despite the travesty of justice that had taken place, Jackson "was calm and undisturbed." Adams, in contrast, was "truly an object of Pity." "He stands alone," Donelson gloated, "at the Ball, the theatre and the circus; but few are seen to welcome him."[33]

"How can a republic last long under such scenes of corruption?" Jackson had previously asked his nephew. "Nothing but the redeeming spirit of a virtuous people, who will arise in the majesty of their strength, and hurl these Demagogues of corruption from their confidence; can redeem our nation from woe, & our republican Government from destruction." Having witnessed the controversial result personally, Donelson could only agree with his uncle's assessment. Jackson had repeatedly warned him that such an event would occur if "demagogues of corruption" were given the opportunity, and he had been right. The result of the 1824 presidential election only made Donelson more determined to help his uncle seize power from the corrupting influences that threatened to destroy the Republic.[34]

32. Hopkins, "Election of 1824," 1:376–81; and Remini, *Course of American Freedom*, 86–95.

33. Remini, *Course of American Freedom*, 98; AJ to WBL, 14 February 1825, in Bassett and Jameson, *CAJ* 3:276; and AJD to John Coffee, 19 February 1825, DLC.

34. AJ to AJD, 17 April 1824, in Moser, Hoth, and Hoemann, *PAJ* 5:395–6.

3

"You Have Not Been a Father to the Orphan"

The outcome of the 1824 presidential election disappointed Donelson and left him in a precarious position. Anticipating Jackson's victory and a possible government appointment, in December 1824, Donelson had ended his law partnership with Thomas A. Duncan. He had been paying scant attention to his clients anyway, so this decision simply reflected the reality of his life. With Jackson's defeat, Donelson now had to decide whether he wanted to open another law office or turn his attention to other ventures that could support his family and solidify his position in Nashville society. While he periodically continued to perform legal services, Donelson decided to try his hand at becoming a successful planter.[1]

Establishing a profitable plantation required Donelson to acquire more land. His decision to do so sparked a conflict that ripped apart the Donelson family. Since at least 1823, Andrew and his brother, Daniel, had been embroiled in a dispute with their stepfather, James Sanders, over an inheritance of land in nearby Sumner County left to them by their grandfather, Daniel Smith. At his death in 1818, Smith had willed the 1,280 acres of land, which had originally belonged to the boys' father, to their mother. Smith did so with the understanding that Andrew and Daniel would share ownership of half, or 640 acres, of the land.[2]

At that point, the land was not a primary concern to Donelson, as he was at West Point. His brother's entrance into the academy in April 1821, however, brought the land inheritance back to the forefront of his mind. Daniel quickly grew dissatisfied with the academy, and by April of the next year sought Jackson's advice about whether he should remain there. Because

1. Satterfield, "Moderate Nationalist Jacksonian," 33–42.

2. Satterfield, *Jackson's Confidant*, 14–5; and AJ to AJD, 5 March 1823, AJD to James Sanders, 24 August 1825, DLC.

he was doing well in his classes, Jackson persuaded him to stay and asked Donelson to support his advice, which he did. In November 1822, Daniel informed Jackson that he had resigned from West Point because he was not being graded fairly. While willing to come home to Tennessee, he told his uncle that he had his heart set on attending Yale College and asked him for his approval and financial assistance in making the transition.[3]

Jackson disagreed with Daniel's reasoning and turned to members of the Donelson family for their assessment of the cadet's position. Andrew and Daniel's maternal grandmother, Sarah Michie Smith, made clear her opposition to the move, emphasizing her late husband's desire that his grandsons receive an "education in a Liberal Manner." (Why Yale could not fulfill that wish is unknown.) She eventually, though reluctantly, agreed to support his move to Yale, although she made it clear that she preferred him to come home. Jackson's meeting with Sanders was less productive. Daniel's stepfather, according to Jackson, remained "silent when consulted" about the matter. Andrew Donelson was not surprised at Sanders's response, telling Jackson with no little sarcasm that his stepfather did not "understand the term *liberal education*." For his part, Donelson wanted his brother to stay at West Point and offered to sell part of the land inheritance as a way of repaying Jackson for funding Daniel's education. "It would be as ungrateful as I know it is foreign to the heart of my brother to tax you, Uncle, with any further contributing on his favour," he assured Jackson.[4]

Although financially strapped from providing an education for several of his wards, Jackson continued to insist that he would find the funds to help Daniel complete his education without having to sacrifice his inheritance. "Nothing but want of means," Jackson promised Donelson, would keep him from providing Daniel with "a liberal education without the sale of his land." He somehow found the money, and spurred on by his relatives' advice, the disgruntled cadet remained at the academy.[5]

3. AJ to JCC, 21 December 1820, in Moser, Hoth, and Hoemann, *PAJ* 4:409–11; AJ to AJD, 31 March 1821, 26 April, 6 August, 11 October, 23 December 1822, in Moser, Hoth, and Hoemann, *PAJ* 5:24–5, 176–7, 212–5, 220–1, 229–31; AJ to AJD, 1, 12, 22 April 1822, DLC; and DSD to AJ, 20 November 1822, JSR.

4. AJ to AJD, 16 December 1822, 8, 21 January 1823, and AJD to AJ, [c. 30 December 1822], JSR; AJ to AJD, 23 December 1822, in Moser, Hoth, and Hoemann, *PAJ* 5:229–31; and AJ to AJD, 5 March 1823, DLC.

5. AJ to AJD, 8, 21 January 1823, JSR; AJ to AJD, 5 March 1823, DLC; and DSD to AJ, JLC.

When Daniel graduated from West Point in 1825 and returned to Davidson County to be near his family, Sanders's reluctance to become involved in his stepson's financial difficulties became clearer. That fall, a debt his brother had accrued led Andrew Donelson to ask Sanders to sign for the obligation. Their stepfather balked at the request. At issue was Sanders's refusal to allow Polly to sign a deed turning over the inherited land to Andrew and Daniel. Sanders accused his oldest stepson of falsely claiming that "I Wished Daniel to Surrender to me a part of the land given him by his grandfather's Will, for an expectancy from me." Sanders made it clear that he believed that the land was rightfully his alone and was willing to fight to maintain control over it.[6]

Sanders's accusation and claim set Donelson off on an angry, bitter tirade that hints at the longstanding resentment that he felt toward his stepfather. Sanders, he argued, had taken advantage of Daniel's absence to try to divest him of his claim to the land. Had he forgotten, Donelson seethed, that his grandfather's will only "appoints you a joint or separate trustee for the specific purpose of conveying?" He continued, "My father built the mill, cleared the land, planted the orchard, put up the dwelling house, leased part of the premises, and died—is this a title for you, and are his orphan children to be driven to the Parish?"[7]

In addition to lambasting Sanders for his conduct toward himself and Daniel, Donelson also pointed out his mistreatment of their mother. If it was necessary to go to court in order to protect their rights, an action that Donelson declared that he did not want to take, then he would do so "with the confidence that you have been unjust to your family, that you have not been a father to the orphan, and that you have wronged their benevolent and innocent mother, *your wife*." Whatever the result, Donelson concluded, "we can vindicate our rights without violating the ties which bind us to our beloved mother—these are sacred with us."[8]

The Donelsons and Sanders eventually agreed to subject the dispute to an arbitration committee composed of local attorneys. The arbitrators, William L. Smith and Henry Crabb, rendered a judgment favorable to the

6. James Sanders to AJD, 14 August 1825, DLC; and Satterfield, "Moderate Nationalist Jacksonian," 39.

7. AJD to James Sanders, 24 August 1825, DLC.

8. Ibid.

Donelson brothers. Swayed by Sarah Michie Smith's statement that her husband intended for the land to go to Andrew and Daniel, Smith and Crabb ordered that the two grandsons receive their share of Smith's land when their mother died. They also gave Polly Sanders sole control over her will "without the consent and cooperation of her husband."[9]

While the preservation of the land inheritance was important, what must have struck Donelson was the difference between how Jackson and Sanders treated him and his brother throughout these two episodes. Jackson acted as a father, advising, encouraging, sustaining, and even sacrificing to support his wards. The bonds of paternalism, honor, and loyalty drew the three men together. In contrast, Andrew and Daniel's relationship with Sanders became even more strained. Sanders's alleged physical abuse of the Donelson boys seemingly exacerbated Andrew's anger over his father's death, producing resentment against his stepfather. That resentment, which Daniel also undoubtedly felt, only increased during the uncertainty over his education. From all indications, Sanders never assisted his stepsons in any capacity, financial or otherwise, which only increased their hostility toward him. His attempt to take away their inheritance, therefore, was only the last in a series of actions that led Donelson to break irrevocably with his stepfather. Unfortunately for the Donelson family, it also appears that, despite their claims of fidelity, Andrew and Daniel remained estranged from their mother until her death in 1857.

Donelson's concern over his and Daniel's land inheritance was not simply a matter of principle, though; he had another motivation for protecting it. He understood that this land would solidify his future prospects in Nashville and Tennessee society. Keeping it only improved his standing among the gentry; losing it meant that he would have to work harder to achieve the status of a gentleman planter. Donelson used the inheritance land, plus the adjoining tract of land given to him by Jackson, to establish a plantation called Ridgeland, located less than a mile from the Hermitage. (This plantation served as the foundation of Donelson's later plantation, Poplar Grove.) The proximity of Donelson's land to the Hermitage allowed

9. Statement by Sarah Michie Smith, 12 August 1825, AJD to James Sanders, 10 September 1825, James Sanders to AJD, 4 November 1825, arbitration agreement, 11 November 1825, arbitration decision, 26 December 1825, DLC; and AJD to James Sanders, [c. 2 November 1825], JLC.

him quick access to Jackson and helped both men maintain their familial and social bonds.[10]

But land was not enough; Donelson also needed to acquire the accoutrements of a planter. In order to do so, he had to borrow money from Jackson. He proved "very industrious," however, and by the winter of 1826, Donelson was looking for an overseer to supervise the planting and harvesting of crops by his slaves and a groom to take care of the "valuable blooded" racehorses he had begun accumulating. Owning and racing horses marked Donelson as a man of wealth, as Jackson's own involvement in the sport demonstrated. At some point, probably in 1826, Donelson also joined the Tennessee militia, rising from captain to the rank of major, a title he retained for the rest of his life. This designation served to enhance the distinction of his military education and service.[11]

Owning slaves was also central to Donelson's ascent to the status accorded a plantation owner. Like most southerners, Donelson found nothing troubling about owning another human being. From his childhood, he had been exposed to the plantation world and the necessity of slaves in maintaining that lifestyle. Not surprisingly, Jackson had taught him that slaves must be kept in line in order to protect their status. Shortly after they arrived in Pensacola in 1821, in fact, Jackson had asked Donelson to supervise the punishment of Betty, Rachel's personal slave. Rachel had written her husband that Betty was "putting on some airs" and disobeying her orders. Jackson gave his nephew blunt instructions. "I have directed [house stew-

10. John Donelson to John Coffee, 16 June 1825, in Atkins, *Emily Donelson,* 108, 109; and Stephen S. Lawrence, "Tulip Grove: Neighbor to the Hermitage," *THQ* 26 (Spring 1967): 3–22.

11. AJ to SH, 22 November, 15 December 1826, 15 February 1827, [SH] to AJ, 5, 13, [28] January 1827, in Harold D. Moser and J. Clint Clifft, eds., *The Papers of Andrew Jackson,* vol. 6, *1825–1828* (Knoxville: University of Tennessee Press, 2002), 235–6, 243–4, 291–3, 256–7, 261–3, 269–71; T[imothy] P[atrick] Andrews to AJD, 18 March 1827, DLC; Kenneth S. Greenberg, *Honor and Slavery: Lies, Duels, Noses, Masks, Dressing as a Woman, Gifts, Strangers, Humanitarianism, Death, Slave Rebellions, the Proslavery Argument, Baseball, Hunting, and Gambling in the Old South* (Princeton, N.J.: Princeton University Press, 1996), 138; Wyatt-Brown, *Southern Honor,* 65, 74, 355; and idem, "AJ's Honor," 8, 20. The question of when Donelson joined the Tennessee militia is an important one that, unfortunately, I have not been able to resolve. A close perusal of the state's militia records during this period failed to produce his membership, but that almost certainly is where this title originated, since Donelson had resigned his army commission as a first lieutenant. For the evolution in titles applied to Donelson, see AJ to WBL, 15 July 1826, 8 March 1828, Moser and Clifft, *PAJ* 6:185–6, 432–3.

ard Ephraim A. Blain] that [at] the first disobedience of orders, that she be publicly whipped," he wrote. "She can behave herself if she will & I have told her that publicly whipped she shall be [at] the first offence." Jackson asked his nephew to "observe her conduct and [at] the first disobedience or impudence under Mr Blain to give her fifty lashes and if he does not perform it, dismiss him, & as soon as I get possession I will order a corporal to give it to her publickly. I am determined to cure her." There is no record of whether Donelson had to carry out Jackson's orders, although he undoubtedly would have.[12]

Jackson also gave Donelson practical experience in the slave trade. When Donelson was studying law at Transylvania, his uncle asked him to find and purchase for his use several young slaves to work at the Hermitage. Jackson gave him specific criteria by which to judge the best potential workers. He wanted "three or four likely negro girls from 15 to 20 [years old] . . . or one or two boys, from 12 to 18 years old." They had to be "of good charector, likely and healthy." Donelson made enquiries and pinpointed three young girls and one young boy as potential slaves for Jackson. The depreciation of Kentucky paper currency convinced Jackson to postpone the purchase, but the experience helped Donelson in future slave purchases.[13]

A final lesson that Donelson learned from Jackson was the power of the plantation owner to decide the ultimate fate of his slaves. Jackson owned a male slave named Gilbert, who on several occasions ran away from Jackson's Big Spring farm in Alabama and the Hermitage. (During one of Gilbert's flights from the Hermitage, Donelson helped Jackson write a newspaper advertisement for his return.) Gilbert's rebelliousness finally cost him his life in August 1827. After Gilbert had been recaptured, Jackson's overseer, Ira Walton, attempted to whip him. The slave, however, attacked Walton, who in return stabbed him several times, resulting in Gilbert's death. When Jackson heard of the incident, he gathered nine men from the community, including Donelson, to judge if Walton had acted in self-defense. The men

12. AJ to James C. Bronaugh, 3 July 1821, in Moser, Hoth, and Hoemann, *PAJ* 5:66–7; and AJ to AJD, 3 July 1821, DLC.

13. AJ to AJD, 21 March, 2 May, 28 June 1822, in Moser, Hoth, and Hoemann, *PAJ* 5:163–4, 177–8, 195–6; AJ to AJD, 1, 12 April 1822, DLC; and AJD to AJ, 14 December 1822, JSR.

determined that he had, and a grand jury subsequently agreed that the overseer was not at fault.[14]

With this experience, Donelson knew what was expected of him. Slavery, with all of its dehumanizing aspects, was going to be a part of the fabric of his daily life as a southern planter. Like his uncle, Donelson understood that slavery was indispensable to helping him achieve and preserve his status among the gentry. It provided the order and stability that was necessary for the preservation of a white-dominated southern society. While Donelson never seems to have experienced the problem with openly defiant slaves that Jackson faced, he also knew that patriarchy, with its inherent propensity toward violence and exaggerated displays of power, was as much as part of plantation life as was paternalism. Jackson, considered an "excellent master to his slaves" by one contemporary, was the model Donelson would try to emulate. All of these things—the land, racehorses, the militia title, and slaves—coupled with his affiliation with Jackson, signaled Donelson's arrival as a member of Nashville's elite society.[15]

Not all in Donelson's life centered on family disputes or social ascension, however. On 6 June 1826, he and Emily welcomed the birth of their first child, Andrew Jackson Donelson Jr., or Jackson, as he was called. (Members of the Donelson family also referred to Jackson Donelson as Jack, which may be where historians and later Donelson descendants have mistakenly inferred his father's supposed nickname.) He and his father enjoyed a close relationship until the young man's death in 1859. Often, in fact, Donelson gave his oldest son advice on finances and reminders to write frequently that closely resembled the lectures Andrew Jackson had given Donelson when he was at West Point and Transylvania University.[16]

Even with all of the events in his personal life distracting him, Donelson's mind was never far from Jackson's presidential ambitions. The 1824 elec-

14. AJ to Egbert Harris, 13 April 1822, in Moser, Hoth, and Hoemann, *PAJ* 4:170–1; advertisement for runaway slave, [September 1824], JSR; and AJ to William Faulkner, 28 August 1827, AJ to Andrew Hays, 30 August 1827, Andrew Hays to AJ, 31 August 1827, AJ to WBL, 1 September 1827, in Moser and Clifft, *PAJ* 6:384, 385–6, 386–7, 387.

15. Memorandum, [1 January 1825], in Moser and Clifft, *PAJ* 6:3–5; Wyatt-Brown, "AJ's Honor," 18; idem, *Southern Honor,* 16; Dickson D. Bruce Jr., *Violence and Culture in the Antebellum South* (Austin: University of Texas Press, 1979), 137; and Chase C. Mooney, *Slavery in Tennessee* (Bloomington: Indiana University Press, 1957), 91.

16. Atkins, *Emily Donelson,* 109–10.

tion and the subsequent "corrupt bargain" had been disappointing and infuriating. For Donelson, Jackson's success in the upcoming presidential contest was also necessary for his own ambitions. He wanted to be a successful planter, but it is likely that he was already looking ahead to a possible political career. Thus the election gave Donelson renewed purpose to help his uncle achieve the nation's highest office.

The 1824 election also may have helped solidify Donelson's political ideology. In an argument presented before a Davidson County grand jury during this period, Donelson expounded upon what he believed were the legal, moral, and political underpinnings of the United States. Donelson began by identifying popular opinion as the "living principle" of government and repeatedly referred to the sovereignty of the people as a fundamental tenet of the nation's political system. He reminded the jury that their forefathers had "plucked from the Iron grasp of tyranny & superstition . . . [the] free institutions, the great principles of freedom & equality, the trial by jury, [and] the sovereignty of the people." He went on to decry the history of countries where "justice and law are swallowed in the criminal enormities of Aristocracy, and monarchism." Donelson additionally emphasized the importance of reason and law to the preservation of the nation's institutions. Donelson's repulsion at Clay's machinations in the House vote and Adams's abetment were evident.[17]

Donelson's contentions clearly showed the influence of his uncle's republican ideology. Jackson had once told him, "My fervent prayers are that our republican government may be perpetual, [and] the people alone by their Virtue, and independant exercise of their free suffrage can make it perpetual." Jackson's version of republicanism embraced the tenets of limited government, popular sovereignty, anti-elitism, no national debt, geographic expansion of the nation, the necessity of public and private virtue in the maintenance of republican government, the reality of conspiracies that sought to undermine that same government, and the preservation of the Union.[18]

17. "Maiden Speech," JLC. This undated and incomplete document is in Donelson's handwriting and seems to have been an argument made before a Davidson County grand jury. Robert B. Satterfield dates it to this period, a logical decision given Donelson's brief legal career.

18. AJ to AJD, 6 August 1822, in Moser, Hoth, and Hoemann, *PAJ* 5:212–5; and Robert V. Remini, *The Legacy of Andrew Jackson: Essays on Democracy, Indian Removal, and Slavery* (Baton Rouge: Louisiana State University Press, 1988), 8–44. Two articles by Robert P. Hay, "Eaton's *Wyoming Letters*," 139–51, and "'The Presidential Question': Letters to Southern Editors, 1823–24," *THQ* 31 (Summer 1972): 170–86,

More than any other document from this period, this statement shows that Jackson had succeeded, through his own rhetoric and choice of educational opportunities for his nephew, in convincing his nephew of the efficacy of republican thought. Donelson's education under Priestley, at West Point, and at Transylvania University had infused him with influential examples, both military and political, from the classical world of Greece and Rome as well as the founding values of the United States. His exposure to Andrew Jackson, however, was the most significant factor in leading Donelson to embrace the republican principles of virtue and popular sovereignty. His uncle's ideology, repeated in written correspondence and in personal discussions, stressed these republican themes. Just as it did for Jackson, the 1824 election undoubtedly removed any doubts that Donelson might have had about the truth of those republican premises.[19]

While Jackson's enemies considered him more a vicious tyrant than a republican hero, Donelson and the Nashville Junto, as a committee of the General's Tennessee advisers came to be called, believed that the Adams-Clay cabal had thwarted the people's will, and they intended to do something about it. A loosely knit group before the 1824 fiasco, the committee now realized the importance of organization and direction. John Eaton was its recognized head (after Jackson), but its membership also included John Overton, Hugh Lawson White, Alfred Balch, William B. Lewis, Sam Houston, and Felix Grundy, and a handful of others, including Donelson. Despite the tension that eventually developed among some of its members, the Junto defended Jackson and attacked Adams. Jackson's cause also benefited from the establishment of a national organ in Washington. The *United*

---

emphasize the characterization of Jackson as the protector and embodiment of republican values. Although Remini argues that the 1824 election transformed Jackson into a supporter of democracy, the General continued to incorporate republican beliefs, symbols, and rhetoric into his political life, most notably during the Nullification Crisis and the Bank War. See Major L. Wilson, "The 'Country' versus the 'Court': A Republican Consensus and Party Debate in the Bank War," *Journal of the Early Republic* 15 (Winter 1995): 619–47; and Richard B. Latner, "The Nullification Crisis and Republican Subversion," *Journal of Southern History* 43 (February 1977): 19–38.

19. For the concepts of virtue and popular sovereignty, see Gordon Wood, *The Creation of the American Republic, 1776–1787* (Chapel Hill: University of North Carolina Press, 1969; New York: W. W. Norton, 1972), 65–70, 596–615; and Drew R. McCoy, *The Elusive Republic: Political Economy in Jeffersonian America* (Chapel Hill: University of North Carolina Press for the Institute of Early American History and Culture, 1980), 48, 65–80.

States Telegraph, edited by St. Louis newspaperman Duff Green, gave the Junto and other Jacksonians a public voice in the nation's capital.[20]

Popular discontent with the House vote and the affirmation that the General had received from voters both before and after the election gave Jackson's supporters confidence that they could make a successful run at the presidency in 1828. To do so, Jacksonians needed to make political alliances that would assure victory. They forged partnerships with two influential politicians: John C. Calhoun of South Carolina and Martin Van Buren of New York. Calhoun, the sitting vice-president under Adams, had strong support in North Carolina, South Carolina, Virginia, and the states in the Northwest. While Calhoun's showing in the 1824 campaign had been weak, his cooperation would enable Jackson to maintain and possibly increase his popularity in these regions. Calhoun's office would also give Jackson a political collaborator in the Adams administration. In return, the South Carolinian benefited greatly from his decision to join with the General, because Clay's appointment to the secretary of state position virtually guaranteed that he would receive the nomination for president when Adams stepped aside. Any hope that Calhoun held for the presidency would not be found in a continued alliance with Adams.[21]

Martin Van Buren was the second addition to the Jacksonian coalition. In fact, Van Buren and his supporters in the Albany Regency, a political faction in New York that he controlled, initiated the move. Van Buren had originally supported William Crawford, but with the Georgian's illness all but eliminating him from political life, the New Yorker needed someone new to champion. Like Calhoun, Van Buren and the Albany Regency saw Jackson as the political future of the nation. Jackson, in turn, realized that the Regency offered organized support in a crucial state. The New Yorkers had established a new form of party politics that emphasized partisan loyalty and discipline as the true test of loyalty to republican principles. The leaders of the Regency believed that they could guarantee their state to Old Hickory

20. Remini, *Course of American Freedom,* 108–9; Gabriel L. Lowe Jr., "John Eaton, Jackson's Campaign Manager," *THQ* 11 (June 1952): 125–47; Louis R. Harlan, "Public Career of William Berkeley Lewis," pt. 1, *THQ* 7 (March 1948): 14–28; and David E. Woodard, "Sectionalism, Politics, and Foreign Policy: Duff Green and Southern Economic and Political Expansion, 1825–1865" (Ph.D. diss., University of Minnesota, 1996), 49–59.

21. Remini, *Course of American Freedom,* 101–2; and Niven, *JCC,* 119.

in the 1828 election. In addition, Van Buren's friendship with newspaper editor Thomas Ritchie, head of the so-called Richmond Junto, presented the tantalizing possibility of bringing Virginia, which had supported Crawford in 1824, into Jackson's column in 1828. Van Buren also began cultivating the idea of supporting Jackson among his North Carolina allies, whose state had gone to Crawford in 1824.[22]

The Jacksonians saw the brilliance of this three-part alliance. It represented all three geographical sections, North, South, and West, and it brought two powerful politicians and their supporters into their coalition. At the same time, Jacksonians ignored the irony of their charges of collusion between Clay and Adams, dismissing their own "combination" as necessary to defeat the enemies of republican government. All that remained was for the Jacksonians to use their strength to the Old Hero's advantage.

As the 1828 election approached, the campaign turned ugly on both sides. Jacksonians accused Adams of fomenting an aristocratic way of life in the President's House. They criticized his purchase of foreign books and newspapers. When they discovered that Adams had purchased a billiard table and chess set for his use, Jacksonians charged him with encouraging gambling. The most scurrilous indictment leveled against Adams was the absurd accusation that he had pimped for the czar while serving at his diplomatic post in Russia.[23]

Adams's supporters were not above spreading their own salacious rumors, which, unlike those of their opponents, were usually grounded in some truth. Jackson's numerous duels allowed his enemies to portray him as violent. Jackson's orders to execute American soldiers during the War of 1812 and British citizens in Florida during the Seminole War simply added to the depiction of him as a murderer. The Adamsites, like the Jacksonians,

22. Michael Wallace, "Changing Concepts of Party in the United States: New York, 1815–1828," *American Historical Review* 74 (December 1968): 453–91; Douglas W. Jaenicke, "The Jacksonian Integration of Parties into the Constitutional System," *Political Science Quarterly* 101 (Spring 1986): 85–108; Mark W. Kruman, "The Second American Party System and the Transformation of Revolutionary Republicanism," *Journal of the Early Republic* 12 (Winter 1992): 509–37; Edward L. Mayo, "Republicanism, Antipartyism, and Jacksonian Party Politics: A View from the Nation's Capital," *American Quarterly* 31 (Spring 1979): 3–20; and John Niven, *Martin Van Buren: The Romantic Age of American Politics* (New York: Oxford University Press, 1983), 179–80.

23. Robert V. Remini, *The Election of Andrew Jackson* (New York: J. B. Lippincott, 1963), 102–5, 117–8.

also introduced a sexual element into the campaign. They portrayed Jackson as a mulatto and the offspring of a prostitute. The crowning achievement of Adams's propagandists, however, consisted of their public revelation that secrecy and scandal shrouded Jackson's marriage. Charges of bigamy and adultery flowed from the pens and mouths of the Adams men. Jackson seethed under the weight of every charge, but the last one struck particularly close to his heart because it involved his beloved Rachel. It took all of the Nashville Junto's efforts to restrain Old Hickory from challenging men to duels or displaying his legendary temper. Doing so, Eaton and others reminded him, would simply substantiate his enemies' accusations.[24]

While only a peripheral member of the Junto, Donelson played a role in its activities during the campaign. In addition to supporting Duff Green's newspaper financially, he continued his unofficial role as Jackson's private secretary, assisting him in answering correspondence and writing public statements. When Jackson's enemies published or alluded to correspondence that they said would incriminate the General in scandals, it was Donelson's responsibility to ascertain the legitimacy and accuracy of such alleged letters and then respond appropriately. In the case of the Jacksons' marriage, he took depositions from private citizens who testified to the legitimacy of the marriage. Rumors concerning Jackson's participation in the Burr Conspiracy compelled Donelson to demand that a Nashville newspaper editor, Boyd McNairy, produce authenticated evidence. When opponents accused Jackson of improperly court-martialing soldiers during the War of 1812, Donelson accumulated correspondence from soldiers who confirmed Jackson's version.[25]

There were times, however, when the circumstances called for Donelson to take more confrontational action. One such incident involved Jackson's

24. Ibid., 151–6; and James C. Curtis, *Andrew Jackson and the Search for Vindication* (Boston: HarperCollins, 1976), 88–9.

25. Satterfield, "Moderate Nationalist Jacksonian," 45–6; Lowe, "John Eaton," 132; draft of AJ's letter to the Tennessee state legislature (coauthored by AJD and JHE), 12 October 1825, JLC; AJ to John H. Morgan and the Citizens of Fayetteville, Tennessee, [6 July 1826], AJ memorial to the Tennessee state legislature, [c. 18 October 1826], Deposition of Elizabeth Brown Craighead, 2 December 1826, Deposition of Mary Henley Bowen, 21 December 1826, AJD to Roger Jones, 29 September 1827, in Moser and Clifft, *PAJ* 6:573, 577, 579, 594; and AJD to Boyd McNairy, 15, 16 August 1828, Boyd McNairy to AJD, 16, 19 August 1828, DLC.

association with the Salt Spring Bubble controversy. During Jackson's tenure as commissioner of treaty negotiations with the Chickasaws, he had helped some of his friends and relatives obtain land involved in the negotiations. Jackson's actions smacked of favoritism, a corrupt practice he now conveniently decried. His denials of wrongdoing produced a negative reaction among some of his former associates in the scheme. Prominent among them was James Jackson (no relation), a former partner who refused to affirm or deny the allegations.[26]

Andrew Jackson told Donelson to visit James Jackson in Florence, Alabama, and convince him to state unequivocally that the General had no knowledge of the financial scandal. Eaton expressed apprehension about the whole idea, especially since Andrew Jackson had authorized his nephew to "make it a personal affair" if James Jackson would not acquiesce to his demands. The certainty that their candidate was winning the election undoubtedly played a part in Eaton and John Coffee convincing Donelson not to confront James Jackson. Donelson appeared satisfied with their argument, telling Coffee that he was "more than gratified to find Uncle disposed to pass by James Jackson without notice."[27]

Donelson's willingness to back down from a potential duel with James Jackson was not a breach of honor, which one might think, but deference to his relationship with Andrew Jackson. The two Jacksons were the main protagonists, and it was up to them whether their dispute resulted in a duel. When Andrew Jackson decided not to pursue the matter, Donelson was obligated to drop it as well. What was important for Donelson's relationship with his uncle was that he was willing to take the field of honor to defend the General's reputation. For Jackson, his nephew's readiness to battle, to serve as his proxy in a duel, was yet another sign of loyalty.[28]

What some voters considered boorish and offensive behavior was to Donelson just a part of politics. He saw that his political future was tied to Jackson's; if his uncle lost a second election, his political influence would de-

26. Satterfield, "Moderate Nationalist Jacksonian," 46–7.

27. JHE to John Coffee, 3, 10 November 1828, RDC; and AJD to John Coffee, 15 November 1828, quoted in Satterfield, *Jackson's Confidant*, 18.

28. Greenberg, *Honor and Slavery*, 62–4; Wyatt-Brown, *Southern Honor*, 349–61; idem, "AJ's Honor," 21–2; Steven M. Stowe, *Intimacy and Power in the Old South: Ritual in the Lives of the Planters* (Baltimore: Johns Hopkins University Press, 1987), 24–30; and Burstein, *Passions*, 140.

cline and leave Donelson with only his plantation and a defunct law practice. Jackson had predicted that his nephew would pursue a successful political career and paid for his preparation to enter that world. Failure now was not an option. The prospect of personal advancement suppressed any qualms that Donelson might have possessed.

The election results confirmed that the strategy employed by the Jacksonians, even though despicable, worked. Jackson's 178 electoral votes easily outdistanced Adams's 83 votes. The popular vote showed Jackson with 139,212 more votes than his opponent. Jackson and his friends had expected a more convincing victory, but this would suffice. Donelson responded in the manner expected of a proud nephew. "How triumphant, how flattering to the cause of the people!" he wrote John Coffee. The unrestrained arrows of assault upon the General's character and career had broken against the rock of the people's will. The "Puritan & black-leg" administration so hated by Jackson's supporters would now give way to the People's Administration, and Donelson would be an important part of it.[29]

Celebration over Jackson's 1828 presidential victory quickly turned to sorrow, however, as his wife, Rachel, died on 22 December. She succumbed to a heart attack brought on by excessive weight, old age, and, in Jackson's eyes, the slanders of a brutal campaign. Indeed, the physical aspects of Rachel's death went unnoticed in Jackson's single-minded determination to blame his enemies. He attributed Rachel's demise to the accusations made against her virtue, an association that would impair his decision making during his first administration.[30]

But that would come later. For now, Jackson and his associates, while grieving for the president-elect's wife, had to ready themselves for the change in government. A celebratory banquet and ball in Nashville had to be cancelled, and Rachel had to be buried. Jackson's grief kept him from answering the many letters that reached the Hermitage, so Donelson continued attending to this correspondence. With preparations finalized, president-elect Jackson and his adopted son, Andrew Jackson Jr., along with Mary Eastin,

29. Remini, *Election of AJ,* 187–8; and AJD to John Coffee, 15 November 1828, James O'Hanlon to AJD, 30 May 1826, DLC.

30. Remini, *Course of American Freedom,* 150–2. Curtis, *Andrew Jackson,* makes the most persuasive argument regarding the connection between Rachel's death and the Eaton affair.

Henry Lee, William B. Lewis, and Andrew, Emily, and Jackson Donelson, set out for Washington on 19 January 1829. Emily reported that in Cincinnati, steamboats greeted their boat, cannons fired, and citizens exulted in the presence of their Old Hero. Jackson complained that night about the pain he was experiencing from shaking so many hands. Adulation was a hard business. The trip lasted three weeks, ending on 11 February, when Jackson entered Washington "as a plain citizen," avoiding the more celebratory plans his friends had laid for his arrival.[31]

Donelson was exuberant. The eight years under Jackson's supervision—first in Florida, then in Tennessee—had served to introduce him to the political world; now he was accompanying his uncle to the national stage. Jackson's election, along with Donelson's acceptance as a member of Nashville's elite, bolstered his future prospects.

31. Remini, *Course of American Freedom,* 152–9; ETD to Mary Purnell Donelson, 29 January 1829, in Burke, *Emily Donelson* 1:164; and Alfred Mordecai to Ellen Mordecai, 11 February 1829, in Sarah Agnes Wallace, ed., "Opening Days of Jackson's Presidency as Seen in Private Letters," *THQ* 9 (December 1950): 368–9.

Part 2

BETRAYAL, SUSPICION, AND DOUBT

Walking downhill toward the Norfolk dock, Andrew Jackson Donelson listened in disbelief. What had been a pleasant vacation in July 1829 was turning gloomy. The beautiful lady on his arm, Margaret Eaton, had just informed him that the president would send him and Emily back to Tennessee if they did not agree to associate socially with her and her husband, Secretary of War John Eaton. He wondered: Was Margaret simply speaking out of anger over Emily's earlier refusal to accept her help when she had fainted? Or, and Donelson cringed at the thought, did she truly know something that he did not? Surely Uncle had not made such a promise to this obnoxious hussy, he thought to himself as they boarded the steamboat that would return the president and his entourage to Washington.[1]

1. AJD to AJ, 25 October 1830, in Bassett and Jameson, *CAJ* 4:189–91.

4

"It Was Impossible That I Could Submit to the Degradation"

One of the first tasks facing the bereaved president when he reached Washington was the composition of his official cabinet. Like previous presidents, Jackson sought to maintain a geographical balance. He also realized the necessity of rewarding the different factions that had aided him in securing the presidency. Most important, Jackson wanted to make sure that he had friends in the cabinet who would be willing to help him fend off partisan attacks.

Achieving this delicate equilibrium proved troublesome and resulted in a cabinet of geographical diversity but not personal cohesiveness. As vice-president, John C. Calhoun represented South Carolina's antitariff planter class. Martin Van Buren, now the governor of New York, became secretary of state. Jackson's close friend and Nashville Junto member, John H. Eaton, received the secretary of war post. William T. Barry, Donelson's former professor at Transylvania University in Kentucky, accepted the postmaster general spot when John McLean, the aspiring presidential contender from Ohio, decided he was better suited for the Supreme Court bench. Jackson gave the U.S. Treasury position to Samuel D. Ingham of Pennsylvania, a reward for that state's support during the recent election. Representing the southern planter class, Senator John Branch of North Carolina became secretary of the navy, and Georgian John M. Berrien, a strong supporter of Indian removal, obtained the position of attorney general.[1]

In addition to his official advisors, Jackson also had informal advisors, including Donelson, who was a part of the so-called Kitchen Cabinet. This unofficial group of advisors consisted of Jackson's closest friends and political associates. In addition to Donelson, the group included, at various times,

1. Donald B. Cole, *The Presidency of Andrew Jackson* (Lawrence: University Press of Kansas, 1993), 26–9.

Van Buren, Eaton, Lewis, Roger B. Taney, Isaac Hill, James A. Hamilton, Amos Kendall, and Francis P. Blair. Compared to his other advisors, though, Donelson was too inexperienced for Jackson to expect much out of him in terms of policy making or political influence.[2]

That was the point, however. Jackson wanted him by his side so that he could become familiar with national politics, grow comfortable interacting with the elite, and make friendships that would benefit his future career. Jackson often asked his nephew to attend the sporadic and generally informal private councils of the Kitchen Cabinet, at which its members plotted strategies to defeat the president's many perceived enemies. He called upon Donelson to draft state papers that identified the policies he believed would keep the Republic safe. He also expected his nephew to maintain his official and personal correspondence, a duty to which Donelson had tended for several years and would continue to look after until Jackson's death. These responsibilities would give his nephew political experience and exposure and, Jackson hoped, help him get ahead. Yet as before, Donelson played a minor, subservient role.

Still, Donelson knew that this was an important time for him and took his tasks seriously. One of his primary responsibilities was to screen the numerous applications for government positions. Over ten thousand federal offices were available for Jacksonian patronage, and the sheer number of those jockeying for desired offices was, at times, overwhelming. At a cabinet meeting shortly before the new administration took office, the president and his advisors decided that Donelson would be in charge of determining which applicants would receive lower-level appointments. Jackson ordered him to maintain a "Book of Applicants" in which he would record the names of job seekers and their sponsors. Jackson emphasized the importance of the individual who recommended an applicant for a position, an approach that job seekers, consisting of both strangers and friends, must have intuitively understood. Dozens of them wrote Donelson, cajoling him with claims of loyalty to the president and other leading Jacksonians. He turned many of

2. For descriptions of the Kitchen Cabinet, see Richard P. Longaker, "Was Jackson's Kitchen Cabinet a Cabinet?" *Mississippi Valley Historical Quarterly* 44 (June 1957): 94–108; Lynn Marshall, "The Strange Stillbirth of the Whig Party," *American Historical Review* 72 (January 1967): 445–68; and Richard B. Latner, "The Kitchen Cabinet and AJ's Advisory System," *Journal of American History* 65 (September 1978): 367–88.

them away, not convinced there was any need to "Cleanse the Augean Stable," as administration journalist Duff Green described the removals.[3]

Although determining appointments to government positions was an important contribution to the Jackson administration, Donelson's writing skills were his biggest asset. During his presidency, Jackson often asked his nephew to compose an important letter or official message from notes or an outline he gave him. The president had to approve everything his nephew wrote, so Donelson's views, if they were included, had to coincide with his uncle's. Yet Donelson was developing writing skills that served an important purpose. Other, more experienced advisers used his drafts as a foundation for their additions, deletions, and modifications to Jackson's own ideas. Donelson's style and expressions may have survived the editing process, but they seemingly were his only substantial contributions to the final product.[4]

Donelson received his first editing assignment almost immediately, as Jackson needed to prepare an introduction of his political agenda for the inauguration. The president-elect outlined his inaugural address, which Donelson helped Eaton and Lewis to revise. It promised something for every part of the Jacksonian coalition: states' rights; a balance among the various economic interests; internal improvements; a strong military; a "just and liberal" Indian policy; and reform of the federal government's patronage system. All would, of course, take place within the strictures of the Constitution, the address promised.[5]

"The Heavens shed a glorious luster on the declining hours of the late chief," one observer wrote, describing John Quincy Adams's last day in office. On 4 March 1829, approximately twenty-one thousand people gathered at the east portico of the Capitol to see his replacement, Andrew Jackson, sworn in as the seventh president of the United States. Although most of these admirers could not hear Jackson's speech, the atmosphere was one of

3. "Outline of principles submitted to the heads of department," 23 February 1829, and AJD to William T. Barry, 15 April 1829, JLC; Leonard D. White, *The Jacksonians: A Study in Administrative History, 1829–1861* (New York: Macmillan, 1954), 307–8; and Satterfield, "Moderate Nationalist Jacksonian," 52–62.

4. Remini, *Course of American Freedom*, 222, 328; and Satterfield, "Moderate Nationalist Jacksonian," 145–6.

5. First Inaugural Address, 4 March 1829, in James D. Richardson, ed., *The Messages and Papers of the Presidents, 1789–1897*, 10 vols. (Washington, D.C.: GPO, 1896–99), 2:436–8.

excitement and approval. Following the ceremony, Jackson and his entourage retired to the President's House for a reception. The mass of people followed, and what unfolded was the wildest scene that Washington society had ever witnessed. Wine flowed copiously. Glasses shattered on the carpet. Muddy boots trampled the furniture, and soiled hands ripped the executive mansion's curtains and wallpaper. "The noisy and disorderly rabble in the President's House," shuddered one Washington socialite, "brought to my mind descriptions I had read, of the mobs in the Tuileries and at Versailles." The exuberant mob pushed forward to see their president. Their insistence on shaking his hand, however, cornered him and forced Donelson and other advisors to help the president escape out a window. "The Majesty of the People had disappeared, and a rabble, a mob, of boys, negroes, women, children, scrambling, fighting, romping" had replaced it, said one observer. Only the deliberate placement of tubs containing punch and liquor on the front lawn saved the mansion from further damage.[6]

The inaugural ball held that night promised a calmer, more genteel affair. Only upper-class Washington society and members of the incoming administration would attend. Jackson, though, would not be there. He was still in mourning, and besides, the day's excitement had taxed his stamina. Instead of initiating a truce between the western interlopers and the established Washington elite, however, the ball commenced the notorious Eaton affair. Twelve hundred guests gathered at Carusi's Assembly Rooms to honor the newly elected president on the night of the inauguration. The Donelsons were there, together with the Calhouns, the Inghams, and the Eatons. What transpired was a foreshadowing of relations over the next few months. Emily Donelson and the cabinet women snubbed John Eaton's wife, Margaret; in fact, they had ignored her at every function that day.[7]

And what was the cause of such snobbish behavior? The reputation of the secretary of war's wife, which was already well established in Washington circles. Margaret O'Neale had been born and raised in the capital, her father a prominent hotel owner and manager. When Congress was in session, his

6. Alfred Mordecai to Ellen Mordecai, 5 March 1829, in Wallace, "Opening Days," 369–71; Edwin A. Miles, "The First People's Inaugural—1829," *THQ* 37 (Fall 1978): 293–307; Margaret Bayard Smith, *The First Forty Years of Washington Society,* ed. Gaillard Hunt (New York: Scribner's, 1906), 295–6; and Remini, *Course of American Freedom,* 178.

7. Remini, *Course of American Freedom,* 178–80; and Smith, *First Forty Years,* 288–9.

rooms were full of politicians. Margaret helped her family tend to the many chores associated with the hotel's upkeep, and as she grew older, she began to attract suitors. An attempted murder-suicide by a beau, several unfulfilled love affairs, and a thwarted elopement indicate the strong attraction many men felt toward Margaret and help explain how rumors of her alleged promiscuity spread throughout the city's society.[8]

Margaret's introduction to John B. Timberlake in 1815 ended her romantic forays. The sixteen-year-old girl and the navy purser married the next year, but Timberlake's financial problems, made more notable by the birth of their three children, tested their marital bliss. At the time of their marriage, he was battling debt incurred during the War of 1812. Timberlake's bad fortune continued when he lost money on a store located next to the O'Neale boardinghouse.[9]

During those years, the O'Neales and Timberlakes befriended Senator John Eaton of Tennessee. Eaton became fast friends with John Timberlake, so much so that Eaton attempted to have the Senate relieve his friend of his war debts. His efforts produced nothing monetary, but they cemented the families' esteem for Eaton. The senator became so close to the Timberlakes that Eaton escorted Margaret to public functions when her husband was away at sea. Timberlake even placed the legal responsibility of his family in Eaton's care by giving him power of attorney. The Timberlakes considered themselves fortunate to have a friend like John Eaton.[10]

In April 1828, however, John Timberlake slit his own throat while on board a ship headed for Spain. He had been gone for almost four years, having left a mere nine months before his last child was born. Margaret believed that her husband had unintentionally killed himself during an asthma attack, but others disagreed. Rumors had already swirled around Washington that Margaret and John Eaton were intimately involved in an illicit relationship. Eaton's solicitude for the family notwithstanding, he and Mrs. Timberlake had been acting inappropriately, the rumors ran. They were seen talking together in low tones, leaning on one another during

8. John F. Marszalek, *The Petticoat Affair: Manners, Mutiny, and Sex in Andrew Jackson's White House* (New York: Free Press, 1997), 32–5; and Margaret Eaton, *The Autobiography of Peggy Eaton* (New York: Scribner's, 1932), 11–3.

9. Marszalek, *Petticoat Affair,* 35–9.

10. Ibid., 37–42.

walks, and conversing outside of socially accepted times and places. Gossip circulated among Washingtonians that Timberlake had committed suicide after finally realizing the treachery of his wife and her lover. Margaret suggested later in life that the tale bearers intimated only that Eaton "loved me when my first husband was living. And that is as far as any rumor ever went regarding him and me." She knew better, of course. People were saying much more than that.[11]

Whatever the true nature of Eaton's and Margaret Timberlake's relationship while Margaret's husband was alive, his death allowed their mutual affection to lead to discussion of marriage, which set off another round of tongue wagging. If John and Margaret had not been engaged in a love affair, why were they moving so quickly toward marriage? Was the "grieving" widow pregnant? Was the guilt of living a lie too much for them?

It was at this point that Andrew Jackson became involved in the public controversy. He had known the O'Neales for five years, holding Margaret in high regard. She reminded Jackson of the vivacious young lady he had met on the Nashville frontier and eventually married so many years ago. When Eaton approached his old friend asking his advice on the proposed marriage, Jackson wholeheartedly supported the idea. "Major, if you love Margaret Timberlake, go and marry her at once, and shut their mouths," he reportedly told him. Eaton used that encouragement to convince his betrothed to consider marrying before Jackson's inauguration. She acquiesced, and on 1 January 1829, less than nine months after John Timberlake's death, Margaret O'Neale Timberlake became Mrs. John Henry Eaton. The reaction among Washington socialites was predictable. "Tonight Gen'l Eaton, the bosom friend and almost adopted son of Gen'l Jackson, is to be married to a lady whose reputation, her previous connection with him both before and after her husband's death, has [been] totally destroyed," one woman commented.[12]

The marriage scandalized Washington society, but all might have been ignored had Jackson not decided to make Eaton a member of his cabinet. The president-elect wanted a Tennessean of stature among his council of advisers, and he considered both Eaton and another friend, Hugh Lawson

11. Ibid., 40–4; and Eaton, *Autobiography,* 48.

12. Marszalek, *Petticoat Affair,* 45–6; Eaton, *Autobiography,* 48; and Smith, *First Forty Years,* 252.

White, for the post. Eaton manipulated White into thinking that Jackson preferred him, so White withdrew his name from consideration. Eaton became secretary of war, and his wife thus rose to a more prominent standing in Washington's elite.[13]

This was shocking. Jackson, the alleged violent, deranged murderer from the western frontier was president, and Margaret Eaton, the supposed whore of Washington, was one of the leading ladies in the administration! The murmuring that had accompanied the Eaton marriage rose to a crescendo. Men and women, both permanent and temporary residents of Washington, could not believe the audacity of the president-elect. Leading figures in the city visited Jackson and cautioned him to rethink his choice of Eaton. A delegation of Tennessee politicians approached him and made a similar request. Jackson ignored them all, attributing the opposition to his old nemesis, Henry Clay, the perceived culprit behind Adams's victory in 1824 and the attacks that led to Rachel's death in 1828.[14]

Washington society was not alone in its opposition to the Eaton marriage and cabinet appointment. To Jackson's dismay, his official and unofficial advisors split over whether to support the Eatons. On one side stood an anti-Eaton faction, composed of Branch, Berrien, and Ingham. Challenging their influence was another faction, composed of Van Buren, Eaton, Lewis, Barry, and Amos Kendall, who was fourth auditor of the Treasury. The pro-Eaton forces defended the besieged secretary of war and his wife on all fronts. Not sharing the president's narrow and emotionally skewed vision, they maintained that Vice-President John C. Calhoun, not Clay, was to blame for the Eatons' troubles. The South Carolinian, they declared, was manipulating the situation for political reasons, specifically, to gain the presidency in 1832.[15]

In reality, Calhoun was not responsible for the public snubbing of Margaret, although he did not like John Eaton, believing he had opposed his alliance with Jackson in 1828. Calhoun was also suspicious of Eaton's relationship with Van Buren, a man he considered a serious rival for the presidency in 1832. (Jackson had stated that he would serve only one term.) Whatever Calhoun's attitude toward the Eatons, it was actually his wife,

13. Cole, *Presidency of AJ*, 27.

14. Marszalek, *Petticoat Affair*, 65–6; and Smith, *First Forty Years*, 252, 282.

15. Marszalek, *Petticoat Affair*, 106–7; and Satterfield, "Moderate Nationalist Jacksonian," 63.

Floride, who set the tone for their association with the new secretary of war and his wife. Very aware of her own rising social standing in Washington and having heard rumors of Margaret's sordid past, Floride was reluctant to associate with them. After ignoring Margaret on Inauguration Day, she accepted a brief visit from the Eatons a few days after but then told her husband that she would not socialize with them again. The Calhouns left for South Carolina soon after that, and the vice-president did not return to the capital until late in the year. Calhoun kept in contact with his supporters in Washington, but there is no evidence that he participated in the Eaton affair during the months of his absence.[16]

Not surprisingly, Donelson found himself caught in the middle of this maelstrom, and a rift among his uncle's closest Tennessee allies complicated his position. There is little doubt that the Tennessee Jacksonians who helped Old Hickory obtain the presidency were clannish and that Jackson was, as one historian has described him, "the old general who stood as the thane, the real and symbolic leader of their clan." The members of the Nashville Junto were in constant competition as they attempted to benefit not only their Old Hero but also themselves. The group closest to the president, which consisted of Willie Blount, Hugh Lawson White, John Overton, William B. Lewis, and John H. Eaton, had dominated the state's politics virtually unchallenged from 1809 to 1819, its members controlling the Nashville Junto and spearheading Jackson's presidential bids in 1824 and 1828. During the 1828 campaign, however, divisions in that group began to appear. Jackson's selection of Eaton over White for secretary of war induced White, Felix Grundy, James K. Polk, and Cave Johnson to challenge the influence of Eaton and Lewis. White and company reiterated their loyalty to Jackson but argued that Eaton and Lewis were seeking to elevate their own standing at the expense of party unity, perhaps hurting the president in the process. Donelson, they were confident, could very well prove to be a key figure in convincing Jackson to rely less on the advice of these two men.[17]

16. Irving H. Bartlett, *John C. Calhoun: A Biography* (New York: W. W. Norton, 1994), 163–5; Niven, *JCC,* 167–8; Richard B. Latner, *The Presidency of Andrew Jackson: White House Politics, 1829–1837* (Athens: University of Georgia Press, 1979), 62–3; and Marszalek, *Petticoat Affair,* 52–4, 66.

17. Ratner, *Tennessee Lieutenants,* 4, chaps. 1 and 2; Remini, *Course of American Empire,* 83–5, 102–3, 124; Paul H. Bergeron, *Antebellum Politics in Tennessee* (Lexington: University Press of Kentucky, 1982), 1–5; idem, "Tennessee's Response to the Nullification Process," *Journal of Southern History* 39 (February

Donelson did, indeed, readily join the anti-Eaton / Lewis faction, a choice that, at first glance, seems surprising. The nature of his relationship with Lewis is unclear, but he had known Eaton for years, Jackson having even placed Eaton in charge of his nephew's move to West Point. At that time, Eaton had expressed a favorable impression of Donelson. Donelson left no opinion of Eaton from this period, but the two men worked together on Jackson's two presidential campaigns without any obvious conflict. Despite Margaret Eaton's later claims that her husband "had no confidence" in Donelson and "had cautioned the General" against him, that seems unlikely. Eaton later remarked to a mutual friend in the middle of the Eaton affair that he held no feelings other than friendship toward Donelson.[18]

What, then, motivated Donelson to join the anti-Eaton faction? As events unfolded, it became apparent that he felt threatened by Eaton and Lewis and their influence with his uncle. Donelson considered himself to be among Jackson's most important confidantes, and his appointment as the president's private secretary probably increased that assessment in his own mind. The actions of Eaton and Lewis threatened this position, however, and may have confirmed in Donelson what he had come to suspect: Eaton, as well as Lewis, viewed him, the youngest member of the Jackson's inner circle of Tennessee advisors, as a lackey, merely there to do their bidding. For a young man who had become comfortable with a position of power close to his uncle, that perceived lack of respect challenged his standing with Jackson.[19]

Donelson had other reasons to side with those opposed to the Eatons. Donelson was aware of the growing romance between his brother and John Branch's daughter, Margaret, which would result in their marriage the next year. He may have felt pressure to protect Daniel's marital intentions. Donelson was also suspicious of Van Buren. He admitted to the New Yorker later

1973): 24–5; Joseph H. Parks, *Felix Grundy: Champion of Democracy* (Baton Rouge: Louisiana State University Press, 1940), 166–73; and Charles G. Sellers Jr., *James K. Polk, Jacksonian: 1795–1843* (Princeton, N.J.: Princeton University Press, 1957), 68–72, 76–92, 95–9, 128–41, 197.

18. Marszalek, *Petticoat Affair,* 85–6, 200–1; JHE to AJ, 20 March 1817, in Moser, Hoth, and Hoemann, *PAJ* 4:103–5; Eaton, *Autobiography,* 92; and John Coffee to AJD, 6 February 1831, in Burke, *Emily Donelson* 1:275–6.

19. Charles Faulkner Bryan Jr., "The Prodigal Nephew: Andrew Jackson Donelson and the Eaton Affair," *East Tennessee Historical Society's Publications* 50 (1978): 98. Eaton and Lewis were former brothers-in-law, having been married to two sisters, Myra Lewis and Margaret Lewis, respectively. See *Dictionary of American Biography,* 20 vols. (New York: Scribner's, 1930), s.v. "John H. Eaton," 3:609–10.

that he had moved to Washington "full of misconception . . . and deeply biassed [*sic*]" against him. Van Buren had originally supported Crawford in the 1824 election, and Donelson had a difficult time believing that he was sincere in his change of heart toward Jackson. Calhoun, on the other hand, had promised to back Jackson immediately following Adams's election. That the Eaton-Lewis clique enthusiastically endorsed the new secretary of state confirmed Donelson's misgivings about Van Buren and encouraged him to support the anti-Eaton faction.[20]

Despite Donelson's political and personal differences, it was his wife, Emily, who set the tone for the Donelsons' reaction to the Eaton marriage. Margaret Eaton called upon the Donelson household shortly after the young couple arrived in Washington in 1829, and Emily returned her call "to please Uncle." But when Margaret "let it be [known] that . . . [the Donelsons] had paid her a visit and they were her best friends," Emily "could not think of visiting her any more." Her opinion of the embattled newlywed worsened because of Margaret's attempts to ingratiate herself. "I have been so much disgusted with what I have seen of her," Emily cringed, "that I shall not visit her again."[21]

Emily was only twenty-one years of age when she became hostess at the President's House, and replacing her Aunt Rachel as hostess was a heady experience. Through her position, Emily encountered Washington's female establishment and its community standards, and in this community, Margaret, the former "barmaid," was an outcast. As a young, impressionable, headstrong woman new to the Washington scene, Emily was no doubt intent on fitting in with those more knowledgeable about the city's social norms. That was not an easy task, since many Washingtonians were not fond of Jackson's rough edges, but joining the gossip about, and ostracism

20. John C. Fitzpatrick, ed., *The Autobiography of Martin Van Buren,* in *Annual Report of the American Historical Association for the Year 1918,* 2 vols. (Washington, D.C.: GPO), 1920), 2:346; and Satterfield, "Moderate Nationalist Jacksonian," 63. Satterfield argues that Donelson pledged to support Calhoun early in Jackson's first administration, but I have been unable to find the evidence (an undated, unsigned note in DLC) that he used to support that claim. Whether or not he explicitly committed his support to paper, Donelson's actions clearly indicated his choice of Calhoun over Van Buren, although it may have been a move more *against* Van Buren than *for* Calhoun.

21. John Donelson to John Coffee, 20 April 1829, ETD to Polly Coffee, 27 March 1829, in Burke, *Emily Donelson* 1:176, 177–9.

of, Margaret was an entry point for her. Additionally, Emily seemed to have possessed a personal aversion to Margaret. Emily claimed that she disliked Margaret upon meeting her on the trip to Washington during the disputed 1824 election. That may or may not have been true, but in 1829, Emily certainly held no love for Mrs. Eaton. She later characterized Margaret as "possessing a bad temper and a meddlesome disposition" and concluded that such behavior "had been so much increased by her husband's elevation as to make her society too disagreeable to be endured." Washington women and their social standards almost certainly encouraged these sentiments.[22]

As for Andrew Donelson, he likely reacted to news of the Eaton marriage with indifference. If Eaton wanted to marry a societal outcast, that was his decision. His appointment to a cabinet post roused Donelson's jealousy, but he kept his emotions under control at first. Eaton's direct questioning of Emily's coolness toward Margaret, however, was the action that provoked Donelson to anger. In early April 1829, just over a month after Jackson's inauguration, John Henry Eaton addressed a letter to Emily in which he informed her that a "little nest of inquirers" was attempting to influence her conduct toward his family. He advised Mrs. Donelson that she was "young and uninformed of the ways and of the malice and insincerity" of her new friends. Hence, he sought to keep her from following their lead and perhaps suffering the same fate as his wife. A follow-up note from Eaton the next day asked for more details as to what Emily's friends had told her about Margaret. This information, he believed, would allow him to make specific accusations against the alleged slanderers.[23]

Eaton's patronizing letters brought a swift and icy response, with Andrew helping his wife compose her rejoinder. "I thank God in all cases where I have need of the council and advice of a friend I have one who is competent to judge for me," Emily began acerbically. She defended her aunt's reputation, which Eaton intimated had been subjected to the same rumors that had befallen his own wife. After upholding her new friends' behavior, Emily concluded with a defense of her own actions. "I do not wish to decide upon

22. Fitzpatrick, *Autobiography of MVB* 2:344; and Catherine Allgor, *Parlor Politics: In Which the Ladies of Washington Help Build a City and a New Government* (Charlottesville: University Press of Virginia, 2000), 215–8.

23. JHE to ETD, 8, 9 April 1829, in Bassett and Jameson, *CAJ* 4:29–30.

any person's character here," she wrote, "nor controul [*sic*] in any way the etiquette of this place."[24]

In order to strengthen this reply, Donelson appended his own comments to Emily's letter. He asserted that his wife had not "given credence to these allegations" against the Eatons. As for their future relations with the secretary of war and his wife, Donelson assured Eaton that "no one can be more ready than myself to pay to yourself and to Mrs[.] Eaton every proper mark of respect, and by my example to recommend the sentiment which justifies it to my family." Anything more than that, Donelson remarked, "my regard for them, and my duty to society does not require me to go."[25]

Donelson's actions suggest that he was trying to maneuver in a political and social arena with which he was not familiar. The arrogance of Eaton's letter riled him, no doubt. How dare John Eaton lecture Emily about her social relations! How dare he try to undermine Donelson's control over his own family! Still, Donelson was unclear to Eaton about his family's social intentions. Would he and Emily socialize with the Eatons only at political functions, or would they also associate with them at other times? Additionally, he left unspoken his political relationship with Eaton. Would the two continue to work together to make the president's administration successful, or had the political gauntlet also been thrown down? The situation seemed to have left Donelson a bit befuddled about how to proceed.

After the heated exchange between Eaton and the Donelsons, communication between the two couples ceased for several weeks. Donelson wrote a close family friend, Gen. John Coffee, that an "unhappy prejudice" surrounded Margaret Eaton. "We have nothing to do with it," he assured Coffee, "but to leave it to its natural course, carefully avoiding its adoption as friends of Major Eaton, and at the same time not seeking to disturb the sentiments of others." Donelson concluded that "indiscretions" caused Washington society to react against the Eatons, and "but for that spirit of malignity so common now in society, would never have been construed as any thing [*sic*] worse."[26]

24. ETD to JHE, 10 April 1829, in Burke, *Emily Donelson* 1:186–7.

25. AJD to JHE, 10 April 1829, in Bassett and Jameson, *CAJ* 4:30.

26. AJD to John Coffee, 15 April 1829, DLC.

While Donelson was well aware of the goings-on in Washington, Tennessee friends kept him apprised of his home state's perception of the Eaton fiasco. A relative, John C. McLemore, informed Donelson that there was "much dissatisfaction at the appointment of our friend Major Eaton" among Jackson's supporters in the state. He warned the president's secretary that some of the state's politicians were discussing the formation of an anti-Jackson party with Governor William Carroll at the head. The result, McLemore advised, would be a "disastrous shock to . . . [Jackson's] standing in Tennessee." He assured Donelson that John Overton, Jackson's old political ally, and other prominent and faithful friends agreed with his assessment.[27]

Such matters were on Donelson's mind when he and Emily accompanied Jackson and the Eatons to Fort Monroe in July 1829. As the *Potomac* traveled toward its destination at Norfolk, Virginia, Emily, who was expecting their second child within the next two months, succumbed to the heat and fainted. Margaret offered her a fan and a cologne bottle, but Emily refused the assistance. Donelson did not witness that exchange, but when Margaret subtly threatened to have the Donelsons exiled to Tennessee, this comment struck a nerve.[28]

It did so because Donelson believed Margaret possessed the influence to carry out her threat. Later, Donelson told Jackson that he knew even before the Norfolk trip that the Eaton imbroglio was straining their relationship. "The truth is," he wrote the president in October 1830, "I had the means of establishing the existence of similar impressions in the society in which I every day moved before that trip, and after it from another unquestionable source." Donelson did not reveal who confirmed Margaret's warning, but he clearly knew that because of his and Emily's actions toward the Eatons, their position with Jackson was becoming tenuous.[29]

The Norfolk trip convinced Donelson that Margaret was deliberately pitting Emily and him against Jackson. Margaret intended to maintain the loyalty of the president, even if his uncooperative family was trampled in

27. JCM to AJD, 5 April 1829, DLC.

28. Burke, *Emily Donelson* 1:202–3, 205; and AJD to AJ, 25 October 1830, in Bassett and Jameson, *CAJ* 4:189–91.

29. AJD to AJ, 25 October 1830, in Bassett and Jameson, *CAJ* 4:189–91.

the process. It was at this point that Donelson determined that "it was impossible that I could submit to the degradation of having a tribune of this character constituted for the purpose of determining within what limits my good behaviour might secure the station which I held."[30]

The "Eaton malaria" affected more than the Donelsons; it continued to spread and infect the social and political life of the capital. Reverend James H. Campbell, who served as pastor for Jackson, Eaton, and Donelson, claimed knowledge that the couple had traveled together and slept in the same room before they were married. Margaret had also allegedly made several comments indicating that her children belonged to Eaton, or, at least, so she wished. In an interview with Donelson and a subsequent meeting with Jackson, Campbell related that a local physician, a Doctor Craven, had told him that Margaret, while still Timberlake's wife, had suffered a miscarriage. Campbell's memory of the dates was vague, but he believed that Timberlake had been away at sea longer than nine months at the time.[31]

Donelson wholeheartedly believed Campbell's account, but Jackson refused to accept it. The minister so exasperated him that the president convened his cabinet on 10 September 1829 for the sole purpose of disputing what he believed were Campbell's baseless accusations against Margaret Eaton. All of the cabinet members, Eaton excepted, attended, as did Donelson, Campbell, William B. Lewis, and Reverend Ezra Stiles Ely, another minister who claimed to know something about the Eatons' indiscretions. Point by point, Jackson refuted Campbell's allegations. When he triumphantly concluded his defense, Jackson asked Ely if he now believed that Margaret was innocent of the charges leveled against her. "On that point, I would rather not give an opinion," Ely rejoined. Jackson snapped angrily, "She is as chaste as a virgin!"[32]

With his administration under attack in his home state, his family, the nation's capital, and even houses of worship, it is little wonder that Jackson sought the source of the conspiracy that he believed his enemies had

30. Ibid.

31. Curtis Dahl, "The Clergyman, the Hussy, and Old Hickory: Ezra Stiles Ely and the Peggy Eaton Affair," *Journal of Presbyterian History* 52 (Summer 1974): 137–55; and memorandum by AJD, 3 September 1829, in Bassett and Jameson, *CAJ* 4:68–72.

32. AJD to John N. Campbell, 12 September 1829, DLC; and Remini, *Course of American Freedom,* 208–9.

formed against him. He initially blamed "Clay and his minions," seeing the present difficulty as an extension of the corrupt practices begun during the 1824 election. As the Petticoat Affair, as it was now called, grew in scope, however, Jackson began to look for other causes of the combination contaminating his administration.[33]

Sometime in the fall of 1829, Jackson finally, and mistakenly, agreed with the pro-Eaton advisors surrounding him that Vice-President John C. Calhoun was the source of his troubles. There appear to have been several reasons for his decision. First, Floride Calhoun was one of the leading ladies in the administration. With both Jackson and Van Buren widowers, it was one of her responsibilities to set the tone for social interaction in the nation's capital. Jackson had noticed her determined snub of Margaret in March and undoubtedly attributed it to the male head of the household. Second, he may already have discovered that Calhoun had not supported his invasion of Spanish Florida in 1818. Then secretary of war, Calhoun had argued that Jackson had superseded his orders and had committed an act of war. Not only that, but he had recommended that the General be censured. Lastly, political insiders suspected, and perhaps even knew, that Calhoun had authored "The South Carolina Exposition and Protest," an essay supporting nullification and opposing the Tariff of 1828. Jackson may have decided that the South Carolinian's extreme states' rights views did not fit his own nationalistic ideology. Whatever his thinking, Jackson marked Calhoun as his enemy, and the Eaton affair, which had started as an attempt by Washington women to regulate their social interactions, became the bloodiest political battle of Jackson's first administration.[34]

Jackson also saw Calhoun's hand in the opposition of his nephew and niece. His suspicions were apparently confirmed when a disgruntled Washington office seeker complained about Donelson's mistreatment of him. Mr. C. Alivater reported to the president that he had related to Donelson a conversation of "treasonable character" that he had overheard among Calhoun, Ingham, and others. Donelson, however, had refused to give it credence and had became so upset at what he deemed "slanderous" accusations

33. Remini, *Course of American Freedom,* 204–5.

34. Marszalek, *Petticoat Affair,* 52–5; Allgor, *Parlor Politics,* 202–3; Niven, *JCC,* 68–71, 167–8; Latner, *Presidency of AJ,* 62–3, 66–72; and idem, "The Eaton Affair Reconsidered," *THQ* 36 (Fall 1977): 330–51.

against Ingham and Branch that he refused to recommend Alivater for a government position. The president apparently believed the angry man's story over that of his nephew. Jackson was convinced that Calhoun was behind the grand conspiracy to discredit his administration, and he was worried that the South Carolinian had duped his nephew.[35]

Donelson could not have disagreed more. He suspected that it was the pro-Eaton clique that was manipulating the president for its members' own dishonorable gain, and thus he chose the side that he thought was looking out for Jackson's best interests. Whatever suspicion he held about the motives of Eaton, Lewis, and company regarding the president, Donelson believed that he ultimately needed to persuade his uncle that he, not they, was protecting Jackson from disloyal friends.

One of the ways to continue proving his loyalty and keep an eye on the Van Buren faction was to continue his duties, which Donelson did. As December 1829 drew near, Jackson presented his nephew with a significant writing task: helping other members of the Kitchen Cabinet compose the president's first annual message. Donelson had contributed to Jackson's inaugural address, but the annual message was more important because it offered a substantial outline of what the president hoped to achieve in terms of policy. Each cabinet officer and department head sent reports to Donelson and his friend from West Point, Nicholas P. Trist, who now worked as a clerk in the State Department. Donelson and Trist then edited and rewrote the reports, submitting them to Jackson for his revisions and final approval.[36]

The annual message submitted to Congress recommended term limits for government officials, including the president, warned against tying the tariff question to "the party conflicts of the day," suggested apportioning to the states the surplus government revenue available after the payment of the national debt, and informed the American people that Jackson had advised the Native American tribes in the South to remove to land west of the Mississippi River. He also hinted that, in the near future, he might seek

35. AJD to C. Alivater, 7 January 1830, DLC; and Satterfield, "Moderate Nationalist Jacksonian," 75.

36. AJD to [JCM], 16 December 1829, DLC; Remini, *Course of American Freedom,* 250–1; Dorothy G. Fowler, *The Cabinet Politician: The Postmasters General, 1829–1909* (New York: Columbia University Press, 1943), 23; Satterfield, "Moderate Nationalist Jacksonian," 42–3, 101; Longaker, "Was Jackson's Kitchen Cabinet a Cabinet?" 103; drafts of first annual message, JLC; and draft of first annual message, 8 December 1829, in Bassett and Jameson, *CAJ* 4:97–104.

the replacement of the Second Bank of the United States. Donelson proudly declared the message "the most popular that has been delivered since the days of Washington."[37]

Unfortunately for Donelson, his reluctance during those months to join his uncle in condemning Calhoun became more complicated with the growing threat of nullification. Passage of a high tariff in 1828 had infuriated many southerners, especially South Carolinians. In response to this so-called Tariff of Abominations, Calhoun had written "The South Carolina Exposition and Protest," which argued that the states were sovereign and could nullify, or void, any federal law that violated a strict, states' rights interpretation of the Constitution. Along with nullification, Calhoun had asserted that states also had the right to secede from the Union if necessary.[38]

The argument over the necessity and constitutionality of nullification became a public spectacle in early 1830, when Senators Daniel Webster of Massachusetts and Robert Y. Hayne of South Carolina turned a debate over public lands into a passionate discussion about the nature of the Union. Hayne defended nullification as a right granted at the time of the nation's founding, while Webster argued that sovereignty resided in the people, not the states. Jackson found the doctrine of nullification appalling and sought an opportunity to state explicitly that the growing nullification movement in South Carolina, led in part by Calhoun, was antithetical to his own views of the nation.[39]

If he had initially possessed any loyalty to Calhoun, which is far from certain, Donelson had abandoned it by 1830, undoubtedly because the vice-president's extreme states' rights position was incompatible with the republican principles of the Jacksonian Democrats. The Jefferson Day banquet, held every 13 April in honor of the third president's birthday, gave Jackson the chance to strike at Calhoun publicly, but it also provided Donelson with the opportunity to show Jackson that he had not left the fold. Calhoun and

37. First annual message, 8 December 1829, in Richardson, *Messages and Papers of the Presidents* 2:442–62; and AJD to [JCM], 16 December 1829, DLC.

38. For the Nullification Crisis, see William W. Freehling, *Prelude to Civil War: The Nullification Controversy in South Carolina, 1816–1836* (New York: Harper and Row, 1966); Richard E. Ellis, *The Union at Risk: Jacksonian Democracy, States' Rights, and the Nullification Crisis* (New York: Oxford University Press, 1987); and Latner, "Nullification Crisis," 19–38.

39. Freehling, *Prelude to Civil War,* 183–6.

other staunch states' rights leaders would be there, so the president wanted to make a strong statement. (Jackson and Calhoun had by this time virtually reached a breaking point over the Eaton imbroglio and the Seminole controversy.) The president turned to Donelson and Van Buren for assistance in preparing a toast that would encapsulate his views. Donelson eagerly agreed to help his uncle. The three men finally settled on "The Federal Union: It must be preserved" as the president's toast. According to reports, Jackson's delivery of this statement at the banquet left Calhoun visibly shaken, but the South Carolinian recovered enough to offer a response that affirmed his commitment to an extreme states' rights position. The split between president and vice-president over nullification was now in the open.[40]

What should have been a triumph for Donelson, however, was not the victory for which he had hoped. His contribution to Jackson's public challenge of Calhoun failed to alleviate his uncle's suspicions about his loyalty. The president continued to doubt his nephew, and Donelson was discovering that regaining his uncle's trust was more difficult than he ever could have imagined.

40. Fitzpatrick, *Autobiography of MVB,* 2:413–4; Satterfield, "Moderate Nationalist Jacksonian," 78; and Remini, *Course of American Freedom,* 234–5.

5

“A House Divided Cannot Stand”

While Jackson remained convinced that John C. Calhoun was conspiring to destroy his administration, Andrew Donelson grew certain that William B. Lewis and Martin Van Buren were behind the controversy. Lewis was, by all accounts, an intriguer, and Jackson relied on him for gathering evidence that reinforced his perception of Margaret Eaton. Van Buren, meanwhile, cultivated the president’s friendship and, Donelson believed, viewed the Eaton affair as an opportunity to advance his political fortunes. Daniel Donelson’s marriage to Margaret Branch, daughter of the navy secretary, drew his brother even further into the anti–Van Buren faction. Meanwhile, Donelson’s relatives, especially John Coffee and John C. McLemore, assured him that the situation was critical in Tennessee and that Jackson was going too far in defending the Eatons. In reply, Donelson sent frequent letters to them relaying his hope that, when it was all over, the events of the Petticoat Affair would “be remembered only as the little inconveniences that disturb any condition of life.”[1]

Donelson had no idea how wrong he would be. In the spring of 1830, Van Buren endeavored to smooth hard feelings by visiting Emily Donelson at the White House and encouraging her to reconcile with Margaret. Emily refused. The situation only worsened in June, when Jackson invited Margaret to eat with him at the President’s House. She replied that she would have to decline his request. “Circumstances . . . are such as that under your kind and hospitable roof I cannot be happy,” Margaret wrote. “I could not expect to be happy at your house for this would be to expect a different course of treatment from part of your family.” Her implication was obvious. Margaret contended that she had “done all in my power to avoid” the “unkind

1. Bryan, “Prodigal Nephew,” 102–4; AJD to John Coffee, 27 August 1829, in Burke, *Emily Donelson* 1:205; and John Coffee to AJD, 3 November 1829, RDC.

treatment" of the president's nephew and niece. As "much injustice as I think they have done me," she noted self-righteously, "I have ever endeavored to return good for evil."[2]

Donelson, who screened Jackson's correspondence, stared at the letter incredulously. Unkind treatment? "The only *unkind treatment* which my family can have p[r]acticed towards Mrs. Eaton," he angrily scrawled at the bottom of her letter before passing it on to Jackson, "is their refusal to acknowledge her right to interfere with their social relations." The rest of Donelson's note to Jackson expressed his frustration:

> All else is imaginary or worse. This letter is abundant evidence of the indelicacy which distinguishes her character, and is disgraceful to her husband. Instead of coming to me as the head of my family for explanations where objections to my conduct were entertained, they have invariably approached the President with childish importunities, first aiming to excite his sympathies, and then to pour upon them the poison which they had concocted for all who did not bow to her commands. Persuasion, personal threats, and finally banishment from the presence of the President, to whom I have stood from my infancy in the relation of son to Father, have served their turn as the wretched expedients in their hands to gratify the vain desire of being understood to possess the controul [*sic*] of his confidence and favor.[3]

Donelson expressed concern about three things: his position as a husband, the Eatons' control of the president, and the Donelsons' own relationship with Jackson. First, Donelson believed that Margaret had attacked his role as the leader of his family and home. In the patriarchal South of Donelson's day, criticism of the male head of a household, especially by a woman, challenged established authority. Donelson's often emotional reactions to Margaret Eaton's accusations, then, were not simply reactions to the implications for him and Emily but for his place in society. Southern patri-

2. Bryan, "Prodigal Nephew," 104; and Margaret Eaton to AJ, 9 June 1830, in Bassett and Jameson, *CAJ* 4:145.

3. AJD to AJ, 10 June 1829, in Bassett and Jameson, *CAJ* 4:145–6.

archy also explains why Donelson considered her behavior "disgraceful" to John Eaton. The actions of the family reflected on the husband, and Margaret, Donelson thought, was dishonoring her husband by challenging his authority.[4]

Donelson also condemned the Eatons' manipulation of the president and its effect on his and Emily's relationship with Jackson. By invoking Rachel Jackson's name and comparing their situation to that of the Jacksons, John and Margaret Eaton "excite[d] his [Jackson's] sympathies" and turned him against his deceased wife's own flesh. Donelson recognized that the Eatons had slowly gained Jackson's ear, persuaded him that he and Emily, his nephew and niece, were standing against him, and convinced the president to consider sending them back to Tennessee. Since Donelson believed himself bound to Jackson by the bonds of family and honor, it is not surprising that he was upset.

If Margaret's letter infuriated Donelson, then events later that month made his disposition worse. Jackson, with the Donelsons accompanying him, returned to Nashville in late June. The Eatons planned to join them along the way. The president's stated purpose was to meet with the Choctaw and Chickasaw leaders and discuss their removal from southeastern lands. Jackson's real reason for the trip, as he revealed to John Coffee, was to attend to the acrimonious relationships "that have coroded [*sic*] my peace, and my mind, and must cease, or my administration will be a distracted one, which I cannot permit."[5]

Jackson was deluding himself. The return to Tennessee merely aggravated the situation. The Jackson party reached Nashville on 5 July 1830, the Eatons not until nearly two weeks later. To avoid contact with the Eatons, who visited frequently from their home in nearby Franklin, and further damage to their strained relationship with Jackson, Andrew and Emily conveniently decided to stay with her mother instead of at the Hermitage or

4. Elizabeth Fox-Genovese, *Within the Plantation Household: Black and White Women of the Old South* (Chapel Hill: University of North Carolina Press, 1988), 63–4; Stephanie McCurry, *Masters of Small Worlds: Yeoman Households, Gender Relations, and the Political Culture of the Antebellum South Carolina Low Country* (New York: Oxford University Press, 1995), 6; and Laura F. Edwards, "Law, Domestic Violence, and the Limits of Patriarchal Authority in the Antebellum South," *Journal of Southern History* 65 (November 1999): 740.

5. Marszalek, *Petticoat Affair,* 128–9; Bryan, "Prodigal Nephew," 105; and AJ to John Coffee, 14 June 1830, in Bassett and Jameson, *CAJ* 4:146.

Springdale. Seemingly oblivious to the effect on his nephew and niece, Jackson organized and accepted invitations to parties, barbeques, and banquets intended to welcome him and his friends home. His intent was to ensure that the secretary of war and his wife received the respect and attention that he believed they deserved. All the while, Jackson kept a sharp eye out for the "intrigue of well disciplined politicians, a combination of the most heterogeneous mass of base enemies and boosom [*sic*] and dear friends" who were attempting to disrupt his administration. Sadly for Donelson, Jackson refused to believe that he had withdrawn his support of Calhoun and that none of the "enemies" identified by the president were manipulating his nephew.[6]

The Donelsons' precarious situation, therefore, only worsened. Jackson told Coffee that duty required that "my household should bestow equal comity to all, and the nation expects me to controle [*sic*] my household." Their refusal to associate with the Eatons even in Tennessee infuriated him and made him even more determined to set them straight. "You know I am immoveable," he wrote William B. Lewis in July. "It may so happen that I shall return to the city in company with my son alone." A week later, the president informed Lewis that "the combination and conspiracy to injure and prostrate Major Eaton, and injure me," was continuing. "That my Nephew and Nece [*sic*] should permit themselves to be held up as the instruments, and tools, of such wickedness," Jackson noted regretfully, "is truly mortifying to me." It was looking increasingly like Margaret was right. If Andrew and Emily would not acquiesce to their uncle's wishes, if they did not get out from under the influence of the "great Magician" Calhoun, then they would be left behind in Tennessee when the president returned to Washington. Jackson even told Lewis to begin finding a replacement for Donelson as his private secretary.[7]

Jackson's anger toward the Donelsons caused great concern among their friends and family. McLemore kept Coffee apprised of the Eatons' alleged conspiracy to come between Jackson and Donelson. Jackson was "about to

6. Marszalek, *Petticoat Affair,* 128–35; and AJ to John Coffee, 20 July 1830, in Bassett and Jameson, *CAJ* 4:164–5.

7. AJ to John Coffee, 20 July 1830, AJ to WBL, 21, 28 July 1830, in Bassett and Jameson, *CAJ* 4:164–5, 165–6, 167.

be made a dupe of the most rascally combination of scoundrels," he observed. As for Donelson, McLemore assured Coffee that "when you are fully in possession of the honest stand A. J. Donelson has taken in regard to this affair and the incalculable injury he has averted by it, and when you see he is about to be sacrificed for his honesty by a set of dam[n] S[coundrels] . . . you will be ready to burst with indignation." McLemore even claimed that the secretary of war had attempted to bribe him with a "loan" of twenty thousand dollars, which he, of course, rejected. The tension was so high that McLemore expected an "explosion" at any moment.[8]

Coffee traveled from Alabama to Nashville, hoping that his presence would help avert the impending outburst predicted by McLemore. He brought Jackson some consolation that the Donelsons would receive the Eatons. When that did not happen, the president gave his nephew an ultimatum. Either Donelson would return to Washington without Emily or stay in Tennessee with her. After some thought, Donelson agreed to go to Washington alone. Someone, perhaps Donelson, suggested that Margaret remain behind as well. Margaret considered the possibility but eventually rejected it. In September 1830, Jackson and Donelson, minus Emily and the children, returned to the capital. John and Margaret Eaton made the trip a month later.[9]

Emily's absence, which Jackson thought would put an end to the division within his household, did little to bring about reconciliation. The president's conditions for Emily's return frustrated Donelson. She would only be allowed to resume her former position as hostess if she was willing to "assume that dignified course that ought to have been at first adopted, of . . . extending the same comity and attention to all the heads of Departments, and their families." Jackson, of course, mentioned not one word about Margaret's responsibility in ending the difficulty.[10]

Donelson's pent-up exasperation and dissatisfaction finally exploded on 25 October 1830. A morning argument with Jackson led him to pen a letter to his uncle protesting the conditions placed upon Emily's return. Donelson

8. JCM to John Coffee, 16, 21 July 1830, RDC.

9. Burke, *Emily Donelson* 1:240–1; and AJ to JHE, 3 August 1830, AJ to WBL, 7 August 1830, AJ to MVB, 12 August 1830, in Bassett and Jameson, *CAJ* 4:168–9, 170–1, 171.

10. AJ to Mary Eastin, 24 October 1830, in Bassett and Jameson, *CAJ* 4:186–8.

reminded Jackson that he and Emily had treated the Eatons with the civility required by social etiquette. Despite that consideration, John Eaton had written Emily a letter in which he accused her of being "under the guardianship of slanderers." While that allegation was insulting, Donelson especially took exception to the insinuation "that my power to hold my place here depended upon my subserviency to the wishes of Mrs. Eaton." Following the incident on the Norfolk trip, Donelson had determined that he and Emily could no longer interact socially with the Eatons as if his position depended upon it. "Honorable as I deem that station," he informed the president, "I scorn to hold it at the will of any one but yourself, or at the expense of those principles with which have grown up my love and gratitude for you." Donelson's decision, then, was simple: his family would not interact socially with Margaret Eaton except in the president's home in Washington. Even should Jackson relent and request that Emily return, Donelson would not allow her to do so except under the conditions he had outlined.[11]

This letter demonstrates Donelson's dilemma. Unquestionably loyal to his uncle, he was, in fact, simply following the advice that Jackson had given him while he was attending West Point. His uncle had warned him repeatedly to choose his friends and acquaintances carefully, taking time to ensure that they were virtuous and worthy of amity. Jackson had even cautioned him against interacting with immoral females. In Donelson's opinion, Jackson's insistence that his nephew and niece intermingle with the Eatons contradicted his uncle's previous counsel. On this point, Donelson had listened and learned well.

One historian describes Donelson as "Andrew Jackson's son in that way. He stubbornly held to his view as a matter of honor, even if it meant opposing the very man who had taught him about honor in the first place." Donelson made it clear that whatever damage his stand might have on his "future prospects," he hoped to show that he "was not tempted by those considerations which usually assail integrity of motive and uprightness of heart." It was an admirable but naïve stance. Donelson did not seem to realize that Jackson did not view his position in the same light. For Jackson, maintaining his administration against his political enemies was paramount. His

11. AJD to AJ, 25 October 1830, in ibid. 4:189–91.

nephew's failure to see that point demonstrated that he did not understand what was at stake.[12]

If Jackson had been thinking clearly, he would have proudly recognized that his nephew had taken his advice about honor and virtue to heart. His stubbornness, however, blinded him to Donelson's reasoning. Instead of viewing his nephew as acting out of virtuous motives, the president saw only a deluded young man caught in the grips of a conspiracy. He wrote Donelson a letter that autumn afternoon insisting that all he had to do was "read the Testimony in [Margaret's] defence" and he would see her innocence. Other "good, virtuous and respectable characters" had called on Margaret Eaton, why could not Emily? As almost an afterthought, Jackson admitted that "all people have a right to select their society, every head of a family have [*sic*] the right to govern their House hold."[13]

Not in Andrew Donelson's case, however. Jackson's paternal authority superseded that of his nephew, he believed, because Donelson's family lived under his roof. Jackson expected Donelson and his family to comply completely with his orders concerning the Eatons, which they apparently were not willing to do. Even though they were living together in the White House, the two estranged men spent the next day exchanging not words but letters. Jackson wished to have a "free, friendly, and full conversation" with his nephew. Donelson, however, had apparently resigned himself to the belief that the president would not relent and asked Jackson to let him know whether he wanted him to stay on as his private secretary or return to Tennessee. "It may be best for you to look to some one to take my place at once," he wrote. In reply, Jackson yet again indicated that he wanted to converse in person.[14]

Despite the president's wishes, the written correspondence within the President's House continued until 30 October. Jackson sent Donelson a long missive in which he agreed that it might be best for his nephew to go back to Tennessee after Congress adjourned. Although he expressed disappointment about Donelson actually leaving his service, Jackson's real regret was

12. Marszalek, *Petticoat Affair,* 140; and AJD to AJ, 25 October 1830, in Bassett and Jameson, *CAJ* 4:189–91.

13. AJ to AJD, [26?] October 1830, in Bassett and Jameson, *CAJ* 4:191.

14. AJ to AJD, 27 October 1830 (two letters), AJD to AJ, 27 October 1830, in ibid. 4:192.

his nephew's "constant melancholy, and abstraction from me" since the beginning of the Eaton affair. He also took offense at Donelson's comment that he had only been a guest in his uncle's house. "When my D[ea]r Andrew were you my guest or how and when treated only as such[?]" Jackson protested. "Review this expression," he chided his nephew, "it is unjust to me, nay, it is Humiliating to us all." He also mentioned his pain at the Donelsons refusing to stay at the Hermitage with him during the summer visit to Tennessee.[15]

Donelson passionately defended his actions. He reiterated his willingness to meet with the Eatons in the President's House but not elsewhere. Donelson charged Jackson with asking him to do something that his conscience would not allow. "You did not when a prisoner in the revolutionary war obey the order of the enemy who had you in his power to clean his boots," he reminded the president, "yet you find fault with my determination merely to keep out of the way of insult." As for the Tennessee trip, Margaret had made it clear that she would not stay under that same roof with the Donelsons. Given Jackson's support of Margaret during that time, "were we not bound from respect even to your feelings not to put ourselves in the way of the honors you intended to pay to Mr. and Mrs. Eaton at the Hermitage?"[16]

In response, Jackson suggested what once would have been unthinkable: that his nephew consider going back to Tennessee permanently. Donelson suspected that one of his rivals was behind the idea and confronted his uncle about rumors in Nashville that had William B. Lewis choosing a replacement for him. Jackson "disavowed having authorized any such inquiry," and Donelson told John C. McLemore that Lewis left himself susceptible to being "flogged" for his actions.[17]

The flood of letters between the two eventually ceased, but only for a few days. Donelson took time in the middle of the exchanges to inform his wife that he likely would be coming home soon. Emily responded over the next few weeks, urging him to stay as long as he thought appropriate. If he did not, his and Jackson's enemies would use it to harm the president and

15. AJ to AJD, 30 October 1830 (two letters), in ibid. 4:193–5, 196.

16. AJD to AJ, 30 October 1830 (two letters), in ibid. 4:195–6, 196–7.

17. AJ to AJD, 30 October 1830 (two letters), in ibid. 4:193–5, 196; and AJD to JCM, 9 January 1831, DLC.

"the whole of the blame will be put on your shoulders." Emily also indicated her willingness to meet with Margaret on social occasions away from the President's House, if that would end the dispute between uncle and nephew. Her encouraging letters "converted . . . into smiles . . . the indignation" that Donelson felt.[18]

The peace that had settled over the president's household lasted only a short time. By 9 November 1830, Donelson and Jackson had again resorted to writing to one another while living in the same house. Donelson kept a personal journal during this period recounting the conversations that they held in November. In one entry, he described a discussion that took place on 10 November. Donelson had repeated to Jackson his resolve to govern his own household affairs and had reiterated that Emily would not visit the Eatons outside of the president's presence. When Jackson protested that his letter caused him "much pain," Donelson argued that he was only trying to defend the president's "fame and [ensure] the protection of my own honor and character."[19]

Other circumstances conspired to keep alive the rift between uncle and nephew. When James Hamilton Jr., a prominent South Carolina politician and leading nullifier, contacted Donelson in November and promised to update Jackson on the situation in his state, the president questioned why his nephew was corresponding with the enemy. For his part, Jackson's denial of involvement in Lewis's subterfuge gave Donelson little comfort. He did not want to believe that his uncle was culpable in the alleged plot and took great pains to make that clear to friends. The trust between the two men had been violated to the point, however, that Donelson, while not vilifying his uncle directly, began criticizing his policies privately.[20]

One of Donelson's complaints about Jackson was the president's continued public feud with Calhoun, which he believed was "impolitic . . . [and] not beneficial to the General's personal fame." He denounced the quarrel and suggested that "the spirit of forgiveness" should have compelled Jackson

18. AJD to ETD, 28 October 1830, in Bassett and Jameson, *CAJ* 4:193; and ETD to AJD, 30 October, 26, 30 November 1830, AJD to ETD, 20 November 1830, in Burke, *Emily Donelson* 1:254, 258–9, 259–60, 255.

19. AJD to AJ, 9 November 1830, JLC; and Statement by AJD, 10–21 November 1830, in Bassett and Jameson, *CAJ* 4:201–2.

20. James Hamilton Jr. to AJD, 3 November 1830, DLC.

to maintain his friendship with the vice-president. "Remember my words," he wrote McLemore, "the movement against Calhoun tho it does not defeat Genl Jackson's election, disorganizes the party, and will make his triumph a personal rather than a political one."[21]

Donelson also decried Jackson's policies regarding nullification in South Carolina and Georgia, which was looking to remove the Cherokee from their ancestral lands. The president's actions were exacerbating the nation's political rivalries, he told McLemore, and creating confusion within the party. "We raise up one after another great engines of opposition. The Tariff, Internal improvements, Bank and lastly the supreme court, against these the popular feeling may sustain and select the General," he observed. "Of what avail will this be after that event," Donelson asked, "if his Presidency does not harmonize the political divisions of the country, sufficiently to secure the ascendancy of his principles?"[22]

Donelson was careful, of course, to insist to McLemore that he still supported Jackson. "I am afraid of awaking your suspicion, that I am more disposed to dabble in Politics, than to discharge my duties. I therefore stop, with the assurance that you misapprehend me, if you ascribe to me any other wish than that of serving Uncle honorably in his arduous tasks," he reassured his friend. Jackson was clearly the target of his disapproval, but Donelson made sure that McLemore understood that he was still loyal to the president.[23]

A partial resolution to the family rift came in early 1831. In mid-January, Donelson wrote Emily that their uncle had finally yielded. While he still defended the Eatons, Jackson had indicated to Donelson that Emily could return whenever her husband believed it proper. The president had also relented on the requirement that his niece and nephew visit the Eatons. Once Congress adjourned, Donelson told his wife, he would come to Tennessee and escort her and their family back to Washington. In the meantime, he cautioned Emily that they would have to "observe our usual silence" on the subject, since Jackson was volatile and circumstances could change at any time.[24]

Donelson set out for Tennessee on 8 March 1831. When he reached his home, a letter from the president, sent only two days after his departure from

21. AJD to JCM, 9 January 1831, DLC.

22. Ibid.

23. Ibid.

24. AJD to ETD, 15 January 1831, in Burke, *Emily Donelson* 1:268–9.

Washington, tempered his elation at seeing his family. Jackson told Donelson that Eaton had been extremely sick when Donelson was leaving Washington and had asked the president why his nephew had not visited him before he left. Why Eaton was so concerned about Donelson's attentions toward him is unclear. It is possible that Jackson received the news from Margaret, who was once again stirring up trouble. Whatever transpired with the Eatons in Washington changed Jackson's mind. He notified Donelson that "as much as I desire you, and your dear little family with me, unless you and yours can harmonise with major [*sic*] Eaton and his family, I do not wish you here."[25]

Donelson was beside himself. The Eaton-Lewis element had used his absence, he believed, to undermine the tenuous relationship he had rebuilt with his uncle. He particularly suspected Lewis of maneuvering to ensconce himself and his daughter as replacements for Jackson's private secretary and official hostess. It looked like Donelson's temporary visit to Tennessee was going to become an exile.

In the early spring of 1831, circumstances in Washington finally seemed to offer a resolution to the entire Petticoat Affair and presented hope for family reconciliation. On 7 April, Eaton took the dramatic step of tendering his resignation to Jackson. Van Buren's followed four days later. Their departure from the cabinet, which Van Buren had orchestrated, would allow the president to request the resignations of its other members, thus purging the advisory body of its malcontents and freeing Jackson to name men more agreeable to his own point of view. With an end to the "Eaton malaria" near, Jackson invited Donelson to resume his position by his side. "I have great need of your aid," he implored. Jackson's conciliatory remarks stemmed in part from a letter that he had received from John Coffee, in which his old friend reminded him that Donelson held "advantages that [were] possessed by few," including "a sence of honor . . . excelled by no man . . . and more knowledge of your business, and of your views generally than any other person."[26]

Donelson intended to visit Washington for only a short time then return home and bring Emily and other family members back to the capital with

25. Bryan, "Prodigal Nephew," 108; and AJ to AJD, 10, 24 March 1831, in Bassett and Jameson, *CAJ* 4:248–9, 251–4.

26. Fitzpatrick, *Autobiography of MVB* 2:403–7; and JHE to AJ, 7 April 1831, AJ to AJD, 19 April 1831, John Coffee to AJ, 28 April 1831, in Bassett and Jameson, *CAJ* 4:257–8, 265–6, 270–1.

him. Jackson, however, changed his mind once again, chiding his nephew for suggesting that "Lewis and Co" were "a set of intriguers." Calhoun's recent break from the administration and his publication of a lengthy statement defending his actions during the Seminole affair gave Jackson more ammunition. Donelson had cast his lot with the Calhounites, who had "alienated you from me, [and] poisoned your mind against my old, and well tried friends." On and on Jackson wrote, refuting (at least in his mind) his nephew's justification for acting as he had toward the Eatons. He reminded Donelson "that a House divided cannot stand." Jackson concluded by notifying him that he would seek a replacement for him as private secretary, someone "who will aid me, and who will think it no disgrace to associate *with me, and my friends.*"[27]

Jackson's distrust of his nephew would have been laughable if it were not so sad. Donelson remained in Washington only a few weeks, during which time the president's mood steadily worsened. Branch published a letter describing the terms under which he had resigned, and his statement made Jackson fume even more. "I hope [Donelson's] eyes are beginning to be opened" to the unfaithfulness of his friends, he wrote Coffee. A final attempt at convincing his uncle to reconsider failed, and Donelson set out dejectedly for Tennessee in mid-June 1831. Jackson's decision to replace him with his nephew's old friend, Nicholas P. Trist, signaled finality to the president's decision.[28]

Donelson took an out-of-the-way route home, traveling to North Carolina in order to visit Branch, a move that annoyed Jackson. A Fourth of July celebration in Washington, at which the participants toasted Emily and the other women who had ostracized Margaret, fueled his anger even more. The president condemned the toast as improper because it used the women solely for "political effect." Calhoun, of course, was behind it all, Jackson suspected. In writing Donelson, he reiterated the necessity of Emily according the Eatons social respect if she wanted to return.[29]

After more than two years of arguments, suspicion, and hurt feelings, the end of the Eaton affair for the Donelsons finally came later that summer.

27. Bryan, "Prodigal Nephew," 109–10; and AJ to AJD, 5 May 1831, in Bassett and Jameson, *CAJ* 4:273–8.

28. Satterfield, "Moderate Nationalist Jacksonian," 93–7; AJ to John Coffee, 26 May 1831, in Bassett and Jameson, *CAJ* 4:285; and Ohrt, *Defiant Peacemaker*, 69, 73.

29. Satterfield, "Moderate Nationalist Jacksonian," 97–8; and AJ to AJD, 10, 11, 27 July 1831, in Bassett and Jameson, *CAJ* 4:310–1, 311–2, 317–8.

John C. McLemore, who, along with Tennessee allies John Bell and Alfred Balch, had been intimately involved throughout the family disagreement, notified Jackson that he and the others believed that the president needed Andrew and Emily by his side. They had convinced the Donelsons to set out for Washington uninvited, with the hope that Jackson would not turn them away. They gambled correctly. Although Jackson groused to Van Buren that he hoped the Donelsons "know my *course,* and my wishes, and I hope, they come to comply," he welcomed his relatives back into his household. They made every effort to appease their uncle by visiting his friends and avoiding those who opposed the Eatons. John and Margaret Eaton's departure for Franklin, Tennessee, in mid-September 1831 aided their efforts.[30]

The Eaton affair marked the low point of Donelson's relationship with Jackson. He and Emily found themselves exiled and berated by their uncle for over two years. The president's long-winded diatribes on proper social intercourse and familial fidelity were exhausting. Instead of addressing his nephew as an adult male who was a member of the southern gentry, Jackson reverted to the paternalistic treatment that had accompanied his lectures on writing frequently and practicing parsimony while Donelson was in school.

Historians offer differing interpretations for Donelson's actions, none of which accord with Jackson's belief that his nephew was a pawn in Calhoun's game of intrigue. In his study of the Eaton affair, John F. Marszalek characterizes Donelson as an "insecure individual" who "wanted to please his uncle, his uncle's political opponents, and society's gentility all at the same time." Charles F. Bryan Jr. finds that Donelson treated the affair "as one of social and moral propriety and . . . leadership within his own family" and viewed his actions as protecting his uncle from an Eaton–Van Buren political conspiracy. This interpretation parallels that of Robert B. Satterfield, Donelson's only biographer to date. Richard B. Latner also finds Donelson fighting a war against the Van Buren political machine intent on unseating Calhoun and raising the secretary of state's standard.[31]

30. JCM and John Bell to AJ, 29 July 1831, AJ to MVB, 5 September 1831, in Bassett and Jameson, *CAJ* 4:323, 346–8; and Satterfield, "Moderate Nationalist Jacksonian," 99–100.

31. Marszalek, *Petticoat Affair,* 139; Bryan, "Prodigal Nephew," 111; Satterfield, "Moderate Nationalist Jacksonian," chap. 4; and Latner, *Presidency of AJ,* 65–6.

Donelson's actions during the Petticoat Affair corroborate each of these interpretations. Jackson's distrust of him certainly made Donelson insecure in his relationship with his uncle. It is also clear that he sought to protect Jackson from what he considered a conspiracy fomented by Van Buren, Eaton, and Lewis. An additional factor was the Donelsons' desire to please socialites in the nation's capital in order to ease their entry into Washington society. At the same time, Donelson fought to shield his own household from the influence of Margaret Eaton, who did not fit Washington (or southern) society's concept of the virtuous woman.

The influence of women over the male political actors in this event, including Donelson, cannot be underestimated. While the men involved viewed the Eaton affair as largely political intrigue, the women certainly did not. And for all of the posturing and maneuvering that took place among the political factions, the women seemed to control much of the discourse, even if it was considered outside of their sphere of influence. Emily's control over her husband's actions is a pertinent example. At the heart of Andrew Donelson's initial refusal to meet with the Eatons socially was Emily's steadfast objection to associating with Margaret. As the arbiter of female morality, it was her decision, not her husband's or her uncle's, whether they would visit the Eatons outside of official functions. Even after she was exiled to Tennessee, Emily held considerable influence over her husband's position. As a condition of her return, she wrote her husband in late 1830, she would agree to see Margaret "sometime[s] officially" in order to satisfy Jackson if Andrew thought it would help "convince him of your desire to please him." In other words, she was willing to compromise in her sphere of influence, the family, in order for him to maintain his position in his sphere, which was politics. Neither he nor Jackson could expect her to concede control over her sphere, however. It may have been the right move in Emily's mind, but it was a poor political decision for her husband's career.[32]

32. Marszalek, *Petticoat Affair,* vii, 237–40; Allgor, *Parlor Politics,* chap. 5; Kirsten Wood, "'One Woman So Dangerous to Public Morals': Gender and Power in the Eaton Affair," *Journal of the Early Republic* 17 (Summer 1997): 254–5; Norma Basch, "Equity vs. Equality: Emerging Concepts of Women's Political Status in the Age of Jackson," *Journal of the Early Republic* 3 (Fall 1983): 308; Sister M. Perpetua Pigott, "Emily Donelson and the Eaton Affair" (master's thesis, Catholic University of America, 1948), 47–56; and ETD to AJD, 30 November [1830], quoted in Atkins, *Emily Donelson,* 192.

Historians have overlooked the importance of virtue and honor in the Eaton affair, especially in interpreting the actions of both Donelson and Jackson. It is obvious that the two men had competing views of what constituted honorable conduct. To be a true republican and southern gentleman, Donelson believed that he had to protect both his virtue and his honor. That meant engaging in relationships that were honorable, relationships that would not disparage his or his family's name. As a head of household, he believed that he had every right, after consultation with Emily, to govern which individuals would come into contact with his family. These were the same principles imparted to him by Jackson during his early days away from home and that regulated southern society.

The difference between Jackson and Donelson lay in their definitions of virtue and honor. Jackson defended Margaret Eaton as personally virtuous because her enemies could not prove otherwise. Donelson, on the other hand, while he may have doubted Margaret's personal virtue, concerned himself with two things: examining her public actions and maintaining his own virtuous conduct. If Margaret were truly virtuous, he believed, then she should have avoided any controversy for the administration by removing herself from the public view. That was simply what virtuous, republican women did—practiced political influence in the home, not in public. Instead, she insisted on continuing the debate while the president suffered. In Donelson's estimation, Margaret's refusal to submit proved that she was not a true republican woman. As for himself, Donelson refused to damage his own virtuous character by associating with someone so antithetical to the republican nature of American life. Official social intercourse was unavoidable; private interaction was not.[33]

The Eaton affair revealed the weaknesses that existed Donelson and Jackson's relationship. The patron-client relationship, one historian notes, was often "brittle because both parties demand complete loyalty, complete trustworthiness. When ambitions diverge or the status and power of the parties substantially change, frustration, jealousy, hurt feelings quickly

33. For descriptions of the representative republican woman, see Linda K. Kerber, *Women of the Republic: Intellect and Ideology in Revolutionary America* (Chapel Hill: University of North Carolina Press for the Institute of Early American History and Culture, 1980); and Mary Beth Norton, *Liberty's Daughters: The Revolutionary Experience of American Women, 1750–1800* (New York: Little, Brown, 1980).

arise." Nothing could be truer for two men who loved one another as father and son. As president and as patron, Jackson had every reason to expect Donelson's acquiescence and deference to his wishes; that Donelson behaved otherwise was, in Jackson's mind, a violation of everything he had taught him about life. Because of his nephew's supposed betrayal of him during the affair, Jackson never fully trusted Donelson again. Donelson's actions affirmed what he had already suspected: his nephew was not cut from the same cloth, and his political success would be limited.[34]

For his part, Donelson emerged from the Eaton affair a wounded son whose confidence in himself and his uncle was never quite the same. In fact, his attempts at cloaking himself in his uncle's mantle suggest a paradox that Donelson faced throughout his life: he needed to prove his value, to himself, to Jackson, and to others, without relying on Jackson's name, yet his path to success had been, and would continue to be, reliant upon his association with his uncle.

34. Wyatt-Brown, "AJ's Honor," 15; and idem, *Southern Honor*, 22.

6

"The Intrigues of Politicians"

The end of the Eaton affair in the fall of 1831 eased the tension between uncle and nephew and allowed the Donelsons to return to Washington. John and Margaret Eaton were back in Tennessee, while Van Buren, whom Jackson had appointed as the new American minister to England, was in London. By December, even William B. Lewis was out of the picture, having decided to move out for the time being. The president's nephew and niece had been restored to their former positions, and Donelson, notwithstanding his earlier misgivings about Jackson's choice of political battles, intended to keep it that way by throwing himself into the political fray.[1]

During the course of the Eaton affair, several crises had developed. One involved the Cherokee in Georgia. Jackson had entered the presidency under pressure from Georgians to rid their state of the Cherokee, and for nearly three years, Jackson, no friend to the Indian, had attempted to do so. The passage of the Indian Removal bill in May 1830 authorized the president to exchange native lands in the Southeast for lands west of the Mississippi River. The Cherokee responded by bringing suit in two cases that reached the U.S. Supreme Court: *Cherokee Nation v. Georgia* (1831) and *Worcester v. Georgia* (1832). In the first case, Chief Justice John Marshall ruled that the Indian tribes in the United States, including the Cherokee, were "domestic dependent nations" subject to national, but not state, jurisdiction. In the latter case, Marshall ruled that the Cherokee Nation was "a distinct community . . . in which the laws of Georgia can have no force."[2]

1. Marszalek, *Petticoat Affair,* 200; Niven, *MVB,* 272; Atkins, *Emily Donelson,* 227; and Louis R. Harlan, "Public Career of WBL," pt. 2, *THQ* 7 (June 1948): 129–30.

2. Remini, *AJ and His Indian Wars,* 226–38, 254–7; and *Cherokee Nation v. Georgia,* 5 Peters 1 (1831) and *Worcester v. Georgia,* 6 Peters 515 (1832), in Henry Steele Commager, ed., *Documents of American History,* 5th ed. (New York: Appleton-Century-Crofts, 1949), 255–8, 258–9.

The Cherokee removal dispute in Georgia had emboldened the South Carolina nullifiers. They believed that if Jackson failed to sustain the state's move to evict the Cherokee and take their land, perhaps the Georgia state government would cast its lot with South Carolina and threaten to secede to preserve its states' rights. That scenario failed to materialize, as a faction of the Cherokee leadership began to negotiate the terms of removal, but when Jackson signed a new tariff bill in July 1832, South Carolina nullifiers concluded that they must act on their own. When the fall elections gave them control of the state legislature, they held a state convention in November, at which delegates passed a nullification ordinance that voided the tariffs of 1828 and 1832, effective 1 February 1833.[3]

As if that were not enough to worry Jackson and his Kitchen Cabinet, the administration faced another problem: the proposed rechartering of the Second Bank of the United States. Jackson had entered the presidency with a decided paranoia about banks based on his own past financial problems, which he blamed on banking in general. In his first three annual messages, he gave the matter scant attention, indicating that he would let Congress deal with the institution. But he also hinted that he was not completely happy with the Bank and had considering not renewing its charter. The president became more determined that he had to address the Bank issue as reports spread that the institution had supported Adams during the 1828 election; however, the Eaton affair proved such a distraction that Jackson set aside those thoughts for a time.[4]

Failing to realize that Jackson had more immediate issues on his agenda, Bank president Nicholas Biddle continued to campaign vigorously to protect his institution. He paid for newspaper articles that defended the Bank's existence and policies and attacked those who opposed them. The breakup of Jackson's cabinet over the Eaton affair only encouraged him further, as most of the new members were decidedly pro-Bank. Despite being warned

3. Edwin A. Miles, "After John Marshall's Decision: *Worcester v. Georgia* and the Nullification Crisis," *Journal of Southern History* 39 (November 1973): 519–44; Freehling, *Prelude to Civil War*, 247–50, 252–4, 260–4; and South Carolina's Ordinance of Nullification, 24 November 1832, in William W. Freehling, ed., *The Nullification Era: A Documentary Record* (New York: Harper and Row, 1967), 150–2.

4. Remini, *AJ and the Bank War*, 49–55; and first annual message, 8 December 1829, second annual message, 7 December 1830, and third annual message, 6 December 1831, in Richardson, *Messages and Papers of the Presidents* 2:462, 528–9, 558.

by the new secretary of the treasury, Louis McLane, not to bring up the issue during a presidential election year, Biddle pushed Congress to recharter the Second Bank in 1832, although its twenty-year contract did not expire until 1836. He was confident that, should Congress go along with his plan and grant the recharter, Jackson would not dare to engage in a fight over the Bank during an election year. Congress rewarded Biddle's certainty when both houses passed a recharter bill over the vehement opposition of the Jacksonian Democrats. Henry Clay, Jackson's challenger for the presidency, trumpeted the bill and challenged his political rival to do something about it.[5]

With a presidential election hanging in the balance, Jackson believed that he had no choice but to strike back against all of his enemies, including Calhoun, Biddle, and Clay, and he called on his nephew to assist him. Donelson spent the early summer months gathering evidence from the states regarding their relationship with the Bank. When Jackson had compiled the necessary resources, he set his advisors to writing the veto. Its composition was largely the work of Amos Kendall, who was growing in importance as a political confidant and counselor to the president. Two members of the new cabinet formed in 1831, Roger B. Taney, the attorney general, and Levi Woodbury, the navy secretary, also contributed. As always, Donelson's contributions were largely limited to editing, although he likely was able to add some evidentiary support for the veto from his investigations. In its final form, the veto message condemned the Bank in the conspiratorial language of republicanism and used emotional and constitutional justification for opposing its recharter.[6]

Donelson also rallied support for the Democratic ticket, which now included Van Buren as Jackson's running mate, during the summer months

5. Remini, *AJ and the Bank War,* 67–81; and Nicholas Biddle to Charles J. Ingersoll, 11 February 1832, in Reginald McGrane, ed., *The Correspondence of Nicholas Biddle Dealing with National Affairs, 1807–1844* (Boston: Houghton Mifflin, 1919), 179–81.

6. Lynn Marshall, "The Authorship of Jackson's Bank Veto Message," *Mississippi Valley Historical Review* 50 (December 1963): 466–77; Donald B. Cole, *A Jackson Man: Amos Kendall and the Rise of American Democracy* (Baton Rouge: Louisiana State University Press, 2004), 165–71; Longaker, "Was Jackson's Kitchen Cabinet a Cabinet?" 103; Marquis James, *Portrait of a President* (Indianapolis: Bobbs-Merrill, 1937), 302; Carl B. Swisher, *Roger B. Taney* (New York: Macmillan, 1935), 194–5; drafts of Bank veto message, JLC; and Bank veto message, 10 July 1832, in Richardson, *Messages and Papers of the Presidents* 2:576–91.

of 1832. Although he was ill during that period and chose to take a trip to the Rip Raps resort in Virginia to recover, Donelson continued his efforts for the party. For example, he encouraged John Branch, who had become governor of North Carolina after his forced resignation from the cabinet, to sustain Jackson and Van Buren. Declaring that the two men differed little in their political views, Donelson urged his old friend not to let past differences hurt his support of the president. He assured Branch that he shared some of his trepidation about Van Buren, which stemmed from the Eaton affair, and regretted the attempt by some Jacksonians to make the president appear subordinate to the New Yorker. Donelson remained convinced, however, that his uncle would continue supporting the principles necessary to maintain the nation's integrity, and it was their duty to support him. "There is scarce room for the operation of illegitimate counsels" during this important election, he reminded Branch.[7]

However much Biddle and Clay expected the Bank issue to hurt Jackson during the election, the incumbent president won the contest convincingly. He beat Clay and the Anti-Masonic candidate, noted attorney William Wirt, by a substantial margin, winning 219 electoral votes to their 49 and 7, respectively. Jackson received almost 700,000 popular votes, over 200,000 more than Clay, with Wirt garnering only 100,000. It was a significant victory.[8]

Without the election to distract him, Jackson focused on the nullification movement in South Carolina. By the time state delegates met to pass their nullification ordinance in November, Jackson had already begun political and military preparations to preserve the Union. His fourth annual message, sent to Congress on 4 December, lulled the South Carolinians into thinking that the president would not act. Jackson barely mentioned the impending crisis and alluded only indirectly to the South Carolina nullifiers. He did, however, affirm his support for "the integrity of the Union" and warned that if some elements in the nation failed to use "moderation and good sense," then "the laws themselves are fully adequate to the suppression of such attempts" to ignore them. Aside from that statement, however, Jackson's mes-

7. AJ to AJD, 30 August 1832, AJD to John Branch, 30 August 1832, DLC.

8. Robert V. Remini, "Election of 1832," in *History of American Presidential Elections,* 4 vols., ed. Arthur M. Schlesinger and Fred L. Israel (New York: Chelsea House, 1971), 1:495–516.

sage, the work of a group of advisors that included Donelson, Van Buren, Kendall, and Taney, appeared to reinforce a states' rights position, particularly in regard to the sale of public lands and a reduction in tariff duties.[9]

Instead of addressing the growing nullification movement at length in his annual message, the president had actually prepared a separate statement on the nullification crisis, which he had Donelson deliver to Congress on 10 December. The Nullification Proclamation, drafted by Jackson, Kendall, Donelson, Secretary of State Edward Livingston, and Secretary of War Lewis Cass, left no doubt as to where Jackson stood regarding South Carolina's actions. Nullification was illegal and "incompatible with the existence of the Union," the message thundered, and its concomitant doctrine of secession endangered the future of the nation. Jackson argued passionately that the people, not the states, were the basis of the United States government. It was thus his duty as chief executive and sole representative of the people's will to enforce the laws of the land and preserve the Union.[10]

Donelson fully supported his uncle's position. His earlier, private criticism of Jackson's policies disappeared as the increasing political division of the nation in 1832 convinced him that the administration and the people would "save the country from the intrigues of politicians and the factions of ambitious office seekers." While supporting Jackson, Donelson still trusted that a compromise could be reached that would avoid conflict. In mid-December 1832, Donelson wrote John Coffee that he hoped that South Carolina would "retrace her steps" and that "the friends of the Union in Congress" would work out an agreement that would reduce the tariff to a satisfactory level. If the two sides could not reach such an arrangement, and if South Carolina "determine[d] to secede or assert the right to nullify," Donelson predicted, "there will undoubtedly be civil war."[11]

9. Fourth annual message, 4 December 1832, in Richardson, *Messages and Papers of the Presidents* 2:591–606; drafts of fourth annual message, JLC; and Ellis, *Union at Risk,* 74–83.

10. Nullification Proclamation, 10 December 1832, in Freehling, *Nullification Era,* 153–63; drafts of Nullification Proclamation, JLC; Longaker, "Was Jackson's Kitchen Cabinet a Cabinet?" 103; AJ to Edward Livingston, 4 December 1832, in Bassett and Jameson, *CAJ* 4:494–5; Charles H. Hunt, *Life of Edward Livingston* (New York: Appleton, 1864), 371–81; and Samuel Tyler, ed., *Memoir of Roger Brooke Taney, LL.D., Chief Justice of the Supreme Court of the United States* (Baltimore: J. Murphy, 1872), 188.

11. AJD to JCM, 9 January 1831, AJD to John Coffee, 26 January, 18 December 1832, AJ to E. G. Davis (drafted by Donelson), 28 January 1832, DLC.

Donelson's fear of impending military clash proved unfounded, but not before the nation experienced some very tense moments. Jackson's volatile relationship with Calhoun finally ended when the vice-president resigned in December. It appeared that the federal government was coming apart. In January, Jackson presented Congress with his Force Bill message, which requested congressional approval to use military action to enforce the nation's laws (although he was not wholly committed to military action at this point). Jackson and his advisors also made a final attempt to bring about reconciliation through legislation. In December 1832, the president ordered Secretary of the Treasury Louis McLane and Tennessee congressman James K. Polk to draft a new tariff bill to remedy some of the grievances held by the nullifiers. Gulian C. Verplanck of New York introduced the bill in the House the following month. It would reduce tariff rates to 1816 levels over a period of two years. Donelson contacted Governor Branch and encouraged him and other southerners to support the tariff bill. Opposition from all quarters was strong, however, and the bill ultimately failed.[12]

By mid-January 1833, the nullifiers were looking for a way to end the crisis, having already postponed the 1 February deadline. The solution to the predicament came from Henry Clay and, surprisingly, John C. Calhoun. While Congress debated the Force Bill, Clay and Calhoun met and agreed on a compromise tariff. It resembled the Verplanck bill but promised to reduce tariff duties at a much slower rate. Jacksonians and even some National Republicans criticized their efforts as merely a ploy to regain lost political influence. Whatever their motivation, the two senators were able to convince enough congressional members to support the tariff that it passed both houses by 1 March 1833. Jackson signed it the following day, ending the crisis.[13]

The resolution of the conflict with Calhoun and South Carolina left Jackson and the Kitchen Cabinet free to turn their attention to the Bank War. After defeating Clay in the 1832 presidential contest, Jackson had decided to remove the government's deposits from the Bank, effectively cutting off

12. Force Bill, 16 January 1833, in Richardson, *Messages and Papers of the Presidents* 2:610–32; Ellis, *Union at Risk,* 99–100, 158–65; Robert V. Remini, *Andrew Jackson and the Course of American Democracy, 1833–1845* (New York: Harper and Row, 1984), 29; and Satterfield, "Moderate Nationalist Jacksonian," 112–3.

13. Remini, *Henry Clay,* 423–35; Niven, *JCC,* 193–4; and Ellis, *Union at Risk,* 166–9.

its main source of money and threatening to destroy it. He asked James K. Polk, one of his loyal Tennessee lieutenants on the House Ways and Means Committee, to convince the other members to recommend the deposits' removal. They failed to deliver, however, and in March 1833, a House report declared the government's deposits safe in the Bank. This annoyed Jackson and spurred him into action. With the assistance of Kendall, Blair, and Roger B. Taney, Jackson prepared a series of questions that he presented to his cabinet on 19 March 1833. He asked whether the present Bank was safe for the government deposits and, if not, how he should address the problem and what actions he should take to replace it with a new institution. The president expected an answer from each of them.[14]

All of the cabinet members except Taney responded that they considered the deposits safe in the Bank as it presently existed. Secretary of Treasury Louis McLane's opinions were particularly favorable toward the financial institution, and as the man who would be responsible for removing the deposits, this presented Jackson with a dilemma. Wanting to find someone more amenable to his thinking on the issue, the president reshaped his cabinet once again. He sent Secretary of State Edward Livingston to France as minister and promoted McLane to fill his position. He then appointed William J. Duane, a Pennsylvanian and reportedly an adamant opponent of the Bank, to the Treasury post. These changes, completed on 1 June 1833, left Jackson with advisors that he thought would sustain his course.[15]

Believing that he now had a loyal cabinet in place, Jackson ordered Kendall to scour the northern and mid-Atlantic states for banks that would be willing to receive government deposits. The president also asked Donelson to help him with two tasks: ascertaining the position of Nashville's Union Bank regarding the Bank of the United States and preparing a memorandum outlining the reasons for removing the government's deposits. Donelson's trip to Nashville proved successful, as Union Bank officials assured the president's nephew that their institution would willingly serve as a repository for the government's deposits when the time came.[16]

14. Remini, *AJ and the Bank War,* 111–3.

15. Ibid., 113–5.

16. Satterfield, "Moderate Nationalist Jacksonian," 117; AJD to ETD, 22, 24 June 1833, AJ to AJD, 5 August 1833, U. R. W. Hill to AJD, 27 August 1833, DLC; and Fletcher M. Green, "On Tour with President Jackson," *New England Quarterly* 36 (June 1963): 209–28.

Donelson returned to Washington in late August 1833 and learned that Jackson was having difficulty with the newest member of his cabinet, William Duane. Reuben M. Whitney, a former Bank director, had assured Donelson that Duane would fully support the president against Biddle's institution. To his chagrin, Jackson had discovered otherwise. The Treasury secretary had taken offense to the president's treatment of him, complaining that Jackson wanted him there simply as a "mere cypher." In a series of letters exchanged throughout June and July, the two men wrangled over whether the secretary of treasury would comply with the president's forthcoming order to remove the government deposits. Jackson believed that as the chief executive he had every right to expect Duane's compliance. The secretary disagreed, arguing that constitutionally and ethically, only Congress could direct him to remove the deposits. Jackson even attempted to bribe Duane by offering him a ministry to Russia if he would resign, a proposition Duane refused.[17]

Finding Duane intransigent on the issue, Jackson next met with his entire cabinet on 17 September 1833 to ask their opinion as an advisory body. Most of the members, with the exception of Taney, were reluctant to remove the government's deposits. They reconvened the next day, at which time Donelson read the paper that he, Jackson, Taney, and Kendall had been working on since the spring. The paper explained the corruption of the Bank that required the deposits' removal and asserted the right of the president to order such action. The other cabinet members reacted first with silence, then a swift exit from the room. Duane, however, remained steadfast, refusing either to remove the deposits or resign.[18]

Faced with an unyielding secretary, Jackson believed that he had no choice but to fire Duane. He sent Donelson to inform Duane that the *Washington Globe* newspaper would announce the deposits' removals on 20 September. Duane, citing illness, asked for one more day, but Jackson

17. Remini, *AJ and the Bank War,* 116–8; idem, *Course of American Democracy,* 65–6, 85–96; and Reuben M. Whitney to AJD, 10 June 1833, DLC. The complete Jackson-Duane correspondence can be found in JLC and William J. Duane, *Narrative and Correspondence Concerning the Removal of the Deposits and Occurrences Connected Therewith* (New York: Burt Franklin, [1838]). Donelson was privy to the dispute since he wrote most of Jackson's correspondence to Duane.

18. Remini, *AJ and the Bank War,* 118–22; Roger B. Taney to AJD, 15 September 1833, DLC; and *Washington Globe,* 23 September 1833.

refused. Further discussions between the president and the secretary proved unfruitful. Duane even appealed to Donelson for help in ending the dispute, but to no avail. Jackson fired Duane, replaced him with Taney, and named Benjamin F. Butler to the attorney general post.[19]

With Duane out of the way, Jackson's path became easier. On 25 September 1833, Secretary of the Treasury Roger B. Taney issued an executive order that declared his intention, on 1 October, to begin depositing government funds into select state banks. The government would pay its operating expenses out of its remaining deposits in the Bank until they were depleted. Jackson's fifth annual message, which Donelson, McLane, and Van Buren helped draft, contained a searing indictment of the Bank that made clear his reasoning. It was "a permanent electioneering machine," the message argued, that threatened to turn the United States political system into one that "the money and power of a great corporation" controlled.[20]

In retaliation, Nicholas Biddle restricted the Bank's credit and began calling in its loans. He hoped to precipitate a financial panic that would force Jackson to relent on the removal of government deposits and compel him to support the Bank's recharter. It initially appeared that Biddle's plan was working. Across the United States, unfounded rumors grew that the nation faced financial collapse. In reality, Biddle had only been able to produce a small recession. When Congress convened in December 1833, however, senators and representatives under the leadership of Clay, Calhoun, and Webster, who opposed the president's policies, moved to take advantage of popular misinformation. They criticized Jackson's banking policies, calling him a "tyrant." With the Whigs in control of the Senate and the Democratic majority in the House disorganized, Clay and his compatriots accumulated enough votes to reject Taney's report recommending the removal of deposits. In a display of their power, the Whig-controlled Senate also passed a censure resolution against "King Andrew I."[21]

19. Remini, *AJ and the Bank War,* 122–4; and AJ to MVB, 22 September 1833, William Duane to AJD, [22] September 1833, in Bassett and Jameson, *CAJ* 5:205–6.

20. Remini, *AJ and the Bank War,* 125–7; Satterfield, "Moderate Nationalist Jacksonian," 124; drafts of fifth annual message, JLC; and fifth annual message, 3 December 1833, in Richardson, *Messages and Papers of the Presidents* 3:19–35.

21. Remini, *AJ and the Bank War,* 125–42.

With the Bank War raging, Donelson defended Jackson's policies. He wrote Edward Livingston, the former secretary of state, and predicted victory over Clay and the pro-Bank forces. "The President will be not only sustained in what he has now done," he confidently calculated, "but he will [also] free the country from an influence dangerous to its morals." Donelson believed as much as any anti-Bank Jacksonian that Biddle's institution was corrupt and jeopardized the nation. "Restraining the evils of monopoly," as Donelson later explained, was the only appropriate response. "Monopolies, exclusive privileges, and restrictives [*sic*] benefiting one portion of the community at the expense of a greater portion," he declared, "are the source of all difficulties which free Governments have to encounter." Without these advantages, "political power would have but little temptation to consult any other objects than those which belong to the greatest good of the greatest number and there would be no minority in any community whose rights would not as a portion of the common interest have its proper agency in limiting and administering the powers of the Government."[22]

When Jackson decided to answer his censure with a "protest" message, he asked Donelson, who usually hand delivered the president's congressional messages to the appropriate body, to take it to the Senate. In a biting condemnation directed against that legislative body, the boldly written message unflinchingly declared that the president was the direct representative of the people and that Jackson was constitutionally correct in his actions concerning the Bank. The House, in the meantime, moved to support the president through a series of resolutions. Led by Polk, representatives voted, along mostly partisan lines, to reject the Bank's recharter, support the removal of deposits, maintain the state banks as depositories, and launch an investigation into the Bank's actions during the recession. Jackson considered himself vindicated.[23]

The Bank of the United States finished out its charter in 1836 and became a Pennsylvania state bank, but the political effects of the Bank War continued to reverberate for many more years. They helped contribute to

22. AJD to Edward Livingston, 7 March 1834, typescript, AJD to [?], 10 July 1836, DLC.

23. Remini, *AJ and the Bank War,* 165–6; idem, *Course of American Democracy,* 152–5; "Protest" message, 15 April 1834, in Richardson, *Messages and Papers of the Presidents* 3:69–93; and Satterfield, "Moderate Nationalist Jacksonian," 124–5.

the creation of the Whig party, which presented the Jacksonian Democrats with a staunch opposition, in the winter of 1833–34. Jackson had made many enemies—nullifiers, pro-Bank men, Native American backers—and this new party gave them a common goal: defeating the president's agenda. In Tennessee, especially, the establishment of the Whig party was costly to Jackson, as his conflict with the Bank caused some of his longtime associates, disaffected by his policies and his treatment of them, to leave the Democratic party and join the opposition.[24]

The emergence of the Whig party was an important development not only for Jackson but also for Donelson. The defection of Hugh Lawson White, John Bell, and other pro-Bank Jacksonians to the Whigs forced Donelson to make a choice. He could join those members of the White faction with which he had been aligned, and break with the president, or he could use the upheaval among his uncle's supporters to keep himself close to Jackson. Fortunately for Donelson, Eaton and Lewis had lost much of their influence with the president, while Polk and Felix Grundy had chosen not to follow White and Bell out of the party, becoming instead two of Jackson's staunchest allies. There is no doubt that Donelson's decision to align with Polk and Grundy in sustaining Jackson was predicated on his support of the president's politics. Like Jackson, he was a staunch believer in a government, supported by the will of the people, committed to fighting the many enemies of republican society. His decision had the additional potential of increasing his visibility as a loyal Jacksonian, convincing his uncle that he was a faithful son and, perhaps, even expunging his reputation as the president's untrustworthy nephew, not unimportant goals for Donelson.

24. Michael F. Holt, *The Rise and Fall of the American Whig Party: Jacksonian Politics and the Onset of the Civil War* (New York: Oxford University Press, 1999), 25–32; Jonathan M. Atkins, *Parties, Politics, and Sectional Conflict in Tennessee, 1832–1861* (Knoxville: University of Tennessee Press, 1997), 32–6; and Bergeron, *Antebellum Politics,* 5.

7

"The Major, like All Weak Persons"

By the fall of 1833, Jackson's supporters were fragmenting. Since the mid-1820s, there had been two distinct pro-Jackson factions in Tennessee: the Eaton-Lewis group, men who had been loyal to Jackson for years and considered themselves his only true friends and most important advisors, and the Polk-Grundy-White group, whose members resented Eaton and Lewis, seeing them as rivals who wanted to manipulate the president for their own ambitions. Jackson's decision to fight Nicholas Biddle and the Bank of the United States and to select Van Buren as his successor caused members of both factions to reevaluate their allegiance to the president and, in some cases, pledge their loyalty to the Whig party.[1]

This realignment in Tennessee produced two of Jackson's most active opponents: Hugh Lawson White and John Bell. Jackson and White had known each other since the state's founding in 1796 and had served together in the War of 1812. During the 1820s, they shared the conviction that Clay and others of his ilk posed a danger to the Republic. Once Jackson ascended to the presidency, however, White began distancing himself from his friend and political ally. Jackson's clear favoritism of Eaton over him for the cabinet infuriated White, as did the president's choice of Van Buren as his successor. White came to view Jackson and his use of patronage as the true threat to

1. Sellers, *Jacksonian,* 197–8. For additional information on the political climate of Tennessee in the 1830s, see also Thomas P. Abernethy, "The Origin of the Whig Party in Tennessee," *Mississippi Valley Historical Review* 12 (March 1926): 504–22; Jonathan M. Atkins, "The Presidential Candidacy of Hugh Lawson White in Tennessee, 1832–1836," *Journal of Southern History* 58 (February 1992): 27–56; Powell Moore, "The Political Background of the Revolt against Jackson in Tennessee," *East Tennessee Historical Society's Publications* 4 (1930): 45–66; idem, "The Revolt against Jackson in Tennessee, 1835–1836," *Journal of Southern History* 2 (August 1936): 335–59; and James Edward Murphy, "Jackson and the Tennessee Opposition," *THQ* 30 (Spring 1971): 50–69.

the Republic's future, and it was enough to cause him to join the Whigs in opposing Jackson's administration.[2]

John Bell, on the other hand, had never been one of Jackson's closest friends, but he had allied himself with men who were, most notably William Carroll. Bell had defeated Felix Grundy in the 1827 congressional election, and as a member of the House of Representatives, he had faithfully supported the president's battles against nullification and for Cherokee removal. His defense of the Bank proved to be his demise among the Jacksonians, however, and Bell and White soon found themselves allied together against their former friend.[3]

Not Donelson, however. Even before going to Washington, Donelson had cast his lot with Polk, Grundy, and White, believing them to be looking out for Jackson's best interests. The Eaton affair only confirmed his judgment and solidified his allegiance to that alliance. Despite his strained relationship with Jackson, Donelson did not abandon his uncle as White and Bell had, preferring to maintain his position with the Polk-Grundy faction. Realistically, there was nowhere else for him to go. Donelson despised the Eaton-Lewis clique, a feeling that some of its members undoubtedly reciprocated, and joining the Whigs was out of the question.

While Jackson continued to favor the Eaton-Lewis faction, Donelson worked closely, as he had always chosen to do, with those whom he considered the president's true friends. The 1833 elections gave him ample opportunity to do so, as both Polk and Grundy were up for reelection. Polk, one of Jackson's staunchest allies in the House, was running against Theodorick F. Bradford for reelection to the House. Bradford, an anti-Jacksonian, tried to use Polk's Masonic membership and the atmosphere of Anti-Masonry that was sweeping the nation to his advantage. Polk, on the other hand, steered the campaign toward an examination of the Bank's corruption. When that tactic failed to elicit the hoped-for support, the embattled congressman turned to the president's nephew for assistance.[4]

2. Ratner, *Tennessee Lieutenants,* 73–82; and Burstein, *Passions,* 209–10.

3. Joseph H. Parks, *John Bell of Tennessee* (Baton Rouge: Louisiana State University Press, 1950), 37–83.

4. Sellers, *Jacksonian,* 200–5; and Joseph M. Pukl Jr., "James K. Polk's Congressional Campaigns, 1829–1833," *THQ* 40 (Winter 1981): 348–65.

Polk asked Donelson to search the State Department's archives and find material that proved Bradford had supported John Quincy Adams before the 1828 election. Polk's intent was to charge his opponent with personal animosity toward Jackson, hoping that the president's popularity would enable him to counter Bradford's attacks. Donelson enthusiastically supported Polk by obtaining proof that when Bradford had sought the position of marshal of West Tennessee in 1827, he had secured letters of recommendation from anti-Jackson politicians to support his application. Donelson sent Polk extracts of letters verifying his opponent's political loyalties but warned him not to use his name. Polk honored Donelson's request, and his evidence helped the Tennessee congressman win reelection over Bradford.[5]

Felix Grundy also approached Donelson for assistance. The state legislature had appointed Grundy to John H. Eaton's vacated Senate seat in 1829, and he was now seeking reelection. Unfortunately, he had several problems that made him a liability. Grundy had allied with the Calhoun faction during the Eaton affair. That decision and his alleged support for nullification in 1830 had led Nashville newspapers to question his loyalty to Jackson. Critics also charged him with failing to protest vociferously when the Senate rejected Van Buren's nomination as minister to Great Britain. Finally, Grundy had used Jackson's frank, supposedly without his knowledge, in distributing his own speeches, placing himself and the president in a precarious political position. It appeared to his opponents that Grundy was intentionally using Jackson for his own selfish purposes. Now out of the cabinet, Eaton had determined that he wanted back in the Senate, but there was no vacancy. Attempts to convince Hugh Lawson White to give up his Senate seat to Eaton and take his place in the cabinet failed, so the Eaton-Lewis-Overton group decided that Eaton's best

5. AJD to JKP, 30 May 1833, JKP to Louis McLane, 24 June 1833, in Herbert Weaver and Paul Bergeron, eds., *Correspondence of James K. Polk*, vol. 2, *1833–1834* (Nashville: Vanderbilt University Press, 1972), 80–2, 87; JKP to AJD, 28 April 1835, in Herbert Weaver and Kermit L. Hall, eds., *Correspondence of James K. Polk*, vol. 3, *1835–1836* (Nashville: Vanderbilt University Press, 1975), 169–72; and Pukl, "JKP's Congressional Campaigns," 364–5. In 1831, a national newspaper had published one of Donelson's letters, mistakenly sent to James Krepps, a Pennsylvania anti-Masonic state senator, allowing former Jackson ally Duff Green, who had aligned with Calhoun, to accuse him of abusing the president's franking privilege. Donelson accepted the blame for the mistake (Satterfield, "Moderate Nationalist Jacksonian," 86–9).

chance to reenter the Senate was to challenge Grundy for his seat in the 1833 election.[6]

Donelson once again found himself in a predicament. Jackson had not publicly declared for either Grundy or Eaton, but Donelson knew that his uncle privately preferred Eaton to win as a statement against his opponents during the Petticoat Affair. Donelson's decision to help Grundy anyway came for several reasons. He could not stomach an Eaton victory, which would remind everyone of his role in the president's difficult first term and would vindicate the former secretary of war. Donelson also identified with Grundy and his troubles, which were similar to those that he had faced. Additionally, he had cast his political lot by allying with Polk and Grundy, and he had no other political options. Despite his support, Donelson had could not offer Grundy substantial help. He did, however, attempt to clarify the franking controversy. During a hurried trip to Tennessee in October 1833, Donelson claimed responsibility for securing Grundy's franks and assured Democrats that he had done so with the full approval of the president. This did not change many minds among Grundy's detractors, but it helped the senator fight off accusations of disloyalty to Jackson. The legislature eventually reelected him after a long political battle lasting fifty-five ballots.[7]

These victories kept two of Jackson's fiercest defenders in the United States Congress. Other Tennesseans, however, had grown dissatisfied with the president and his political decisions. Jackson's decision to fight the Bank caused John Bell some consternation, since he was the director of its Nashville branch and had used it for personal loans. Bell's failure to support the president's banking policy allowed Polk and Grundy to question his loyalty to Jackson. Bell subsequently complicated his standing in the party when, in 1834, he challenged and defeated Polk in the election for Speaker of the House. Knowing that he was in a precarious political position with the administration, Bell publicly affirmed his devotion to Jackson, whom he continued to call his friend, giving Van Buren's continued prominence as the reason for his disloyal actions.[8]

6. Parks, *Felix Grundy,* 182–213; and Sellers, *Jacksonian,* 196–8.

7. Parks, *Felix Grundy,* 206, 214–5; Sellers, *Jacksonian,* 198–202, 205–6; and Marszalek, *Petticoat Affair,* 201–7.

8. Atkins, *Parties, Politics, and Sectional Conflict,* 35–6; and Parks, *John Bell,* 68–72.

Van Buren's candidacy was also causing some discomfort among Jackson's Tennessee and southern supporters. Many suspected that Van Buren had plotted Calhoun's alienation and the cabinet's reshaping during the Eaton affair, all in an effort to maneuver himself into place as Jackson's successor. He was also a New Yorker, and there were questions about his commitment to protecting slavery, a combination that the president's supporters found difficult to accept. However, Jackson supported him and wanted him to become president, so most of his political lieutenants fell into line behind him.[9]

Even Donelson decided to back Van Buren. Despite his reservations about the vice-president during the Eaton affair, he and the New Yorker had become political associates. Donelson's change of heart regarding Van Buren was attributable to several factors. First, while they had been on opposite sides of the Petticoat Affair, Donelson's personal ire had been directed at Eaton and Lewis, not Van Buren. True, he had initially distrusted the New Yorker, but his distrust had not been personal, which kept animosity between the two men from building. Second, once the Eaton imbroglio ended and Jackson endorsed Van Buren as his successor, Donelson realized that to advance politically, he had to align with his uncle. Should the New Yorker win the presidency, the president's nephew would have to rely on his good graces for a political appointment. And third, supporting Van Buren offered a way for Donelson to restore Jackson's trust in him. With formerly faithful friends falling away, he knew the president would be watching to see if his nephew would repeat his earlier mistake of disloyalty. Donelson was not going to let that happen again.

Donelson may have thrown his wholehearted support to Van Buren, but Whigs in Tennessee and elsewhere were determined to undermine his chances in the 1836 presidential election. They emphasized that the New Yorker's candidacy threatened the elevation of a southerner, much less a Tennessean, as many hoped, to the presidency. His reluctance to stand against Jackson during the Bank War also marked him as simply the president's puppet. With antagonism growing against Jackson, Hugh Lawson White allowed his name to enter the public domain as a potential presidential nominee. His candidacy, orchestrated by Bell, received the endorsement of

9. Niven, *MVB*, 394–5; and William G. Shade, "'The Most Delicate and Exciting Topics': Martin Van Buren, Slavery, and the Election of 1836," *Journal of the Early Republic* 18 (Fall 1998): 459–84.

an unofficial December 1834 caucus of Tennessee's congressional members (excepting Grundy and Polk).[10]

Jackson and Donelson took active roles in opposing White and supporting Van Buren. They attended Tennessee's state constitutional convention in 1834, where Jackson reminded the delegates of his recent fight against the Bank. During the receptions and dinners that followed, he and Donelson canvassed for Van Buren's nomination and election, assuring their friends that the New Yorker, not White, stood for the republican principles propounded by Jackson. Some of Donelson's friends wrote him and agreed with the president's assessment, assuring his nephew that White had no possibility of winning the election for the Whigs. One relative encouraged him to continue writing to his Tennessee friends, because his letters would have "great influence" in convincing them to support Van Buren. Not all agreed, apparently, as some of the Donelson family favored White.[11]

White's candidacy posed a serious threat to Van Buren's chances in Tennessee, so Donelson joined others in spearheading the establishment of a Jacksonian newspaper in Nashville, one that would trumpet the New Yorker's virtues as a presidential contender. White's supporters had gained control of the city's major Democratic newspaper, the *Nashville Banner,* firing its editor, Samuel H. Laughlin, for promoting Van Buren as Jackson's successor. Establishing a loyal administration newspaper had not only become a political necessity for the Democrats but also offered a chance for Donelson, by helping finance the party organ, to curry favor with both Jackson and Van Buren.[12]

Donelson, Polk, and Laughlin first sought to purchase one of the existing Nashville papers. When that attempt failed, Laughlin, along with another editor, Medicus A. Long, established the *Nashville Union,* a newspaper that would give "unqualified support of all such principals [*sic*] upon which the national government should be administered." Laughlin served as editor, while Long became business manager and publisher. The new editor,

10. Atkins, "Hugh Lawson White," 33–6; and Thomas Brown, "From Old Hickory to Sly Fox: The Routinization of Charisma in the Early Democratic Party," *Journal of the Early Republic* 11 (Fall 1991): 339–70.

11. *Washington Globe,* 26 August 1834; and JCM to AJD, 20 December 1834, DLC.

12. SHL to JKP, 8 January 1833, 20 October 1834, in Weaver and Bergeron, *CJKP* 2:11–3, 534–7; and Robert B. Satterfield, "The Uncertain Trumpet of the Tennessee Jacksonians," *THQ* 26 (Spring 1967): 83.

unfortunately, was a chronic alcoholic, and in December 1834, one of his bouts with drinking delayed the gathering of the necessary printing materials until after the New Year. Other setbacks kept the first issue from reaching print until early April 1835.[13]

Donelson was not only a primary founder of the *Union* but also expected to be an important source of information, editorials, and moral support for the newspaper. Laughlin asked both Polk and Donelson to provide correspondence and information from the major cities in the East. The president's nephew also hoped to function as a conduit directly from Jackson to his fellow Tennesseans, a service that would improve his relationship with Jackson and increase his own political influence within the state and the party.[14]

An illness in March 1835 kept Donelson from traveling to Tennessee as he had planned, but he recovered enough to go there in April. Jackson had sent him on a mission: convince Robert M. Burton, a Wilson County lawyer, to run against John Bell in the House election. Jacksonians had unsuccessfully attempted to persuade William Carroll and several others to challenge him, so they had turned to Burton. The president imparted to Donelson the importance of reminding Tennesseans of the nation's republican principles and encouraged him to relay that same message to Burton. The lawyer continued expressing his reluctance to enter the contest, and Donelson could not induce him otherwise. Whatever hope of Burton's candidacy remained vanished when he fought a brawl in his hometown of Lebanon, Tennessee, and promptly withdrew from the race, leaving Bell unchallenged.[15]

While in Tennessee, Donelson also tried to find a delegate willing to travel to Baltimore for the Democratic National Convention, set for May 1835.

13. Frank W. Williams Jr., "Samuel Hervey Laughlin, Polk's Political Handyman," *THQ* 24 (Winter 1965): 359–60; Paul H. Bergeron, "James K. Polk and the Jacksonian Press in Tennessee," *THQ* 41 (Fall 1982): 257–60; Satterfield, "Uncertain Trumpet," 84; Samuel G. Smith to JKP, 20 September, 20 November, 18, 28 December 1834, in Weaver and Bergeron, *CJKP* 2:493–5, 555–9, 580–1, 613–4; and SHL to AJD, 1 March 1835, DLC.

14. Williams, "Samuel Hervey Laughlin," 359–60; Bergeron, "JKP and the Jacksonian Press," 257–60; Satterfield, "Uncertain Trumpet," 84; Samuel G. Smith to JKP, 20 September, 20 November, 18, 28 December 1834, in Weaver and Bergeron, *CJKP* 2:493–5, 555–9, 580–1, 613–4; and SHL to AJD, 1 March 1835, DLC.

15. SHL to JKP, 9 February 1835, in Weaver and Hall, *CJKP* 3:92–3; SHL to AJD, 1 March 1835, AJD to ETD, 23, 29 April 1835, AJ to AJD, 2, 12 May 1835, DLC; Parks, *John Bell,* 106–7; and Sellers, *Jacksonian,* 274–5.

Despite Jackson's harangues and Donelson's visits, no prominent Tennessee Democrat wanted to make the trip, reportedly because they were too busy, but more likely because the Whigs had accused their opponents of holding a convention that sought to "dictate" the president's successor. The absence of a Tennessee delegate with strong Jacksonian ties resulted in supporters of Richard M. Johnson persuading Edmund Rucker, a Tennessean who happened to be in the city on other business, to cast the state's votes for their vice-presidential candidate. Johnson, considered a political liability because he had a mulatto mistress, defeated the other prominent nominee, William C. Rives of Virginia. Although Van Buren received all 265 available votes for president at the convention, Donelson's trip to Tennessee had proven to be a disappointment.[16]

Donelson returned to Washington in May, but he did not have time to dwell on the disappointment of his trip. Another, more important battle had begun. Bell and White supporters had turned their attention to defeating Polk in the fall congressional elections. Polk once again asked Donelson for help. The congressman's old nemesis, Theodorick Bradford, seemed his likely challenger, and Polk wanted his friend to send him official copies of the evidence he had used against Bradford in the previous election. Donelson hurriedly complied, but the evidence proved unnecessary, as Bradford never officially entered the contest. Like Bell, Polk ran unchallenged.[17]

Donelson's work for the Democratic party in 1835 made him an easy target for critics in Tennessee looking to weaken Van Buren's presidential candidacy. The *Nashville Republican,* which supported the White-Bell alliance, was particularly malicious in leveling charges of conspiracy and corruption at the president's nephew. Its editors initially made an accusation that someone was using Jackson's franking privilege, without his permission, to distribute newspapers criticizing White. The editors then accused Donelson

16. AJ to AJD, 12 May 1835, DLC; Sellers, *Jacksonian,* 271–5; Remini, *Course of American Democracy,* 255; Richard C. Bain, *Convention Decisions and Voting Records* (Washington, D.C.: Brookings Institution, 1960), 20–3; Thomas Brown, "The Miscegenation of Richard Mentor Johnson as an Issue in the National Election Campaign of 1835–1836," *Civil War History* 39 (March 1993): 5–30; *Washington Globe,* 11, 22 June 1835; Joel H. Silbey, "Election of 1836," in *History of American Presidential Elections,* 4 vols., ed. Arthur M. Schlesinger and Fred L. Israel (New York: Chelsea House, 1971), 1:584, 591, 596; and AJD to William C. Rives, 12 June 1835, William C. Rives Papers, Library of Congress.

17. Sellers, *Jacksonian,* 275, 283; and JKP to AJD, 28 April 1835, in Weaver and Hall, *CJKP* 3:169–72.

by name of neglecting his duties in the land office to send out the franked papers. They also branded him a corrupt politician who was using Jackson's name to gather support for Van Buren, an act in which, they alleged, the president would never engage. Donelson's motivation, they concluded, was to ensure Van Buren's election and gain a foreign mission for himself. "The Major, like all weak persons," a September editorial derisively claimed, "has a constant itching for intermeddling with things and subjects above his caliber, and a few soft words and fair promises" from Van Buren "would almost set him on his head."[18]

The *Republican*'s editors were still not finished with Donelson. They accused him of being a "partisan" of Calhoun during the president's first administration, suggesting that he was a covert nullifier. Other Whig newspapers joined the attack. The editors of the *National Banner and Nashville Whig* claimed that its rival, the *Nashville Union*, "*cares nothing for Gen. Jackson, provided it can bolster up Van Buren and his tools! It cares nothing for the President's veracity, provided it can sustain that of Major Donelson!*" Jackson and Donelson moved quickly to refute the charges. The president insisted that his friend, the painter Ralph E. W. Earle, and his son, Andrew Jackson Jr., had franked most of the public documents and newspapers and that Donelson had participated only on occasion and solely "at my request." Donelson, in his own defense, sarcastically accepted the "vast influence" that he allegedly held over the president and accused the "great rascal" Bell of working surreptitiously to supply the *Republican* with editorials and information to use against the administration, a charge its editors denied.[19]

Donelson's conduct during the Eaton affair was an unpleasant, but not an unexpected, avenue of criticism. He defended his support for Calhoun by telling the *Republican*'s editors that he had expressed his opinions openly to Jackson. When the vice-president had broken with Jackson over the nullification issue, Donelson reminded his critics, he had immediately withdrawn his support, a disingenuous claim on his part. The *Republican* repeatedly

18. *Nashville Republican,* 7, 18, 28 July, 8 August, 1, 8, 12, 15 September 1835.

19. Atkins, "Hugh Lawson White," 27–56; *National Banner and Nashville Whig,* 2 November 1835; AJ to James Gwin, 8 August 1835, in *Nashville Republican,* 1 September 1835; AJD to SHL, 15 August, 28 September 1835, in *Nashville Union,* 31 August, 16 October 1835; and AJD to JKP, 29 September 1835, JKP to AJD, 18 October 1835, in Weaver and Hall, *CJKP* 3:314–5, 336–8.

used baseless insinuations against its enemies, he fumed, and its charge that he was a nullifier was unfounded. What his actions actually showed, Donelson concluded, was that he was "not afraid to entertain an opinion" contrary to the president's own and that Jackson was not the "dictating man" depicted by Bell. Donelson dismissed the entire debate as a ploy by *Republican* editor Washington Barrow to exact revenge for a failed attempt to obtain a government position.[20]

The Whig charges against Donelson had hit close to the mark, however. The *Republican*'s characterization of him as a sycophant hurt, and it purportedly led him to challenge Barrow to a duel, although the truth of that report is unclear. To his opponents, including former friends, Donelson was "weak" and dim-witted, giving his loyalty to anyone who promised him something in return. They attacked his virtue and honor by highlighting his self-interest and ambition. While there is no evidence that Donelson had asked for a foreign mission or any other reward for assisting Van Buren, his actions in supporting Polk and Grundy and founding the *Union* indicated his desire to improve his political standing in the party. His opportunities to have a meaningful influence on Jacksonian politics had been limited so far, so he was casting about for a chance to demonstrate his talents.[21]

The attacks on Donelson coincided with the fall elections, which were a disaster for the Democrats. Polk won reelection, but Bell and other pro-White candidates trounced their Democratic opponents in the August elections. To make matters worse, the Tennessee General Assembly unanimously reelected White as senator. The legislators not only gave Jackson's enemy another six years in Washington but also refused to consider a matter that the president considered very important. He had requested that the legislature instruct the state's senators to help expunge his censure from the Senate journal. Not only would Jackson receive some satisfaction from having the censure removed, but he also hoped to embarrass White, who had committed himself to opposing the expunging. When the issue came up, the legislature, instead of taking up the resolutions, tabled them. Donelson repeated to

20. AJD to SHL, 15 August 1835, in *Nashville Union,* 31 August 1835; and Bergeron, *Antebellum Politics,* 43.

21. DSD to AJD, 26 October 1835, Bettie M. Donelson Papers, Tennessee State Library and Archives, Nashville (hereafter cited as BDP); and Wyatt-Brown, "AJ's Honor," 14–5, 24.

Polk a rumor then circulating among Tennessee Democrats that William B. Lewis, his old nemesis from the Eaton affair, was working with Bell to block the president's wishes, a charge that Lewis denied to Jackson.[22]

Dissatisfied with the Tennessee elections, Donelson, from his post in Washington, moved to ensure Polk's election as Speaker of the House of Representatives. His opponent in the election was John Bell, and a victory would bring sweet revenge for the Tennessee Democrats. Donelson reassured Polk that his friends in Middle Tennessee wanted him to succeed and encouraged him to make certain that his supporters in the House were present for the balloting. Polk was confident that he would win, despite the intrigues of men bent on his failure. His optimism proved correct. When Congress convened in December 1835, Polk defeated Bell on the first ballot with 132 out of a possible 222 votes. His victory guaranteed that Jackson would have a strong influence in the House for his remaining months as president.[23]

With Polk firmly ensconced in power, Donelson turned his attention back to the presidential campaign. In addition to White, two other contenders had emerged: Daniel Webster, nominated by the Whigs, and William Henry Harrison, a War of 1812 military hero chosen as the candidate of Pennsylvania Whigs and Anti-Masons. The presence of three Whig presidential aspirants threatened to send the election to the House of Representatives, where even Polk might not be able to save Van Buren. Rallying the Democratic ranks around the party standard became imperative.[24]

White's candidacy was the most worrisome. Donelson had already confided to Edward Livingston in April 1835 that White's popularity was "unfortunately delusive to some who have heretofore acted with us." By pre-

22. Parks, *John Bell,* 111; Sellers, *Jacksonian,* 283–4; Atkins, *Parties, Politics, and Sectional Conflict,* 48–9; AJD to JKP, 24 September 1835, in Weaver and Hall, *CJKP* 3:307–8; and Harlan, "Public Career of WBL," pt. 2, 140.

23. AJD to JKP, 28 August, 24 September, 20 October 1835, JKP to SHL, 6 September 1835, JKP to AJD, 22 September, 18 October 1835, in Weaver and Hall, *CJKP* 3:277–8, 307–8, 341–2, 283–6, 303–7, 336–8; SHL to AJD, 21 October 1835, Tennessee Documentary Project, James D. Hoskins Library, University of Tennessee, Knoxville (hereafter cited as TDH); and Sellers, *Jacksonian,* 292–7.

24. Silbey, "Election of 1836," 1:584–5; Donald B. Cole, *Martin Van Buren and the American Political System* (Princeton, N.J.: Princeton University Press, 1984), 268–9; and Richard P. McCormick, "Was There a 'Whig Strategy' in 1836?" *Journal of the Early Republic* 4 (Spring 1984): 47–70.

senting himself as a "*no party man*," White was catering to "the taste of the Whigs and Nullifiers." His claims that he was remaining true to the republican principles of the Jacksonians were false, since the "honest laborer in an honest cause is content with success." When Van Buren became president, Donelson promised, there "will be no ground under his administration for the operation of those men who under cover of friendship for the man do all in their power to bring his measures into disrepute."[25]

Donelson worked for Van Buren from Jackson's side in Washington. He focused mainly on swaying Tennessee's votes into the Democratic column. For example, when John Catron, an influential Jacksonian jurist in Tennessee and later a justice on the U.S. Supreme Court, informed Donelson that "the planting people" in the state needed reassurance that Van Buren would not attempt to restrict or eliminate their source of labor, he provided the *Nashville Union* with congressional speeches that indicated Van Buren's opposition to the abolition of slavery in the District of Columbia. Donelson considered such concern unwarranted and attributed it to desperation on the part of the Whigs to organize a strong southern faction to defeat the Democratic nominee. When White's supporters further attempted to undermine the New Yorker's Jacksonian ties by associating him with John Quincy Adams and Daniel Webster, the "two high priests of Federalism," Donelson declared that support for the Tennessee Whig came from "thousands of rank Federalists and Nullifiers in the South," both groups that had proven dangerous to the nation's republican principles.[26]

Donelson also helped to solidify Jackson's hard-money policy, an area that hopefully would assist Van Buren in his efforts against the pro-Bank Whigs. In June 1836, Congress passed the Deposit Act, which required an increase in the number of deposit banks and the distribution of the government surplus that had accrued during Jackson's second administration. This

25. AJD to Edward Livingston, 13 April 1835, AJD to Lewis Randolph, 9 August 1835, DLC.

26. Satterfield, "Moderate Nationalist Jacksonian," 154–5; *Nashville Union*, 7, 28 January 1836; John M. McFaul, "Expediency vs. Morality: Jacksonian Politics and Slavery," *Journal of American History* 62 (June 1975): 24–39; Shade, "Most Delicate and Exciting Topics," 459–84; Michael Feldberg, *The Turbulent Era: Riot and Disorder in Jacksonian America* (New York: Oxford University Press, 1980), 43–7; Leonard L. Richards, "*Gentlemen of Property and Standing*": *Anti-Abolition Mobs in Jacksonian America* (New York: Oxford University Press, 1970); and John Catron to AJD, 11 February 1836, AJD to [John Catron], 1 March 1836, DLC.

move coincided with an increase in British capital imports and an overabundance of Mexican silver and made it appear that the surplus distribution caused the rise in inflation that accompanied the international financial maneuverings. The president attempted to curb the inflation by requiring specie for payments of public lands, which many Americans believed had become the center of the speculative mania and was causing the country's economy to grow too quickly. After informing his cabinet of his decision, Jackson asked Donelson to help Senator Thomas Hart Benton, who had unsuccessfully attempted to introduce similar legislation in the past, draft the order. Issued on 11 July 1836, the Specie Circular, as the executive order was called, required specie payments, with some exceptions allowed, for the purchase of public lands. Jackson's stated purpose was to restore hard money to the country, but he also probably wanted to maintain economic stability until after the fall's presidential election.[27]

In his eagerness to secure Van Buren's election, Jackson decided to travel across Tennessee in August 1836, making stops in White's home region in the eastern part of the state before proceeding to the Hermitage. The result could not have been more disastrous. Whig charges of "dictation" appeared correct as the sitting president campaigned for his successor. Whig newspapers, still wary of attacking Jackson directly, maintained that the trip was not his doing but that of his "managers," a group that included Donelson and Polk.[28]

When the election was held in early November, White won a decisive victory in Tennessee. Van Buren fared poorly in East and West Tennessee and, by a narrow margin, lost even Middle Tennessee, home to Jackson,

27. Peter Temin, *The Jacksonian Economy* (New York: Norton, 1969), 22–3, 172–7; Remini, *Course of American Democracy,* 317–29; Thomas Hart Benton, *Thirty Year's View; or, A History of the Workings of the American Government for Thirty Years, from 1820 to 1850,* 2 vols. (New York: D. Appleton, 1857), 1:676–7; Richard H. Timberlake Jr., "The Specie Circular and Distribution of Surplus," *Journal of Political Economy* 68 (April 1960): 109–17; idem, "The Specie Circular and Sales of Public Lands: A Comment," *Journal of Economic History* 25 (September 1965): 414–6; Harry N. Scheiber, "The Pet Banks in Jacksonian Politics and Finance, 1833–1841," *Journal of Economic History* 23 (June 1963): 196–214; and Bray Hammond, *Banks and Politics in America: From the Revolution to the Civil War* (Princeton, N.J.: Princeton University Press, 1957), 455.

28. Remini, *Course of American Democracy,* 330–2, 336; Sellers, *Jacksonian,* 299–303; Atkins, *Parties, Politics, and Sectional Conflict,* 50–4; JKP to AJD, 9 August, 3 September 1836, in Weaver and Hall, *CJKP* 3:696–7, 713–4; *National Banner and Nashville Whig,* 15 August 1836; and Silbey, "Election of 1836," 1:596.

Donelson, and Polk. The state's voters apparently believed Whig charges that Jackson had abandoned his republican principles and that White was more "Jacksonian" than even Old Hickory. Uncertainty over Van Buren's slavery views also lessened his appeal in the state. Thankfully for the Democrats, the national election went decisively in favor of Van Buren, although his showing was weaker than Jackson's had been in the previous two elections.[29]

Donelson was ecstatic. Van Buren had won, and his victory assured the Jackson Democrats of another four years at the head of the government. The new president would likely need his services in some capacity. Donelson had been working hard to position himself for political advancement. His alliance with prominent party members, such as Polk and Grundy, had enabled him to gain more experience with local, state, and national elections, and his association with the *Nashville Union* was making clear that writing political rhetoric was one of his strengths. Whatever the Whigs might think, any position that Donelson obtained would not be because of nepotism but because he deserved it.

29. Remini, *Course of American Democracy,* 330–2, 336; Sellers, *Jacksonian,* 299–303; Atkins, *Parties, Politics, and Sectional Conflict,* 50–4; JKP to AJD, 9 August, 3 September 1836, in Weaver and Hall, *CJKP* 3:696–7, 713–4; and Silbey, "Election of 1836," 1:596.

8

"Depressed in Spirits"

While serving his uncle in Washington, Andrew Donelson also found it necessary to spend time looking after plantation business back in Tennessee. His family was growing, and Donelson believed that "farming," as he called it, promised a more profitable source of future income than any that he had found in working for the government of the United States. Initially, Jackson had written Donelson personal checks to cover his family's expenses while in Washington; this financial support largely ended in March 1833, however, when his nephew landed a position in the General Land Office signing public land warrants for a monthly salary of $125. Such modest income probably seemed insufficient for someone who considered himself a member of elite southern society, although given Donelson's questionable financial decisions, he was fortunate to have it. So while helping Jackson fend of his political opponents, Donelson also devoted his attention to enhancing his personal fortunes as a planter.[1]

Being a successful southern planter required finding a dependable overseer, particularly when the land's owner was absent for months at a time. On the day Jackson and Donelson left for Washington in January 1829, the two men signed a contract with Graves Steele in which they authorized the latter to oversee their plantations that year, with the possibility of extending his service for another three years. Steele found that the task required more work than he had anticipated, as Jackson's business associate, Charles J. Love, informed Donelson that the overseer wanted more money for managing the two plantations. Love assured Jackson's nephew that Steele treated the slaves well and that their crops were promising. But relative James G. Martin J. wrote him otherwise, indicating that while Steele had "little trouble" with

1. Satterfield, "Moderate Nationalist Jacksonian," 55–6, 113; and Edward Livingston to AJD, 7 March 1833, DLC.

Jackson's slaves, he had encountered "some" trouble with Donelson's. Donelson chose to relieve Steele of further duties on his plantation, although he continued to work at the Hermitage. Donelson's next several overseers were apparently no better, although they did well enough to lead Emily to predict that the family would make forty thousand dollars on their Middle Tennessee crops in 1830.[2]

Emily may have been too optimistic in her assessment, but her husband was making some money, as his purchase of slaves during this period indicates. Before leaving for Washington, Donelson bought seven slaves from his brother-in-law, John C. McLemore. With Jackson's help, he acquired two more slaves (a young boy and girl) in early 1831. Unfortunately, Donelson was no better at keeping thorough records of slave life on his plantations than he was at preserving financial records. From the scattered evidence that remains, it appears that his slaves suffered the usual maladies that pervaded their ranks. Some also ran away, an action that produced concern among southern planters, including Donelson, who often expressed consternation at the lack of loyalty displayed in such an action. Not surprisingly, the slaves on Donelson's plantation received minimal attention unless they transcended their assigned roles as docile, functioning laborers.[3]

Still, things were not going as smoothly as Emily thought. Her husband's plantation in Haywood County, Tennessee, which he had received from Jackson in the mid-1820s in a land exchange, struggled in the early 1830s. Unpaid taxes led the local sheriff to put the plantation up for auction in both 1830 and 1831. Donelson convinced one of his business associates to pay the taxes for him and promised to reimburse him at a future date. Only in his early thirties, Donelson was already finding that owning a plantation and

2. Agreement among AJ, AJD, and Graves W. Steele, 19 January 1829, AJ to AJD, 22 August 1829, in Bassett and Jameson, *CAJ* 4:2–3, 65–6; AJD to ETD, 26 July 1829, MVB to AJD, 27 July 1829, AJ to AJD, 22, 26 August 1829, Charles J. Love to AJD, 22 August 1829, agreement between AJD and Archibald Pool, 22 October 1829, ETD to AJD, 4, 30 October, 30 November 1830, DLC; Remini, *Course of American Freedom,* 250–1; and Satterfield, "Moderate Nationalist Jacksonian," 42–3, 101.

3. Bill of sale between JCM and AJD, 5 January 1829, William Watson to AJD, 13 June 1829, [?] to AJD, 27 October 1830, AJD to ETD, 15 January, 6 February, 10 June 1831, AJD's order to purchase slaves, 14 June 1831, [D. F. Armstrong?] to AJD, 6 December 1832, DLC; AJD to [Lewis Jones], 7 March, 21 June 1831, Arthur Holbrook Collection, Milwaukee County Historical Society, Milwaukee, Wisc.; Peter J. Parish, *Slavery: History and Historians* (Boulder, Colo.: Westview Press, 1989), 64–6; and James Oakes, *The Ruling Race: A History of American Slaveholders* (New York: Knopf, 1982; New York: Vintage, 1983), 188–90.

slaves was no guarantee of financial success. Whether he consciously admitted it to himself, he was also discovering that he did not possess the financial acumen planters found crucial to turning a profit.[4]

This was an unfortunate shortcoming, because the Donelson family was rapidly growing larger. Son Jackson was joined on 31 August 1829 by daughter Mary Rachel (later renamed Mary Emily). John Samuel and Rachel Jackson followed on 18 May 1832 and 19 April 1834, respectively. Emily often commented on young Jackson's wildness, while Mary Emily was her father's "red bird," which may have been a reference to her hair color. Not unexpectedly, all of the children suffered from illness at various times, which worried their parents.[5]

The Donelson children all survived these health scares, giving them the chance to learn from their father and their esteemed great-uncle what would make them successful representatives of their family and their region. Undoubtedly remembering his uncle's emphasis on education, Donelson encouraged his oldest son to study so that he could "entitle himself to the praise of being a Jackson boy." Donelson also warned his wife not to coddle young Jackson too much; he needed to spend time with his tutor, Mr. Brent. With Brent, Donelson declared, "his morals will be well attended to" and "he has a prospect of becoming quite a scholar."[6]

These lessons were not exclusive to Jackson Donelson. According to Mary Donelson's memoirs, Uncle Jackson "encouraged us to talk and ask questions" at the supper table and "shielded us from punishment when naughty," much to Emily's chagrin. Jackson's response: "I think Emily, with all due deference to the Good Book, that love and patience are better disciplinarians than rods." This lesson likely only served to spoil the children, but other lessons were more serious in their consequences. For example, three of the children received slaves from Andrew Jackson: for Jackson Donelson, a "bright mullato boy—about 10 (ten) years old"; for Mary, an eight-year-

4. AJ to AJD, 22 August 1829, in Bassett and Jameson, *CAJ* 4:2–3, 65–6; AJD to ETD, 26 July 1829, MVB to AJD, 27 July 1829, AJ to AJD, 22, 26 August 1829, Charles J. Love to AJD, 22 August 1829, DLC; Remini, *Course of American Freedom*, 250–1; and Satterfield, "Moderate Nationalist Jacksonian," 42–3, 101.

5. ETD to AJD, 4, 30 October, 26 November, 22 December 1830, 31 January 1831, 21 July 1834, AJD to ETD, 9, 21 January, 7 September 1831, AJD to Dr. Samuel Hogg, 26 August 1834, DLC.

6. AJD to ETD, 20 December 1830, 29 April 1835, 10 May 1835, DLC.

old girl named Emmeline; and for Rachel, two girls, Louisa and Sophia, both "about 16 yrs. [old]." (Why John did not receive a slave as well is unknown.) These gifts reinforced the Donelson children's position as the offspring of the gentry class.[7]

Jackson also continued to look out for the children's father in his 1833 last will and testament. The president made generous bequeathals, granting Donelson a one-hundred-acre tract north of his current residence, ten slaves valued at three thousand dollars for Jackson Donelson, a sword given to the Hero of New Orleans by the state of Tennessee, and one-third of any cash left after Jackson's estate was settled. The rest of Jackson's estate went to his adopted son, Andrew Jackson Jr.; both Andrews were appointed as executors. Donelson had reason to hope that his uncle continued to value him, despite their differences over the Eaton affair.[8]

Another indication that Jackson held his nephew in high regard was his contribution to the building of his new home. Begun in 1834, the Poplar Grove mansion and name replaced that of Springdale. Architects Joseph Reiff and William Hume worked with Jackson and Donelson to draw up plans for the new house, with additional input from Emily. Reiff and Hume built the new mansion in Greek Revival style, following recommendations made by Boston architect Asher Benjamin, whose writings were making Greek Revival a popular choice for new homes. On his trips home, Donelson updated Emily on the mansion's progress, assuring her that she "would be pleased with it." Its construction was completed in 1836, giving the Donelsons a place to which they could return once Jackson finished his term.[9]

During these years, Andrew Donelson's relationship with his wife was tested by the strains of separation amid the turmoil of the Eaton affair. While exiled to Tennessee, Emily often wrote to him that she feared that he was sick or depressed and wanted to be with him to lift his spirits. As their separations grew longer, she became more "melancholy." Emily criticized her husband for his short letters, telling him, "It seems to me you leave much

7. Mary E. D. Wilcox, *Christmas under Three Flags* (Washington, D.C.: Neale, 1900), 26, 35; and Atkins, *Emily Donelson,* 232, 332.

8. AJ's will, 30 September 1833, JLC.

9. AJD to ETD, 23, 29 April, 10, 20 May 1835, DLC; Stockly Donelson to AJD, 5 June 1836, BDP; Lawrence, "Tulip Grove," 8–14; and Atkins, *Emily Donelson,* 266–7, 274–5.

unsaid[,] so much you might have said, and I am sometimes afraid you do not feel so sensibly as I do our separation. . . . When I hear that you are getting on so well without me I feel dissatisfied." Donelson assured her that he was well and that he thought of her often. "'Think not beloved,'" he quoted an unknown poet, "'time can break the spell around us cast, or absence from my bosom, take the memory of the past.'" Their separations became less frequent after the Eaton affair, with Donelson traveling only once or twice a year to Tennessee to check on his and the president's affairs there. Still, there was an undercurrent of tension in Andrew and Emily's relationship that suggested her realization that serving, and proving his loyalty to, Uncle was of such importance to her husband that he willingly sacrificed time with his wife and family.[10]

Donelson's unwillingness to leave his father figure and cleave to his wife became very apparent during Jackson's second administration, particularly its last two years. He tried hard to balance his work in the Land Office with his service to Jackson, often to the detriment of his family. Sometimes, after making a political trip for his uncle, Donelson found himself overwhelmed with Land Office paperwork, forcing him to ask for help from other departments. Other times, his duty to Jackson left him too busy even to check on his plantation in Tennessee, and he had to request help from relatives.[11]

While Donelson fought the enemies of Jackson and Van Buren in 1835 and 1836, his wife, Emily, grew increasingly ill. She had suffered from poor health for her entire life, but her condition had become more chronic since the birth of their daughter, Rachel, in 1834. As Emily's physical condition deteriorated, it became necessary for her to return to Tennessee and their new home at Poplar Grove. She departed from Washington in the late spring of 1836. Donelson intended to follow her home after he had resolved matters at the Land Office, planning to resign his office in anticipation of the

10. ETD to AJD, 30 October, 26 November 1830, 23 February 1831, AJD to ETD, 1 January 1831, DLC. The tension between a husband and a wife caused by the husband's sense of public duty is a common theme in the early Republic. One of the best examples is that of the Wirts, analyzed by Anya Jabour in her *Marriage in the Early Republic: Elizabeth and William Wirt and the Companionate Ideal* (Baltimore: Johns Hopkins University Press, 1998).

11. Satterfield, "Moderate Nationalist Jacksonian," 124; AJD to ETD, 2 November 1834, JCM to AJD, 20 December 1834, AJD to Edward Livingston, 13 April 1835, DLC; and AJD to Stockly Donelson, 1 June 1835, TDH.

administration's end. He further delayed his trip home in order to verify that the new furniture the couple had purchased would arrive at Poplar Grove from Pittsburgh and then traveled to nearby Baltimore to examine several slaves he and Andrew Jr. were considering for purchase.[12]

Donelson returned to Tennessee in early August 1836 with the expectation of going back to Washington with Emily and his uncle in early September. Emily, however, experienced a "rupture of a blood vessel" that kept her from making the return trip to the capital. More seriously, she was suffering from tuberculosis, or "consumption," as it was normally called at this time. A bacterial disease of the lungs that particularly struck young women, tuberculosis was the most dangerous disease in the United States between 1800 and 1860. It spread through coughing and sneezing, and its symptoms included a low-grade fever and expectoration of blood from the lungs. Emily had exhibited symptoms of the disease from birth, and they were worsening.[13]

Donelson remained with his wife at their home until mid-October 1836. When Emily's physician, Dr. Laurence, predicted that she would recover enough to travel by December, Donelson set out for Washington. He arrived on 20 October, with an enormous backlog of forty thousand land warrants awaiting his signature before he could relinquish his post to Andrew Jackson Jr. He signed nearly three thousand warrants a day and assisted in the preparation of Jackson's final annual message. The president, who suffered a near-fatal hemorrhaging of his own on 19 November, was not as involved in the latter stages of the message's preparation as he would have liked. The responsibility for its completion, therefore, fell on Donelson and Amos Kendall. Jackson wanted to excoriate Representatives Balie Peyton, a fellow Tennessean, and Henry A. Wise of Virginia for their scurrilous and, many times, petty attacks on Speaker of the House Polk, but Donelson apparently convinced him to eliminate that section. (Jackson later regretted its absence, lecturing his nephew that "a temporizing policy will destroy

12. Burke, *Emily Donelson* 2:70; AJD to ETD, 14 June 1836, in ibid. 2:105; AJD to ETD, 2, 11 July 1836, DLC; and Linda Bennett Galloway, "Andrew Jackson, Jr.," pt. 2, *THQ* 9 (December 1950): 322.

13. AJD to ETD, 2 November 1834, in Burke, *Emily Donelson* 2:71–2; AJ to AJ Jr., 9, 17 September 1836, JLC; SHL to JKP, 15 September 1836, in Weaver and Hall, *CJKP* 3:730–1; and Jack Larkin, *The Reshaping of Everyday Life, 1790–1840* (New York: Harper and Row, 1988), 78–81.

any one who adopts it.") Kendall and Donelson disagreed as well, debating whether to acknowledge the failure of the state banks to administrate properly the government's deposits. Kendall, who eventually won the argument, wanted to downplay the problem, while Donelson thought it best to concede that using the state banks had been an "injustice and a bad policy." Despite these differences, the two men completed the message to Jackson's satisfaction.[14]

Andrew Donelson's mind, however, was never far from Emily. Her doctor's assurances and his own hopes aside, Emily's condition was serious, and Andrew knew it. He wrote her frequently, encouraging her and advising her to follow the orders of Jackson's physician, Dr. Hunt, who recommended that she take "elixir vitriol[,] . . . blisters alternately on the breast and between the shoulders[,]" and a diet of light fruit, milk, and mush. Because of Jackson's need for his nephew to sign the land warrants and help with the annual message, Donelson chose not to go home in mid-November. The delay greatly troubled Emily, but to ease his concerns, she assured him that her health was improving.[15]

Such misplaced optimism may have convinced Donelson that he could tarry longer than his planned departure date of 22 November 1836. His uncle's illness also weighed in his decision. Donelson's loyalty and dedication to Jackson was laudable, but here it cost him. Just one day after writing Emily that he would be home on 1 December, Donelson received his last letter from her. In it, she reassured him that she was feeling better. But Emily was wrong—her illness was progressing rapidly. Lulled into a false sense of security, Donelson informed his wife that he would be unable to leave before 1 December due to Jackson's sudden illness and the need to prepare the annual message. He promised her that they would travel to a warmer climate, probably New Orleans, when he returned and she had recovered adequately. Donelson finally left for Tennessee on 3 December, arriving on the twenty-

14. AJD to ETD, 13, 28 October 1836, AJ to ETD, 21 October 1836, in Burke, *Emily Donelson* 2:114–5, 118, 116; AJ to ETD, 31 October 1836, in Bassett and Jameson, *CAJ* 5:433; AJ to AJD, 29 December 1836, DLC; Satterfield, "Moderate Nationalist Jacksonian," 151–2; Sellers, *Jacksonian,* 307–10, 315–7; eighth annual message, 5 December 1836, in Richardson, *Messages and Papers of the Presidents* 3:236–60; and Remini, *Course of American Democracy,* 370–1.

15. William Donelson to AJD, 12 October 1836, AJD to ETD, 21, 23, 28 October 1836, DLC.

first, a week later than expected and two days too late to see his wife alive for the last time. Emily died on the afternoon of the nineteenth, watching out the window for her husband's arrival, according to family reports. Donelson buried his wife next to her father and sister on 22 December.[16]

Emily's death devastated Donelson. At first, he displayed a remarkable resilience. He wrote Jackson on the day of her funeral that he expected to go to the Hermitage and inquire about the president's affairs the following day. Although he was able to look after some "indispensable business" and eventually resumed his place by the outgoing president's side in Washington early in 1837, Donelson continued to grieve, leading Jackson to observe as late as March 1837 that his nephew was "depressed in spirits" and had no "lively interest in politics." Jackson himself expressed regret that he had kept Donelson "three days longer than I wished him to aid me in compleating my message" and had been "the cause of your detention from her."[17]

Donelson unquestionably experienced guilt associated with his absence during Emily's last days. Instead of being by her side and helping her obtain better medical treatment, he instead chose to place his political career above his concern for Emily's health. It was a common choice for aspiring politicians to make, but that did not lessen the personal loss to Donelson. Jackson's presidency, which began as a time of optimistic anticipation for the young man, ended with disappointment, regret, and grief, which he expressed in a memorial to his young wife:

> The virtues which made her the object of [her family's] love and affection and secured for her the respect and admiration of all who knew her, and which gave her that good name which endureth forever,

16. AJD to ETD, 10, 20, 27 November 1836, ETD to AJD, 11 November 1836, AJ to ETD, 1 December 1836, James G. Martin to John Donelson Coffee, [December 1836], AJD to AJ, 23, [22] December 1836, in Burke, *Emily Donelson* 2:121–2, 123, 122, 125–6, 127, 130–1; AJ to Maunsel White, 2 December 1836, and AJ to AJD, 10 December 1836, in Bassett and Jameson, *CAJ* 5:440–1, 441; and *Washington Globe,* 20 January 1837. Donelson's letter of the twenty-third must be misdated. Emily died on Monday, 19 December. Andrew arrived, by his own account, on Wednesday, the twenty-first. Emily was buried the next day, which could only mean that she was buried on 22 December 1836.

17. AJD to ETD, 23, [22] December 1836, AJ to MVB, [March 1837?], in Burke, *Emily Donelson* 2:130–1, 139; AJ to AJD, 6 December 1836, AJD to AJ, 31 December 1836, DLC; and AJ to Mary Polk, 22 December 1836, quoted in Remini, *Course of American Democracy,* 370.

no tombstone can record. . . . She was beautiful in person, meek in temper, pure and ardent in attachment, circumspect in deportment, always charitable and humane. A being so perfect in her nature the world could not slander nor the tongue of the malicious injure.[18]

18. ETD memorial, n.d. [Winter 1836–37], DLC.

9

"An Advancement Disproportioned"

Even though Donelson was still mourning Emily's death, his uncle wanted him back in Washington as soon as possible to help arrange his personal affairs for the trip back to the Hermitage. There was also a political matter that demanded Donelson's attention. During the recent presidential campaign, Hugh Lawson White and his supporters had accused Jackson of offering White the vice-presidency under Van Buren if he would withdraw his own candidacy and support the president's chosen successor. That charge, Jackson exclaimed, was "*false and a positive libel,*" and he ordered his nephew to "meet the charge in any way you deem proper." Donelson, however, ignored the request. When accusations of Jackson's improper use of patronage also surfaced in Congress, the president again asked Donelson to answer the allegations. Once more, his nephew did nothing. It is impossible to say whether Donelson was perturbed at Jackson for his impatience or if he was still blaming himself for not reaching Poplar Grove in time to give Emily some comfort.[1]

Whatever the case, the political world was moving forward. While he was still mourning Emily's death, rumors reached Donelson that Van Buren was going to ask him to serve as his secretary of war, which he did in early 1837. In making his offer, the president-elect praised Donelson profusely. Then Van Buren changed his mind. In his autobiography, Van Buren wrote that he did so after consulting "a discreet and disinterested friend" in Tennessee. The friend, he remembered, had "thought that the appointment would cause a surprise on the part of the public and would be regarded as an advancement disproportioned to the stations he had before occupied." In other words, would friends and foes alike look at Donelson's appointment as a sop to

1. AJ to AJD, 11, 24, 31 January, 23 February 1837, in Bassett and Jameson, *CAJ* 5:449–50, 451–2, 456, 460; AJ to AJD, 23 February 1837, DLC; and Robert T. Lytle to AJ, 26 February 1837, JLC.

Jackson? Van Buren mentioned the concern to the president, who indicated that "the same idea had passed through his own mind, but that he had not felt himself at liberty, under the circumstances, to suggest it." With this advice fresh in his mind, Van Buren informed Donelson of his withdrawal of the offer, attributing his decision to staunch opposition from "mutual friends."[2]

When notified of Van Buren's decision, Donelson had no alternative but to comply. In a letter to the president-elect, Donelson agreed it was important to avoid the appearance that he was receiving a position simply because of his relationship with Jackson. Such participation in Van Buren's cabinet would only revive Whig charges of "dictation." To save face, he told the New Yorker that he had written his uncle "such a letter . . . as would induce you, even if the judgment of mutual friends had created any doubt in your mind, to come to the decision which had been adopted." Despite Donelson's statement, no record of this correspondence with Jackson exists. No doubt, he was more disappointed than he indicated. His career had led up to this moment, and when it seemed that he was about to ascend to a powerful position, it had been taken away from him.[3]

Jackson's agreement with Van Buren must have particularly frustrated Donelson. His uncle had convinced him early in life that he would hold the highest positions in the nation, but when an opportunity arose for his advancement, Jackson apparently believed him unprepared for the job. He could understand his uncle's opposition to him over the Eaton affair—that had been about loyalty and honor, concepts Donelson well appreciated, even if he did not agree with Jackson in that particular instance—but this situation was different. His uncle, it must have seemed to Donelson, cared more about maintaining his reputation and legacy through Van Buren's administration than helping his nephew achieve the fame that he had predicted.

After some delay due to his daughter Rachel's illness, Donelson did make it to Washington in time to witness Van Buren's inauguration, but he did not

2. MVB to AJD, [8 February 1837], Martin Van Buren Papers, Library of Congress, Washington, D.C. (hereafter cited as VBL); Fitzpatrick, *Autobiography of MVB* 2:346–7; AJD to MVB, 21 February 1837, in Fitzpatrick, *Autobiography of MVB* 2:346–7; W. S. Derrick to NPT, 13 February 1837, NPTP; MVB to JKP, 21 February 1845 (two letters), James K. Polk Papers, Library of Congress, Washington, D.C. (hereafter cited as PLC); and James C. Curtis, *The Fox at Bay: Martin Van Buren and the Presidency, 1837–1841* (Lexington: University Press of Kentucky, 1970), 57.

3. AJD to MVB, 21 February 1837, in Fitzpatrick, *Autobiography of MVB,* 346–7.

linger to accompany Jackson home. Polk was left to travel back to Tennessee with the recently retired president. Back at the Hermitage, Jackson finally persuaded his nephew to proceed with the desired attacks on the Whigs. Donelson reluctantly agreed, telling Van Buren that "the game is not worth shooting, and I shall endeavor to dissuade him from the purpose." Jackson, of course, would not relent, so Donelson wrote the editorials denouncing White's actions. The decision only prolonged an issue that should have ceased with the 1836 presidential election. Jackson considered it important, however, since Tennessee would experience another round of state elections in the fall of 1837.[4]

The outcome of those elections would depend in large part on the nation's economy. The United States in 1837 continued to experience economic contraction. The Deposit Act and the Specie Circular that Jackson had supported the previous year had failed to stop the nation's growing financial problems. The Whigs, who had initially blamed Jackson, now accused Van Buren of increasing the severity of this Panic of 1837. Donelson had helped Senator Thomas Hart Benton draft the Specie Circular, and now he moved to defend it publicly. In a *Nashville Union* editorial, he criticized White's use of the circular in condemning Jackson's "corrupt" administration. "It seems to have been his opinion, that this order was issued, not only to favor speculation and break all the banks in the country, but to secure Mr. Van Buren's election," he wrote. Why, then, did he not bring these accusations to Congress when Jackson was in office, Donelson asked sarcastically. It was "folly and childishness."[5]

Privately, however, Donelson expressed worries about the circular's effect, "which has not been so much the cause as the pretext for the complaints that are made in the money market," he wrote Van Buren. "It would be a god send if this means of annoyance could be silenced by some step on your part which would have the effect of giving to purchasers of the public lands the customary facilities of credit thro specie paying Banks," he encouraged

4. *Washington Globe,* 9 March 1837; AJD to JKP, [4, 18 March 1837], in Herbert Weaver and Wayne Cutler, eds., *Correspondence of James K. Polk,* vol. 4, *1837–1838* (Nashville: Vanderbilt University Press, 1977), 74, 79–80; AJD to MVB, 3 April 1837, AJ to AJD, 10 April 1837, DLC; AJD to MVB, 17 May 1837, in Bassett and Jameson, *CAJ* 5:479; and *Nashville Union,* 22, 27 July 1837.

5. Major L. Wilson, *The Presidency of Martin Van Buren* (Lawrence: University Press of Kansas, 1984), 44–56; AJD to JKP, 20 July 1837, in Weaver and Cutler, *CJKP* 4:187–8; and *Nashville Union,* 22 July 1837.

the new president, "at the same time that it maintained the policy declared by the General in respect to the disuse of small bills and the gradual restoration of the constitutional currency." It is probable that the panic was affecting his own finances and, as a result, his ideas about the nation's economic policies.[6]

After conversations with Jackson, Donelson decided not to send the letter, as he later told Van Buren, because he was "not competent to discuss" the issue. Jackson had apparently cornered his nephew and convinced him to drop the subject. In the end, he kept Donelson quiet, and Van Buren kept the circular as policy. Donelson never uttered his opinions publicly, but Jackson's treatment of him must have reinforced his impression that his uncle did not have faith in him and did not think him capable of shaping national policy.[7]

Donelson was right about one thing—it was becoming increasingly clear that a healthy economy was crucial to the success of both Van Buren's administration and the Democratic party. The Panic of 1837 had begun taking its toll even before Van Buren's ascension to the presidency; now, he faced its full effect. In May, New York banks suspended specie payments, and other banks across the country followed their lead. In an attempt to stabilize the specie standard, Van Buren took control of the Treasury and called a special session of Congress for September to discuss the panic and the government's response to it. The president also formulated a plan for an independent treasury, which would completely divorce the Treasury from the banking system. In Tennessee, the president's actions met with some trepidation. Felix Grundy, for example, proclaimed, "The friends of the administration . . . [were] wholly at a loss as to the views of the Executive Government upon the subject" of the suspension of specie payments.[8]

While Van Buren was concerned with the effect of his economic policies on the nation, Donelson viewed their consequences on Tennessee's upcom-

6. AJD to MVB, 3 April 1837, DLC; and AJD to MVB, 17 May 1837, VBL.

7. AJD to MVB, 17 May 1837, VBL; Wilson, *Presidency of MVB,* 52–4; Levi Woodbury to AJD, n.d. [1837], MVB to AJD, 6 September, 4 October 1837, DLC; AJD to JKP, 20 July 1837, JKP to AJD, 6 August 1837, Weaver and Cutler, *CJKP* 4:187–8, 198–9; and message to the special session of Congress, 4 September 1837, in Richardson, *Messages and Papers of the Presidents* 3:324–46.

8. Wilson, *Presidency of MVB,* 54–60; Cole, *MVB,* 297–301; Felix Grundy to Levi Woodbury, 1 June 1837, Levi Woodbury Papers, Library of Congress; and Remini, *Course of American Democracy,* 429–30.

ing fall elections. The state's Democratic party incorrectly believed that the previous year's defection of supporters to the White candidacy was an aberration. When it became apparent that the Whigs were a permanent feature of the state's political landscape, the Democrats sought out new candidates to try to reverse the situation. For governor, the Democrats ran Gen. Robert Armstrong, one of Jackson's favorites but a man John Catron called "radically defective in intelligence," against the incumbent, Newton Cannon. In the congressional races, Polk ran unopposed in the Ninth District, while Cave Johnson fought off the candidacy of Gen. Richard Cheatham in the Eighth District. In the Seventh District, home to the Hermitage and Poplar Grove plantations, the Democrats initially had no one to challenge the incumbent, John Bell, Jackson's former ally. Eventually, party leaders drafted Lebanon attorney Robert L. Caruthers, but his candidacy quickly floundered. The Democrats then considered their perennial nominee, Robert M. Burton, but swiftly discarded the idea. They needed someone with name recognition to oppose Bell, someone who could draw voters to the polls. Why not Andrew Jackson Donelson? someone suggested.[9]

As attractive as a Donelson candidacy looked to some Democrats, the idea went nowhere. John Catron, who spoke for a group of state leaders that included Felix Grundy, David Craighead, and William Carroll, nixed the idea immediately. He thought that Bell was too strong and Donelson, who was "a stranger" to the voters of the district, had little chance of defeating him. Another concern, Catron told Jackson, was that "the relation in which Major D. stands to yourself personally, and to the character of the administration, would make his defeat the subject of great exultation to the adversary, and of equal mortification to our friends." It would be better, he concluded, to allow the moderate citizens who had voted for White to return to "their old principles" of their own accord rather than risk the controversy that would accompany Donelson's candidacy.[10]

9. Sellers, *Jacksonian,* 321–6; Joseph M. Pukl Jr., "James K. Polk's Congressional Campaigns of 1835 and 1837," *THQ* 41 (Summer 1982): 120–3; Atkins, *Parties, Politics, and Sectional Conflict,* 55–65; Grant, "Cave Johnson," 204; John Catron to JKP, 16 April 1837, JKP to AJ, 16, 21 June 1837, Felix Grundy to JKP, 18 June 1837, in Weaver and Cutler, *CJKP* 4:90–2, 147–8, 156–7, 151; and John H. Dew to AJ, 16 June 1837, JDC.

10. John Catron to AJ, 21 June 1837, JDC; and JKP to AJ, 21 June 1837, in Weaver and Cutler, *CJKP* 4:156–7.

Donelson disagreed with Catron that it was best to leave the election uncontested. "It seems that we have no one who is willing to try the question," he observed to Jackson, "or who thinks that he can unite the votes of those who are opposed to Bell." The two men must have discussed the issue that evening, and Donelson may have broached the idea of running against Bell. If he did make that suggestion, however, his uncle convinced him otherwise. Donelson informed Polk the next day that he "would be very willing *myself* to risk the contest with Mr. Burton" but for the reluctance of "our Nashville friends" to support him.[11]

Donelson must have been flabbergasted. Once again, friends had been unwilling to support his political promotion, and once again his uncle had concurred. One historian's description of Jackson's early ambition could easily describe that of Donelson as well: he possessed "a zeal for public acceptance . . . [and] to be regarded by his community as an accepted authority. . . . [He] aimed to become more visible." To do that, Donelson believed, required him to advance politically. Now that Jackson had retired, Donelson thought it crucial that he obtain some means of maintaining his public visibility. Holding a political office was one avenue, because "in those times [it] opened doors to power and riches when opportunities were so limited for those just aspiring to enter the ranks of the upper class." Donelson could count himself a member of the Nashville gentry, but to remain there and advance further he needed to make a name for himself, separate from Jackson. At the same time, he was eager to use his uncle's name to make that reputation, just as he always had.[12]

Donelson was discovering how complicated his relationship with Jackson really was. Despite his earlier expectations, Jackson did not seem disposed to see his nephew achieve his political ambitions. The General may have believed, as one historian sees it, that "any brisk trading of offices, emoluments, privileges, and special treatment for the performance of useful favors smacked of demeaning commercialism, greed, and corruption." In other words, Jackson may have agreed with his nephew: Donelson needed to make his own reputation. It also seems probable that Jackson did not think

11. AJD to AJ, 22 June 1837, JDC; and AJD to JKP, 23 June 1837, in Weaver and Cutler, *CJKP* 4:157–8.

12. Burstein, *Passions,* 25.

his nephew astute enough to win the election, and a loss would damage both of their reputations.[13]

The absence of Donelson or any other opponent for Bell did not dampen the enthusiasm of the state's Democrats, especially in the middle section of the state, to win the fall elections. They were determined to beat the Whigs, and they looked to receive substantial support in the campaign from the *Nashville Union.* The party organ, though, proved less than helpful. It had failed to challenge adequately the White candidacy in 1836, and it repeated its poor showing in 1837. Most of the blame for this failure belonged to the *Union*'s editor, Samuel H. Laughlin, who, in addition to succumbing often to his weakness for alcohol, spent inordinate amounts of time traveling in search of subscribers. In his absence, Donelson had to help Congressman A. O. P. Nicholson and John Catron, Jackson's recent appointment to the U.S. Supreme Court, write editorials for the paper.[14]

The *Union*'s weakness as political ally had led Donelson to try to revive it following the 1836 election. The paper had been floundering in a morass of debt, despite his contributions and those of Polk, Catron, and other Tennessee Democrats. In late December 1836, Donelson informed Jackson that, after meeting with Nashville's prominent religious publisher, Joel M. Smith, and hearing tales from him of Laughlin's drinking and financial problems, he had determined to meet with the editor and find some suitable arrangements to keep the Jacksonian cause "in a proper light before the people." Donelson's efforts had been unsuccessful, leaving Laughlin at the head of the *Union.*[15]

In the spring of 1837, the Democrats had finally taken decisive action. Laughlin still refused to give up his editorship, despite promises to do so, but pressure from the party's leadership finally forced him to relinquish his

13. Wyatt-Brown, "AJ's Honor," 15–6.

14. A. O. P. Nicholson to JKP, 20 December 1835, 31 January 1836, SHL to JKP, 18 November 1835, 9 January, 12 April, 3 August 1836 (two letters), in Weaver and Hall, *CJKP* 3:400–1, 477–80, 363–5, 432–4, 579–85, 687–9; SHL to JKP, 5 January 1837, in Weaver and Cutler, *CJKP* 4:11–6; A. O. P. Nicholson to AJD, 21 January 1837, AJD to AJ, 31 December 1836, 1 January 1837, DLC; Bergeron, "JKP and the Jacksonian Press," 261–4; Satterfield, "Uncertain Trumpet," 84–6; and Williams, "Samuel Hervey Laughlin," 361–8.

15. SHL to JKP, 12 April, 3 August 1836 (two letters), in Weaver and Hall, *CJKP* 3:579–85, 687–9; SHL to JKP, 5 January 1837, in Weaver and Cutler, *CJKP* 4:11–6; A. O. P. Nicholson to AJD, 21 January 1837, AJD to AJ, 31 December 1836, 1 January 1837, DLC; Bergeron, "JKP and the Jacksonian Press," 261–4; Satterfield, "Uncertain Trumpet," 84–6; and Williams, "Samuel Hervey Laughlin," 361–8.

position, although he left the newspaper with six thousand dollars in debt. In May 1837, Donelson, Catron, and other leading Democrats entered into negotiations with an interested buyer, Robert Nesbit. They agreed to pay half of the four thousand dollars Nesbit offered Laughlin for the subscription list and the name of the paper. (The former editor would have to cover the remaining debt himself.) After some negotiation, Nesbit took charge of the newspaper in early July, with John O. Bradford, an Episcopal divinity student from Kentucky, serving as editor. During the transfer of proprietorship, Donelson and others wrote the paper's editorials.[16]

The results of the August elections indicated that even a change at the *Union* had not been able to rally Tennessee Democrats. In a repeat of the 1835 debacle, Whigs once again soundly defeated Jackson's supporters. Cannon won the gubernatorial race by some twenty thousand votes. Bell ran without opposition. Polk was able to secure another term, but Cave Johnson went down to defeat. Another candidate Donelson had hoped would win, William Trousdale of Gallatin, also lost. In the end, the Whigs secured ten of the state's thirteen seats in the House. The Democratic ticket was an almost complete failure.[17]

It was a bitter defeat. Jackson blamed the "temporising policy" of Felix Grundy and the *Union* and the "imbecile councils, [*sic*] of the Nashville politicians." A defection from within their own family particularly galled Donelson and Jackson. William Donelson, Emily's brother, had voted a straight Whig ticket. Jackson, not surprisingly, saw him as the tool of a "pigmy combination" intent on embarrassing him in his own district. He expressed "mortification" that William would "aid in prostrating the rising fame" of his brother-in-law, an ironic statement given Jackson's own

16. John Catron to JKP, 16, 22 April and 17 June 1837, SHL to JKP, 4, 24 May 1837, James Walker to JKP, 2 June 1837, Daniel Graham to JKP, 17 June 1827, Felix Grundy to JKP, 18 June 1837, JKP to AJ, 22 June 1837, JCM to JKP, 27 June 1837, John O. Bradford to JKP, 8 July [1837], 22 July [1837], JKP to AJD, 12 July 1837, AJD to JKP, 20 July 1837, in Weaver and Cutler, *CJKP* 4:90–1, 96–8, 148–9, 110–1, 126–7, 134–6, 150–1, 151, 157, 162–3, 172, 188–9, 175–8, 187–8; John Catron to James Walker, 30 May 1837, PLC; Bergeron, "JKP and the Jacksonian Press," 264–5; Satterfield, "Uncertain Trumpet," 86–7; and Williams, "Samuel Hervey Laughlin," 367–8.

17. Sellers, *Jacksonian*, 325–6; Bergeron, *Antebellum Politics*, 48–50; Grant, "Cave Johnson," 204; Atkins, *Parties, Politics, and Sectional Conflict*, 62–5; Walter T. Durham, "William Trousdale," in *The Tennessee Encyclopedia of History and Culture*, ed. Carroll Van West (Nashville: Rutledge Hill Press, 1998), 994–5; and AJD to JKP, 20 July 1837, JKP to AJD, 6 August 1837, in Weaver and Cutler, *CJKP* 4:187–8, 198–9.

reluctance to advance his nephew's career. In 1834, John C. McLemore had warned Donelson that members of his and the president's family opposed some of Jackson's policies; now, his prediction had been proven true.[18]

Disappointment over the election results was still on Donelson's mind as he set out for Washington later that same month. While in the nation's capital, Donelson stayed with Van Buren, who encouraged him to continue his political efforts. "Our friends are in good spirits," Donelson reported to his brother, "and are really much stronger than I was prepared to expect." The political climate there, however, only served to illustrate how disoriented things had become in his home state. "In no quarter of the Union but Tennessee do the people take the side of the Banks against the Government," he regretfully admitted.[19]

Donelson's comment was pure hyperbole, of course; many Tennesseans opposed the Bank. As he recognized, however, the specter of the Bank dominated the political landscape of Tennessee in the late 1830s. During the legislative session that fall, the economy became the main point of contention. The state's Whig party was divided over the Bank issue, giving Democrats, despite their numerical disadvantage, hope that they could control the legislative session. The Whigs were able to unify and vote instructions to the state's senators, Felix Grundy and Hugh Lawson White, that bound them to oppose Van Buren's independent treasury plan; however, they were unsuccessful in committing them to support a new national bank. Tennessee Democrats took advantage of their opponents' weaknesses, passing a bill that reestablished a uniform currency to replace the state's confusing system of payment and credit. They also were able to approve a measure that created a new state bank, pledged the new bank's profits to subsidize educational institutions, and increased the state's internal improvements program. The Democratic plan not only endeared them to Tennessee citizens beleaguered by the panic's effects but also highlighted the difficulty faced by the Whigs.[20]

At the request of Polk, Donelson moved to take advantage of the weakened Whigs. John Bell, whose recent journey through the northern states had finally revealed his support of the Whigs, was Donelson's first target.

18. AJ to Andrew J. Hutchings, 5 August 1837, AJ to JKP, 6 August 1837, in Bassett and Jameson, *CAJ* 5:502–3, 503–4; and JCM to AJD, 20 December 1834, DLC.

19. AJD to [DSD], [20] October 1837, DLC.

20. Atkins, *Parties, Politics, and Sectional Conflict,* 65–71.

Democratic friends in the North sent Polk evidence of Bell's true affiliation, which he then forwarded to Donelson with the request that he place them in the *Union.* Polk's lack of confidence in Joshua Cunningham, who succeeded Bradford as editor of the newspaper in November 1837, was evident from his admission that he had "no personal acquaintance with the new Editor of the Union, and know of no one whom I can so safely trust with these suggestions as yourself." Donelson reminded him that they "must be patient and not expect too much" of Cunningham and assured him that the information on Bell was having "a good effect."[21]

Donelson also sought to revive the state's party by reminding its members of their ideological goals. At a Democratic party public meeting held at the Nashville courthouse on 30 December 1837, he introduced a set of resolutions that highlighted the republican underpinnings of the party and reinforced its principles. The preamble to the resolutions opened with the claim that "the Federal party have [*sic*] resolved upon another attempt to bring into discredit the great principles upon which the Republicans have ever been united." It continued by reminding the attendees that "the people themselves, who are the real source of all power, and for whose benefit alone all governments out to be established, [should] examine carefully the principles which are involved, and . . . dispose of them as shall best promote their true interest and permanent prosperity." The resolutions themselves emphasized the differences between the two parties, particularly on economic issues, and praised Van Buren's proposal for an independent treasury "as the surest means of attaining for the people a sound currency." An address penned by Donelson that was later printed in the *Nashville Union* continued in the same ideological vein: Democratic leaders such as Jackson and Van Buren were defending the Republic against corruption by trying to rein in banks, while Whig leaders, such as Bell, were "Hartford Convention Tories and Blue Light Federalists" who wanted to see a national bank established for their own financial and political gain.[22]

21. Sellers, *Jacksonian,* 344–7; JKP to AJD, 12, 18 December 1837, 3 January 1838, AJD to JKP, 28 December 1837, in Weaver and Cutler, *CJKP* 4:286–8, 296–8, 312–3, 304–5; and Bergeron, "JKP and the Jacksonian Press," 267, 270.

22. JKP to AJD, 18 December 1837, 3 January 1838, AJD to JKP, 28 December 1837, 4, 24 January 1838, James Walker to JKP, 31 December 1837, Samuel Mitchell to JKP, 2 January 1838, in Weaver and Cutler,

Donelson's writings during this period were his first significant public expressions of his political ideology. They established a pattern that his later editorials and speeches would follow. Donelson always appealed to the republican foundations of the nation, stressing the sanctity of the Union and the need to avoid both extremist policies and politicians. At nearly every opportunity, he invoked the founders and his uncle as examples for Americans to emulate politically. The enemies of the Union, on the other hand, were soundly denounced in ideological terms as grave threats to future of the United States. Often verbose and always thorough, Donelson made sure that those who read or heard his words knew that he was a staunch believer in, and defender of, the Republic.

Believing that his rhetoric would great political effect in convincing Tennesseans that the economy was better off in the hands of the Democrats, Donelson turned his attention to the upcoming 1839 state elections. Polk's national stature had grown to the point that some Democrats wanted him to run for the vice-presidency in 1840, which they ultimately expected would lead to the presidency. The key for Polk was to become more visible, since he had already reached the height of his power in the House. Winning the governorship of Tennessee would allow him to maintain his status while strengthening the Democratic party in Tennessee.[23]

Donelson worked vigorously to accomplish both of these goals. He was intent on "prov[ing] that the state [of Tennessee] is where she has always been, in the Republican faith." His primary concern was helping the party find suitable candidates to campaign under the Democratic banner. Unseating Bell in the Seventh District was a top priority. As early as February 1838, William Carroll had indicated his willingness to run against Bell, and in December of that year, he told Jackson's nephew that he would challenge the Whig if Donelson could ascertain his chances of success in Wilson County. Although Carroll informed Democratic leaders that he was suffering from

---

CJKP 4:296–8, 312–3, 304–5, 314, 338–9, 306–7, 311–2; Satterfield, "Moderate Nationalist Jacksonian," 174–7; "Resolutions of Nashville Democratic Committee," 30 December 1837, quoted in Satterfield, "Moderate Nationalist Jacksonian," 174–6; draft of "Address of the Republican General Committee of Davidson County, to the People of Tennessee" and "Address of the Republican General Committee of Davidson County, to the People of Tennessee," in *Nashville Union,* 27 January 1838, DLC.

23. Atkins, *Parties, Politics, and Sectional Conflict,* 72–3; Sellers, *Jacksonian,* 350–3; and John Catron to AJD, 4 January 1839, DLC.

rheumatism, which might keep him from running, Democrats pinned their hopes on him anyway. When it became apparent that Carroll would not enter the race against Bell and the "Whig wigwam," Donelson unsuccessfully attempted to change his mind.[24]

Carroll's withdrawal forced the Democrats once again to turn to Robert M. Burton, who reluctantly agreed to oppose Bell. His campaign was a disaster. Donelson attended a Lebanon meeting between the two candidates at which the Whig representative, in a tactic that he used repeatedly, dominated the proceedings by speaking until dark, leaving his Democratic challenger little time to respond to charges against Van Buren and his party. In a *Union* article, Donelson attempted to belittle Bell's speech, but the incumbent's superior speaking skills were apparent to all those in attendance. As the campaign progressed, Burton tried to compensate for his deficiency by researching the issues more thoroughly than his opponent, asking Donelson to send him "Holland's Life of Van Buren—all of Judge White's speeches on the Bank . . . also Bell's speech at Hartford." He also requested the use of Donelson's "pistols, some balls—caps etc.," an indication of the tenseness of the meetings.[25]

Andrew Jackson remained confident throughout the 1839 campaign of "a speedy return by the state to the republican fold." For the most part, he was right. Polk beat Cannon and became governor, and Democrats were able to win bare majorities in both houses of the Tennessee General Assembly. Their number in the U.S. House also increased from three to six. As for Burton, in whom Donelson inexplicably seemed to have more confidence than anyone else, the well-armed candidate failed to find enough political

24. Bergeron, *Antebellum Politics,* 53; Atkins, *Parties, Politics, and Sectional Conflict,* 73–8; Sellers, *Jacksonian,* 358–60; Jonathan M. Atkins, "William Carroll," in *The Tennessee Encyclopedia of History and Culture,* ed. Carroll Van West (Nashville: Rutledge Hill Press, 1998), 129–31; William Carroll to AJD, 4 December 1838, AJ to AJD, 7 December 1838, DLC; AJD to JKP, 6 October 1838, William Carroll to JKP, 17 February, 30 November 1838, in Weaver and Cutler, *CJKP* 4:573–4, 368–70, 623–6; Robert Armstrong to JKP, 6 February [1839], William Carroll to JKP, 8 February 1839 (summary), AJ to JKP, 11 February 1839, in Wayne Cutler, Earl J. Smith, and Carese M. Parker, eds., *Correspondence of James K. Polk,* vol. 5, *1839–1841* (Nashville: Vanderbilt University Press, 1979), 48–9, 55, 61–3; and Robert Armstrong to AJ, n.d. [late 1838 or early 1839], JDC.

25. Sellers, *Jacksonian,* 359–60; Parks, *John Bell,* 159–60; Joel M. Smith to JKP, 30 March 1839, PLC; Jeremiah George Harris to AJD, n.d. [14 April 1839] and 19 April 1839, Robert M. Burton to AJD, 6 May 1839, DLC.

ammunition to unseat Bell. The Tennessee Democratic party, however, had achieved most of its objectives, seemed poised to send Polk to Baltimore as its vice-presidential choice, and appeared ready to reclaim the state for the Old Hero.[26]

Even after the campaign was over, Donelson continued to try to improve the political prospects of the Democratic party. He still believed that the Whigs, through their advocacy of a national bank, presented a threat to the republican principles of the United States. His assessment appeared correct when, in October 1839, Tennessee's banks, which had resumed specie payments, followed the lead of eastern banks and suspended them. At the same time, they moved to restrict currency circulation. With the decrease in the amount of money available, Tennesseans saw property values and prices plummet. Those with large debts particularly felt the pinch, as creditors began pressuring them for payments that were hard to make and seized their property when they did not find the means to pay.[27]

Democrats, of course, accused Whigs and the Bank of causing the Panic of 1839. Donelson saw it as his duty to help Democrats defeat the "monied aristocracy" of Whiggery, thus protecting the people from corrupt manipulation and financial ruin. To achieve that result, he helped his uncle write letters in response to political questions and public invitations, a task he had been performing for almost fifteen years. The theme of these letters and speeches remained the same: the Whigs, through their corruption and greed, were the cause of the state's and nation's problems, and the Democrats, with their devotion to republican principles, offered the only remedy to cure the political and financial ills. Both Jackson and Donelson intended all of these efforts to bolster the party's prospects in 1840.[28]

While Donelson worked with Jackson during the winter of 1839–40, Van Buren asked him to come to Washington. Since the president's renomination by the Democrats was virtually undisputed, he probably wanted to get Donelson's opinion on his standing in Tennessee and discuss the possibility of placing Polk on the ticket. There was no question as to the

26. AJ to MVB, 2 May 1839 (two letters), VBL; and Sellers, *Jacksonian,* 373–4.

27. Atkins, *Parties, Politics, and Sectional Conflict,* 88–92.

28. Holt, *American Whig Party,* 109–11; AJ to AJD, 28 September 1839, 18 June 1840, DLC; and AJ to AJD, 10 December 1839, in Bassett and Jameson, *CAJ* 6:41–2.

Tennessee governor's republican principles and his agreement with Van Buren. The question was, could Polk's influence guarantee Van Buren's victory?[29]

Donelson was convinced that it could. After talking to Francis P. Blair, William B. Lewis, and other Democrats and calculating the votes, he believed that Polk could defeat the sitting vice-president, Richard M. Johnson, and any other candidate who emerged. Donelson's confidence in Polk was unfounded. By the time of his meeting with Van Buren, Polk's campaign for the vice-presidential nomination was already faltering. The Whig convention had followed the Democrats' earlier example and nominated a War of 1812 hero, William Henry Harrison, for president. In order to counter Harrison's military career, it was almost impossible for the Democrats to choose anyone except Johnson (also a famous veteran of the war with England) for the vice-presidential spot. Polk would not only have to overcome Johnson's military credentials but also have to fend off challenges from other politicians, such as Secretary of State John Forsyth of Georgia and Secretary of War Joel R. Poinsett of South Carolina, who were similarly or even better qualified than he was.[30]

Not realizing his erroneous analysis, Donelson returned to Tennessee from his consultation with Van Buren intent on garnering support for Polk. Circumstances, however, intervened to hinder his work. The state Democratic convention had already selected Donelson as a delegate to the national convention, scheduled to start in Baltimore on 5 May 1840, but he declined to go because of the poor health of his chronically ill youngest daughter, Rachel. The Tennessee delegates who attended worked desperately to gain Polk's nomination, but their efforts ultimately failed. The convention renominated Van Buren as expected but passed a resolution refusing to nominate a vice-presidential candidate. Through the columns of the *Nashville Union*, Donelson attempted to convince the public that Polk was a viable candidate, but Polk, realizing that any agitation for the vice-presidency on his part would

29. MVB to AJD, 23 December 1839, DLC; Sellers, *Jacksonian*, 400–6; and JKP to David Hubbard, 7 February 1840, in Cutler, Smith, and Parker, *CJKP* 5:386–8.

30. AJD to AJ, 4 March 1840, Francis P. Blair to AJ, 17 March 1840, WBL to AJ, 21 March 1840, JLC; AJD to JKP, 4 March 1840, in Cutler, Smith, and Parker, *CJKP* 5:400–1; and Sellers, *Jacksonian*, 406–18.

only damage his political future, withdrew from the contest. Donelson was disappointed, but he moved quickly to support the Van Buren–Johnson ticket. He was a member of the state committee that published addresses and defended the party's policies. He also wrote campaign speeches for Jackson, who either delivered them in person, if healthy, or mailed them with his regrets when his health would not allow him to travel.[31]

Admonitions about the danger the Whigs posed to the nation's future failed to convince voters, however. Harrison carried the national election easily, winning nearly 1.28 million popular and 234 electoral votes to Van Buren's 1.13 million popular and 60 electoral votes. In Tennessee, the Whig candidate polled over 12,000 more votes than his Democratic opponent. Van Buren's defeat was bitter for the Democrats, especially for Donelson. Since returning to Tennessee in 1837, he had actively campaigned to defeat the Whigs. Moderate Democratic success in the state elections, particularly Polk's 1839 victory in the gubernatorial contest, rewarded his efforts. In 1840, however, the state and the nation rejected Van Buren, Jackson's chosen successor and the architect behind the construction of the Democratic party. The declension of the party was a blow to Donelson's future prospects, both political and financial.[32]

31. Jeremiah George Harris to AJD, 20 February 1840, DLC; JKP to SHL, 1, 2 April 1840, Alexander O. Anderson to JKP, 14 April 1840, Felix Grundy to JKP, 15, 23 April 1840, SHL to JKP, 29 April (two letters), 2, 3, 6 May 1840, Aaron V. Brown to JKP, 2 May 1840, [3 May 1840], Pierce B. Anderson, 6 May 1840, JKP to AJ, 9 May 1840, in Cutler, Smith, and Parker, *CJKP* 5:414–5, 415–7, 423–7, 427–8, 428–9, 429–31, 431–2, 433–6, 437–8, 440, 432–3, 436, 439–40, 445–7; AJ to AJD, 8 September, 8 October 1840, DLC; *Nashville Union,* 14 September 1840; Sellers, *Jacksonian,* 413–8; Bain, *Convention Decisions,* 27–8; Satterfield, "Moderate Nationalist Jacksonian," 186; and Remini, *Course of American Democracy,* 467–9.

32. William N. Chambers, "Election of 1840," in *History of American Presidential Elections,* 4 vols., ed. Arthur M. Schlesinger and Fred L. Israel (New York: Chelsea House, 1971), 1:681, 690; and Atkins, *Parties, Politics, and Sectional Conflict,* 112–6.

10

"The Hard Times Have Been a Little Harder with Me"

Donelson was never a good businessman. His tax troubles in West Tennessee in the early 1830s were simply one episode of many that demonstrated that financial acumen was not one of his strengths. All was not his fault, of course. Donelson's financial difficulties substantially mirrored those of other Tennesseans during this period. Between 1836 and 1845, the value of land and slaves in the state dropped over 20 percent. Cotton prices fell as low as three cents per pound, and the prices of surplus crops, such as corn and pork, also declined. It was hard for any planter to make money during the Panic of 1837 and in its aftermath. The one advantage that Donelson possessed was his ability to depend upon Jackson to supply financial resources in times of need. Or so he thought. He would discover that even his uncle's generosity had its limits.[1]

Donelson accrued considerable debt during the late 1830s and early 1840s. Some of it was related to his political activities, in particular, his efforts at keeping the *Nashville Union* afloat. The money he and others had contributed to keep the newspaper solvent since its founding in 1835 was not producing a profitable return. In late August 1839, the *Union*'s proprietor, Joel M. Smith, decided to sell the paper, news that caused considerable concern among Democratic leaders, especially Donelson and Catron, both of whom had invested heavily in the paper. The two men attempted to convince the current editor, Jeremiah George Harris, to purchase the organ, but he insisted that he could not both write editorials and solicit contributions and subscriptions. To keep the *Union* afloat and protect their investments, a group of five men, including Donelson, finally stepped in and took over ownership in November 1839.[2]

1. Atkins, *Parties, Politics, and Sectional Conflict,* 89–90.

2. John Catron to AJD, 29 August [1839], DLC; Jeremiah George Harris to JKP, 29 August 1839, Joel M. Smith to JKP, 15, 31 August, 24 September 1839, Robert Armstrong to JKP, 4 September [1839], Cave

This politically associated debt was only one part of Donelson's troubles, however. In the fall of 1837, he visited Washington on a business trip intended to settle a debt with Robert M. Henderson, from whom Donelson, his brother, Daniel, and an associate, R. W. Williams, had borrowed forty-five hundred dollars for an unknown investment. He also had outstanding debts left from his time in Washington and considerable obligations related to his children's education. His plantations proved less profitable than he anticipated, undoubtedly hurt by the nation's economic downturn. Donelson's pursuit of horseracing and horse breeding was also a failure. He had always anticipated recouping some of his losses through victories at the racetrack, which he then believed would lead to a demand for breeding his horses. Donelson never succeeded in making horses a profitable source of income, however, and the expenses associated with raising and racing them only added to his indebtedness.[3]

Floundering in a financial morass, Donelson repeatedly sought to obtain relief from his uncle, but the debts of Jackson's adopted son, Andrew Jackson Jr., left the former president without the available credit to aid Donelson. Jackson's son, according to his biographer, "seemed to show a complete lack of understanding of business and constantly failed to heed his father's sound advice." Jackson even had to sell some of his land in order to free himself from seven thousand dollars of Andrew Jr.'s debts.[4]

Probably at his uncle's prompting, Donelson turned to President Martin Van Buren for financial assistance in 1838, requesting a personal loan of several thousand dollars. The president, prompted by Jackson and undoubtedly hoping to solidify his support in Tennessee, agreed. By June 1838, Van Buren was able to inform Donelson that his New York associate and loyal Jacksonian, Churchill C. Cambreleng, would send him three thousand dollars for twelve to eighteen months. Van Buren quickly paid off Cambreleng's loan, leaving Donelson indebted to him alone. Donelson used the money to help pay off debts related to his investment in the *Union* and to purchase a

---

Johnson to JKP, 19 November 1839, in Cutler, Smith, and Parker, *CJKP* 5:216–7, 190, 218–9, 249–50, 227–8, 304–7; and Satterfield, "Uncertain Trumpet," 89. The group that purchased the *Union* probably consisted of Donelson, Robert Armstrong, Polk, Cave Johnson, and Felix Grundy.

3. Satterfield, "Moderate Nationalist Jacksonian," 189–92; [AJD to MVB], 3 April 1837 (fragment), AJD to [DSD], [20] October 1837, JCM to [AJD], 8 January 1839, DLC; AJ to MVB, 2 May 1839, VBL; and Wyatt-Brown, "AJ's Honor," 8.

4. Galloway, "AJ, Jr.," pt. 2, 310–23.

plantation in Mississippi. James K. Polk and his brother, William H. Polk, offered to sell him a farm in Yalobusha County, near Coffeeville, but Donelson turned down that proposal because of the farm's inflated price. Instead, he bought a plantation, minus the slaves, from the estate of the recently deceased Thomas Ivy in Chickasaw County, Mississippi. The land cost $6,151, of which Donelson paid a security of one-third, or $2,050.33.[5]

Donelson's finances, always precarious, had come to consume most of his time. In 1839, he unsuccessfully appealed to his old adversary, William B. Lewis, for help with a debt that he and Andrew Jackson Jr. had incurred to William A. Eliason in 1836. Stymied on that front, the next year, Donelson asked Van Buren to make additional loans of $10,000 and $2,000. Faced with his own financial problems, Van Buren was only able to give him the $2,000 loan. By the end of the year, Donelson owed various creditors at least $15,451 and perhaps more.[6]

To Jackson's credit, he tried to help his nephew out of his difficulty. Before Donelson made a trip to Washington in 1840, Jackson wrote Van Buren, assuring him that his nephew's property, consisting of his two plantations, crops, and slaves, was worth nearly $60,000. (Donelson owned a minimum of 106 slaves, worth at least $37,900.) He even asked that the president provide his nephew with a government position. Donelson, in fact, may have visited Washington with that expectation, based on Jackson's encouragement and a misinterpretation of Van Buren's suggestion that the nation's capital would provide "a suitable theatre" for his talents. No appointment was forthcoming, however.[7]

5. MVB to AJD, 11, 13 May, 11, 28 June, 22 July, 11, 25 August 1838, AJ to MVB, 1 May 1838, MVB to Gorham A. Worth, 10 August 1838, MVB note regarding loan to AJD, 8 October 1838, VBL; AJD to JKP, 6 October 1838, in Weaver and Cutler, *CJKP* 4:573–4; and William Polk to AJD, 11 September 1838, deed of sale to AJD, 26 November 1838, DLC.

6. Satterfield, "Moderate Nationalist Jacksonian," 191–2; WBL to AJD, 28 October 1839, MVB to AJD, 23 December 1839, AJ to AJD, 15 February 1840, AJ to MVB, 15 February 1840, DLC; agreement between William A. Eliason, AJD, and AJ Jr., 20 September 1836, JDC; AJ to MVB, 21 May 1840, VBL; and account statement between AJD and MVB, [28 May 1846?], Martin Van Buren Papers, Chadwyck-Healey Collection, Library of Congress, Washington, D.C. (hereafter cited as VBC).

7. MVB to AJD, 23 December 1839, AJ to MVB, 15 February 1840, and tax list, n.d. [1840s], DLC; and AJ to MVB, 21 May 1840, VBL. Marsha Mullin, chief curator at the Hermitage, confirmed that the undated tax list cited here belonged to Donelson and was from the 1840s. Marsha Mullin, e-mail to author, 15 July 2005.

Jackson willingly offered his name and estate as collateral to assist Donelson in obtaining loans, but he could not offer more substantial help. His son, Andrew Jr., remained financially incompetent, having since 1838 accrued numerous debts that Jackson felt obligated to pay. In 1840, his son's financial mismanagement forced Jackson to sell Hunter's Hill, his original home in Davidson County. Junior's bad decisions led the Whigs "to circulate the wildest stories respecting [Jackson's] pecuniary affairs," Donelson informed Van Buren in 1841, although he believed his uncle's estate was completely debt free and worth one hundred thousand dollars. The General thought otherwise, believing that it was beyond his means to assist Donelson when his own affairs were in such dire straits. When his uncle was not able to provide the requested financial support, Donelson could only interpret it as Jackson failing to follow through on his promise, nearly two decades old, to help him succeed in the world. Donelson must have partially blamed Andrew Jr. The former president was giving his adopted son plenty of financial assistance to pay off foolish debts, while Donelson, his talented nephew with promising political prospects, languished in debt just down the road. Donelson likely resented the situation.[8]

Donelson's financial woes only worsened in the 1840s. His crops in Mississippi failed to produce enough profit for him to pay off the Van Buren debt, and in April 1841, all he could do was make promises about future payments. "The hard times have been a little harder with me [than Jackson]," Donelson informed his benefactor, "because I had purchased property on credit, and chose to devote some of my cash means to the republican cause." Not to worry, he assured Van Buren, "I have only to use a little economy, and with one more good crop, or at furthest two, I shall be out of debt, and have quite a handsome estate." For the next several months, Van Buren, who was himself living the life of a retired gentleman farmer, repeatedly asked him to pay off his loans. His frustration increased to the point that he told Donelson that he was willing to settle, at least for now, for a promised one-thousand-dollar payment, which would barely pay the interest owed. "Don't

8. AJ to AJD, 8 September 1840, WBL to AJD, 28 October 1839, DLC; Galloway, "AJ, Jr.," pt. 2, 310–25; AJ to WBL, 11 November 1839, AJ to AJD, 10 December 1839, 19 February 1840, in Bassett and Jameson, *CAJ* 6:40, 41–2, 52–3; WBL to AJ, 21 March 1840, JLC; and AJD to MVB, 23 April 1841, VBL.

trouble yourself about any more," Van Buren assured his friend. Even that small request was ignored.[9]

Donelson finally found some potential relief from his financial plight, and some domestic happiness, when he married his second cousin, twenty-six-year-old Elizabeth Anderson Martin Randolph, in 1841. Jackson had counseled him in 1840 to "seek out a discret [*sic*] Lady for a partner and Marry. This can alone make you happy at home, and enable you to raise your charming little daughters and keep them under your own roof." His advice mirrored not only his own view of marriage but also that of a society that expected widowers to remarry, usually by choosing much younger wives who could bear more children and enhance "paternal prestige."[10]

Born on 17 August 1815, Elizabeth was the daughter of Catherine Donelson, Emily Donelson's older sister. She had attended Nashville Female Academy as an adolescent and, during Jackson's presidency, had often stayed with the Donelsons in Washington and Tennessee. Elizabeth, in fact, had been one of the primary care givers for her dying aunt Emily in the winter of 1836, an act that Donelson could not help but appreciate. In 1835, Elizabeth married Meriwether Lewis Randolph, son of Thomas Mann Randolph Jr. and one of Thomas Jefferson's grandsons. Randolph had accepted Jackson's appointment to become the territorial secretary of Arkansas in February 1835, but his premature death in September 1837 left Elizabeth a widow. Their only child, Lewis Jackson Randolph, died before the age of five.[11]

According to one family matron, the romance between second cousins Andrew and Elizabeth began at young Lewis's deathbed. As she recounts it, Donelson witnessed the young widow and mother "crushed by her grie[f] . . . and put his arm about her and led her out of the room[;] then and there a new love was awakened in the heart of each." Some such scene may have occurred; what is certain is that by early 1840, the two were discussing a fu-

9. Reeve Huston, "The 'Little Magician' After the Show: Martin Van Buren, Country Gentleman and Progressive Farmer, 1841–1862," *New York History* 85 (Spring 2004): 93–121; AJD to MVB, 23 April 1841, VBL; account statement between AJD and MVB, [28 May 1846?], VBC; MVB to AJD, 28 April, 13 June, 12 October, 26 November 1841, DLC; and AJD to AJ, 4 March 1841, JDC.

10. AJ to AJD, 19 February 1840, in Bassett and Jameson, *CAJ* 6:52–3; and Wyatt-Brown, *Southern Honor*, 205.

11. Jonathan Daniels, *The Randolphs of Virginia* (Garden City, N.Y.: Doubleday, 1972), 265–7; and Burke, *Emily Donelson* 2:62–3, 67–70, 72, 84, 99–102, 122.

ture together. Their courtship was not all pleasant, however. Whether out of political, personal, or romantic jealousy, one of Emily's brothers, Stockley, took it upon himself to inform Elizabeth that her beau was not serious in his "matrimonial intentions." The actions of Stockley, who had earned Jackson's wrath by becoming a Whig and accusing several of his slaves of murder, elicited an impassioned response from Donelson. "Allow me to say that no one can do me justice who presents me as entertaining any other sentiment or feeling respecting you than what is consistent with the highest respect for your numerous virtues," he assured Elizabeth, "and the most tender regard for you both as a friend and relation." Donelson was able to convince her of his intentions, and they married on 10 November 1841. John C. McLemore declared Donelson a "lucky man"; in his estimation, "I never saw a finer & more intelligent woman; she has indeed every virtue and accomplishment that could be desired to make an intelligent man like yourself happy."[12]

This marriage was not made purely for personal happiness, however. Much like with his marriage to Emily, Donelson saw an opportunity to strengthen his ties within the Donelson clan. Elizabeth provided his children with a maternal figure and him with the chance to produce more offspring. Elizabeth possessed another positive attribute as well: her first husband's death had left her in control of several thousand acres of land spread across a handful of counties in Arkansas. For a man who struggled to make ends meet, this wealth must have played some role in his decision to pursue Elizabeth.[13]

Within a year, the newlyweds were celebrating the birth of their first child, Daniel Smith Donelson. Of course, four other children also demanded their attention. Within two years, sixteen-year-old Jackson followed his father's example, entering West Point as a cadet in 1844. Thirteen-year-old Mary had been attending a girl's school in nearby Lebanon, where she studied music and other domestic tasks with which females were expected to become familiar. Ten-year-old John and eight-year-old Rachel presumably stayed at

12. AJD to ERD, 9 March 1840, JDC; notes by Pauline Wilcox Burke, n.d., Jeremiah George Harris to AJD, 25 November 1841, MVB to AJD, 26 November 1841, JCM to AJD, 19 December 1841, DLC; and Remini, *Course of American Democracy*, 452–3.

13. Tax records, 1842–49, Andrew Jackson Donelson Papers, Tennessee State Library and Archives, Nashville (hereafter cited as DTL); and entries in the journal of James G. Martin Jr., 1843–46, DLC.

home with their parents, although by January 1844, Rachel was enrolled in a nearby school.[14]

Donelson's marriage to Elizabeth did not provide immediate relief from his financial troubles, however, and he grew very concerned about his indebtedness to Martin Van Buren, to whom he now owed over $6,200. The New Yorker was scheduled to visit Tennessee in April 1842, and as part of the delegation sent to accompany him from Kentucky to Tennessee, Donelson knew that there was no avoiding the issue. Although the records are unclear, it is possible that Donelson made the overdue $1,000 payment at this time. Whatever transpired, the two men, along with Jackson, had a friendly visit. The former presidents and Donelson discussed the party's political future and the 1844 presidential election. When it came time for Van Buren's departure, Donelson traveled with him as far as Nashville, where he turned south toward his Mississippi plantation.[15]

Van Buren's visit had one lasting effect on the Donelson family. According to family oral tradition, during his time in Tennessee, the New Yorker suggested that Donelson rename his house. He and Emily had named their house Poplar Grove after the nearly one hundred tulip poplar trees that surrounded the house and nearby acreage. While walking with Donelson one afternoon, Van Buren supposedly asked his host the name of his home. When informed that it was Poplar Grove, the former president, impressed by the buds that were then blooming, remarked that Tulip Grove seemed a more suitable name for his home. "Since that time," according to one interested observer, "the name Tulip Grove has been used." With a new wife and the beginnings of a new family, Donelson may have found the new name of the home that he had once shared with Emily, if only for a short time, refreshing.[16]

Renaming his home did not give Donelson a fresh start with his creditors, however. Later that summer, he visited Philadelphia, then New York,

14. Lawrence, "Tulip Grove," 14; and MED to AJD, [1841], AJ to ERD, 17 January 1844, WBL to AJD, 3 July 1844, DLC.

15. Account statement between AJD and MVB, [28 May 1846?], VBC; Robert Armstrong to JKP, 22 April 1842, 25 April [1842], 4 May [18]42, in Wayne Cutler and Carese M. Parker, eds., *Correspondence of James K. Polk*, vol. 6 (Nashville: Vanderbilt University Press, 1983), 44–5, 45, 58–9; John C. Niven, *MVB*, 487–94; and Sellers, *Jacksonian*, 466–7.

16. Lawrence, "Tulip Grove," 16–7.

in search of financial relief. Not surprisingly, Van Buren's debt was not his only financial obligation. He also owed William A. Eliason's widow, Mary, over $5,000, while Robert M. Henderson's son was pressing for a $1,600 payment on that past-due loan. While visiting Van Buren at his home, Donelson finally obtained the requested $10,000 from the former president's New York friend, John P. Beckman. The terms of the loan required Donelson to mortgage Tulip Grove and get Jackson as cosignatory. Donelson used the Beckman money to pay the interest on the Eliason loan, but he continued to ignore his debt to Van Buren.[17]

Donelson's actions throughout this period suggest that he was, at the very least, financially incompetent. At times, he was even disingenuous about the money others loaned him, such as when he used the Beckman money not to pay off Van Buren, as he had promised he would, but to invest in his Mississippi plantation. Betting on next year's crop for an enormous windfall was a popular game among southern planters, and one that rarely worked for Donelson. Just as troubling, he ignored pleas for payment from William Eliason's daughter, who claimed that her and her mother's very existence depended upon his repayment of her father's loan. (Donelson had even refused to return to her a sixty-dollar bank note that he had supposedly forgotten to sign.) Donelson's financial conduct was sometimes calloused, frequently questionable, and usually ill-advised. It also, at times, negatively affected his political career, prompting him to make choices that led others to question his motives.[18]

17. Robert Henderson to DSD, 22 January 1842, J. N. Armstrong to AJD, 6 July 1842, Certificate by AJ, 18 July 1842, AJD to ERD, 4 August 1842, MVB to ERD, 4 August 1842, Mary S. Eliason to AJD, 25 August 1842, MVB to AJD, 19 September 1842, WBL to AJD, 2 January, 31 July 1843, DLC; AJD to ERD, 21, 24, 29 July 1842, AJ's and AJD's note to John P. Beckman, 1 [?] 1842, JDC; R. W. Latham to AJ, 10 December 1843, JLC; account statement between AJD and MVB, [28 May 1846?], VBC; and Satterfield, "Uncommon Nationalist Jacksonian," 194.

18. Account statement between AJD and MVB, [28 May 1846?], VBC; and Mary S. Eliason to AJD, 25 August 1842, DLC. Donelson finally made a payment of one thousand dollars to Van Buren sometime between 1842 and 1845.

Andrew Jackson Donelson as a young man.
Courtesy The Hermitage: Home of President Andrew Jackson, Nashville, TN

Andrew Jackson Jr., the president's adopted son and Donelson's cousin (ca. 1830s).
Courtesy The Hermitage: Home of President Andrew Jackson, Nashville, TN

Donelson's first wife, Emily (1831).
Courtesy The Hermitage: Home of President Andrew Jackson, Nashville, TN

Donelson's second wife, Elizabeth (ca. 1840s).
Courtesy William Donelson

Tulip Grove, Donelson's home near the Hermitage.
Courtesy The Hermitage: Home of President Andrew Jackson, Nashville, TN

Andrew Jackson, Donelson's uncle, patron, and mentor, 1845.
Courtesy The Hermitage: Home of President Andrew Jackson, Nashville, TN

Campaign banner depicting Know-Nothing party 1856 presidential and vice-presidential candidates, Millard Fillmore and Andrew Jackson Donelson.
Courtesy The Hermitage: Home of President Andrew Jackson, Nashville, TN

Part 3

PROVING HIS WORTH

Donelson sat in Uncle's chair and read the despatch again. Texas. This diplomatic mission was what he had been waiting for all these years. Tyler and Calhoun wanted him to meet with Houston and the other Texas government officials there at Washington-on-the-Brazos and convince them that casting their lot with the United States was their best option. It was going to be a decision "of the very first magnitude," and he was going to receive the credit for its success. Jackson's hand rested on his shoulder, and Donelson looked up. The gleam in his uncle's eyes said it all. His nephew was about to change the destiny of America.[1]

1. JCC to AJD, 16 September 1844, in J. Franklin Jameson, ed., *Correspondence of JCC,* in *Annual Report of the American Historical Association for the Year 1899,* 2 vols. (Washington, D.C.: GPO, 1900), 2:614–5; and JCC to AJD, 17 September 1844, in William R. Manning, ed., *Diplomatic Correspondence of the United States: Inter-American Affairs: 1831–1860,* 12 vols. (Washington, D.C.: Carnegie Endowment for International Peace, 1935), 12:80–1.

11

"In Bad Spirits and Mortified"

President William Henry Harrison's unexpected death on 4 April 1841, brought on by exhaustion and exposure to the elements during his first month in office, plunged the Whig party into disarray. Several prominent Whigs, including Senator Henry Clay and Secretary of State Daniel Webster, had expected to control the new president, but Harrison's death resulted in the vice-president, John Tyler, taking the reins of government. Tyler was no pushover, and his determination to set his own course wrecked any hopes of backroom manipulation by Clay and company. As a states' rights Virginian, Tyler had been an early admirer of the Kentucky senator, but as president, he declared his independence by vetoing two banking bills that Clay strongly supported. The presidential cabinet, with the exception of Webster, resigned in protest, leaving Tyler without party support and the Whigs wondering how their party had lost control of the executive branch that it had so recently won.[1]

This political infighting gave hope for all Democrats, but especially those in Tennessee. They saw the Whig party's confusion in Washington and its factionalism in their own state as a boon. If James K. Polk could win the 1841 gubernatorial race, they reasoned, the party would be back on solid footing. Democratic optimism wavered, however, once the Tennessee Whigs selected James C. "Lean Jimmy" Jones as Polk's challenger. The upstart politico consistently outmaneuvered the veteran Polk in the campaign, and the election result hit the Democrats hard. They lost the governorship, one of their House seats, and control of the general assembly, although they were

1. Norma Lois Peterson, *The Presidencies of William Henry Harrison and John Tyler* (Lawrence: University Press of Kansas, 1989), 31–43, 57–87.

able to hold onto the majority in the state senate by one crucial vote. It was a demoralizing defeat.[2]

While financial and personal affairs commanded much of Donelson's attention during these years, he continued to keep an eye on political developments. As one of Polk's longtime supporters and with two of his Whig brothers-in-law, Meredith P. Gentry and Robert L. Caruthers, involved in the 1841 state elections, Donelson kept up with the progress of the campaign. He certainly stayed abreast of national politics. Following Harrison's death and Tyler's assumption of the presidency, Democrats began calculating how they could take advantage of the Whigs' disorganization in Washington, which *Nashville Union* editor Jeremiah George Harris predicted would lead to "the downfall of the dummies." Jackson was especially interested and maneuvered to gain influence within the Tyler administration. Despite having thought little of Tyler in the past, he now envisaged that "the whole republican democratic party will sustain him throout [*sic*] the union." Testing the waters, Jackson asked Donelson to convey to the president his approval of the veto of Clay's bill attempting to eliminate the Independent Treasury and establish a new national bank.[3]

Donelson did as Jackson requested. Tyler wrote back, thanking both men for "the approbation you expressed at my recent course in relation to the Bank." The embattled president characterized himself as "a republican of the Jeffersonian school" who, from the beginning, had supported Jackson's stand against the Bank's recharter, conveniently neglecting to mention that he had opposed Jackson's 1833 decision to remove the government deposits from the Bank. Donelson did not indicate that he supported Tyler, but he had a reason for toning down his uncle's criticism. By moderating Jackson's disapproval of the administration's economic policy, Donelson may have been maneuvering for a political appointment. One of his acquaintances, Timothy P. Andrews, had recommended that Donelson, who was considering speculation in government or military contracts, instead seek out a political

2. Jeremiah George Harris to JKP, 13 December 1841, in Cutler, Smith, and Parker, *CJKP* 5:784–7; Sellers, *Jacksonian*, 429–44; and Atkins, *Parties, Politics, and Sectional Conflict*, 116–8.

3. Jeremiah George Harris to JKP, 3 September 1841, in Cutler, Smith, and Parker, *CJKP* 5:752–3; AJ to WBL, 19 August 1841, in Bassett and Jameson, *CAJ* 6:120–1; AJ to AJD, 9 September 1841, DLC; Remini, *Course of American Democracy*, 474–6; and Peterson, *Presidencies*, 67–72.

office, especially since "Mr. Tyler is hard pushed to get popular or honest men for office." Donelson's friendly letter to Tyler gave him the opportunity to visit the president on a trip to Washington during the summer of 1842, at which time he broached the subject of a government position. Once again, however, he was disappointed, as no offer developed at that time.[4]

It also was hard to remain optimistic for the Democratic party. In the 1841–42 legislative session, Tennessee Democrats had caused an uproar by blocking the seating of the state's two U.S. senators, a situation that would remain unresolved until 1844. This senatorial appointment controversy, along with the continuing economic depression, contributed to the Democratic party's dismal showing in the state's August 1843 elections. Polk's attempt to reclaim the governor's seat from "Lean Jimmy" Jones fell short; in fact, his margin of defeat increased. The Whigs also secured an eight-seat majority in the legislature and control of both houses. The only good news for Democrats was their gain of a majority of Tennessee's eleven congressional seats, but that was of little comfort. The Whigs had retained their control of the state, and the Democrats needed strong leadership from Donelson and other prominent Democrats to unseat them.[5]

Even as he struggled with his debts, Donelson worked with other Democratic leaders to try to revitalize the party. In October 1843, he helped form a committee to strengthen Polk's claim to the 1844 vice-presidential nomination. Despite Polk's losses in the two previous gubernatorial elections, Tennessee Democrats believed that the former governor was still their strongest candidate. If Polk could win the vice-presidency, they surmised, he could use his influence to bring Tennessee back into the Democratic column. "Polk is the strongest, as well as the truest man that can be taken up in the south or west," Jackson reminded Van Buren in November 1843. "He will give you more strength than any other man." Richard M. Johnson's candidacy, on the other hand, would "be a dead weight to you as it was before."[6]

4. John Tyler to AJD, 16 November 1841, Timothy P. Andrews to AJD, 2 September 1842, DLC.

5. Atkins, *Parties, Politics, and Sectional Conflict,* 118–25; and *Nashville Union,* 11 August 1843.

6. William H. Polk to JKP, 16, 22 October 1843, JKP to AJD, 19 October 1843, SHL to JKP, 20 October, December 1843, JKP to MVB, 30 November 1843, Robert Armstrong to JKP, 22 December [1843], in Cutler and Parker, *CJKP* 6:345, 352–3, 347–9, 350–1, 379–81, 364–6, 390–1; AJ to MVB, 29 November 1843, in Bassett and Jameson, *CAJ* 6:245–6; and diary entry, 18 October 1843, in St. George L. Sioussat, ed., "Diaries of S. H. Laughlin of Tennessee, 1840, 1843," *Tennessee Historical Magazine* 2 (1916): 70–1.

Following Jackson's lead, Tennessee Democrats Aaron V. Brown and Robert Armstrong approached Donelson with the idea that he write prominent national Democratic leaders, including Silas Wright of New York, and give them an ultimatum. If Van Buren's supporters did not nominate Polk for the vice-presidency at the 1844 national convention, he was directed to threaten, then Tennessee's delegation would cast its presidential votes for Van Buren's leading rival, Lewis Cass of Michigan. Polk encouraged Donelson's efforts by reminding him, "Our friends at the North and East, should understand the true state of things in this part of the Union, and take bolder ground before the public in reference to the Vice Presidency." It was especially important, he noted, "that the ground should be preoccupied [*sic*] before Col. J[ohnson] concludes to fall back upon it." Donelson, however, apparently never fulfilled their request.[7]

The holding of a state Democratic convention on 23 November 1843 offered an opportunity to validate Polk's position, and Donelson's relationship to Jackson ensured him a prominent place in that event. An informal committee, composed of Laughlin, Armstrong, William Polk, West H. Humphreys, Judge Samuel Powell, and others, met on 20 October and recommended Donelson as the delegate to the national convention from the Eighth District, now composed of Davidson, Sumner, and Smith Counties. The Davidson County Democratic Convention, which met on 6 November, then selected Donelson as a delegate to the state convention. There he had the pleasure of assisting Laughlin and West H. Humphreys in composing Polk's address to the convention.[8]

The state gathering went smoothly. The nearly 230 delegates passed resolutions endorsing Polk as the vice-presidential nominee and promising to support the national convention's choice for president. They could not, however, agree on instructions that would force Tennessee's national delega-

7. William H. Polk to JKP, 22 October 1843, JKP to AJD, 19 October 1843, SHL to JKP, 20 October, 18 December 1843, JKP to MVB, 30 November 1843, Robert Armstrong to JKP, 22 December [1843], in Cutler and Parker, *CJKP* 6:352–3, 347–9, 350–1, 379–81, 364–6, 390–1; and diary entry, 18 October 1843, in Sioussat, "Diaries of SHL," 70–1.

8. JKP to Edmund Burke, 8 October 1843, J. G. M. Ramsey to JKP, 12 October 1843, SHL to JKP, 20 October 1843, William H. Polk to JKP, 22 October 1843, David Craighead to JKP, [6 November] 1843, JKP to SHL, 17 November 1843, JKP to MVB, 30 November 1843, in Cutler and Parker, *CJKP* 6:339–40, 342–3, 350–1, 352–3, 357–8, 360–1, 364–6.

tion to vote as a unit once its members reached Baltimore. An "anti–Van Buren feeling" was noticeable enough for Whig reporters to take notice, and there may also have been significant support for Cass. The convention chose thirteen delegates to send to the national convention in May 1844, but Donelson, surprisingly, was not one of them. Instead, he would serve as an alternate to Samuel R. Anderson of Sumner County.[9]

What led the convention to snub Donelson as a national convention delegate is unclear. The move surprised Polk, who told Van Buren, "Your friend *Andrew J. Donaldson* [*sic*] should have been the *Delegate* instead of the *Alternate* from the Nashville District." Davidson County Democrats had endorsed him in October, but the state delegates apparently did not share their enthusiasm for Jackson's nephew. Perhaps they determined that possessing Old Hickory's name was no guarantee of success. Prominent Tennesseans at the convention also may have known about his debts to Van Buren and thus questioned his loyalty to Polk's candidacy.[10]

Polk still valued Donelson, however, and expected him eventually to serve as a delegate. In the meantime, he asked Jackson's nephew to travel north and visit loyal newspaper editors and leading politicians. Ohio was a particularly important state, according to Polk, because Johnson had just been there campaigning for the second spot on the Democratic ticket. The state was "at this moment, the point of most interest" in determining the vice-presidential nominee. Polk had already suggested that Donelson write politicians Thomas Hart Benton, William Allen, and Benjamin Tappan and newspaper editors Moses Dawson and Samuel Medary and ask them to use their "controlling influence" over the Ohio Democrats. A personal visit from Donelson would be even more effective, he reasoned. Laughlin, without elaborating further on his reservations, questioned whether it would be appropriate for Donelson to make such a journey. In any case, Donelson declined the opportunity, saying he had to visit his Mississippi plantation. Polk considered sending someone else, but no one made the journey, and, to his disappointment, the Ohio convention endorsed Van Buren and Johnson.[11]

9. Charles G. Sellers Jr., *James K. Polk, Continentalist: 1843–1846* (Princeton, N.J.: Princeton University Press, 1966), 13–4; and *Nashville Republican Banner,* 24 November 1843.

10. JKP to MVB, 30 November 1843, in Cutler and Parker, *CJKP* 6:364–6.

11. JKP to AJD, 20 December 1843, Robert Armstrong to JKP, 22 December [1843], SHL to JKP, 29 December 1843, JKP to SHL, 29, 30 December 1843, William H. Polk to JKP, 31 December 1843, JKP to AJ,

Donelson had chosen a crucial time to disappear from the campaign. He spent the early part of 1844 traveling to his Mississippi plantation, then down to New Orleans. He claimed personal business as his reason for leaving Tennessee. With Van Buren's loan accumulating an annual interest of 15 percent, Donelson needed to make his plantation profitable soon; the former president and other creditors would not wait forever. He also felt slighted by the Democrats' unwillingness to select him as a delegate. It was becoming an all-too-familiar pattern, this reluctance to give him a prominent role within the party. The combination of these factors makes it easy to understand how Donelson could put his personal affairs before the Democratic cause.[12]

While Donelson was away in Mississippi, Democrats considered the major issues facing their party. The future of Texas emerged as the defining concern. Originally a part of Mexico, Texas had declared its independence from the Mexican government in 1836. The Lone Star Republic had proven self-sufficient and had grown into an attractive and potentially prosperous neighbor for the United States. Calls for its annexation had remained constant since 1836, however, and the rhetoric escalated in 1843 and 1844. Prominent Democrats argued that annexation would benefit both northerners and southerners by allowing slavery to expand, thus keeping the southern institution safe and northern states free from slaves.[13]

President Tyler also seized upon the matter in an attempt to win the 1844 election. A president without a party, Tyler held little hope of securing either the Whig or the Democratic nomination, much less of winning the election, unless he could find some issue to galvanize popular support. Tyler's attempts to negotiate a treaty with Texas in 1843 and 1844 forced the two major parties to address the annexation question. The rhetoric em-

---

25 December 1843, in Cutler and Parker, *CJKP* 6:382–4, 390–1, 396–7, 397–8, 402–3, 403–4, 392–3; and SHL to JKP, 1, 11 January 1844, William H. Polk to JKP, 1 January 1844 (two letters), Robert Armstrong to JKP, [7 January 1844], JKP to SHL, 9 January 1844, in Wayne Cutler and James P. Cooper Jr., eds., *Correspondence of James K. Polk,* vol. 7 (Nashville: Vanderbilt University Press, 1989), 3–5, 24–5, 5–6, 6–7, 11–2, 19–21.

12. SHL to JKP, 25 December 1843, in Cutler and Parker, *CJKP* 6:393–5.

13. Sellers, *Continentalist,* 40–9; John H. Schroeder, "Annexation or Independence: The Texas Issue in American Politics, 1836–1845," *Southwestern Historical Quarterly* 89 (October 1985): 137–64; and Richard Bruce Winders, *Crisis in the Southwest: The United States, Mexico, and the Struggle over Texas* (Wilmington, Del.: Scholary Resources, 2002), 71–89.

ployed by both Whigs and Democrats also made the Texas matter important. Proslavery Democrats warned that the British were trying to acquire Texas for themselves, hoping to abolish slavery there and ultimately in the entire American South. Antislavery Whigs, conversely, cautioned the American people against supporting southern efforts to annex Texas because it would only lead to slavery's expansion.[14]

By the time Donelson returned from Mississippi to Tulip Grove on the evening of 23 April 1844, Texas was about to become the central issue in American politics. On 12 April 1844, the United States and Texas had agreed to the terms of an annexation treaty. When the treaty was sent to Congress on the twenty-second, Calhoun included with it copies of confidential British correspondence denying Whitehall's interest in influencing American slavery and his own response justifying slavery and warning of a British conspiracy to rid Texas of slavery. When Benjamin Tappan leaked the treaty and Calhoun's correspondence to the press on 27 April, a fierce public debate erupted.[15]

Tennessee Democrats were primed to take up the annexation cause in order to preserve their peculiar institution, and they looked to Martin Van Buren as their champion. Van Buren disappointed annexation proponents, however, when on 27 April he had a letter published in the *Washington Globe* that asserted his opposition to immediate annexation. His letter coincided with the publication of a similar letter by the probable Whig nominee, Henry Clay. This correspondence, intended to remove annexation from the fall campaign, backfired for both men. The Democrats faced a crisis within their party—should they support the New Yorker regardless of his position, or should they find another candidate to replace him? In all sections

14. Schroeder, "Annexation or Independence," 150–5; Peterson, *Presidencies,* 207–9; William J. Cooper, *The South and the Politics of Slavery, 1828–1856* (Baton Rouge: Louisiana State University Press, 1978), 183–98; William W. Freehling, *The Road to Disunion,* vol. 1, *Secessionists at Bay, 1776–1854* (New York: Oxford University Press, 1990), 274–425; and David E. Narrett, "A Choice of Destiny: Immigration Policy, Slavery, and the Annexation of Texas," *Southwestern Historical Quarterly* 100 (January 1997): 270–302.

15. SHL to JKP, 24 April 1844, in Cutler and Cooper, *CJKP* 7:107–9; Atkins, *Parties, Politics, and Sectional Conflict,* 127–8; Remini, *Course of American Democracy,* 491–7; Sellers, *Continentalist,* 56–61; Schroeder, "Annexation or Independence," 154–5; Niven, *JCC,* 275–7; and JCC to Richard Pakenham, 18 April 1844, in Clyde N. Wilson, Shirley Bright Cook, and Alexander Moore, eds., *The Papers of John C. Calhoun,* vol. 20, *1844* (Columbia: University of South Carolina Press, 1991), 273–8.

of the country, including Tennessee, Democrats denounced Van Buren and pledged to support a candidate dedicated to making Texas part of the United States. Some Democratic politicians, such as Benton and William Allen of Ohio, rallied to Van Buren's defense, but the tide of opinion was turning decidedly against the New Yorker.[16]

Donelson quickly became involved in the debate. For the first few weeks after his return from Mississippi, he was in meetings with Jackson and other Democrats. On the day that Donelson arrived home, Jackson had actually been conversing with Benjamin F. Butler, a New York lawyer and one of Van Buren's closest political friends, and Tennessee associate Robert Armstrong about the former president's prospects of defeating Clay in the fall election. Jackson's views on annexation were well known; he had made clear his support of it in recent correspondence with political associates across the nation. News of Van Buren's letter, therefore, darkened the mood at the Hermitage. Armstrong noted that Van Buren's revelation left Donelson "in bad spirits and mortified," while Laughlin reported that Jackson's "dander is up." After considering his options, on 10 May, Jackson had Donelson summon Polk to visit him. "The division in our ranks threatened by conflicting views about the annexation question," Donelson wrote, "must be obviated in time for the convention at Baltimore." He hinted to Polk that he knew what step Jackson was about to take: "I am particularly anxious that the ground occupied by the Genl should be thoroughly understood by you. What he may now say if not modified by disclosures recently made will produce important results."[17]

Having received Jackson's summons, Polk, accompanied by Armstrong, set out for the Hermitage. Along the way, they met Donelson, who was riding into Nashville to deliver a letter from Jackson, to be published in the *Union,* separating himself from Van Buren and calling for the immediate annexation of Texas. Instead of continuing on, Donelson turned around and

16. Sellers, *Continentalist,* 60–6; Remini, *Course of American Democracy,* 497–8; idem, *Henry Clay,* 638–41; Niven, *MVB,* 516–29; and Michael A. Morrison, "Martin Van Buren, the Democracy, and the Partisan Politics of Texas Annexation," *Journal of Southern History* 61 (November 1995): 695–724.

17. JKP to Cave Johnson, 18 March 1844, SHL to JKP, 26, 24 April 1844, Robert Armstrong to JKP, 7 May [1844], 10 May [1844], Leonard P. Cheatham to JKP, 7 May 1844, AJD to JKP, 10 May [18]44, in Cutler and Cooper, *CJKP* 7:89–91, 107–9, 109–10, 123–4, 131, 124–5, 131–2; SHL to JKP, 10 May 1844, PLC; Remini, *Course of American Democracy,* 498–502; and Niven, *MVB,* 524, 527, 532.

rode back to the Hermitage with them. Once there, all three men met with Jackson, who expressed his extreme dissatisfaction with Van Buren, Benton, and other Jacksonians who hesitantly supported or completely resisted Texas annexation. By publicly opposing annexation, Jackson declared, Van Buren had nullified his chance of regaining the executive office. Without a united front on the Texas question, it seemed certain that the Democrats would find it difficult to seize the presidency from the Whigs. This possibility was unthinkable to Jackson. The Democrats must have "an annexation man [who] reside[s] in the Southwest," he said. Polk fit this qualification, and, therefore, Old Hickory wanted him to become the Democrats' presidential nominee.[18]

After Polk left, Jackson directed his nephew, who was now a delegate due to Samuel R. Anderson's resignation, to campaign actively at the convention. Donelson was to use his uncle's name to ensure Polk's nomination. Jackson's decision to support the Tennessean instead of the New Yorker left Donelson in an awkward position. His uncle wanted Polk because, unlike Van Buren, Polk supported annexation and had proven himself loyal in recent years. But Donelson could see the strengths and weaknesses of both men. Polk had Jackson's backing and was ideologically in line with many other southern Democrats; however, he had also lost the last two elections in which he was a candidate. Van Buren had his own problems, including his ideological break over annexation and his loss in the 1840 presidential election, but he had been a successful standard-bearer for the Democrats in the past.[19]

In what was a difficult choice, Donelson ignored his financial obligations to Van Buren and opted to support Polk. His ideological justification was that Polk supported annexation and slavery, whereas Van Buren's recent statements made questionable his commitment to these Democratic principles. As a southern slaveholding Democrat, Donelson understood that annexation was a vital issue for himself and those like him. The land in Texas would allow the spread of slave labor and the cash crops that it produced. Territorial expansion also promised to preserve the future of republican government in the United States and, particularly, the South, a government

18. JKP to Cave Johnson, 13 May 1844, in Cutler and Cooper, *CJKP* 7:134–6; Remini, *Course of American Democracy*, 498–502; and AJ to FPB, 11 May 1844, in Bassett and Jameson, *CAJ* 6:285–7.

19. Sam W. Haynes, *James K. Polk and the Expansionist Impulse* (New York: Longman, 1997), 91–103.

in which slavery upheld the "collective honor and individual liberty" of white southerners.[20]

As Jackson also had pointed out, the New Yorker was not electable in the South, and the Democratic party could not afford another presidential defeat. In addition to these reasons for opposing Van Buren, Donelson had to obey Jackson and assist Polk if he had any hopes of furthering his political career. Working for Van Buren at the national convention would challenge Jackson's authority publicly, something Donelson had avoided since the Eaton affair. He was not about to make that mistake again, so he made the logical choice.[21]

Explaining his decision to Van Buren was another story, however. Van Buren had brought this on himself, but Donelson had to be careful that he did not cut all ties to his benefactor. Before he left for Baltimore, he wrote the New Yorker. "It is inexplicable to me how this question [of annexation] could have been forced to such importance," he complained, "without a knowledge on the part of some of us of your views and feelings." He explained that he had been away from Nashville most of the year on personal business, not expecting that it would be necessary to "give but little attention to general politics . . . as the choice of the Democratic party seemed to be almost unanimous for you." He expressed disappointment with Jackson for pressing the issue of Texas annexation when it "would be injurious to the party," but, tellingly, he did not promise to work for Van Buren at the convention. In a draft letter, Donelson noted that he still had "hope that there is room to repair the error," but in the letter he sent, he only told Van Buren, "I am in trouble and amazement beyond expression, and have hardly the heart to go to the convention."[22]

Donelson stayed home an extra day in order to tone down Jackson's rhetoric in the letter intended for the *Nashville Union,* then he delivered it to the newspaper's offices and set out for Baltimore on 15 May. Even before Donelson reached the convention site, however, the divisiveness that underlay the party gathering surfaced. Informal preconvention conferences by the state delegations revealed that Van Buren had the majority of the dele-

20. Thomas R. Hietala, *Manifest Design: Anxious Aggrandizement in Late Jacksonian America* (Ithaca, N.Y.: Cornell University Press, 1985), chaps. 1, 4, and 6; Michael F. Holt, *The Political Crisis of the 1850s* (New York: John Wiley, 1978; W. W. Norton, 1983), 40–45; and Wyatt-Brown, "AJ's Honor," 18.

21. Remini, *Course of American Democracy,* 499–501.

22. AJD to MVB, 14 May 1844, VBL; and AJD to MVB, 14 May 1844 (draft), DLC.

gates' support. Yet there was a movement underway to force the convention to accept the precedent set at the first Democratic nominating convention in 1832, which stipulated that a nominee had to garner two-thirds of the delegates' votes to claim victory. When the convention opened on 27 May, anti–Van Buren factions were able to elect a speaker, Hendrick B. Wright of Pennsylvania, who assured them control of the proceedings. They then forced through a resolution binding the delegates to the two-thirds rule. This action signaled the end of Van Buren's fading chances. He would presumably win a majority of the votes on the first ballot, but his stance on the annexation issue had undercut any realistic chance he had of winning two-thirds of the delegates' votes. It appeared inevitable, then, that Van Buren would have to withdraw his name so that a viable candidate could attain the two-thirds majority needed to secure the nomination.[23]

The Tennessee delegation in Baltimore consisted of thirteen men. Polk had instructed five of them (Donelson, Laughlin, Gideon Pillow, Cave Johnson, and William G. Childress) to support a Van Buren–Polk ticket; only if it looked like the New Yorker would not get the nomination were they to present his own name for the presidency. When the Tennessee delegates present caucused on 23 May, before the convention began (and before Donelson had arrived), it became apparent that they were divided, with support for Van Buren on one side and support for someone, anyone, besides the New Yorker, on the other side. After much debate, the delegation decided to vote for Silas Wright as a compromise candidate and push for Polk's nomination as vice-president. Wright had already promised not to accept the offer, but the Tennessee delegates believed they could convince him to do otherwise. Pillow reported on the twenty-fifth that they were "still waiting for further developments and light before we act or determine what we will do." Cave Johnson told Polk, "It is probable that Donelson[,] Pillow[,] & myself will scarcely yield Van whilst he is kept up by his friends."[24]

23. AJD to MVB, 14 May 1844, VBL; AJD to AJ, 14 May 1844, DLC; JKP to Cave Johnson, 14 May 1844, in Cutler and Cooper, *CJKP* 7:136–8; Remini, *Course of American Democracy,* 500–2; *Nashville Union,* 16 May 1844; Sellers, *Continentalist,* 76–85; Charles G. Sellers Jr., "Election of 1844," in *History of American Presidential Elections,* 4 vols., ed. Arthur M. Schlesinger and Fred L. Israel (New York: Chelsea House, 1971), 1:763–6; Bain, *Convention Decisions,* 31–3; and Paul H. Bergeron, *The Presidency of James K. Polk* (Lawrence: University of Kansas Press, 1987), 16.

24. Sellers, *Continentalist,* 76, 81–7; and Gideon J. Pillow to JKP, 22 May 1844, 24 May [18]44, 25 May [18]44, SHL to JKP, 23 May 1844, Cave Johnson to JKP, 24 May [1844], 25 May 1844, William G.

Donelson arrived on the twenty-fourth, and it was presumably he, probably at Jackson's direction, who convinced the Polk contingent to change tactics. When the convention began and the balloting commenced, the Tennesseans' strategy materialized. The state's votes consistently went to Cass, with "solid support" and only "1 or 2" votes going to other candidates. With two of the five Polk delegates (Pillow and Laughlin) voting for Cass, and the other three (Donelson, Johnson, and Childress) for Van Buren, their purpose became obvious. Johnson, Pillow, and other members of the Polk contingent were dividing their votes between Van Buren and Cass to keep both of them from winning the nomination. It was obvious that Van Buren was not going to win the nomination, so they were biding their time, waiting for the opportune moment to spring their compromise candidate—Polk.[25]

Ballot after ballot over the first two days resulted in Van Buren winning a majority of the votes but not the necessary two-thirds. Finally, on the evening of 28 May, the break for which Polk's camp had been waiting came. George Bancroft of Massachusetts approached Donelson and Pillow on the convention floor with a proposal. Massachusetts and New Hampshire wanted to introduce Polk's name as a nominee in order to defeat Cass. The two Tennessee candidates assured Bancroft that if he could get the New England delegations' endorsement for Polk, they would secure the backing of Tennessee, Mississippi, and Alabama. The three then left the convention hall to meet with the Ohio and New York representatives, adjourning before midnight with the promise of Ohio's allegiance and New York's tacit agreement to support Polk.[26]

The next morning, Polk's nomination took off. On the eighth ballot, he received 44 votes to Cass's 114 and Van Buren's 104. The New England states began switching their votes to Polk on the next ballot, followed by New York and Virginia. By two o'clock that afternoon, the delegates had unanimously selected Polk as their presidential nominee. Silas M. Wright received the

---

Childress to JKP, 25 May 1844, in Cutler and Cooper, *CJKP* 7:145–7, 151–3, 155–7, 147–9, 149–51, 154–5, 153–4.

25. Sellers, *Continentalist,* 89–92; idem, "Election of 1844," 1:766–7; and W. G. Childress to JKP, 28 May 1844, JKP.

26. Satterfield, "Moderate Nationalist Jacksonian," 220–2; and George Bancroft to JKP, 6 July 1844, in M. A. De Wolfe Howe, *The Life and Letters of George Bancroft,* 2 vols. (Port Washington, N.Y.: Kennikat Press, 1971), 1:253.

vice-presidential nomination, but when he declined, George M. Dallas of Pennsylvania accepted it. The delegates then passed resolutions opposing the Bank of the United States, supporting state, as opposed to national, regulation of slavery, and calling for the "reoccupation of Oregon and the reannexation of Texas, at the earliest practicable period." They also reaffirmed their republican foundation. "The liberal principles embodied by Jefferson in the declaration of independence, and sanctioned in the constitution, which makes ours the land of liberty, and the asylum of the oppressed of every nation," they declared, "have ever been the cardinal principles in the democratic faith."[27]

After the convention announced Polk's nomination, the bombastic Pillow took most of the credit. "I held you up before the convention, as the '*Olive Branch of peace,*'" he bragged, "and all parties ran to you as to *an ark of safety.* I was up nearly all night last night in bringing about *this result.* I had many *difficulties* to *encounter.* But I faltered not." His friend's nomination, he declared, "was the *result & force* and *power of circumstance,* which I seized hold of & wielded, as I think with *no little skill* & judgment." Pillow also claimed that he "got no help on the work which was done last night from our home people. I communicated the plan & prospect to some of them & they had *no faith* in the *thing* & so expressed themselves."[28]

Pillow's arrogance grated on the nerves of Laughlin, Johnson, and Donelson, all of whom had played a crucial role at the convention. For Donelson, however, it had been a difficult endeavor. Historian Charles G. Sellers describes Donelson as "congenitally so lacking in self-confidence that he was not very effective in this kind of situation." That characterization misses the complexity of Donelson's position. He had clearly wanted Van Buren to re-

27. Sellers, "Election of 1844," 1:770–2; "Proceedings of the Democratic National Convention," in idem, "Election of 1844," 849–52; and John M. Belohlavek, *George Mifflin Dallas: Jacksonian Patrician* (University Park: Pennsylvania State University Press, 1977), 86–8.

28. Ed Frank, "Gideon Johnson Pillow," in *The Tennessee Encyclopedia of History and Culture,* ed. Carroll Van West (Nashville: Rutledge Hill Press, 1998), 735; Bergeron, *Presidency of JKP,* 16; Eugene I. McCormac, *James K. Polk: A Political Biography* (Berkeley and Los Angeles: University of California Press, 1922), 235–8; Charles A. McCoy, *Polk and the Presidency* (Austin: University of Texas Press, 1960), 41–2; Gideon J. Pillow to JKP, 29 May 1844 (2 letters), in Cutler and Cooper, *CJKP* 7:162–4; George Bancroft to JKP, 6 July 1844, in Howe, *George Bancroft* 1:253; and Elwood Fisher to JCC, [April?] 1845, in Chauncey S. Boucher and Robert P. Brooks, eds., *Correspondence Addressed to John C. Calhoun, 1837–1849,* in *Annual Report of the American Historical Association for the Year 1829* (Washington, D.C.: GPO, 1930), 289.

ceive the nod before the convention, but the New Yorker had made such an outcome impossible. Donelson had orders from Jackson to carry out at the convention, orders that he could not refuse personally, politically, or ideologically. He played his role at the convention, but it was almost certainly a half-hearted effort.[29]

In writing to Van Buren after the convention ended, Donelson attributed the proceedings at Baltimore to "chicanery" to which the New Yorker's friends "were obliged to assent." He proclaimed that the result had produced in him "a bleeding heart and spirits barely able to carry me home." Donelson's emotional outburst appears overly dramatic, but it was probably genuine. No doubt, though, he also had in mind the debt he owed Van Buren. In the early part of his letter, Donelson had asked his friend for more time to pay off his loans. Donelson was still in a precarious financial situation, and if the New Yorker suspected that his Tennessee friend had been dishonest about his loyalty to him, he might demand repayment of the loans.[30]

Donelson apparently did not reveal his struggles to Jackson, choosing instead to announce Polk's triumph in glowing terms. "The dark sky of yesterday has been succeeded by the brightest day democracy has witnessed since your election," he gushed. To say otherwise would have been foolish. Jackson needed to know that his nephew had worked hard to fulfill his orders. So did Polk, because should he win the presidency, Donelson wanted him to think that he had been one of his most loyal lieutenants and deserved a reward.[31]

After the convention ended, Donelson returned to Tennessee, where he found an electorate still torn between its strong Whig ties and a native son. Whigs argued that the voters had rejected Polk on two different occasions because of his failure to support republican principles. He was as much a demagogue as Jackson had been, they claimed. Polk's elevation to a higher office would merely visit his excessive ambitions over the entire country in-

29. Thomas H. Winn, "Cave Johnson," in *The Tennessee Encyclopedia of History and Culture,* ed. Carroll Van West (Nashville: Rutledge Hill Press, 1998), 485–6; Satterfield, "Moderate Nationalist Jacksonian," 221–2; McCoy, *Polk and the Presidency,* 40–2; McCormac, *JKP,* 238–40; Williamson Smith to JKP, 29 May 1844, in Cutler and Cooper, *CJKP* 7:164–5; Sellers, *Continentalist,* 93; and Jeremiah George Harris to George Bancroft, 13 September 1887, in Sellers, *Continentalist,* 114.

30. AJD to MVB, 2 June 1844, VBL.

31. AJD to AJ, 29 May 1844, in Bassett and Jameson, *CAJ* 6:296.

stead of just his home state. Democrats countered by attaching the name "Young Hickory," which the Whigs used derisively, to Polk. Yes, they agreed, their candidate was a Young Hickory, a man committed to the republican principles of Andrew Jackson. Polk offered the promise of rescuing the nation from the clutches of the corrupt, aristocratic Whigs.[32]

The core issues for Democrats nationally and in Tennessee continued to be annexation and slavery. Many Tennesseans had either economic or personal ties to Texas, and it became imperative that the people understood where Polk stood. To help them, Donelson and the other members of the Nashville central committee issued an invitation for a Democratic "Mass Convention" on 24 July 1844. The primary purpose of the meeting was to demonstrate to the other states that "Tennessee is safe for Polk and Dallas." Donelson busied himself preparing letters of invitation to Democratic leaders across the nation.[33]

A movement by discontented Democrats, however, forced the Nashville committee to reschedule the July meeting. Following the Baltimore convention, Van Buren Democrats in Congress joined with Whigs to defeat the annexation treaty in the Senate, vote down the tariff-reducing and southern-supported McKay bill, and very nearly overturn the "gag rule" that kept Congress from debating antislavery petitions. These actions infuriated Congressman Robert Barnwell Rhett and other South Carolina congressional members. Rhett called for nullification of the Tariff of 1842 and threatened to take over the Nashville meeting and force the attendees to discuss secession. Donelson assured Polk that he would write northern friends and convince them that the South Carolinians would not capture the July meeting, but Robert Armstrong later informed him that the meeting had to be postponed until 15 August because "it could not have been well Controled" in July. The committee's official explanation for the delay was that they needed time to make "more bountiful preparation" for a larger-than-expected attendance.[34]

32. Atkins, *Parties, Politics, and Sectional Conflict,* 129–35.

33. *Nashville Union,* 11 June 1844; and AJD to JKP, 14 June 1844, in Cutler and Cooper, *CJKP* 7: 251–2.

34. Niven, *JCC,* 279–82; Remini, *Course of American Democracy,* 505–6; AJD to JKP, 14 June 1844, Robert Armstrong to JKP, 25 June [1844], JKP to AJD, 26 June 1844, in Cutler and Cooper, *CJKP* 7:251–2, 280–1, 286–7; Jeremiah George Harris to JKP, 28 June 1844, PLC; and *Nashville Union,* 29 June 1844.

Donelson and Polk's other advisors had several concerns. One was the tariff. Donelson had met with Dallas following the nominating convention, at which time the vice-presidential nominee had told him that the tariff was the most important issue in Pennsylvania, a pivotal state in the upcoming election. Donelson passed on that information to Polk, and Pennsylvania Democrats confirmed his warning. Isaac G. McKinley, editor of the *Harrisburg (Pa.) Democratic Union,* wrote Polk, "All we ask in Penna is a *Revenue tariff,* so adjusted as to afford protection to our iron, coal, & manufactures." Gubernatorial nominee Henry A. P. Muhlenberg concurred, urging the Tennessean to "devise some mode of giving us in Pennsylvania some moderate declaration respecting a revenue tariff[f] . . . embracing the principle of discriminating duties & incidental protection." Polk responded to Pennsylvania Democrats' concerns by sending two letters to John K. Kane of Philadelphia, a Van Buren supporter who had requested the Democratic nominee's views on the tariff. In these letters, Polk declared, "I am opposed to a tariff for protection *merely* and not for revenue." He had given his "support to the policy of General Jackson's administration on this subject," voting against the 1828 tariff and in favor of the 1832 and 1833 tariffs. Donelson expressed his pleasure with Polk's statements, declaring that they would "kill Clay," the Whigs' presidential candidate.[35]

Southern extremists' threatened takeover of the Nashville meeting also caused Polk's campaign managers concern. Polk himself asked Donelson and former *Nashville Union* editor Jeremiah G. Harris to prepare an address that would soothe the minds of northerners leery of attending a rally controlled by the party's radical wing. Their statement made clear that the August meeting in Nashville would be a gathering for the entire Democratic party, not just southern discontents. The address, which avoided mention of the tariff because of its potential divisiveness, depicted Polk as "the stern and unflinching republican, whose public and private virtues so eminently qualify him for the" presidency, and lauded the Van Burenites, who to "secure harmony and unite all the republican strength in support of the great principles" had graciously assented to Polk's nomination for the benefit of

35. Belohlavek, *George Mifflin Dallas,* 92; Isaac G. McKinley to JKP, 3 June 1844, Henry A. P. Muhlenberg to JKP, 3 June 1844, JKP to John K. Kane, 19 June 1844 (two letters), AJD to JKP, 1, 16 July 1844, in Cutler and Cooper, *CJKP* 7:191–3, 183, 193–5, 265–7, 267–8, 303–4, 351; and Sellers, *Continentalist,* 116–28.

the Democratic party. Donelson and Harris further declared that the annexation issue was a national, not a sectional, question on which all Democrats could agree in order to "secure to us peace, harmony, and increased prosperity." The authors interwove national interest with republican ideology to convince their fellow party members that Polk would ensure the continuation and expansion of the United States political system, especially those principles near and dear to the hearts of Democrats.[36]

To substantiate his claim about the Van Burenites' support of Polk, Donelson urged Van Buren to attend the Nashville meeting. He also slyly suggested that doing so would repair the New Yorker's reputation within the party. Since Polk had pledged not to seek reelection, Donelson predicted that in the next election Van Buren would almost certainly receive the Democratic nomination "as vindication for the injustice resulting from the scenes of 1840." In 1848, he reminded his friend, there will be "no Texas question to disturb the harmony of our party" and undermine Van Buren's return to glory. Donelson concluded with an admonition for Van Buren, should he not be able to visit Tennessee, to send the Nashville committee "a cheering letter." "There is a providence in the circumstances which brought about the nomination of Polk," he concluded, "that will punish those who have been treacherous to Republicanism, and reward the faithful and true." Van Buren responded favorably, sending a letter that endorsed the Polk-Dallas ticket and reiterated the republican tenets of the Democratic party.[37]

Donelson also tended to a myriad of other duties during the campaign. He wrote numerous private letters himself and for Andrew Jackson, reassuring Democratic doubts about which faction was in control of Polk's campaign. He encouraged Laughlin and Harris to put together a campaign biography for Polk that emphasized the Democratic candidate's republican ideology. "The people want the facts," Donelson insisted. He also occasionally submitted articles to the *Nashville Union*, now under the editorial direction of John P. Heiss, and attended local Democratic rallies. When the

36. JKP to AJD, 26 June 1844, Jeremiah George Harris to JKP, 29 June 1844, AJD to JKP, 1 July 1844, in Cutler and Cooper, *CJKP* 7:286–7, 298–9, 303–4; Jeremiah George Harris to JKP, 28 June 1844, JKP; and *Nashville Union*, 2 July 1844.

37. AJD to MVB, 8 July 1844, MVB to Nashville Central Committee, 29 July 1844 (published in a Gallatin, Tennessee, newspaper), VBL.

Whigs tried to use some of Andrew Jackson's pro-annexation correspondence to depict him and Polk as "dictators," Donelson assured Polk that he would screen Jackson's outgoing letters more carefully.[38]

Donelson additionally helped party leaders plan for the pivotal August meeting. When the great day finally arrived, an estimated fifty thousand men and women gathered on the fifty-acre Camp Hickory near Nashville. After partaking in a banquet spread on tables that reportedly stretched two miles long, the meeting came to order. Donelson, as the leading member of the Committee of Arrangements, announced the officers who would preside over the meeting. President Cave Johnson opened with a rousing speech that included a promise to preserve the Union. Other speakers, including Lewis Cass, spoke throughout the day. Not everyone could attend the meeting, of course. Van Buren, Bancroft, Buchanan, and several others sent their regrets to Donelson, and some, such as Van Buren, transmitted letters to be read before the assembly. Whether writing or speaking, Democratic leaders emphasized the party's unity and the necessity of annexing Texas. The *Nashville Union,* stressing these themes, declared the meeting a great success.[39]

Inexplicably, Donelson left for his Mississippi plantation once the meeting ended. In the midst of a hard-fought campaign and on the cusp of a

38. SHL to JKP, 8 May 1844, Jeremiah George Harris to JKP, 19 July 1844, AJD to JKP, 8 July 1844, PLC; SHL to JKP, 5, 14 July 1844 (summary), Robert Armstrong to JKP, 25 June [1844], 10 July 1844, [16 July 1844], 22 July [18]44, JKP to AJD, 11 July 1844, Jeremiah George Harris to JKP, 25 June, 12 July 1844 (summary), 17, 23, 31 July 1844, AJD to JKP, 14 June 1844, 1, 16, 24, [25], 29 July 1844, JKP to George Bancroft, 20 July 1844, AJ to JKP, 23 July 1844, John P. Heiss to JKP, 29 July 1844, JKP to John P. Heiss, 31 July 1844, in Cutler and Cooper, *CJKP* 7:313–7, 347–8, 280–1, 330–1, 350–1, 377–8, 343–4, 281–3, 345, 357–8, 386–8, 416–8, 251–2, 303–4, 351, 391–2, 394, 408–10, 372–3, 389–91, 410–1, 418–9; AJ to AJD, 17 July 1844, in St. George L. Sioussat, ed., "Selected Letters, 1844–1845, from the Donelson Papers," *Tennessee Historical Magazine* 3 (1917): 135; Nashville Central Committee to Levi Woodbury, 22 July 1844, Levis Woodbury Papers, Library of Congress, Washington, D.C.; Nashville Central Committee to MVB, 17 June 1844, VBC; Lewis Cass to AJD, 29 July 1844, THB to AJD, 10 August 1844, DLC; Sellers, *Continentalist,* 104–5; and Williams, "Samuel Hervey Laughlin," 386–8.

39. JKP to AJD, 26 June, 3, 13 August 1844, Jeremiah George Harris to JKP, 29 June, 31 July 1844, AJ to JKP, 29 June 1844, Robert Armstrong to JKP, 30 June 1844, [16 July 1844], 19 July [18]44, 22 July [18]44, 4 August [18]44, 5 August [18]44, AJD to JKP, 1, 24, [25] July, 5 August 1844, SHL to JKP, 5 July 1844, JKP to Cave Johnson, 16 July 1844 (summary), William E. Cramer to JKP, 21 July 1844, in Cutler and Cooper, *CJKP* 7:286–7, 428–9, 450, 298–9, 416–8, 299–300, 301–2, 350–1, 363–4, 377–8, 436–7, 437–8, 303–4, 391–2, 394, 438–9, 313–7, 351, 376–7; George Bancroft to AJD, 6 July 1844, James Buchanan to AJD, 17 July 1844, in Sioussat, "Selected Letters, 1844–1845," 135–6, 136–7; WBL to AJD, 3 July 1844, DLC; and *Nashville Union,* 9, 23 July, 17 August 1844.

possibly momentous victory, Donelson decided it was imperative to give more attention to his finances. Perhaps he was also tired of mundane political tasks, thinking that his talents were being underutilized. His friends and associates, including Jackson, must have wondered if Donelson was ever going to commit himself to a task and prove that he could bring it to a successful end. It was little wonder that some of them were reluctant to give him more serious responsibilities when he had trouble completing the minor duties assigned to him.

12

"I Could Not Withhold My Aid"

Donelson was still in Mississippi when word reached him that Tilghman A. Howard, the recently appointed chargé d'affaires to Texas, had unexpectedly died, and President Tyler wanted Donelson to take his place. The president wrote Jackson to inform him of the appointment. Expressing a hope that Donelson would not delay accepting the post, Tyler also provided his reasons for choosing Jackson's nephew. They were not surprising. "Independent of my great regard for Major Donalson, I was much incited to the appointment from the fact of his being intimate with President [Sam] Houston and above all being a member of your family and in your close confidence. This I doubt not will have a controuling influence with Genl. Houston and incline him, if he entertains any feelings antagonistical to the U. States and favourable to England, to pause ere he declares against annexation."[1]

After reading Tyler's letter, Jackson hurriedly wrote to Donelson, urging his nephew to return to Tennessee. When Donelson arrived home on the evening of 1 October, he read Tyler's letter and the accompanying despatches from Secretary of State John C. Calhoun. Calhoun emphasized that the issue of Texas annexation "must be decided in the next three or four months." He authorized Donelson to reassure the members of the Texas government that his nation would negotiate in good faith and that the United States would adopt an aggressive posture toward Mexico regarding any threatened invasion. Calhoun additionally instructed Donelson to warn Houston's admin-

1. John Tyler to AJ, 17 September 1844, in Bassett and Jameson, *CAJ* 6:319–20; Robert Armstrong to JKP, 25 September 1844 (summary), Jeremiah George Harris to JKP, 26 September 1844, AJ to JKP, 26 September 1844, in Wayne Cutler, Robert G. Hall II, and Jayne C. DeFiore, eds., *Correspondence of James K. Polk,* vol. 8, *September-December 1844* (Knoxville: University of Tennessee Press, 1993), 120, 127–8, 129–30; and Annie Middleton, "Donelson's Mission to Texas in Behalf of Annexation," *Southwestern Historical Quarterly* 24 (1921): 251.

istration that, because of constitutional limits, the United States would not be able to act decisively unless Mexico actually attacked Texas. As for the appointment's financial benefits, the government would pay Donelson an annual salary of forty-five hundred dollars, half of which he would receive immediately. Congress would also provide him an additional forty-five hundred dollars to pay travel expenses.[2]

Donelson accepted the appointment with appropriate reluctance, telling Calhoun that it would come "at a great sacrifice of my private interests." He assured the secretary of state, however, that as "a good citizen . . . I could not withhold my aid" and agreed to leave for Texas as soon as he could. Annexation was important to him ideologically and politically, and to have a hand in bringing the Lone Star Republic into the Union was an attractive endeavor. As a condition of his acceptance, Donelson asked that he be allowed to return home during the winter "to complete the arrangement of my private affairs." His last statement revealed another purpose for taking the position: he needed the money.[3]

Donelson's financial problems were well known. Calhoun's South Carolina friend, James Hamilton Jr., wrote the secretary of state that "some domestic circumstance [i.e., his financial debts] may make it inconvenient for Major Donelson to accept the mission." In fact, just the opposite was true. Van Buren had already written Donelson begging him to pay his debt, which had grown to over six thousand dollars. Jackson wrote back that his nephew had accepted the mission, and the "Major requested me to say to you, that as he passed thro[ugh] Neworleans [*sic*], he would make arrangements, based upon his cotton crop, to remit to his N.York debt six thousand dollars." Despite Jackson's guarantee, his nephew never made the payment. When Blair also wrote Jackson, asking about one of Donelson's bank drafts that "had not been punctually paid, and . . . [was] protested," the General assured his old friend that Donelson would pay the debt. "The Major has had great trouble . . . in mon[e]y Matters," he notified Blair. Before leaving

2. JCC to T. A. Howard, 10 September 1844, JCC to AJD, 17 September 1844, in Manning, *Diplomatic Correspondence* 12:78–9, 80–1; JCC to AJD, 16 September 1844, in Jameson, *Correspondence of JCC* 2:614–5; AJ to [JKP?], 26 September 1844, in Cutler, Hall, and DeFiore, *CJKP* 8:129–30; and AJ to MVB, 2, 22 October 1844, VBL.

3. AJD to JCC, 2 October 1844, in Wilson, Cook, and Moore, *PJCC* 20:16–7.

for Texas, Andrew Donelson sent Blair and John C. Rives the requested $2,517.10, which William B. Lewis was to use in paying off Donelson's debt to the Eliason family. Van Buren, meanwhile, received nothing. Before the newly appointed chargé left for Texas, he placed his personal affairs in the hands of his brother, Daniel, and brother-in-law, William Donelson.[4]

Donelson also consented to go to Texas because it furthered his political ambitions. He was ready to move forward and achieve what he had always desired—a prominent political post in an important situation. While holding a ministership to a foreign nation was the highest diplomatic position at that time, being a chargé was a significant diplomatic appointment. He had to realize, however, that Tyler selected him only because of his relationship with Jackson and Houston. The president had said as much in his letter to Jackson. So while Donelson at last received some recognition, the Tyler administration expected him to serve as Jackson's spokesperson.[5]

Regardless of the motivation behind his appointment, Donelson understood that this was a moment of great importance for the United States. Texas annexation had become the key issue in the presidential campaign, and after years of maneuvering and posturing by both Texas and the United States, Americans were waiting to see how the victor, either Polk or Clay, would resolve the Lone Star Republic's future, since prior presidents, including Jackson and Van Buren, had failed to bring resolution. Jackson had taken office in 1829 with an eye toward attaining Texas. He considered Texas an ideal location upon which to place dislocated Native Americans from the southern and eastern states. When Texas won its independence from Mexico in the 1835–36 revolution, with significant help from Tennesseans, including Sam Houston, it appeared to most observers that the United States would move quickly to absorb the region as a new territory. Jackson, however, moved circumspectly on the annexation issue. He was aware that the Whigs would seize upon his friendship with Houston to levy charges of dictation. He also wanted to be careful that he did not hurt the 1836 election chances of his handpicked successor, Martin Van Buren, a northerner some southerners looked upon with suspicion because of uncer-

4. AJ to FPB, 17 October 1844, in Bassett and Jameson, *CAJ* 6:325; AJ to MVB, 2, 22 October 1844, VBL; MVB to AJD, 5 October 1844, FPB and John C. Rives to AJD, 30 October 1844, DLC; account statement between AJD and MVB, [28 May 1846?], VBC; and Satterfield, "Moderate Nationalist Jacksonian," 256.

5. Peter Bridges, *Pen of Fire: John Moncure Daniel* (Kent, Ohio: Kent State University Press, 2002), 65–7.

tainty about his commitment to protecting slavery. Recognizing these limitations, Jackson moved away from annexation and entrusted the issue to his successors. Before leaving office, however, he granted official recognition to Texas. Van Buren was too concerned with the repercussions of the Panic of 1837 to respond to the Texas government's formal request for annexation in 1837.[6]

Not until 1843 and John Tyler's presidential administration did the United States again seriously consider Texas annexation. Under Sam Houston's leadership, the Texas government renewed its pressure on the United States for such action, while at the same time opening informal discussions with Mexico and Great Britain. As rumors of British interest in Texas reached Washington, Tyler and his supporters became agitated. If Great Britain annexed Texas, then British abolitionists already active there might not only do away with slavery in that territory but also try to influence the South toward freeing its own slaves.[7]

In reality, Great Britain was more interested in the economic stability of Mexico than it was the abolition of slavery in Texas or even the annexation of the Republic itself. Convincing Mexico to accept and recognize Texas independence would help further British economic interests in the two North American countries. Additionally, an independent Texas republic would stymie American expansion, which was threatening to destabilize British-Mexican commercial relations. Although the abolition of slavery was a concern for the British government, since it had recently done away with the institution in its colonies, the perception that Great Britain was conspiring to eliminate slavery in Texas was more a function of American, specifically southern, fears than any specific British policy.[8]

6. Schroeder, "Annexation or Independence," 139–47; John M. Belohlavek, *"Let the Eagle Soar!": The Foreign Policy of Andrew Jackson* (Lincoln: University of Nebraska Press, 1985), 218–38; Narrett, "Choice of Destiny," 273–84; Remini, *Course of American Freedom,* 352–68; George P. Garrison, "The First Stage of the Movement for the Annexation of Texas," *American Historical Review* 10 (October 1904): 72–96; and Joel H. Silbey, *Storm over Texas: The Annexation Controversy and the Road to the Civil War* (Oxford: Oxford University Press, 2005), 13–7.

7. Schroeder, "Annexation or Independence," 148–54; Narrett, "Choice of Destiny," 288–92; and David M. Pletcher, *The Diplomacy of Annexation: Texas, Oregon, and the Mexican War* (Columbia: University of Missouri Press, 1973), 113–35.

8. Lelia M. Roeckell, "Bonds over Bondage: British Opposition to the Annexation of Texas," *Journal of the Early Republic* 19 (Summer 1999): 260, 267.

Nevertheless, British interest in Texas concerned proslavery southerners enough to spur them to push for a conclusion to the long-simmering annexation issue. Throughout early 1843, Texas chargé d'affaires Isaac Van Zandt and U.S. Secretary of State Abel P. Upshur seriously discussed annexation. Their efforts bore fruit in the summer months, when President Houston ordered Van Zandt to hint that Texas was considering a Mexican proposal, supported by Great Britain, that would recognize its independence. If this plan bore fruit, the United States could lose all hope of acquiring the republic. The United States had to decide if it wanted to risk losing Texas by not genuinely negotiating for annexation.[9]

The pressure worked. In October 1843, Upshur sent Van Zandt a message stating the United States' desire to begin final negotiations for Texas annexation. Houston directed Van Zandt to respond that Texas, Mexico, and Great Britain had already begun negotiating and that any disruption might cause Mexico, with Britain's tacit support, to invade Texas. Houston clearly wanted the Tyler administration to guarantee that the United States would complete its own negotiations and help repel any Mexican military invasion. Upshur made no explicit promises, but he convinced Van Zandt to proceed.[10]

Upshur and Van Zandt completed a preliminary treaty, but Upshur's sudden death in early 1844 left the completion of the process to John C. Calhoun, a decision that boded well for annexation supporters. Although initially leery of taking a post in Tyler's unsuccessful administration, Calhoun accepted the State Department appointment because he was dedicated to adding Texas to the United States. He, like many of his fellow South Carolinians, believed that its acquisition would give slavery new life and increase the South's political influence. Working with the new Texas envoy, J. Pinckney Henderson, Calhoun finalized a treaty that proposed several points: Texas would become a territory of the United States under the existing constitutional guidelines; Texas would turn over its public land and property to the United States in exchange for payment of its public debt, limited to a maximum of ten million dollars; and the Texas-Mexico boundary would

9. Eugene C. Barker, "The Annexation of Texas," *Southwestern Historical Quarterly* 50 (July 1946): 61–2.

10. Ibid., 62–3; and Schroeder, "Annexation or Independence," 153–4.

remain ambiguous and subject to change after annexation. After receiving minor concessions, Hou ;ton and other Texas leaders agreed to the preliminary treaty, the U.S. and Texas negotiators signing it on 12 April 1844.[11]

With an eye on the presidential campaign, members of the Senate debated the preliminary treaty from April until June 1844, and the tone of the discussion left many observers uncertain as to how the senators would vote. Senators requested reports, maps, and other information from Tyler, and at one point, fearing war, they asked the president if he had moved any military forces near the Texas-Mexico border. Tyler replied that, indeed, he had made war preparations.[12]

Tyler's reply and the fallout from the publication of Calhoun's accompanying correspondence to Richard Pakenham clinched the treaty's defeat. On 8 June, the senators rejected it by a vote of thirty-five to sixteen. All but one Whig voted against the treaty, as did eight Democrats. The Texas issue had placed the Whigs in a difficult position. They feared the matter would sway many ambivalent southerners to vote with the Democrats for annexation during the upcoming presidential election. On the other side, the eight Democrats resisted annexation for personal and constitutional reasons. Senator Thomas Hart Benton of Missouri, for example, held a personal vendetta against Calhoun because of prior disagreements, but he also argued that annexation would provoke an unconstitutional war against Mexico. Other Democrats cited the constitutional issue, the loss of status within the European community, and the dictations of Jackson.[13]

After the Senate's rejection, Tyler tried a new tack. He argued that the United States government did not need a treaty to annex territory. An act of Congress, originating in the House, held just as much constitutional authority as a treaty ratified by the Senate. Tyler hoped to place annexation before the voters in the 1844 presidential election, but since the House would adjourn shortly, not to meet again until December, this approach provided no immediate solution. Still, he wanted an American representative in Texas

11. Pletcher, *Diplomacy of Annexation,* 136–8; Barker, "Annexation of Texas," 63–4; Schroeder, "Annexation or Independence," 154; Department of State circular, 29 February 1844, in Richardson, *Messages and Papers of the Presidents* 4:333; and Niven, *JCC,* 270–4.

12. Reply to the 13 May 1844 resolution concerning annexation, 15 May 1844, in Richardson, *Messages and Papers of the Presidents* 4:316–8.

13. Schroeder, "Annexation or Independence," 156; and Pletcher, *Diplomacy of Annexation,* 147–8.

to continue advocating for the annexation cause, and this was Donelson's charge.[14]

Donelson, accompanied by his brother-in-law, James G. Martin Jr., left Tulip Grove on 21 October 1844 and arrived by steamboat in New Orleans eight days later. While in the city, he took time to write his wife back home, reassuring her that they would soon be together again. If Polk was elected, he would be home by 1 February 1845; if not, he would have to stay until the situation became "well defined." After waiting a week for the steamboat to arrive, Donelson finally set off for the Texas port city of Galveston on 7 November, arriving three days later. After talking briefly with some prominent citizens, Donelson wrote Calhoun that the people there felt nothing but "cordial friendship and good will to the United States," and he expected to receive the same treatment from the Texas government.[15]

Donelson's initial optimism regarding the republic's endorsement of annexation increased over the next few days. As he made his way on horseback to the Texas capital of Washington-on-the-Brazos, Donelson encountered enthusiastic support for annexation. "The further I advance into this country," he reported, "the stronger is the evidence of the anxiety of the people for incorporation into our union." He surmised that "so strong is the attachment of the great body of Texans to our Union, that I am not sure they might not be induced to stand the hazards of another war with Mexico" instead of choosing to ally themselves with Great Britain or another country. Donelson captured the spirit of the people on this occasion, as most Texans had voiced their desire to become part of the United States since obtaining independence in 1836.[16]

14. Schroeder, "Annexation or Independence," 156; Barker, "Annexation of Texas," 64–5; and John Tyler to House of Representatives, 10 June 1844, in Richardson, *Messages and Papers of the Presidents* 4:323–7.

15. AJ to MVB, 22 October 1844, VBL; Jeremiah George Harris to AJD, 20 July 1844, AJD to ERD, 30 October, 7 November 1844, DLC; Justin H. Smith, *The Annexation of Texas* (New York: Barnes and Noble, 1941), 314–5; Robert Armstrong to JKP, 10 July 1844, 19 July [18]44, AJD to JKP, 16 July 1844, Jeremiah George Harris to JKP, 19, 25 July 1844, William E. Cramer to JKP, 21 July 1844, Jeremiah Y. Dashiell to JKP, 27 July 1844, in Cutler and Cooper, *CJKP* 7:330–1, 363–4, 351, 367–8, 395–6, 376–7, 405–8; AJD to JKP, 8 July 1844, JKP; AJD to JCC, 11 November 1844, in Manning, *Diplomatic Correspondence* 12:371–2; and Stewart Newell to Richard K. Crallé, 12 November 1844, in Wilson, Cook, and Moore, *PJCC* 20:242–4.

16. AJD to JCC, 18 November 1844, AJD to John Tyler, 18 November 1844, in Wilson, Cook, and Moore, *PJCC* 20:316–7, 317–20; and Smith, *Annexation of Texas,* 161.

Donelson believed that continued Texas support for annexation depended upon the presidential elections in the United States. Shortly after accepting the Texas post, Donelson told Polk that if the voters elected Clay, "how undefined become all the speculations respecting the existence of slavery. What a dark clould [*sic*] will at once hang over the prospect of all our southern states. Great Britain will forthwith resume her projects for the abolition of slavery, and with the aid of Webster and Adams will consider that her game is insured." All of "the leading interests of our country" would find better protection through Polk's election, because he defended slavery and "identified with the preservation of Republican principles and the promotion of the public prosperity." In sum, Polk's election would secure the endorsement of the Texas citizens, but a Clay victory would doom the annexation process.[17]

Fortunately for Donelson and other annexation supporters, a majority of American voters supported the Democratic platform. Polk won the presidency over Clay by an electoral count of 170 to 105. The popular vote totals were exceptionally close: 1,337,000 for the Democratic candidate, 1,299,000 for the Whig nominee, and 62,000 for the Liberty party hopeful, James G. Birney. New York had proven to be the decisive state, with Birney likely siphoning off enough popular votes to give Polk its thirty-six electoral votes and the election. The Democrats also gained control of both houses of Congress.[18]

Donelson had worked toward Polk's victory while in Tennessee; now, it would give him additional help in pursuing annexation. "If you are elected," he had written Polk shortly before voters went to the polls, "I shall use the fact as decisive of the wish of the people of the U[nited] States to incorporate Texas immediately into our Union, and shall calculate that the response to this wish on the part of the Government of Texas will be such as to shut out effectively all machinations of Great Britain and other powers to defeat it."[19]

Donelson did not learn of the election's result until December 1844. In the meantime, he worked to counteract the presence of annexation

17. AJD to JKP, 6 November 1844, in Cutler, Hall, and DeFiore, *CJKP* 8:276–7; and AJD to the editor of the *Nashville Union,* 11 October 1844, in *Nashville Union,* 15 October 1844.

18. Bergeron, *Presidency of JKP,* 19–20.

19. AJD to JKP, 6 November 1844, in Cutler, Hall, and DeFiore, *CJKP* 8:276–7.

opponents in and around the Texas government. Upon reaching Galveston in November 1844, he discovered that Houston's administration, undoubtedly tired of Washington's vacillation over its relationship with the Lone Star Republic, was ignoring the public's pro-annexation proclamations. George W. Terrell, who served dually as a member of Sam Houston's cabinet and as minister to France, and James Reily, the new Texas minister to the United States, stated unequivocally to the chargé that they opposed annexation. Other members of the government held this view as well, Donelson reported. He also had to deal with the fickle leadership of Sam Houston. Houston had served as the republic's first president following the 1836 revolution and had pushed for annexation upon taking office. After the Jackson and Van Buren administrations turned down inquiries about unifying the two countries, Houston determined to make Texas successful on its own, which he did. He left the presidency in 1838 but was reelected in 1841. During his second term, Houston vacillated on the annexation issue, but now convinced that Mexico intended to invade and reconquer his nation, Houston once again looked to procure a promise of protection from another country. He preferred the United States, but there was always Great Britain and France.[20]

It became Donelson's responsibility to convince Houston to accept annexation by the United States. A sense of urgency prevailed because Houston's term was nearing its end and Secretary of State Anson Jones was about to become the republic's new president. Jones possessed his predecessor's uncertain support for annexation, but Donelson would not be able to use Jackson's friendship as leverage with him as he could Houston. It became extremely important for Donelson to make a strong case for annexation in order to gain Houston's approval or at least force the incoming Jones administration to follow his predecessor's lead.[21]

Shortly after arriving at the Texas capital, Donelson met unofficially with Houston. In the company of several members of his government, the presi-

20. AJD to JCC, 23 November 1844, in Manning, *Diplomatic Correspondence* 12:373–4; George W. Terrell to Anson Jones, 12 November 1844, in Anson Jones, *Memoranda and Official Correspondence Relating to the Republic of Texas, Its History and Annexation* (New York: D. Appleton, 1859; New York: Arno Press, 1973), 398–9; Pletcher, *Diplomacy of Annexation,* 177; Remini, *Course of American Democracy,* 493–4; Llerena Friend, *Sam Houston: The Great Designer* (Austin: University of Texas Press, 1954), 78; and James L. Haley, *Sam Houston* (Norman: University of Oklahoma Press, 2002), 278–82, 286–8.

21. Pletcher, *Diplomacy of Annexation,* 163–4, 205.

dent denounced the United States' slow course regarding annexation. Once his government friends departed, however, Houston changed his tone. He inquired about Jackson's health, becoming emotional in the process. The chargé replied to this emotion by tying annexation to Houston's old friend. Donelson told the Texas president that Jackson saw the issue as the "great question of the day" and hoped that Houston would act, in response, with "wisdom and experience." Houston insisted his course would mutually benefit both countries; he only hoped to obtain favorable terms for Texas. Their conversation continued well into the night and convinced Donelson that Jackson's old ally was simply a tired politician who wanted to retire in an economically safe and viable territory, preferably in the new U.S. state of Texas.[22]

Donelson's initial conversation with Houston demonstrated why Tyler had appointed him as the U.S. chargé to Texas. The president wanted Donelson to use his uncle's name to pressure the Texas president into accepting the United States' terms. After initially failing to budge Houston from his position, Donelson must have realized that even that influence only went so far. To his credit, he did not let his disappointment dissuade him from working toward his goal. Still, there was only so much he could do without help from home. Facing opposition at the highest levels of the Texas government, Donelson advised Calhoun to urge Congress to adopt legislation proposing annexation and to send it to the Texas legislature before its adjournment date. Such a move would allow the Texas Congress time to pass comparable legislation and the Texas people the opportunity to vote their approval. If the United States neglected to move quickly, Donelson warned, then Great Britain and other countries might have the time to convince Houston and other influential Texas politicians that annexation was not in their best interest.[23]

Foreign agents were, in fact, already in place. William Kennedy, the British consul in Texas, was working to convince key Texas politicians, such as Sam Houston and Anson Jones, to listen to British overtures. He also tried to gain Britain better access to Texas markets, end the practice of slavery by introducing free labor, and encourage British immigration into Texas. Charles Elliot, British chargé to Texas, was an even more formidable

22. AJD to JCC, 24 November 1844, in Manning, *Diplomatic Correspondence* 12:375–8.

23. AJD to JCC, 23 November 1844, in ibid. 12:373–4.

adversary. Since his arrival in 1842, he had contrived to reach an agreement among Great Britain, Mexico, and Texas that would include Mexican recognition of Texas' independence; the republic's pledge to remain independent of other countries, especially the United States; and Britain's promise to assume the debts of slaveholders if they emancipated their slaves. Despite his efforts, Elliot's proposal, which he advocated until the United States finally annexed Texas, had thus far come to naught.[24]

Donelson recognized the danger inherent in such diplomatic activity. "Every day's delay is adding strength to the hands of those who are playing the game for the ascendency [*sic*] of British influence in this Republic," he reported to Calhoun. "Not that the people are averse to union with us, or are willing to obtain their independence by the sacrifice of any of the principles which are recognized as essential to the American idea of liberty. . . . [But] without forecast to unravel the real designs of Great Britain—without information to penetrate the motives," annexation's opponents might convince the citizens of Texas to delay indefinitely the two republics' union. Gaining Texas was "necessary not only to give us strength—but to save these brave and patriotic people from the hazards of more and doubtful struggles for liberty & independence." Donelson was certain that "the object dearest to their hearts is annexation . . . and support of it will overrule any combination that may be formed against it."[25]

Donelson's first public opportunity to argue his case for annexation came when Houston and President-elect Jones officially received him on 29 November 1844. In a speech given upon presenting his papers to the Texas government, Donelson highlighted the two countries' common bonds. The republic's struggle for independence, the chargé remarked, reminded him of that of the American colonists. "I cannot but look upon [the Texas people] as brothers, who in their struggle for liberty and independence, have proved that they are the worthy descendents [*sic*] of the heroes of Bunker Hill and Yorktown," Donelson said. Now, however, an opportunity had arisen to join these two great republics. They had been "given time for a more perfect development of those causes which are at work in their internal structure, as

24. Narrett, "Choice of Destiny," 286–91; and Pletcher, *Diplomacy of Annexation,* 82–4, 116–8.

25. AJD to JCC, 23 November 1844, in Manning, *Diplomatic Correspondence* 12:373–4; and AJD to John Tyler, 18 November 1844, in Wilson, Cook, and Moore, *PJCC* 20:317–20.

well as external relations," he declared, and now it was time "to harmonize their progress, if not to unite their destiny."[26]

Houston responded to Donelson's speech by asserting that the people of Texas had on several occasions attempted to unite with the citizens of the United States but with no success. "They have done all they could do," he pronounced, "and the failure which has occurred, is, I assure you, sir, attributable to no want, on their part of the most earnest disposition to see the desired union speedily and fully accomplished." Donelson's informal conversation and his formal speech had not changed Houston's mind.[27]

Houston's reprimand of his native land continued in his valedictory speech to the Texas people. The retiring president resolutely reiterated his belief that the United States and Texas should remain separate. Noting that the United States had "spurned" the republic on two different occasions, Houston urged Anson Jones's incoming government to "maintain her position firmly as it is, and work out her own salvation. Let her legislation proceed upon the supposition that we are to be and remain an independent people." If Texas became part of the United States, Houston warned, that would "only degrade" the republic's standing in the eyes of the world. He concluded that Texas should only unite with the United States if that nation "open[ed] the door" for it to enter. Until then, "we have our destiny in our own hands, and may become a nation distinguished for its wealth and power." Houston had issued the challenge; it was now up to the United States to respond. Donelson understood the fact clearly.[28]

Finding Houston unwilling to concede that annexation to the United States was favorable for both nations, Donelson next addressed the Texas Congress. He began by pledging U.S. support to the republic and promising to testify to his "countrymen that the 'lone star' which Texas has adopted as the emblem of her deliverance from oppression shines with a lustre as bright as their own stars." His uncle would agree with his sentiments, Donelson informed them, because he had convinced his nephew of the same. When Jackson had first publicly announced his pro-annexation views in February

26. AJD's speech to SH [29 November 1844], in Amelia W. Williams and Eugene C. Barker, eds., *The Writings of Sam Houston,* 8 vols. (Austin: University of Texas Press, 1938–43), 4:391–2.

27. SH's speech to AJD, [29 November 1844], in ibid. 4:389–91.

28. SH's valedictory speech, 9 December 1844, in ibid. 4:401–5.

1843, Donelson recalled, he had privately opposed them. "I was by his side when his letter to the Honorable A[aron] V[.] Brown was written," he remembered, "and was among those who doubted the propriety of mixing the great measure of annexation with the party issues then existing in my country." Jackson, however, had convinced him that annexation was crucial to keeping Texas out of foreign hands. "Delay will be opportunity to the monarchies of the old world to embarrass a young Republic palsied with war and oppressed with the burdens of debt and the measures necessary to gain organization to her Government," he had argued. "That Republic has a right to our sympathies."[29]

Jackson's ideological advocacy of annexation at that time and since had convinced Donelson of its necessity, he told the assembly. He emphasized that he, along with his fellow Americans, now understood the importance of acquiring Texas. "The people of the United States[,] after the most mature reflection[,] have decided that the importance of annexation was not overrated, as one of security not only to the lives of the United States, but to this whole continent, if it is destined to be, as we trust it is[,] the home of freedom and the asylum of the oppressed." Although the rest of Donelson's speech is lost, his position was clear. He initially opposed annexation because it threatened to cloud the focus of the Democratic party; however, Jackson had convinced him that the United States had no other recourse but to save the republic; to do otherwise would be dishonorable.[30]

As Donelson stood firm on annexation, President Tyler, who regarded Polk's election as a mandate from the American people, pressed Congress to acquire Texas. In his fourth annual message to Congress, he once again outlined the reasons for annexation. Mexico threatened war with Texas, endangering American interests, and the people had spoken by selecting the expansionist Polk as the next president. "Free and independent herself, she [Texas] asks to be received into our Union. It is a question for our own decision whether she shall be received or not," Tyler wrote. His message persuaded annexation supporters in Congress to take up a joint annexation resolution, which the Senate began deliberating on 9 December 1844.

29. AJD to Texas Congress, n.d. [late November or early December 1844], DLC.

30. Ibid.; AJD to ERD, 28 November 1844, DLC; and AJ to AJD, 2 December 1844, in Bassett and Jameson, *CAJ* 6:334–6.

Disagreement about the nature of the resolution quickly brought the Senate to an impasse. On the twelfth, the House of Representatives initiated its own annexation debates. The assumption of Texas citizens' debts, the role of slavery in the territory, and the dispute over the border between Texas and Mexico—all came to the forefront as issues for representatives to debate. There was also the question of whether a joint resolution was even constitutional. As in the Senate, there was no quick or easy solution.[31]

While Congress pondered its choices, Donelson left Washington-on-the-Brazos and headed for New Orleans. He had requested a leave to take care of "some private business." Donelson carried with him a list of five conditions that the Texas government wanted incorporated into an annexation treaty with the United States. First, the republic desired complete recognition as a U.S. territory. Next, the United States needed either to assume all of the republic's debts at the time of annexation or allow it to retain the land necessary to pay those debts. Third, Texas gave the United States permission to divide it up into several states, if necessary. Additionally, inhabitants on the borders of Texas and the United States should receive compensation if their land claims changed because of annexation. Lastly, the United States should redeem Texas' public bonds at face value. Donelson believed the list, proposed by Houston and officials in the Jones administration, provided opportunities for compromise.[32]

In his report to Calhoun, Donelson warned the secretary of state of the need for a speedy outcome. His concerns were realized when he encountered the British chargé to Texas, Charles Elliot, in New Orleans. Elliot had a new offer for the republic's consideration. The British overture pledged to maintain Texas independence and promised economic reciprocation if its government postponed negotiations with the United States. Donelson feared that although the Jones government had assured him of its commitment to continue negotiations with the United States, any delay endangered the prospects of favorable settlement with Texas.[33]

31. Fourth annual message, 3 December 1844, in Richardson, *Messages and Papers of the Presidents,* 4:340–5; Peterson, *Presidencies,* 251–2; Bergeron, *Presidency of JKP,* 54–5; Pletcher, *Diplomacy of Annexation,* 180–2; and Silbey, *Storm over Texas,* 2–3.

32. AJD to JCC, 24 December 1844, in Manning, *Diplomatic Correspondence* 12:389–91.

33. Ibid. 12:389–90.

Donelson had another reason to write Calhoun at this time. He informed the South Carolinian that he was going to approach his uncle about helping the two enemies mend their political differences. Jackson wanted nothing to do with the effort, and Donelson had to apologize to Calhoun for reopening a "[case] that cannot be settled by argument." Inexplicably, he blamed John Branch, one of the anti-Eaton cabinet members from Jackson's first administration, for even broaching the subject with his uncle, believing that "if I have done wrong he must be responsible."[34]

Donelson's oldest son, Jackson, later recalled that his father and great-uncle had been "alienated" from each other in 1845. The reopening of the Calhoun-Jackson feud may have precipitated that estrangement, which plagued the two men's relationship to the day Jackson died in his bed at the Hermitage. Regardless, it was simply a continuation of the complex bond that these two men shared, and Donelson's willingness to lay blame at the feet of an outsider, in this case a man who had been intimately involved in the Eaton dispute, is not surprising.[35]

Donelson was in New Orleans only a short time, leaving there in late December 1844 and returning to the Texas capital, where a letter from Calhoun awaited him. The secretary of state applauded the chargé's accomplishments: "The important points were to secure the confidence of the Government of Texas and to keep open the question of annexation, in both of which your efforts have been entirely successful." He also reported that the House of Representatives had taken up the annexation question and appeared ready to deal conclusively with the issue.[36]

But now a new problem arose. Tyler had appointed Duff Green, Calhoun's close friend and former editor of the *United States Telegraph*, as U.S. consul at Galveston in September 1844, a decision he quickly regretted. While Donelson was in New Orleans taking care of financial problems, Green meddled in U.S. relations with Mexico to the point of almost inciting a war between the two countries. He approached members of the Texas

34. AJD to JCC, 26 December 1844, in Wilson, Cook, and Moore, *PJCC* 20:627–9; and AJD to JCC, 24 March 1845, in Clyde N. Wilson, Shirley Bright Cook, and Alexander Moore, eds., *The Papers of John C. Calhoun*, vol. 21, *1845* (Columbia: University of South Carolina Press, 1993), 442–3.

35. Satterfield, "Moderate Nationalist Jacksonian," 320–4.

36. JCC to AJD, 9 January 1845, in Wilson, Cook, and Moore, *PJCC* 21:71–2.

government and proposed that the Texas Congress grant charters to various land companies that he planned to form. Part of the charter would include the right to raise an army, composed of U.S. soldiers and sixty thousand Native Americans, to defend Texas and conquer the Californias and parts of Mexico. When President Jones balked at the proposal, Green first attempted to bribe him, then threatened to start a revolution if Jones refused to go along with his scheme. The Texas president, supported by his cabinet, responded by revoking Green's credentials and, according to one report, threatening to "seize a pistol that lay on a table nearby and blow his brains out." Fortunately, instead of resorting to violence, Jones appealed to Donelson for help.[37]

Although suffering from an influenza attack that left him convalescent and close to death, Donelson was not about to let Green muck up all of his hard work. He contacted the troublesome consul and demanded that he make a public apology to the Jones administration. Green explained away the entire episode as a misunderstanding, claiming that Jones had misunderstood him, and argued that he, not the president, was "the injured party." Donelson assured Jones and an agitated Ebenezer Allen, acting secretary of state for Texas, that Green, who had resigned his consular position and stated his intention to become a Texas citizen, had acted as an individual and not as a U.S. agent. The French chargé, Alphonse de Saligny, found Donelson's explanation "badly devised" and thought "they could have trumped up something better" to rationalize Green's blackmail. British chargé Elliot warned Jones that Green had "some official mission *behind* Major Donelson's chair." Unaware of this foreign criticism, and despite it, Donelson finally prevailed upon Green to admit reluctantly, but publicly, his culpability in the crisis.

37. Duff Green to JCC, 27, 30 September, 7, 9 October 1844, in Manning, *Diplomatic Correspondence* 12:368–9, 369, 369–70, 370–1; Dubois de Saligny to François Guizot, 8 January 1845, in Nancy N. Barker, ed., *The French Legation in Texas,* 2 vols. (Austin, Tex.: State Historical Association, 1971–3), 2:605–8; AJD to Anson Jones, 6 December 1844, Ebenezer Allen to AJD, 6 January 1845, AJD to Ebenezer Allen, 6 January 1845, in George P. Garrison, ed., *Diplomatic Correspondence of the Republic of Texas,* in *Annual Report of the American Historical Association for the Years of 1907 and 1908,* 2 vols. (Washington: GPO, 1908, 1911), 2:325–6, 332–4, 335–7; Duff Green to JCC, 8 December 1844, in Wilson, Cook, and Moore, *PJCC* 20:505–7; Ebenezer Allen to AJD, 4 January 1844 [1845], in Wilson, Cook, and Moore, *PJCC* 21:73–5; Ebenezer Allen et al. to Anson Jones, 30 December 1844, in Jones, *Memoranda,* 412–3; Woodard, "Sectionalism, Politics, and Foreign Policy," 161–7; Peterson, *Presidencies,* 246–54; and Glenn W. Price, *Origins of the War with Mexico: The Polk-Stockton Intrigue* (Austin: University of Texas Press, 1967), 38–44.

By leaving his post, even with permission, Donelson had potentially allowed a misguided troublemaker to undermine his annexation efforts.[38]

Fortunately, the tension between Texas and the United States eased, and there were no lingering consequences for Donelson. Satisfied with his success so far and believing that the annexation process would not move forward until Polk took office, in January 1845, Donelson again requested and received a leave of absence. He originally planned to meet Elizabeth in New Orleans, but when he found that she was still in Tennessee, he started home. Donelson wanted to see his family, and his personal affairs still need tending, as his previous leave had produced no relief. Rumors were also circulating that Polk wanted to offer him an alternate government position, possibly even a cabinet post. Finally, and perhaps most important, Donelson had received news that General Jackson's "life hangs on a thread." This might be his last chance to visit Uncle.[39]

38. AJD to [Ebenezer Allen], 20 January 1845, Duff Green to AJD, 20 January 1845, Rob[er]t H. Williams, A. S. Thruston, and Jos[eph] C. Meggerson to Duff Green, 1 January 1845, Ebenezer Allen to AJD, 21 January 1845, in Garrison, *Diplomatic Correspondence* 2:346–7, 347–8, 348–9, 350–1; Anson Jones's proclamation, [31 December 1844], AJD to JCC, 9, 27 January 1845, Duff Green to JCC, 21 January 1845, E[lisha] A. Rhodes to JCC, 22 January 1845, AJD to Elisha A. Rhodes, 16 January 1845, Duff Green to AJD, 20 January 1845, AJD to JCC, 25 January 1845, in Wilson, Cook, and Moore, *PJCC* 21:75, 72–3, 211–4, 168, 179, 199–200, 198–9; Duff Green to [AJD], n.d. [January 1845], DLC; Alphonse de Saligny to François Guizot, 20, 26 January, 1 February 1845, in Barker, *French Legation* 2:612–3, 614–5, 616–8; Charles Elliot to Anson Jones, 14 January 1845, AJD to Anson Jones, 23 January 1845, in Jones, *Memoranda,* 413–4, 418; Woodard, "Sectionalism, Politics, and Foreign Policy," 167–8; Peterson, *Presidencies,* 249; and Price, *Origins of the War,* 45–8.

39. AJ to ERD, 16 January 1845, AJD to H. McLeod, 21 January 1845, in Sioussat, "Selected Letters, 1844–1845," 149, 149–50; and AJD to JCC, 27, 30 January 1845 in Wilson, Cook, and Moore, *PJCC* 21: 211–4, 232–3.

13

"His Soul Is the Very Seat of Honor"

Donelson was clearly worried as he headed for Tulip Grove in late January 1845. His past debts, plus the declining profitability of his plantations' crops, had placed him in difficult financial straits. His brother, Daniel, and brother-in-law, William Donelson, had been unable to avoid losing an unpaid three-thousand-dollar debt claim against him and could not keep creditors from two other debts. An additional problem was Donelson's overseer in Mississippi, "a great scamp" who had created another two thousand dollars in debt. Jackson also warned his nephew that Van Buren was pressing for payment on his loan and suggested selling the Mississippi plantation as a way to pay off his debts. Donelson rejected his uncle's proposition, still hoping to turn the plantation into a profit maker. Jackson's situation was not much better. "Poverty stares us in the face," he lamented. The combined cotton production from the Hermitage and Tulip Grove plantations for the year totaled thirty-seven thousand pounds, but the market price was only yielding four cents a pound. After paying their overseer's salary and liens against their cotton, Jackson reported that he, Andrew Jr., and Donelson had only thirty-six dollars remaining. Jackson's own financial problems meant he would once again be unable to help his nephew pay Van Buren or any other creditor.[1]

Donelson instead had to look to Polk for help. Both his wife and his uncle had written him in December 1844 that the president-elect was considering Donelson for a cabinet post. Elizabeth Donelson described Polk's victorious reception in Tennessee and related a rumor that Polk was going to appoint her husband his secretary of war. "I do not know that a place in

1. AJ to ERD, 16 January 1845, AJ to AJD, 10 [16?] February 1845, in Sioussat, "Selected Letters, 1844–1845," 149, 151–2; AJ to AJD, [16 February 1845?], in Bassett and Jameson, *CAJ* 6:367–8; ERD to AJD, 1, 17 January, 3 February 1845, JDC; and Satterfield, "Moderate Nationalist Jacksonian," 278.

the cabinet will be offered," she cautioned, "but if it is, accept it, as it will suit us better than a foreign mission." Living in Washington, she reminded Donelson, would allow them to be together, as well as give them "the opportunity of placing our children at the best schools." Jackson, meanwhile, assured his nephew that Polk possessed "the utlmost [*sic*] friendship for you, and your interest and wishes will be carried into effect as far as can be with propriety. I find that he would like to have you near him; But he will have some dificulty [*sic*] in arrangeing his cabinet." The most important thing, Polk had told Jackson during their discussion, was for him to have a united cabinet, one with "no aspirant to the presidency in it."[2]

Donelson had not only Jackson's cautious endorsement and Polk's seeming approval but also the support of Democrats from across the nation, which he hoped would prove helpful. Newspaperman Francis P. Blair and Donelson's Mississippi associate, William M. Gwin, urged him to take the cabinet position if offered. His old comrade, Nicholas P. Trist, believed that, if elected, Polk could do no better than to appoint Donelson secretary of war or as head of another department. His selection would give the president a close and "confidential" friend and provide "an additional link and bond of affinity between the administration of the 'Old Hickory' and that of the 'Young Hickory.'" Even Donelson's former enemy, William B. Lewis, thought that his appointment would benefit the Polk administration and the Democratic party. Other Democrats wrote Polk directly to campaign for Donelson. Memucan Hunt, an important Texas government official, wanted the president-elect to appoint Donelson secretary of war because his relationship with Jackson would please Texas citizens. Vice-president-elect George M. Dallas believed him an "admirable" choice for the post, although he admitted that he saw "nothing to justify a preference" for Donelson on a list that included Robert Armstrong; William Allen, a Democratic senator from Ohio; and William O. Butler, a former Democratic representative from Kentucky.[3]

2. ERD to AJD, 1 December 1844, JDC; and AJ to AJD, 2 December 1844, in Bassett and Jameson, *CAJ* 6:334–6.

3. AJ to AJD, [February 1845?], WBL to AJ, 1 January 1845, FPB to AJ, 3 January 1845, in Bassett and Jameson, *CAJ* 6:367–8, 352–3, 354–7; William M. Gwin to AJD, 12 December 1844, Barry S. Patton to AJD, 13 December 1844, Barry S. Patton to AJ, 13 December 1844, DLC; and Memucan Hunt to JKP, 1 January 1845 (summary), George M. Dallas to JKP, 10 January 1845, in Wayne Cutler and Robert G. Hall II, eds., *Correspondence of James K. Polk,* vol. 9, *January-June 1845* (Knoxville: University of Tennessee Press, 1996), 7–8, 34–7.

It was Martin Van Buren, however, who wrote the most flattering recommendation for Donelson. The New Yorker informed Polk that he would have appointed Donelson to a seat in his own cabinet, but for Donelson's "modesty, and an apprehension on his own part that he would [be] regarded by the people of Tennessee as having been prematurely advanced out of favor to the Genl." Van Buren thought that those criticisms had dissipated by this time. He praised Donelson profusely:

> There is not a man in the Country who could render you such varied, & useful service. His talents are of the very highest order, his soul is the seat of honor, & he is by far too sagacious to be humbugged by the rouges, whatever may [be] their calibre. It has not fallen to the lot of many to have better opportunities to become well acquainted with the real character[,] capacities and disposition of the public men of the Country. He is always composed & firm, writes for all practical & useful purposes as well as any man I know & could make himself useful to you in a thousand ways[.]

No doubt, Van Buren saw that having an ally in Polk's cabinet would help his interests in the 1848 election, and he probably wanted Donelson to find a permanent post so he could repay his lingering debt.[4]

Unconvinced by these recommendations, Polk decided against giving Donelson the cabinet appointment. One can only speculate as to why. Perhaps Polk thought that if he placed the General's nephew in his cabinet, the Whigs would charge the former president with dictation and Polk with acquiescing to his influence. Polk also undoubtedly wanted a fresh start, free from Tyler's own cabinet members and Jackson's public influence, but not his private advice. There was also the question of Donelson's qualifications. Except for his West Point education and a short stint with Jackson in Florida over two decades earlier, he had not been involved with the military in any capacity, and his political experience was unimpressive compared to other potential candidates. Donelson's irresponsible absences must have influenced Polk's decision as well. Jackson's nephew was a hard worker when

4. MVB to JKP, 11 February 1845, in Cutler and Hall, *CJKP* 9:99–100.

he was at a task, but who knew when he would decide to take off on his ever-pressing "personal business"? He had done so twice with Polk in 1844. The risk was just too great to take with the important War Department, so Polk selected William L. Marcy of New York, a War of 1812 veteran, former state judge, and governor, for the post.[5]

Upon learning of Polk's misgivings about Donelson, Jackson reconsidered his nephew's financial situation. He was in serious need of a position that would prove financially profitable; heading an executive department, Jackson decided, did not fit that condition. At the same time, Donelson needed some prestigious station that would keep his name before the public. After an exchange of letters with the president-elect, Jackson informed his nephew that, when Polk took office, he would make him a "full minister to some foreign court." Donelson must not be disappointed; a foreign ministry would provide him with a regular salary and the prominence needed to advance politically.[6]

Donelson was confused. Every indication had led him to think that Polk wanted him in his cabinet; now, the president-elect had changed his mind. He first received the news when he reached New Orleans in January 1845 and found a letter from Jackson informing him of the change in plans. Once Donelson made it to Tulip Grove and had time to see his uncle at the Hermitage, he wrote Polk: "It appears that without any knowledge or agency of mine some of my friends had suggested my name for the War office, and the Genl informs me [that] your kind feelings disposed you to comply with their suggestion." After having a "full conversation" with Jackson, Donelson wrote Polk affirming the decision. "I have no political aspirations, and certainly none that could lead me to consider the high office referred to as not demanding talents and experience greatly above mine," he demurred. "My only ambition is to repair now, by a life of economy, the mistakes of early years, and lay up, if possible, something for the education of my children, and the support of old age," he confided. "This consideration and duty

5. Sellers, *Continentalist,* 272; and "William Learned Marcy," in *Biographical Directory of the United States Congress.* Donelson may also have been a victim of the developing rivalry between the Polk–Van Buren factions of the Democratic party. See Silbey, *Storm over Texas,* 96–111.

6. AJ to JKP, 10 January 1845, in Cutler and Hall, *CJKP* 9:37–9; AJ to WBL, 4 February 1845, in Sioussat, "Selected Letters, 1844–1845," 150–1; and AJ to AJD, [16 February 1845?], in Bassett and Jameson, *CAJ* 6:367–8.

would induce me to accept public employment where it might aid this object, but not at the hazard of postponing the claims of others whose weight of character or greater efficiency would be a surer guarantee for the advancement of the public interest." Jackson wrote Polk the same day, confirming Donelson's agreement with the decision and asking the president-elect to remember to provide his nephew with a foreign post. "The Major appears satisfied," he concluded.[7]

Actually, Donelson had every reason to be dissatisfied. His answer to Polk was disingenuous, claiming that he had "no political ambitions." Of course he did; why else did he and Jackson continue to discuss the possibilities for his political career? Donelson must also have recognized that neither his uncle nor the president-elect had much faith in his abilities, which must have rankled him. He kept those feelings to himself, however, and when he finally responded to Polk, he simply parroted Jackson's arguments for why he should decline the position: his poor health, his financial instability, and the inevitable Whig charges of dictation. Once again, Donelson was not willing to challenge his uncle over a political matter.

With no chance at a cabinet position, Donelson turned his attention back to annexation, as events in Congress were pushing the process forward. During Donelson's vacation, members of the outgoing Tyler and the incoming Polk administrations had been working together to find a compromise. After some argument over the details, on 25 January 1845, the House of Representatives adopted a version of the proposed joint resolution that would make Texas a state (with the United States retaining the right to divide it into several states), allow Texas residents to decide whether slavery would be included in the state's constitution, and promise to settle Texas' boundaries at a later date. The vote of 120 to 98 in favor of this resolution indicated an uneasy acceptance of its provisions.[8]

In the Senate, Thomas Hart Benton had for the past year been working to undermine support for annexation. He believed that such a course of action would only exacerbate tensions between Mexico and the United States

7. AJD to JKP, 1, 15 February 1845, AJ to JKP, 15 February 1845, in Cutler and Hall, *CJKP* 9:80, 103–4, 104–5.

8. Peterson, *Presidencies,* 255–7; Pletcher, *Diplomacy of Annexation,* 180–1; Silbey, *Storm over Texas,* 3; AJD to JCC, 26 December 1844, in Wilson, Cook, and Moore, *PJCC* 20:628–9; and AJD to AJ, 24, 28 December 1844, in Bassett and Jameson, *CAJ* 6:348–9, 349–50.

and between proslavery and antislavery forces. On 5 February, however, he suddenly changed his mind. Under pressure from Donelson, Jackson, Blair, and Polk, and perhaps having more faith in Polk than in Tyler, Benton revised his earlier anti-annexationist stance and introduced a version of the joint resolution that asked simply for the formation of a state "out of the present Republic of Texas . . . as soon as the terms and conditions of such admission, and the cession of the remaining Texan territory to the United States," could be reached by both governments.[9]

Benton's softening on annexation seemed to be the break that pro-annexation congressmen needed. In late February, with Polk in town awaiting his inauguration, Senator Robert J. Walker of Mississippi introduced a compromise resolution giving the president the flexibility of choosing annexation under the authority of either the House bill or Benton's Senate resolution. The measure passed the Senate by a 27 to 25 vote on February 27. The next day, the House approved the compromise by a 132 to 75 count. Looking to salvage his administration's reputation, Tyler signed the resolution, indicating that the inclusion of Texas into the Union only awaited the Lone Star Republic's approval.[10]

News of the joint resolution reached Nashville in early March 1845, the report undoubtedly surprising the vacationing chargé. To him, it had seemed more likely that Polk's administration, not Tyler's, would bring about annexation. Calhoun, however, had spurred Tyler's swift action with a warning that the British were acting vigorously to derail the process within the Texas government. Now that the U.S. Congress and president had acted, it fell to Donelson to convince the Texas government to accept the measure. He felt unsure because its leaders had been ambiguous about their intentions, but he held resolutely to the belief that the republic's citizens would press for the annexation resolution's acceptance.[11]

9. Pletcher, *Diplomacy of Annexation,* 180–1; AJD to AJ, 28 December 1844, in Bassett and Jameson, *CAJ* 6:349–50; Thomas H. Benton to AJD, 10 January 1845, in Sioussat, "Selected Letters, 1844–1845," 148–9; Elbert B. Smith, *Magnificent Missourian: The Life of Thomas Hart Benton* (Philadelphia: J. B. Lippincott, 1958), 194–203; Peterson, *Presidencies,* 255–7; and Silbey, *Storm over Texas,* 80–8.

10. Peterson, *Presidencies,* 256–7; Bergeron, *Presidency of JKP,* 54–5; Pletcher, *Diplomacy of Annexation,* 181–2; and Silbey, *Storm over Texas,* 3–5, 80–8.

11. Middleton, "Donelson's Mission," 265–6; and AJD to JKP, 18 March 1845, in Bassett and Jameson, *CAJ* 6:383–5.

On 8 March, Donelson set out for New Orleans at a leisurely pace. He intended to check on his Mississippi plantation along the way, but heavy rain and flooding made the roads impassable. His health was also still a concern. "I am not in a situation to swim creeks, or stand much exposure to the weather," he wrote his wife from Florence, Alabama. "Be not uneasy about my health. My last lesson will not soon be forgotten." Only after it appeared that he would be unable to visit his plantation did Donelson's pace toward Texas quicken. Donelson had another matter to ponder on his way to New Orleans. As he was leaving Tulip Grove, he had received a letter from Pennsylvania Democrat Simon Cameron, who said that Polk wanted him to become editor of a new administration newspaper in Washington. Unsure about the offer's legitimacy and worried about its effect on the Democratic party, Donelson asked Jackson for his opinion on what he should do. He continued on to his destination, hoping that, this time, his uncle would be supportive.[12]

By the time Donelson reached New Orleans on 17 March, a despatch from Calhoun awaited him, followed two days later by a letter from Polk. The now-departed secretary of state told the chargé to inform the Texas government that the joint resolution was the best that they could expect. Donelson was also to urge the Texas government to adopt the resolution without amendment; if its members insisted on changes, they should submit legitimate reasons. It was imperative, the despatch concluded, that Donelson set out immediately and "urge speedy and prompt action on the subject. . . . Your presence, intelligence, activity and influence are confidently relied upon to counteract" the British manipulation that almost assuredly would follow news of the annexation resolution.[13]

Polk's letter, on the other hand, ordered Donelson to wait until James Buchanan, the new secretary of state, sent him modified instructions. These reached Donelson on 24 March in the hands of Arkansas congressman Archibald Yell, a staunch Polk supporter. Buchanan directed the chargé, in orders similar to those of Calhoun, to convince Jones and the Texas Congress to accept immediate annexation and work out any differences after the fact, trusting in the United States' integrity. Otherwise, annexation

12. AJD to AJ, 9 March 1845, and AJD to ERD, 10 March 1845, DLC.

13. JCC to AJD, 3 March 1845, joint resolution annexing Texas to the United States, [1 March 1845], in Wilson, Cook, and Moore, *PJCC* 21:398–400, 400–2.

opponents would use the delay to their advantage. Polk "confidently expects that you will exert your well known ability and energy to secure this auspicious result by every honorable means within your power," Buchanan told Donelson.[14]

Jackson, meanwhile, was corresponding with Polk about the proposed newspaper position for Donelson. Polk's letters helped Jackson understand better what the administration was asking of his nephew. Polk did not want Donelson to start a new newspaper, as mutual friends had reported; instead, he wanted him to take over Francis P. Blair's editorship of the *Washington Globe.* "The Globe[,] it is manifest[,] does not look to the success or the glory of my administration so much as it does to the interests, and views of some prominent men of the party [Van Buren and Benton], who are looking to succeed me in 1848," Polk told Jackson. He believed that if Donelson assumed the *Globe* editorship, "all the sections of the party would be at once reconciled and satisfied." Donelson would also discover, said Polk, that he could make money at the position, which he knew was a major concern for Jackson's nephew.[15]

Without waiting for Jackson's opinion, Donelson had determined to write Polk himself. He had decided to reject the offer for several reasons. Firing Blair would only weaken the party, he said, and, besides, "I have too much distrust of my abilities to undertake a task of such responsibility, requiring a discipline and tact so foreign to my past pursuits." His "chief solicitude" now, Donelson told Polk, was "to repair the losses to which I have been subjected by a long connection with politics. In this respect my position has been unfortunate, borne along as you have been aware by circumstances from which I could not separate without apparent harshness to the Genl [Jackson]." Without even waiting to hear Jackson's reasons for rejecting the offer, Donelson had determined that he could not do the job. Surprisingly, even Polk's promises of financial salvation had not convinced him to accept the editorship.[16]

14. JKP to JCC, 6 March 1845, JKP to AJD, 7 March 1845, in Cutler and Hall, *CJKP* 9:176, 180; and JB to AJD, 10 March 1845, in Manning, *Diplomatic Correspondence* 12:85–8.

15. JKP to AJ, 17 March 1845, in Cutler and Hall, *CJKP* 9:197–9; Sellers, *Continentalist,* 274–8; and Elbert B. Smith, *Francis Preston Blair* (New York: Free Press, 1980), 163–7.

16. AJD to JKP, 18 March 1845, in Cutler and Hall, *CJKP* 9:205–7.

Still in New Orleans, Donelson wrote Polk what he had learned there about the current political atmosphere in Texas. When the annexation news reached Galveston, Yell had reported that several Texas newspapers "came out furious and intemperate against it." The administration's newspaper, the *Washington (Tex.) National Register,* also adamantly opposed the annexation resolution. Donelson, however, believed that even if the newspapers accurately reflected the Jones administration's viewpoint, "I cannot doubt that of the people of Texas. They anxiously desire annexation, and I feel no doubt of the result whenever the question is submitted to them." He was confident that the people of Texas would not fail him or the annexation process.[17]

Donelson left New Orleans for Texas on the afternoon of 24 March 1845 aboard the steamboat *Marmora.* In Galveston and Houston, he received disturbing information. Surprised by news of the annexation resolution, the British and French diplomats were increasing their pressure on the Jones administration. Fearing that they might be losing control of the situation, Elliot and Alphonse de Saligny, the French chargé, hurriedly left Galveston for the Texas capital on 25 March, mere hours after Donelson had started for the city. There, the two foreign envoys met with Jones and the new secretary of state, Ashbel Smith, and presented them with the probability of Mexico recognizing the Texas republic's independence if it rejected U.S. annexation. President Jones agreed to open negotiations and instructed Smith to prepare to visit England, where he would work with British officials toward a peaceful settlement with Mexico.[18]

Oblivious to their strategy, Donelson set off for the Texas capital. As he neared Washington-on-the-Brazos, he crossed paths with Elliot and de Saligny as they were leaving the town and asked the two men when the Texas Congress would convene. Learning that there were no immediate plans to meet, the American chargé rode into the city, Elliot's and de Saligny's

17. AJD to JKP, 18, 19 March 1845, Archibald Yell to JKP, 23 March [18]45, in Cutler and Hall, *CJKP* 9:205–7, 207–8, 227–9; and AJD to JB, 1, 3 April 1845, in Manning, *Diplomatic Correspondence* 12:397–9, 399–400.

18. AJD to JB, 1, 3 April 1845, in Manning, *Diplomatic Correspondence* 12:397–9, 399–400; Archibald Yell to JKP, 26 March 1845, in Cutler and Hall, *CJKP* 9:236–8; Ephraim D. Adams, *British Interests and Activities in Texas, 1838–1846* (Gloucester, Mass.: P. Smith, 1963), 197–211; Middleton, "Donelson's Mission," 266–70; Alphonse de Saligny to François Guizot, 18, 24 March, 1 April 1845, in Barker, *French Legation* 2:636–7, 637–8, 638–48; and Friend, *SH,* 150–1.

suspicious behavior failing to alert him to their conspiracy. Once in Washington-on-the-Brazos, he discovered only evasive answers to his questions. He was finally able to gain an audience with President Jones, who explained that Secretary of State Smith was taking a leave of absence and Attorney General Ebenezer Allen was now serving in his place as the Texas government's prime negotiator. When Allen stated that he, too, was taking a leave of absence, Donelson observed that he had "an apprehension that there existed some settled scheme of delay, or of manoeuvre, to promote the imputed project of a Treaty with France and England." Jones, however, assured Donelson that his suspicions were unfounded.[19]

After further discussion with Jones and Allen, the chargé proclaimed himself perplexed and decided to ascertain from Sam Houston what was afoot. Reports had reached him that the former Texas president, who still wielded considerable influence, now wanted the Texas government to delay immediate annexation in favor of further negotiations. If these rumors were true, Donelson told Buchanan, it was "unfortunate," but he did not think that even Houston's opposition could defeat the measure now. The former president was in Montgomery, Texas, however, noticeably avoiding an encounter with the U.S. diplomat. Blaming floods, bad road conditions, and family business for his absence, Houston wanted to avoid Washington until Jones had made a decision regarding annexation. His evasiveness presented a large obstacle, since it was upon him that Donelson "mainly rel[ied] to bring the question to the earliest practicable settlement." Yell had warned Polk earlier that "Houston is looked upon as occupying a doubtful position," but Donelson had brought with him a letter from Jackson to Houston that "he thinkes [*sic*] will settle that matter." While not meeting with Donelson personally, in a series of letters written between 3 and 9 April, the Texan outlined his objections to several sections of the annexation offer. Houston recommended that a commission made up of negotiators from both countries settle the issue, rather than having one country then another decree the conditions under which they would agree to annexation. He argued that he supported annexation if it occurred on "terms mutually beneficial to both countries," but he did not like the fact that "the *terms are dictated,* and the

19. Alphonse de Saligny to François Guizot, 1 April 1845, in Barker, *French Legation* 2:638–48; and AJD to JB, 1 April 1845, in Manning, *Diplomatic Correspondence* 12:397–9.

conditions absolute," which displayed a lack of respect on the part of the United States.[20]

After receiving Houston's reply, Donelson set out to visit him in Montgomery. He hoped that a personal meeting would convince the Texan to support annexation publicly. Donelson was wrong; the meeting did not go well. Houston maintained his position, leaving the chargé with the impression as he left that "if the adoption of our proposals depended upon his vote, it would be lost." Houston's position perturbed Donelson. He later complained that Houston, who "has not given the question the support I expected," had always encouraged annexation, but only on increasingly better terms for Texas. The former Texas executive did not realize that the British agitation for abolition in his republic "might put it out of the power of the Democratic party to pass a better bill for Texas at the next session of Congress." The opportunity for annexation was now, Donelson exclaimed. If Houston and other Texas politicians failed to take advantage of the proffered terms, no matter how unsatisfactory they appeared to some, there might not come another occasion.[21]

Whereas Donelson's dealings with Houston caused him disappointment, his interview with Jones on 12 April 1845 bolstered his hopes. The Texas president told the American chargé that the American proposal did not provide enough benefits to Texas; however, he believed that duty compelled him to convene Congress and call a convention that would allow the Texas citizens to decide their country's fate. Jones hoped that the legislative session would continue long enough for Elliot to return with an alternative plan, but he realized that public opinion in Texas sided strongly with U.S. annexation. Donelson realized the importance of public opinion and encouraged it where he could. Out of propriety, he declined invitations to attend the

20. AJ to AJD, 12 March 1845, SH to AJD, 3, 6 April 1845, in Sioussat, "Selected Letters, 1844–1845," 153–4, 154–5, 155–6; AJD to JKP, 18 March 1845, Archibald Yell to JKP, 26 March 1845, in Cutler and Hall, *CJKP* 9:205–7, 236–8; AJD to JB, 1, 3, 12 April 1845, in Manning, *Diplomatic Correspondence* 12:397–9, 399–400, 400–2; AJD to ERD, 2 April 1845, DLC; SH to AJD, 9 April 1845, in Williams and Barker, *Writings of SH* 4:410–7; AJD to JCC, 24 April 1845, in Wilson, Cook, and Moore, *PJCC* 21:504–6; Pletcher, *Diplomacy of Annexation,* 196; and Sellers, *Continentalist,* 222–3.

21. AJD to JB, 12 April 1845, in Manning, *Diplomatic Correspondence* 12:400–2; SH to AJD, 9 April 1845, in Williams and Barker, *Writings of SH* 4:410–7; AJD to JCC, 24 April 1845, in Wilson, Cook, and Moore, *PJCC* 21:504–6; AJD to ERD, 4, 16 April 1845, DLC; and [AJD] to Thomas Ritchie, 28 May 1845, in Sioussat, "Selected Letters, 1844–1845," 157–8.

many pro-annexation meetings, but he cheerfully received and answered letters from interested Texans. The chargé always tried to present himself as a diplomat observing but not influencing public opinion. Those with whom he communicated knew differently. Donelson was working hard to make sure that all Texans recognized annexation as the only beneficial course they could take.[22]

With the Texas Congress scheduled to meet in mid-June, the people's convention set for early July, and the Texas people approvingly discussing annexation, Donelson took the opportunity to go to Galveston in early May 1845, where he met with a consortium of American agents sent there by President Polk. Yell, who had accompanied the U.S. chargé on his return trip from New Orleans in March 1845, had been in the city for several weeks. Another agent, Charles A. Wickliffe, postmaster general in Tyler's cabinet, "took a very active part in negotiating the Treaty, last year," Polk noted, and "has my confidence." The third individual, U.S. Navy commodore Robert F. Stockton, was "rabidly expansionist," according to Polk's major biographer. Their official mission consisted of convincing prominent Texas politicians to accept annexation, although Donelson also asked them to ascertain the likelihood of a threatened Mexican invasion.[23]

This Mexican menace especially concerned President Jones and the Texas government. They asked Donelson what his government would do to protect them in the time between annexation and Texas' actual inclusion into the United States. Aware of the danger himself, Donelson recommended that Jones ask Polk to place American troops along the Mexican border. Not waiting on Jones to act, however, Donelson advised Buchanan to ready the troops in the Arkansas territory and along the Red River. "If war be declared against us," he observed, "Texas will be its theatre, and the earlier we are in possession of the commanding points on the Rio Grande,

22. AJD to JB, 12, 16, 29 April, 6 May 1845, in Manning, *Diplomatic Correspondence* 12:401–2, 405, 405–7, 408–9; Pletcher, *Diplomacy of Annexation,* 194–5; Annie Middleton, "The Texas Convention of 1845," *Southwestern Historical Quarterly* 25 (1921–22): 26–62; idem, "Donelson's Mission," 271–3, 277–84; and AJD to ERD, 2, 4 April 1845, Hugh McLeod to [Archibald Yell], 9 April 1845, A. W. Canfield to AJD, 12 April 1845, DLC.

23. JB to Charles A. Wickliffe, 27 March 1845, AJD to JB, 29 April 1845, in Manning, *Diplomatic Correspondence* 12:88–90, 405–7; JKP to AJD, 28 March 1845, in Cutler and Hall, *CJKP* 9:240–3; Sellers, *Continentalist,* 221–3; and Bergeron, *Presidency of JKP,* 57–9.

the sooner we shall be able to bring it to a close." Donelson assured Buchanan that he would "be prepared to give immediate notice with such suggestions in regard to the route and positions of our force" once the Texas Congress met and approved annexation. With Donelson's advice fresh on his mind, Buchanan was prepared for Allen's official request on 19 May 1845 for military protection. A few days later, Buchanan informed Donelson that he would "consider it to be both his right and his duty to employ the army" whenever Texas agreed to immediate annexation. Polk had already taken the precaution of locating part of the navy near Veracruz and in the Gulf of Mexico and had positioned three thousand troops on the U.S.-Texas border "to act without a moment's delay." Allen and the Texas government could rest easy.[24]

While Donelson was overseeing defense preparations, Yell wrote Polk that everything was proceeding as expected. "Nothing but a Providential interfearence can prevent Annexation," he predicted. Yell had just seen Houston, on his way to the Hermitage to visit Jackson, and found him willing to acquiesce to annexation, if not actively support it. Donelson deserved all of the credit for this conversion, Yell believed. "Every thing [*sic*] that was necessary to consumate [*sic*] the object so much desired has been done by our worthy and talented Charge D'Affaires. No other man in the Union could have affected so much," he observed. "His peculiar relation to the Old Hero of the Hermitage as well as the Hero of *San Jacinto,* and his acquaintance with the members of Congress of Texas, as well as the temperement [*sic*] of the people and the various cliques and factions, give him the power to do more than any other man could have done."[25]

Unaware of these compliments, Donelson nevertheless agreed with Yell's assessment of Texas' political atmosphere. So confident was Donelson of success that he requested permission for a leave of absence to commence shortly after the 16 June meeting of Congress. He was actually already in Louisiana, visiting his old friend, Edward G. W. Butler, in Iberville and

24. AJD to JB, 11 May 1845, Ebenezer Allen to AJD, 19 May 1845, in Manning, *Diplomatic Correspondence* 12:409–10, 410–1; JB to AJD, 23 May 1845, in John Bassett Moore, ed., *The Works of James Buchanan,* 8 vols. (Philadelphia: J. B. Lippincott, 1909), 6:159–60; JKP to AJ, 27 April 1845, AJD to JKP, 11 May 1845, in Cutler and Hall, *CJKP* 9:320–2, 365–6; and AJD to ERD, 2 April 1845, DLC.

25. Archibald Yell to JKP, 5 May 1845, in Cutler and Hall, *CJKP* 9:346–7.

hoping to make a trip to his Mississippi plantation. He feared leaving the New Orleans area should any annexation matter demand his attention, however. Donelson also wanted to travel to Nashville to see the gravely ill Jackson and his own family and to take care of his never-ending financial problems. "I feel that the little public good I can do is but a poor excuse" for not visiting Tulip Grove, he wrote.[26]

Indeed, Donelson inexplicably chose the most important moment of the negotiations to abandon his post. It was not his supreme faith in popular support for ratification that induced him to leave but a personal dilemma. The *Globe* situation had finally been resolved. Throughout April, Polk had urged Donelson to reconsider his rejection of the editorship. The incoming administration and the Democratic party needed him to take the position, the president argued. Donelson would not have to invest any of his own money, and Polk assured him that he and his prospective coeditor, Thomas Ritchie of Virginia, would receive the congressional printing. "You would make a fine fortune in a very short time and that without any risk except your time," he wrote the chargé. Polk also continued to press Jackson for his help in convincing Donelson to accept the *Globe* editorship. Donelson persisted in rebuffing Polk's entreaties, but he also began to show signs of warming to the idea. While in New Orleans on 11 May, he repeated his reasons for rejecting the offer, highlighting his own inexperience. "Am I fitted for such an association—would it be right for one so unused as I am to an exercise of this kind to share its responsibility and reward with him [Ritchie] who will bring into the field so much more experience and wisdom?" he asked demurely. Donelson requested that Polk consider postponing the decision until July, when he expected to return from his Texas mission. That would enable him time to "consult with Genl Jackson" and Elizabeth about what course he should take.[27]

Polk was not willing to wait. While Donelson vacillated, Jackson supported Blair throughout the dispute and tried to convince the president to change his mind. As for Donelson replacing Blair, Tennessee friends reported that Jackson did not want his nephew involved in the affair. When Blair re-

26. AJD to JKP, 11, 14 May 1845, in ibid. 9:366–7, 372–3; and AJD to ERD, 24 May 1845, DLC.

27. JKP to AJ, 26 March 1845, JKP to AJD, 28 March 1845, AJD to JKP, 11 May 1845, in Cutler and Hall, *CJKP* 9:233–5, 240–3, 366–7.

luctantly agreed to withdraw from the newspaper, Jackson still thought it a mistake, but he grudgingly agreed to sanction the *Globe*'s sale to Ritchie and *Nashville Union* editor John P. Heiss. Blair and his partner, John C. Rives, ceased publication of the *Globe* on 30 April 1845, and the following day, Ritchie and Heiss introduced the *Washington Union* in its place.[28]

The *Globe* incident, which distracted Donelson during his final months in Texas, was one of the most telling indications of the paradoxical tensions in Donelson's life. Editing the Polk administration's newspaper would have given him a public position of some influence, one that accentuated his writing talents. It also would have provided him, if Polk can be believed, an answer to his financial woes. Even that possibility, however, did not convince Donelson to accept the position. Instead, he vacillated over accepting the newspaper editor's position—seemingly because he knew that Jackson opposed the move. Thus continued Donelson's unwillingness to challenge his uncle's wishes for his career, despite his admission to Polk that his "long connection to politics" had caused him considerable financial loss. His aversion to showing an "apparent harshness to the Genl [Jackson]" paralyzed his independence. His comments clearly indicate that he thought his relationship with Jackson had, and continued to, cost him significant financial gains, both in the amount of time that politics took away from his personal business and by Jackson's apparent unwillingness to help him obtain a more prominent and profitable position. Not that Donelson was being completely honest, as he had political aspirations. But he seemed unable to find a way to assert his independence without jeopardizing his relationship with his uncle.[29]

When Donelson expressed his desire to visit Tulip Grove in May, then, it was shortly after he had found out that Polk would not wait on his return to replace Blair at the *Globe.* He had just surrendered a position that promised him, on paper, a way out of his grim financial duress. Donelson was questioning his confidence in Jackson, who he believed had undermined his career, and Polk, who seemed ready to give up on him altogether. It is little

28. JKP to AJ, 27 April 1845, JKP to AJD, 6 May 1845, Jeremiah George Harris to JKP, 6, 7, 9 April 1845, Robert Armstrong to JKP, 7 April 1845, AJ to JKP, 7 April 1845, in ibid. 9:320–2, 350–3, 255–6, 262, 271–3, 256–7, 263–4; FPB to AJ, 24 March 1845, in Bassett and Jameson, *CAJ* 6:388–9; Sellers, *Continentalist,* 274–8; Smith, *Francis Preston Blair,* 163–7; and Remini, *Course of American Democracy,* 515–6.

29. AJD to JKP, 18 March 1845, in Cutler and Hall, *CJKP* 9:205–7; and Wyatt-Brown, "AJ's Honor," 14–6.

wonder that he appeared unwilling to commit the necessary physical energy and mental resources necessary to see his Texas mission through to the end.

Polk, ironically, cautioned the chargé about his overconfidence and ordered him to remain in Texas "until the object of your mission is consummated." The president had discovered Ashbel Smith's secret mission to England to discuss the Texas-Mexico peace plan with the British government. The president insisted that Donelson attend the June meeting. "I fear you may be too sanguine about the assent of *Texas* to our terms of annexation," he noted. Donelson's presence at the gathering was necessary to counteract any foreign influence, including the British, French, and Mexican ministers and some of the "leading men of Texas, [who] are secretly opposed to the measure and are only restrained from making open resistance to it, by the popular opinion of the masses." For these reasons, Donelson had to stay close by, despite his other desires. "This is *the* great question of the times," Polk exclaimed.[30]

The risk of foreign interference that concerned Polk became a reality in late May and early June 1845. British chargé Charles Elliot returned from Mexico City with despatches containing Mexico's formal recognition of Texas. While the general population remained determined to support U.S. annexation, British and Texas officials, including Jones, Kennedy, and Allen, welcomed the news as a last chance to stave off the inevitable. In response to the Mexican overture, President Jones issued a proclamation sanctioning peace with Mexico and promised to present the Mexican proposal at the July convention. Mexico's proposition came too late, however. The citizens of Texas clamored loudly for U.S. annexation and showed little regard for Elliot's plan.[31]

Learning of Mexico's offer of recognition while still in New Orleans, Donelson hurried back to Texas. Despite the internal conflict with which he was wrestling, he seemingly found the fortitude to finish the job. His first move was to make preparations in case an invasion followed the Texas

30. JKP to AJD, 6, 26 May 1845, in Cutler and Hall, *CJKP* 9:350–3, 408–10; and JB to AJD, 3 June 1845, in Moore, *Works of JB* 6:164–5.

31. Ebenezer Allen to Anson Jones, 5 June 1845, in Jones, *Memoranda*, 466–8; Charles A. Wickliffe to JB, 13 June 1845, in Manning, *Diplomatic Correspondence* 12:408–9; Sellers, *Continentalist*, 226–7; Adams, *British Interests and Activities*, 217–8; and Pletcher, *Diplomacy of Annexation*, 195–6.

Congress' approval of annexation to the United States. He asked the Polk administration to send more troops to Fort Jesup, Louisiana, near the Texas border and to order the commander of those forces to remain nearby and in constant communication with the U.S. chargé. Rumors circulated that over eight thousand Mexican troops were massing on the border with Texas. If the convention approved annexation and Mexico invaded, Donelson wanted a military force nearby to react.[32]

Polk advised Donelson that as soon as the Texas convention approved annexation, "I shall regard Texas as a part of our Union: all questions of Constitutional power to defend and protect her, by driving an invading Mexican army out of her Territory, will be at an end, and our land and naval forces will be under orders to do so. . . . The assent of the Convention is all we want." The president also gave Donelson the discretion to make the war decision. If Mexico invaded, Polk granted the chargé the authority to "repel the invaders of Texas." To support Donelson, Polk ordered Gen. Zachary Taylor and his troops to a position along the Sabine River, the lower part of which served as the border between Louisiana and Texas.[33]

Of particular concern for both the United States and the Texas governments was Robert Stockton's feverous activity. Upon his arrival in Galveston in mid-May 1845, the commodore had exceeded his orders by encouraging pro-annexationist sentiment among the Texas people. Accompanied by Texas militia commander, Gen. Sidney Sherman, he then visited President Jones and requested permission to raise troops for offensive operations, expressing his intention to capture the Mexican port at Matamoros and send troops into the disputed Rio Grande territory. His obvious aim was to give the United States the opportunity to use its professed defensive stance as a pretext to an offensive war.[34]

32. AJD to ERD, 24 May 1845, Zachary Taylor to AJD, 20 July 1845, DLC; AJD to JB, 2, 4, 13 June 1845, in Manning, *Diplomatic Correspondence* 12:422–4, 424–6, 434; Charles A. Wickliffe to JKP, 3, 4 June 1845, in Cutler and Hall, *CJKP* 9:422–5, 425–8; Pletcher, *Diplomacy of Annexation,* 254–5; and Bergeron, *Presidency of JKP,* 62–3.

33. JKP to AJD, 15 June 1845, in St. George L. Sioussat, ed., "Letters of James K. Polk to Andrew J. Donelson, 1843–1848," *THQ* 3 (1917): 67–8; Pletcher, *Diplomacy of Annexation,* 254–5; and Bergeron, *Presidency of JKP,* 62–3.

34. Charles A. Wickliffe to JB, 20 May 1845, AJD to JB, 24 May, 2, 4 June 1845, in Manning, *Diplomatic Correspondence* 12:412–5, 419–20, 422–4, 424–6; Jones, *Memoranda,* 48–52; Sellers, *Continentalist,*

Donelson, taken aback by Stockton's blatant aggression, tried to maintain control of the situation. He misled Buchanan, saying Stockton had "taken no step susceptible of construction as one of aggression upon Mexico—nor will he take any unless ordered to do so." He had talked to the commodore, warning him not to make any aggressive movements during this crucial time, and Stockton would remain under his watchful eye until after the Texas Congress met, Donelson promised. Stockton appears to have abandoned his scheme, not because of Donelson but because of the issuance of Jones's peace proclamation on 4 June 1845. With peace officially in place, the commodore lost interest in inciting a war. He remained in Texas until 23 June, then headed back to Washington.[35]

In his memoirs, Anson Jones blamed Donelson for providing the atmosphere that allowed Stockton's belligerent actions. "Major Donelson was always 'boring' me to ask for protection, protection, protection! (and conjuring up stories of Mexicans coming,) and I always laughed at him and the idea." The American chargé, however, had finally manipulated Ebenezer Allen into asking for troops, Jones claimed, then had used that pretext to bring "down an army and a navy upon us, when there was not a hostile foot, either Indian or Mexican, in Texas; not (as afterwards became apparent) to *protect* Texas, . . . but to insure a *collision* with Mexico. . . . The protection he had in view was *immediate and aggressive*." Donelson's despatches indicate just the opposite; he took a defensive, not offensive, posture.[36]

In the midst of Stockton's bluster and Donelson's watchfulness, the Texas Congress met on 16 June to discuss the United States' annexation proposal and the Mexican offer of independence. Jones had promised to support whichever alternative they chose. After some debate, both houses voted unanimously to accept the U.S. offer and reject that of the Mexican government. They also affirmed the calling of the July convention. Allen informed Donelson of the results and congratulated him on his "energies and tallents [*sic*] [that] have been so ably and faithfully devoted to the success of that

224–8; Pletcher, *Diplomacy of Annexation*, 197–200; Bergeron, *Presidency of JKP*, 58–9; and Price, *Origins of the War*, 105–20.

35. AJD to JB, 24 May, 2, 4 June 1845, in Manning, *Diplomatic Correspondence* 12:419–20, 422–4, 424–6; AJD to Anson Jones, 2 May 1845, Ebenezer Allen to Anson Jones, 3 May 1845, in Jones, *Memoranda*, 457–8, 458; and Price, *Origins of the War*, 130–52.

36. Jones, *Memoranda*, 53; Bergeron, *Presidency of JKP*, 59; and Price, *Origins of the War*, 118–52.

cause. . . . It must be particularly gratifying to observe the harmony and unanimity with which this Resolution has passed."[37]

Satisfied with the outcome, Donelson again indicated a wish to retire from his mission. The burden of his finances continued to worry him. Bearing in mind Polk's earlier admonitions, however, he decided to stay until after the July convention met. He busied himself with arranging a trip to Austin, where the convention would meet, and preparing for the movement of troops that would follow the close of the meeting. A recurrence of the fever incapacitated Donelson for five days, but he recovered sufficiently by 30 June to answer Allen's queries about military protection. Allen was very anxious about Mexico's response to annexation and the availability of U.S. troops for defense. Donelson reminded him that he had already promised that three thousand U.S. troops would protect Texas. To alleviate Allen's nervousness and in anticipation of Mexico's military response to annexation, Donelson sent Gen. Zachary Taylor guarded recommendations regarding the placement of troops. He advised Taylor to move his troops to San Antonio, Corpus Christi, and another location in between these two towns. He pointedly warned the general to exercise restraint. "It should be distinctly understood that your action will be strictly defensive and aimed at the protection of the rights of Texas," he wrote. Donelson had already predicted to his wife that "war will be prevented if my diplomacy can prevail."[38]

While Donelson was deciding how best to protect Texas, the republic held its popular convention on 4 July to decide the annexation issue. On the first day of the convention, the delegates voted to accept annexation by the United States. Arriving a day later, Donelson responded to the convention's vote with a declaration stating that, by its approval, Texas had gained his nation's military support. The convention then prepared a new constitution to present to the United States and authorized the submission of these

37. Middleton, "Donelson's Mission," 290–1; and Ebenezer Allen to AJD, 23 June 1845, joint resolution of Texas Congress accepting annexation, 23 June 1845, in Manning, *Diplomatic Correspondence* 12:434–6, 435–6.

38. Smith, *Annexation of Texas,* 455–6; Charles A. Wickliffe to JB, 13 June 1845, AJD to JB, 23 June 1845, Ebenezer Allen to AJD, 26, 28 June 1845, AJD to Ebenezer Allen, 30 June 1845, in Manning, *Diplomatic Correspondence* 12:433–4, 437–8, 438–40, 440–1, 441–3; and AJD to Zachary Taylor, 28 June 1845, AJD to ERD, 21 June 1845, DLC.

and other issues to the Texas people. Donelson declared the convention a success. "Thus is dissipated all the schemes of Foreign powers to raise a party in Texas adverse to annexation," he notified Buchanan, "and thus has this gallant state vindicated her appreciation of the principles of liberty and of the necessity of union with us in order to preserve those principles."[39]

Donelson left Austin on 11 July and proceeded toward Galveston. He visited Corpus Christi along the way, presumably to check on Taylor's compliance with his and Buchanan's orders. He reached New Orleans in mid-August 1845, having left Texas without waiting for popular ratification of the convention proposals. (The populace eventually voted overwhelmingly for annexation.) Polk and Buchanan had given him permission to return to the United States so long as nothing occurred that called for his immediate intervention, and Donelson had used that as a pretext to abandon his post. The effects of his several bouts with the fever lingered, and he still had not been able to settle his numerous financial debts. Seeing his wife and children and finding a means to increase his wealth, Donelson decided, were more important to him than watching a fait accompli.[40]

Andrew Jackson did not live to see the culmination of Donelson's efforts in Texas. He had died on 8 June, only days before the Texas Congress gave its approval of United States annexation. Donelson's wife, Elizabeth, was with him, as was their son, John. On his deathbed, Jackson motioned John to come near. As the young teenager moved closer, Elizabeth recounted, the dying patriarch "kissed him and gave him his blessing and parting admonitions[.] He told him not to weep for him[,] that he hoped to meet him in Heaven & that he must be a good boy, obey his parents, keep the Sabath [*sic*] holy, and not neglect his salvation." It was a benediction that resembled the one that Jackson had sent John's father. In his last letter to Donelson, the dying Old Hero conveyed his affection to his once young, now middle-aged, protégé: "My dear Major, live or die you have my blessing and prayers for your welfare & happiness in this world."[41]

39. Middleton, "Texas Convention," 32–4; Smith, *Annexation of Texas,* 458–9; and AJD to Thomas J. Rusk, 6 July 1845, AJD to JB, 6 July 1845, in Manning, *Diplomatic Correspondence* 12:446, 447–8.

40. AJD to Ebenezer Allen, 16 July, 14 August 1845, in Manning, *Diplomatic Correspondence* 12:453–4, 458–9; JKP to AJD, 27 July 1845, in Sioussat, "Letters of JKP to AJD," 69; and JB to AJD, 28 July 1845, in Moore, *Works of JB* 6:211.

41. Account of AJ's death recorded by ERD, n.d. (transcript), AJ to AJD, 28 May 1845, DLC.

In what must have been a devastating blow to Donelson's expectations concerning his uncle's affection for him, Jackson's final will, last amended in June 1843, bequeathed to him only a sword given to the Hero of New Orleans by the state of Tennessee and the admonition to "use it when necessary in support and protection of our glorious Union, and for the protection of the Constitutional rights of our beloved country should they be assailed by foreign enemies or domestic traitors." Composed in 1833, his uncle's original will had left Donelson land, slaves, cash, and the sword. In the end, however, everything of monetary value went to Andrew Jackson Jr., something that Jackson said he did because it was what Rachel would have wanted. While Donelson heeded Jackson's admonition to protect the Union in his future political career, the cautionary statement did nothing to alleviate his current precarious finances. It also demonstrated for the final time his uncle's failure to provide for him. For all practical purposes, Jackson's sword, name, and expectations were his only legacy to Donelson.[42]

Before he died, Jackson had written Polk, "*All* [is] safe & Donelson will have the honor of this important Deed. But my Dr Col[.], the sacrifice to his private affairs has been great." Jackson's words were prescient. For almost nine months, Donelson worked to bring about Texas annexation, and he ultimately succeeded in his goal. For helping achieve that objective, Donelson deserves credit. These months as chargé to Texas were also a disappointment, however. Jackson's interference with his nephew's political career had caused Donelson much consternation during his time in Texas. In addition, the mission had not been as financially profitable as he had hoped, and his debts distracted him at crucial times. With his uncle's death in June 1845, Donelson now possessed the opportunity to free himself from the constraints of Jackson's oversight yet still use his uncle's name to his advantage. As he pursued his political ambitions, however, Donelson found it imperative to keep a close eye on the financial benefits that accompanied his advancing career.[43]

42. AJ's will, 7 June 1843, in Bassett and Jameson, *CAJ* 6:220–3; and Remini, *Course of American Democracy,* 483–5.

43. AJ to JKP, 26 May 1845, in Cutler and Hall, *CJKP* 9:410–1.

14

"The Fatal Error in My Life"

Confident that the annexation process would succeed without him, in September 1845 Donelson traveled directly from New Orleans to Washington, where he updated Polk and Buchanan on the Texas situation and the prospects of war with Mexico. Despite a bout of illness that left him "prostrated," he was able to make several social engagements. Politics and society, however, were a secondary purpose of the trip. Donelson was feeling the pressure of his ever-increasing debts and spent some of his time in the city searching for a definitive solution to his problems. Looking to help his old colleague, *Washington Union* editor John P. Heiss proposed that Donelson become part of a business venture involving the building of a naval yard in Memphis. A group of New York and Pennsylvania businessmen wanted a Tennessean to serve as a liaison in the state, but, surprisingly, Donelson declined the opportunity. Despite that decision, he optimistically promised his wife, Elizabeth, "I am looking ahead to see what is attainable for us in the future, and what is most consistent and proper, considering our poverty and the interests of our children."[1]

Donelson seemed to have an eye on a political, rather than a business, solution to his financial woes. The president, honoring Jackson's request that he provide his nephew an opportunity to recover "the sacrifice to his private affairs," offered Donelson the position of minister to Prussia. The post paid nine thousand dollars annually and an outfit, or advance, of another nine thousand to defray the cost of moving and travel expenses. Donelson hoped, with proper management, to do well on this salary. His longtime friend, Nicholas P. Trist, had assured him that in Berlin, his annual expenses would only total five thousand dollars. "With the same economy that we

1. AJD to ERD, 24, 27 September 1845, John P. Heiss to AJD, 15 September, 20 October 1845, DLC; and diary entries, 20, 21, 24, 27, 28 September 1845, in Milo M. Quaife, ed., *The Diary of James K. Polk During His Presidency, 1845 to 1849,* 4 vols. (Chicago: A.C. McClung, 1910), 1:37, 37–8, 39–40, 41–4, 44.

have practiced," Donelson assured his wife, "something will be made by the movement."[2]

Now possessing some certainty about his future, Donelson left Washington for Tulip Grove in early October 1845. He and Elizabeth had filled their letters with regret over their separation; now they were finally together again. The reunion quickly became secondary, however, as Donelson fended off his creditors and readied himself for his new position. Donelson's first concern became finding a way to pay off his longstanding debts to Van Buren and Beckman. In July 1845, the former president had apologized for contacting Donelson while he was "engaged in such important business" but reminded him of his failure to make a payment on the Beckman loan. By October, however, Beckman had lost his patience. "Your total failure in your engagements with the Dr.[,] aggravated by your omission to take any notice of his repeated letters had [so] irritated him," Van Buren informed Donelson, that the former president had to "work hard" to convince Beckman to give him one more chance. Van Buren pleaded with Donelson to write his creditor personally and explain his situation, at the same time reminding the Tennessean of his debt to him, which then stood at over four thousand dollars.[3]

With a disgruntled creditor threatening to take legal action against him, Donelson visited his Mississippi plantation in November to ascertain the feasibility of selling it. He found that, with the price of cotton so low, it would be impossible to do so profitably at that time. Returning in January 1846, he was intent on selling his cotton in Mobile, Alabama, at whatever price he could obtain. The impending war with Mexico bolstered Donelson's confidence that the price of cotton would rise due to foreign demand, but his optimism proved unfounded. The price stayed at about seven cents, leading Donelson to tell Elizabeth not to sell his Tulip Grove cotton in Nashville. "It will be useless to ship it, if prices are no better," he lamented. "We are poor," he told her. "My cotton at present prices will [do] but little in the payment of my debts."[4]

2. AJ to JKP, 26 May 1845, in Cutler and Hall, *CJKP* 9:410–1; JB to AJD, 26 April 1846, in Diplomatic Instructions, German States, vol. 14, DSA; AJD to JKP, 20 February 1846, PLC; and AJD to ERD, 22 February 1846, DLC.

3. MVB to AJD, 10 July, 8 October 1845, DLC.

4. AJD to JKP, 4 November, 20 December 1845, 27, 31 January, 20 February 1846, PLC; and AJD to ERD, 8, 17, 22 February 1846, DLC.

Finding no financial salvation in Mississippi, Donelson turned to another possible source of income. His marriage to Elizabeth had given him access to several thousand acres of Arkansas land. While he was in Mississippi attempting to sell his cotton, Donelson asked Elizabeth's brother, James G. Martin, to look into putting the Arkansas land on the market, hoping to use the proceeds to alleviate his financial burdens. Martin agreed to help his brother-in-law and journeyed to Arkansas in February 1846 with the intention of selling most, if not all, of the Randolph-Donelson land. Confusion over land titles and legal obstacles, however, frustrated his efforts. Squatters refused to vacate the land they now claimed as their own. Several people held legal title to different parts of the Randolph-Donelson land, a common occurrence in territories. Even more exasperating was the interested parties' refusal to purchase the land from Martin without Elizabeth's written permission. In the end, Martin only succeeded in selling approximately six hundred acres for $1,020, most of it allocated in installments over four years. After paying back taxes, he gained his brother-in-law only $906, none of it in cash. This amount was hardly the windfall that Donelson had expected when he sent Martin to Arkansas.[5]

With other sources of income seemingly exhausted, Donelson pressured Polk for an official announcement of his appointment, a move that would provide him with his outfit and salary. "It is a troublesome matter for me to put my business in such a situation that I can leave it," Donelson reminded Polk. "The sooner you make my nomination the better, as until that event is settled I shall not put my private affairs in the condition that I wish them to be during my absence." Polk promised him in February 1846 that he would make the nomination "at a[n]y time that you may desire" and proposed early April as the target date. Giving in to Donelson's pleas, however, Polk nominated him on 4 March. The current minister, Henry Wheaton, who also happened to be the United States' senior diplomat, would remain at his post until early May, leaving his neophyte replacement plenty of time to order his affairs before he left.[6]

5. Satterfield, "Moderate Nationalist Jacksonian," 340–1; and Arkansas land tax receipts, n.d., DTL.

6. AJD to JKP, 4 November 1845, 31 January, 20 February 1846, PLC; JKP to AJD, 9 February, 5 [4] March 1846, in Sioussat, "Selected Letters, 1844–1845," 70–1, 71; *Washington Daily Union,* 18 March 1846; and Elizabeth F. Baker, *Henry Wheaton: 1785–1848* (Philadelphia: University of Pennsylvania Press, 1937), 151–2.

While preparing to leave for Berlin, Donelson finally rid himself of the burden of the Beckman loan. Beckman's son wrote Donelson in early March, asking for his immediate attention to the matter. A letter from Van Buren followed shortly thereafter, informing Donelson that Beckman was indeed considering legal action against him, and as before, only the New Yorker's intervention had prevented it. Donelson's continued refusal even to write his creditor an explanation, he lectured, was only making matters worse. Facing the possibility of losing Tulip Grove if he did not resolve the situation, Donelson obtained loans of $1,000 from Washington newspaperman John P. Heiss and $10,000 from Mississippi planter William M. Gwin; with these, he was able to pay the principal and interest, totaling $12,479.61, on the Beckman loan. Despite such considerable effort, Donelson remained in debt, only now he owed two friends rather than a stranger.[7]

With his finances settled for the moment, Donelson traveled to Washington in anticipation of his trip. While waiting for Elizabeth and their four underage children to join him, he met with Baron Gerolt, the Prussian minister to Washington. Donelson did not impress the baron, who found him "ignorant and unprepared" for a diplomatic mission. Donelson also witnessed the patriotic fervor that greeted news of the opening of hostilities between the United States and Mexico. Previously leery about the United States prosecuting a war with Mexico, Donelson now gave his approval. He congratulated Buchanan "on the prospect thereby opened of an early negotiation with Mexico by which peace may be restored, and the questions in dispute with that unfortunate nation honorably settled."[8]

Donelson and his family left New York for Berlin on 12 June 1846, intent on taking the least expensive route. Elizabeth's continued poor health, however, compelled them to take a more direct route, leading to their arrival in Berlin on 5 July, earlier than expected. Donelson carried with him limited instructions. He was to conclude negotiations with Bavaria and Saxony over the "mutual abolition of the *droit d'aubaine* [seizure of a deceased foreigner's property by the state] and taxes on emigrants." Those were his only specific

7. T. Beckman to AJD, 9 March 1846, DLC; MVB to AJD, 15 April 1846, VBL; and AJD to John P. Heiss, 16 January 1846 (promissory note), AJD to William M. Gwin, 14 May 1846 (promissory note), note by John P. Beckman, 23 May 1846, Henry Horn to AJD, 20 May 1846, DTL.

8. Baker, *Henry Wheaton,* 296; AJD to JKP, 20 February, 21 May 1846, PLC; and AJD to JB, 31 May 1846, in Despatches from United States Ministers to the German States and Germany, Prussia, vol. 4, DSA.

instructions, although Wheaton had also been in the process of waiting for the U.S. Senate to ratify a treaty that would allow for the "mutual extradition of fugitives from justice"; presumably, Donelson would complete those negotiations as well. Polk had also undoubtedly instructed the new minister to ascertain European reaction to the war with Mexico.[9]

The Donelsons entered a Germany resistant to the nationalist and liberal forces shaping other parts of the European continent. Composed of thirty-nine states, Germany was divided into spheres of influence between the two largest states: Prussia and Austria. The German Confederation, consisting of thirty-eight German states, including Prussia, Austria, Bohemia, and Moravia, provided political unity to its members. Economic unity came from the Zollverein, a customs union established in 1834 under Prussian auspices to reduce duties and increase trade. (Austria was excluded from the Zollverein.) German monarchs still opposed relinquishing their rights to a centralized government, the state parliaments, or the people. In Prussia, King Friedrich Wilhelm IV, after initial indications that he would support reform, had so far failed to match the liberals' expectations.[10]

From the early days of Donelson's mission, it was apparent that he was inadequately prepared to serve as a diplomat in Europe. As Gerolt had observed, Donelson's knowledge of German affairs was sparse. He read and wrote, but did not speak, French and German, which many times left him searching for the right response to events about which he had little or no understanding. Donelson's time as chargé in Texas had not prepared him for the demanding everyday duties of a diplomat, and he had to learn the intricacies of European commercial relations and political alliances while on the job. Weeks of inactivity in Berlin also left him plenty of time to worry

9. JB to AJD, 26, 27 April 1846, in Diplomatic Instructions, DSA; AJD to JB, 30 March, 31 May 1846, in Despatches, vol. 4, DSA; AJD to JKP, 21 May 1846, PLC; diary entry, 20 April 1846, in Quaife, *Diary of JKP* 1:339–42; Common Council of New York City, 5 May 1846, AJD to Common Council, 5 May 1846, DLC; AJD to NPT, 26 June 1846, NPTP; AJD to JB, 7 July 1846, DPL; and Satterfield, "Moderate Nationalist Jacksonian," 344.

10. Peter Jones, *The 1848 Revolutions* (Harlow, U.K.: Longman Group, 1991; New York: Addison Wesley Longman, 1998), 29–42; William Otto Henderson, *The Zollverein* (London: Frank Cass, 1959), 93–4; William Carr, *A History of Germany, 1815–1945* (New York: St. Martin's Press, 1969), 29–30; James J. Sheehan, *German History, 1770–1866* (Oxford: Clarendon Press, 1989), 595–6, 621–8; Agatha Ramm, *Germany, 1789–1919: A Political History* (London: Methuen, 1967), 166–7; and Koppel S. Pinson, *Modern Germany: Its History and Civilization* (New York: Macmillan, 1954), 82.

about his financial affairs back home. The expected windfall that his diplomatic post was supposed to generate did not materialize immediately, and he constantly complained to Buchanan about his poverty and inability to save money.

Donelson had reason to worry. Shortly after arriving in Berlin, he received warnings from relatives that his finances back home were still dangerously weak. Daniel, who was overseeing his brother's finances while he was away, wrote Donelson that he needed $10,000 immediately to begin paying off his brother's debts, which he estimated at $17,300, "far greater than I anticipated." He advised Donelson to secure a $25,000 loan, which he could then use, with the profits from the year's cotton crop, to stabilize his position. Donelson's brother-in-law, James G. Martin Jr., reported that while the cotton crop looked promising, he had been unable to sell more land in Arkansas. By July 1847, Daniel was warning his brother that he either had to sell his property, presumably in Mississippi, or mortgage his land and property to pay off debts that had risen to nearly $25,000.[11]

Even with Donelson in Europe, his creditors continued to hound him for payment. Van Buren, who had exhibited tremendous patience, sent a letter through the State Department threatening to turn his bond over to another New York creditor unless he immediately paid the $777.72 interest due. Donelson also received a letter from John H. Eaton, his old nemesis, regarding an 1841 debt totaling $541. Donelson had ignored his requests, leading the courts to enter a judgment against him. Hoping to appeal to the minister's sense of southern honor and republican virtue, Eaton lectured him. "Justice and right between man & man, are first duties, where the capability of performing them, is professed, as is your case," he explained. "I can not doubt that you will remit [the requested money] to me, as I have requested, [so] that this *old*—this *antiquated* affair, of honor amongst friends, may be ended." As with Van Buren, Donelson did not answer Eaton's warning.[12]

Donelson apparently did not respond to any of these entreaties, but the letter from his brother concerned him enough to seek financial help.

11. DSD to AJD, 3 August, 4 September 1846, 3 July 1847, BDP; and James G. Martin Jr. to AJD, 9 December 1846, DTL. Thanks to Doug Spence for directing me to the BDP collection.

12. MVB to AJD, 24 February 1847, JHE to AJD, 13 May 1847, DLC; MVB to Francis P. Blair, 2 May 1847, MVB to AJD, 2 May 1847, VBC; and John C. Rives to MVB, 12 May 1847, VBL.

In November 1846, he made an unauthorized trip to London to see his old Tennessee acquaintance, Robert Armstrong, now the U.S. consul at Liverpool. Armstrong was unable to assist him, however, and Donelson's trip only reminded the Polk administration of his propensity to become distracted. His failed trip to London and Van Buren and Eaton's threatening letters led Donelson to request a month-long leave of absence for June 1847 so that he could visit the United States and address his financial affairs. After discussing the situation with Buchanan, Polk rejected Donelson's application. He and Buchanan had decided that "during the war with Mexico, it is important that the United States should be represented at all the Courts of Europe, and that your absence from *Berlin,* at this juncture[,] might prove detrimental to our interests." "It would not be safe for you to leave *Berlin* at the present time," Polk informed him. "I hope through your brother *Genl.* [Daniel] *Donelson* or some other friend you may be enabled to arrange your private business in the U. States satisfactorily, without the necessity of your personal presence." The president attempted to soothe his friend's displeasure by reminding him that he had turned down similar requests from other U.S. diplomats. Disappointed, Donelson had no choice but to acquiesce.[13]

Thwarted in his plans to visit the United States, Donelson again asked Armstrong for help. His friend pronounced himself unable to make the "money arrangements" requested of him. No further correspondence regarding the monetary dispute between Van Buren and Donelson exists, so the Tennessean must finally have satisfied his debts, though not without a cost. Donelson and Van Buren ended their correspondence and, presumably, their longstanding political and personal association. As for Daniel's warnings, successful cotton crops apparently kept Donelson afloat, and he gave up asking his brother to send money.[14]

When not looking after his finances, Donelson tended to his official duties, which included negotiating treaties. One in particular, a new commercial treaty with the Zollverein, caused him trouble. In 1844, Wheaton had

13. AJD to JB, 16 November, 22 December 1846, 15 May 1847, James Buchanan Papers, Historical Society of Pennsylvania, Philadelphia (hereafter cited as JBP); AJD to JB, 16 November 1846, 24 June 1847, in Despatches, vol. 4, DSA; J. N. Armstrong to AJD, 12 November 1846, DLC; and JKP to AJD, 29 December 1846, in Sioussat, "Letters of JKP to AJD," 72–3.

14. Robert Armstrong to AJD, n.d. [27 April 1847], 9 July 1847, DLC.

attempted to conclude an agreement with the German commercial union that would lower the German tariffs on U.S. tobacco, eliminate duties on U.S. cotton imported into participating German states, and maintain the current tariff on U.S. rice. The Zollverein states approved sending the treaty to the U.S. Senate, but under pressure from non-Zollverein states, Great Britain, and Whig senators, the Senate refused on several occasions to ratify the treaty.[15]

Donelson hoped to reopen these negotiations with the Zollverein. Shortly after arriving in Berlin, he notified Buchanan that he believed the Prussian government was ready to discuss a more favorable treaty than the one Wheaton had negotiated. Donelson spent enormous energy and time collecting data and communicating with German officials about the present tariff rates and the benefits and drawbacks of certain changes in trade. Buchanan and Baron Gerolt, the Prussian minister at Washington, finally signed a protocol in February 1847 reopening discussions, and Buchanan notified Donelson of the change. The secretary of state, however, never authorized Donelson to open negotiations in Berlin, telling him only to familiarize himself with the data.[16]

Donelson interpreted Buchanan's letters differently. In early June, he asked permission to negotiate the commercial treaty. Then, without waiting for authorization, he plunged ahead. Later that month, Donelson happily announced that he had almost completed a letter to the Prussian minister of foreign affairs, Baron von Canitz, that would become the basis of a new and favorable commercial treaty. He then sent Buchanan a copy of his correspondence with Canitz, which outlined the changes necessary for a successful completion of negotiations and his rationalizations for them. Donelson not only opened unauthorized communication with Canitz but also met

15. Baker, *Henry Wheaton,* chaps. 27–30.

16. JB to Baron Gerolt, 25 February 1846, Protocol of Conference between United States and Prussia, 23 February 1847, JB to AJD, 26 February, 13 May 1847, in Moore, *Works of JB* 6:376–7, 7:224–6, 227, 302–3; JB to AJD, 23 July, 14 August 1846, 26 February 1847, in Diplomatic Instructions, DSA; AJD to JB, 15, 19 July, 12 August, 1, 9, 13, 14 September, 19 October, 1, 15 December 1846, Bodelschwing to AJD, n.d. [27 August 1846], AJD to [Bodelschwing], 29 August 1846, AJD to J. G. Flüget, 31 August 1846, AJD to Baron von Canitz, 18 April (translated copy), 18 May 1847 (copy), DPL; AJD to JB, 16 November 1846, 20 January 1847, AJD to Baron von Canitz, 19 January 1847 (translated copy), Baron von Canitz to AJD, 12 April 1847 (translated copy), in Despatches, vol. 4, DSA; and Satterfield, "Moderate Nationalist Jacksonian," 360.

with the Prussian minister of commerce, industry, and public works, Robert von Patow, who agreed to convey Donelson's treaty stipulations to the Zollverein states.[17]

Donelson clearly, and deliberately, misread Buchanan's instructions. On 12 July, he acknowledged that Canitz wanted him to negotiate, but he was waiting for the administration to send him "the necessary power." In a message dated the next day, he notified the State Department of his meeting with Patow and renewed his request, repeated ten days later, for negotiating powers, indicating that he had spoken with Prussian officials without Buchanan's knowledge. As late as August 23, Donelson maintained his request for authorization. Although he was asking permission to do so, he had actually already opened talks with the Prussian government.[18]

Donelson's correspondence and actions puzzled Buchanan. The secretary of state consulted Polk, then dashed off a letter to his minister in Berlin. "I have examined with care my despatch to you of the 13th May last . . . and I confess I can not discover from what portion of it you could have drawn such an inference" to open negotiations, he wrote. Buchanan chastised Donelson for not recognizing the implication of the documents enclosed in his despatch, which prohibited U.S. ministers from entering such negotiations. He tempered his criticism, but Donelson could not fail to detect the rebuke.[19]

Donelson reacted with restrained umbrage. He claimed, despite his earlier admission, that he "never used" Buchanan's instructions "as authority" for opening negotiations with the Zollverein. Canitz, he assured Buchanan, knew that the treaty discussions were informal and only intended "to elicit information which would enable the two governments to come to some just and satisfactory arrangement." Donelson demonstrated his true motives, however, when he admitted that "although I had not your authority for the supposition that a convention satisfactory to the President and Senate

17. AJD to JB, 3, 6 June, 1, 8 July, 23 August, 2 September, 20 October 1847 (two letters), AJD to Baron von Canitz, 8 July 1847, AJD to Robert von Patow, 1 September 1847, J. L. Tellkampf to AJD, n.d. [October 1847], DPL; AJD to JB, 24 June, 12, 13 July 1847, in Despatches, vol. 4, DSA; and Theodore S. Hamerow, *Restoration, Revolution, Reaction: Economics and Politics in Germany, 1815–1870* (Princeton, N.J.: Princeton University Press, 1958), 151.

18. AJD to JB, 12, 13 July 1847, in Despatches, vol. 4, DSA; AJD to JB, 23 July, 23 August, 2 September 1847, DPL; and AJD to JKP, 13 July 1847, JKP.

19. JB to AJD, 7 August, 12 October 1847, in Moore, *Works of JB* 7:382–4, 431–2.

might be concluded on the basis suggested, I did not feel that I was thereby withheld from indulging or acting upon such a supposition, subject to your future approbation and direction." Surprisingly, Donelson then criticized Buchanan for sending vague instructions that allowed him to infer incorrectly that he should proceed with diplomatic discussions.[20]

Buchanan did not respond to Donelson's baited replies. He had made his point clear—Donelson was not to discuss formally or informally any treaty between the United States and Prussia. His reluctance to entrust the minister with those powers partially came from a fear of repeating the mistakes of the previous legation, which during the Tyler administration had blundered away an opportunity to settle the issue. More important, Polk and Buchanan possessed little regard for Donelson's diplomatic skills. They advised Donelson throughout his ministry only to observe, rarely giving him the authority to do anything else. Polk and Buchanan viewed him as unqualified to conduct himself appropriately or independently. During his time as chargé in Texas, Donelson had proven himself irresponsible at times, and his actions regarding the commercial treaty only confirmed their judgment, as did his future requests for the same authority.[21]

Donelson was fortunate that Polk did not recall him. Several factors seemed to save the disobedient minister from that ignominious fate. For one, the president could not have asked for a better spectator. Despite his faults, Donelson was a keen observer, and he sent excruciatingly detailed reports of the happenings in Germany. Polk's loyalty to Jackson also may have played some part in saving Donelson from an embarrassing recall. Even in death, Old Hickory, who valued honor and loyalty, apparently had an influence over his supporters. Polk may also have felt beholden to Donelson

20. AJD to JB, 20 October 1847 (two letters), 3 November 1847, J. L. Tellkampf to AJD, n.d. [October 1847], DPL.

21. Baker, *Henry Wheaton,* 254–74; AJD to JB, 11 January, 3 April 1848, DPL; AJD's speech at Bremen, n.d. [December 1847], in Despatches, vol. 4, DSA; AJD to Anton von Schmerling, 24 July 1848 (copy), AJD to JB, 26 July, 3, 8–9 October 1848, Anton von Schmerling to AJD, 29 July 1848, in Despatches from United States Ministers to the German States and Germany, Federal Government of Germany, vol. 1, DSA; AJD to JB, 1 August 1848, n.d. [received 5 November 1848], 26 November, 14 December 1848, JBP; JB to AJD, 7, 15 August, 30 October, 6 November 1848, and 17 February 1849, in Moore, *Works of JB* 8:152–4, 167–9, 232–3, 237–9, 342–3; and AJD to JB, 19 December 1848, 9 January, 11 March 1849, in Despatches from United States Ministers to the German States and Germany, Prussia, vol. 5, DSA.

for his previous political support, and he might have been apprehensive about making an enemy out of a prominent Tennessean with strong ties to Jackson. For some or perhaps all of these reasons, Polk kept Donelson in Prussia, albeit with trepidation.

As for Donelson, his deliberate disobedience of Buchanan's instructions was puzzling. When he received them, instead of requesting immediate clarification as one would do if confused, Donelson approached Canitz and Patow and then asked the Polk administration to sanction his discussions. Perhaps his experience as chargé to Texas had emboldened him, leading him to believe that he had more flexibility in his orders than he possessed. Or maybe he was just bored. He had been in Prussia since July 1846 and, when not worrying over his finances, had spent much of his time at pedestrian tasks. These menial duties might have failed to satisfy Andrew Jackson's nephew, a man who had just negotiated one of the greatest land acquisitions in U.S. history. Then again, it is possible that Donelson was just trying to prove that he deserved the diplomatic appointment. As with his time in Texas, he must have recognized why he was in Prussia. Polk had given him the position only at Jackson's request. Donelson's mission to Texas had been successful, true, but Polk's decision to send him to Berlin did not seem to have been predicated on that achievement. Donelson might have believed that he needed to show himself a competent diplomat, and negotiating this commercial treaty gave him the opportunity to do that.

When he was not looking after his official duties or openly defying the Polk administration, Donelson kept an eye on developments in the Mexican-American War. Most European diplomats criticized the war, he reported, but some, such as natural scientist Alexander von Humboldt, Friedrich Wilhelm IV's personal adviser, assured Donelson that they supported the United States. Von Humboldt especially expressed confidence in the United States' management of the war, but he identified slavery as a potential obstacle to its success. It "leads him to doubt the capacity of our union to bear a much greater extension," he declared, an opinion with which Donelson disagreed: "If let alone, it [expansion] will be found to be the amelioration of a necessary servitude, in the direction of which the U. States ought to be applauded rather than censured." Donelson further bragged that, by employing slave labor, his nation "will have accomplished more for the black race than all the nations of the earth can ever expect to do for the same race, existing as a separate people in Africa." Instead of slavery threatening the Republic, he argued, it strengthened the United States by spreading its institutions to a "less-enlightened" people and keeping republican government, for white men at least, intact.[22]

Donelson derived great satisfaction from news of progress in the war with Mexico. "I rejoice in the success of our arms in Mexico, and trust in God that the war will be soon terminated," he wrote Buchanan in the summer of 1847. He still considered his diplomatic functions mundane, although he tended to them diligently. A revolutionary storm was moving across Europe, however, that provided him with an opportunity not only to observe the cataclysmic events that transformed the face of the Continent but also to relate those changes to the triumph of his own nation's republican experiment.[23]

The 1848 revolutions that swept across Europe developed from a series of interrelated economic, political, and social factors. Europe's population had been growing rapidly, taxing both emerging urban centers and the outlying rural areas. The French Revolution of 1789 unleashed democratic forces when Napoleon Bonaparte and his armies marched across the Continent, and the conservative political backlash that followed Napoleon's downfall left both liberals and nationalists primed to challenge the power of the European monarchs. That opportunity arrived for the German states in the 1840s. Crop failures and the collapse in railway construction prompted middle-class supporters of German liberalism to call for change. But the German governments, most of which remained opposed to liberal reforms, reacted slowly, if at all, to the clamor for the constitutional protection of rights and greater popular participation in government.[24]

Donelson watched these developments affect the German states, but the Prussian king's actions initially led him to discount talk of revolution there.

22. AJD to JB, 22 December 1846, 8 January 1847, JBP; second annual message, 8 December 1846, in Richardson, *Messages and Papers of the Presidents* 4:471–506; Thomas Nipperdey, *Germany from Napoleon to Bismarck, 1800–1866,* trans. Daniel Nolan (Princeton, N.J.: Princeton University Press, 1996), 429–30; and AJD to JB, 28 September, 24 October 1846, 4, 20 February 1847, DPL.

23. AJD to JB, 16 November, 22 December 1846, 8 January, 21 February, 15 May 1847, JBP; and AJD to JB, 24 June 1847, in Despatches, vol. 4, DSA.

24. Jones, *1848 Revolutions,* chaps. 1–6.

Upon his arrival in Berlin, Donelson believed that Friedrich Wilhelm IV was moderate and conciliatory, but he soon realized the king was not committed to a change in government. At a meeting of the Prussian legislative assembly in April 1847, the king, to Donelson's dismay, reasserted his absolutist claims. Wilhelm's ideas were out of step with the times, Donelson thought, and his refusal to address his subjects' immediate concerns only exacerbated existing problems.[25]

During the winter of 1847–48, Donelson observed in a letter to Buchanan that political change in Europe seemed imminent. His observation was prescient. In early March 1848, news reached Berlin that French king Louis Philippe had abdicated his throne and a republic had replaced the monarchy. Donelson excitedly conveyed to Buchanan his impression of the revolutionary proceedings, emphasizing their effect on the German states. The events in France "have astounded all classes of society" in Berlin, he reported. Many members of the Prussian Diet were advocating Germany's unification under a strong central government, Donelson observed, but the Prussian people appeared reluctant to embrace revolution as a solution to their problems.[26]

Some German citizens, however, drew strength from the French example. In Mannheim, liberals demanded a number of rights, including a free press, equitable taxation, loyalty of the army to a constitutional government, accountability of government ministers, and, most important, the convening of the German Diet to address their concerns. In Heidelberg and Cologne, speakers called for the recognition of the new French republic, the formation of a national Prussian assembly, and a popular government. In Berlin, meanwhile, popular restlessness also increased. Donelson observed on 8 March that troop movements to suppress potential riots within the city indicated that "the Government will betray no hesitation in the use of the most extreme measures, if they become necessary, to enforce the legal

25. AJD to JB, 19 July 1846, 20 February, 13, 20 April, 5 May 1847, 9 May 1849 [1847], DPL; Pinson, *Modern Germany,* 82–3; Carr, *History of Germany,* 37; Peter Stearns, *1848: The Revolutionary Tide in Europe* (New York: W. W. Norton, 1974), 34; Richard W. Reichard, *Crippled from Birth: German Social Democracy, 1844–1870* (Ames: Iowa State University Press, 1969), 41–2; and Hamerow, *Restoration, Revolution, Reaction,* 75–93.

26. AJD to JB, 30 October [November], 10 December 1847, 11, 29 January, 26 February, 4 March 1848, DPL; AJD to JB, 8 November 1847, in Despatches, vol. 4, DSA; and Carr, *History of Germany,* 41–2.

authority." The Prussian people resented the military reinforcements, which represented the king's absolutist power and overt distrust of the citizenry.[27]

Even with such ominous events swirling around him, Donelson continued to focus on his financial problems. He requested a two-month leave of absence in February 1848, absurdly insisting that he planned to negotiate a treaty with the Zollverein in Washington. Actually, he wanted, once again, to check into his debts, claiming that he barely possessed enough money to enable his son, Jackson, to purchase passage to Berlin. Polk denied Donelson's request because of the outbreak of the French revolution but promised him that, if the situation in Europe calmed by the summer, then he could return home for a short time.[28]

In relating his difficulty in helping Jackson make the trip to Berlin, Donelson strongly advised his son to take care of his finances, even telling him to record daily expenditures to keep from accruing debt. "Let it be your maxim in the commencement of your career to live within your means," he told his oldest son. "Consider that the basis of all morality and religion. The fatal error in my life was to be seduced into habits which were beyond my income."[29]

Financial stability did not come to Donelson, and neither did the anticipated political tranquility in Europe. Instead, revolution shook the Prussian capital on 18 March 1848, forcing Donelson to give his attention, for a time at least, to his mission. From 13 to 17 March, the citizens of Berlin clashed with royal troops in the city's streets. Shaken by the turn of events, on the eighteenth, Friedrich Wilhelm IV attempted to calm the situation by granting the people an audience. The king publicly conceded several rights: freedom of the press, the assembly of the German Diet, the German Confederation's reorganization, and a written constitution. Crowds gathered

27. Carr, *History of Germany,* 41; Veit Valentin, *1848: Chapters of German History* (London: George Allen and Unwin, 1940; reprint, trans. Ethel Talbot Scheffauer, Hamden Conn.: Archon Books, 1965), 178; Nipperdey, *Germany from Napoleon to Bismarck,* 530; Rudolph Stadelmann, *Social and Political History of the German 1848 Revolution,* 2d. ed., trans. James G. Chastain (Athens: Ohio University Press, 1975), 46–52, 55–6; AJD to JB, 8, 10 March 1848, DPL; AJD to Charles Graebe, 7 March 1848 (copy), in Despatches, vol. 4, DSA; and Hajo Holborn, *A History of Modern Germany, 1840–1945* (New York: Knopf, 1969), 52.

28. AJD to JKP, 22 February 1848, PLC; AJD to Jackson Donelson, 5 March 1848, JDC; and JKP to AJD, 2 April 1848, in Sioussat, "Letters of JKP to AJD," 72–3.

29. AJD to Jackson Donelson, 5 March 1848, JDC.

outside the palace heard his speech and cheered his words, but when shouts called for the military's removal from Berlin, Friedrich Wilhelm IV ordered the throng dispersed. Gunshots rang out, barricades appeared, and casualties quickly grew. By the time peace was restored to the city the following day, 230 people had died. The king, realizing that he faced a worse fate than Louis Philippe if he did not react quickly, appealed for an end to the bloodshed, promising to remove the military and bow to the people's demands.[30]

From his Berlin apartment, Donelson watched these dramatic events unfold. His prediction of peace had proven wrong. Local citizens and diplomatic friends constantly updated him on the revolution's progress, and he even ventured out to do his own reconnaissance when the fighting ended, although he was careful to avoid participating in political activities. Donelson kept the Polk administration up to date with frequent despatches, sometimes writing late into the night, his observations revealing a diplomat overwhelmed by the surrounding circumstances. The revolution's violence especially startled and repulsed him. During a lull in the fighting on 18 March, Donelson pessimistically calculated its effect. "The whole spectacle is a humiliating lesson to us all," he remarked. "We see on the one hand that great curse of the age, a standing army ready with its terrible power to crush the people, the guilty as well as the innocent[;] on the other[,] both the monarch and the people, when the force is withdrawn, incapable of maintaining order."[31]

Following the bloody 18 March clash, the Prussian monarchy quickly embraced liberal reforms. Friedrich Wilhelm IV withdrew his troops, allowed Berlin's residents to form their own militia to guard his palace, and consented to replace his current cabinet with liberal ministers. Yet tension in Berlin did not disappear completely. The people, seeking a scapegoat for the violence, forced the hurried exit of Prince Wilhelm, the king's brother, heir, and the future emperor, to London on a "diplomatic" mission. It was common knowledge among the people that he was plotting a coup d'état to

30. Stadelmann, *German 1848 Revolution,* 56–61; and Nipperdey, *Germany from Napoleon to Bismarck,* 530–1.

31. AJD to JB, 18–9, 28, 30–1 March 1848, DPL; and JB to AJD, 5 April 1848, in Moore, *Works of JB* 8:41.

restore the absolutist rule of Friedrich Wilhelm IV. The prince would have been "torn to pieces" if he had remained, Donelson remarked.[32]

In early April, Friedrich Wilhelm IV ordered the Prussian Diet to convene and discuss Germany's political unification. He had previously entertained ideas of a unified Germany, but the current political atmosphere made it imperative that Prussia and the other German states discuss the idea more fully, not only to maintain internal harmony but also to dissuade other European powers from intervening. In the days leading up to the Diet's meeting, Donelson approvingly commented on German interest in America's republican system. Prussians besieged him for copies of the U.S. Constitution, he said, and the people "openly avowed" a federal government modeled after the United States, "defined as ours is by a written constitution." Donelson attended the Diet's opening session on 2 April and pronounced himself satisfied with its stated intention to establish a constitutional monarchy in Prussia and to allow the people to select delegates to a national assembly in Frankfurt.[33]

Much of the revolution's ultimate success depended upon the progress of this Frankfurt assembly. The members who eventually took their seats on 19 May, however, were not united in their goals or the means to achieve them. Moderate liberals wanted to make gradual changes to the existing order, perhaps even retaining the monarchy in some form; radicals pressed to remake completely the present political system into a republic. During the opening days of the meeting in St. Paul's Church, liberals succeeded in electing their candidate, Heinrich von Gagern, as the provisional president, solidifying their control of the Frankfurt Parliament.[34]

During the late spring and summer months of 1848, each day seemed to bring news from Berlin and Frankfurt that kept Donelson guessing as

32. AJD to JB, n.d. [March 1848], 20 March 1848, 21–2 March 1849 [1848], 23–5 March 1848, AJD to Baron Canitz, 21 March 1848, DPL; Stadelmann, *German 1848 Revolution,* 62–3; Carr, *History of Germany,* 43–4; and Nipperdey, *Germany from Napoleon to Bismarck,* 531.

33. Holborn, *History of Modern Germany,* 31–2, 50–1; AJD to JB, 21–2 March 1849 [1848], 23–5, 28, 30–1 March, 1–2, 6, 8, 11 April 1848, DPL; and AJD to JB, 10 April 1848 (two letters), in Despatches, vol. 4, DSA.

34. Frank Eyck, *The Frankfurt Parliament, 1848–49* (New York: St. Martin's Press, 1968), 28–56, 84–8, 103; and Theodore S. Hamerow, "The Elections to the Frankfurt Parliament," *Journal of Modern History* 33 (March 1961): 15–32.

to the success of a unified Germany. In Prussia, Friedrich Wilhelm IV retreated from his promises of reform and used the military to suppress protesting crowds and return Prince Wilhelm from his exile. The people also seemed undecided about their support for political reform. Donelson polled those living in his building and reported that none of the four voters there "comprehend[ed] the character of the sacred right" of suffrage, believing themselves "not capable of advising the King or his Government." When the new, popularly elected Prussian Diet met in late May, its members bowed to the king's will and produced a constitution that Donelson called "totally incompatible with the principle of representation, as understood with us," leading him to doubt whether 20 percent of the Berlin population truly supported a republican party. Reports from Frankfurt only increased Donelson's gloom. He estimated that only 84 of the 512 delegates were republicans. Almost a month into the assembly's first session, he predicted that if Prussia and other German states did not institute a "strong Federal government," then they would crush "the germ of republicanism."[35]

Donelson saw some hope, however. "As revolutions are said to produce the characters necessary to conduct them," he told Buchanan, "so we may hope that there will be found in the occasion which calls for these assemblies men capable of turning them to the advantage of popular liberty." A Prussian representative at Frankfurt introduced a constitution that, with a few exceptions, mirrored that of the United States, and other delegates indicated their support for, if not a pure republic, then at least a constitutional monarchy. It was a small step toward liberty, and it satisfied Donelson.[36]

Convinced that liberal reformers would eventually unite the German states, on 30 June 1848, Donelson repeated his request to Buchanan, first sent in April, that Polk allow him to open diplomatic relations with the Frankfurt Parliament. He argued that it was imperative that he be in Frankfurt to present his credentials when the new government emerged. Donelson was now asking for two missions: his present ministerial position in Berlin and a new diplomatic appointment to Frankfurt. Donelson's request, while couched in

35. AJD to JB, 21, 30 April, 1, 13–5 May 1848, DPL; Carr, *History of Germany,* 44; Nipperdey, *Germany from Napoleon to Bismarck,* 531; AJD to JB, 25–28 May, 4, 5, 11, 30 June, 15 July 1848, in Despatches, vol. 4, DSA; and Eyck, *Frankfurt Parliament,* 190–7, 202–5.

36. AJD to JB, 21 April, 1, 5 May 1848, DPL; and AJD to JB, 5, 24 June 1848, in Despatches, vol. 4, DSA.

language emphasizing the necessity of an experienced, republican minister at Frankfurt, also contained an unspoken but almost certain motivation. Donelson undoubtedly hoped that his salary would double, from nine to eighteen thousand dollars, and that he would receive an extra outfit of nine thousand dollars. The additional money would not only defray the expenses that Donelson faced while trying to sustain what was now a family of eight (another son, Martin, had been born in June 1847, and Jackson and John, who had been attending school in the United States, joined the rest of the family in Berlin in 1848) but also allow him to pay his debts in the United States.[37]

After receiving Polk's consent, Buchanan granted Donelson's request. The president appointed him "Diplomatic Representative of the United States" to the Frankfurt provisional government. Polk, however, wanted Donelson to maintain his residence in Berlin and travel between there and Frankfurt as needed. Buchanan made no mention of an extra salary or outfit, although he promised that the administration would reimburse him for his personal travel expenses. Donelson, no doubt, assumed that it was forthcoming.[38]

37. AJD to JB, 3 April 1848, DPL; and AJD to JB, 30 June, 1, 15 July 1848, in Despatches, vol. 4, DSA.

38. JB to AJD, 24 July, 3, 7, 15 August 1848, in Moore, *Works of JB* 8:130–1, 150–1, 152–4, 167–9; and diary entry, 5 August 1848, in Quaife, *Diary of JKP* 4:53–8.

15

"A Silent and Vigilant Sentinel"

James Buchanan's July 1848 despatch containing Donelson's new appointment reached the minister not at Berlin, as expected, but at Frankfurt. Donelson had impetuously decided to travel there in order to ascertain the political climate. Despite his continued financial duress, however, he also took his family on a vacation along the way, a strange choice for someone who continually proclaimed his poverty. They traveled to Baden, where his older children left to visit Switzerland and Italy. Donelson justified his decision by remarking that "nothing important could be immediately transacted with this Government."[1]

Donelson finally arrived at Frankfurt in early September 1848 and discovered that he had appeared just in time to observe the provisional government's first major crisis. Having been at war with Denmark earlier in the year, Prussia and the German Confederation signed a seven-month armistice with their foe in August. Public opinion, which had been confident of a German victory, turned against the provisional government, despite the fact it had been virtually excluded from any part in the negotiations. Members of the Frankfurt Parliament who opposed the truce forced the provisional government's head, Archduke Johann of Austria, to form a new cabinet, but they were unable to prevent a slim majority in their body from approving the peace agreement. Angry German citizens responded with riots that government troops in Frankfurt and Berlin quashed with deadly force.[2]

1. AJD to JB, 8 July 1848, in Despatches, vol. 4, DSA; AJD to JB, 26 July, 2 September 1848, in Despatches, vol. 1, DSA; and AJD to John Samuel Donelson, 15 August 1848, AJD to [John Samuel Donelson], 3 September 1848, DLC.

2. AJD to JB, 2, 6–11, 14, 17–8, 19, 21–3 September 1848, in Despatches, vol. 1, DSA; and Eyck, *Frankfurt Parliament,* 162–3, 288–311.

Donelson observed the chaos with dismay. Violent demonstrations threatened the Frankfurt government's survival and any hope of unifying Germany. Donelson expressed the inconceivability of forming a republic in the midst of such popular protest. Remembering the events in France earlier in the year, he insisted that the proclamation of a republic now "is an appeal to arms." By physically attacking the government, the German people were endangering their own future. As repugnant as it was to Donelson to see the Frankfurt government "enforce its orders at the point of the bayonet," he declared himself "satisfied that the power which enforces [the Parliament's orders] aims to establish a system that will in the end be an improvement on those which it changes."[3]

Circumstances in Germany kept Donelson busy throughout the fall of 1848, but by November, he was complaining again. He wanted to travel between Berlin and Frankfurt as ordered, Donelson wrote, but the lack of additional compensation made the travel impossible. "The responsibilities of my mission are greatly increased, and with them my expenses," he remarked. He tried to make his point by appealing to Buchanan's sense of propriety, telling him, "I know very well that it is not desirable for our ministers to imitate the extravagance of those of the European Governments." He slyly added, however, that "no American, situated as I am at this time, can escape the numerous demands which are made upon him, as the representative of the nation which is looked to so confidently as the source of the great reform movement which is now agitating this country."[4]

Donelson also asked for another leave of absence. He promised Buchanan that his visit to the United States would be short and he would return to Frankfurt as soon as possible "to help on the great cause of the Representative principle." Still, Donelson could not help but end with a gripe, noting that "it is too much for me to encounter the service and expense now thrown upon me without any compensation." The Polk administration ignored his complaints and denied both his leave and his request for compensation. "Your appointment was made to secure you the place at Frankfurt, in case our Diplomatic relations with Prussia should cease: and it

3. AJD to JB, 17–8, 19, 21–3, 25 September 1848, Despatches, vol. 1, DSA.

4. AJD to JB, 4 November 1848, in Despatches, vol. 5, DSA.

was a pretty general impression in the Senate that this appointment would not produce an additional expenditure," Buchanan responded. He assured Donelson that Congress would probably grant him his requested outfit when his mission ended. Until then, he would just have to be patient and stay in Germany.[5]

As he was wrangling with Buchanan over his compensation and leave, Donelson received news from Washington that heightened his concern about his future. Whig candidate Zachary Taylor had defeated the Democratic nominee, Lewis Cass, in the presidential election. The Whig victory galled Donelson, as did the campaign of former president Martin Van Buren, who held the top spot on the ticket of the Free-Soil party, an antislavery political group. Donelson's mood soured further following a December diplomatic dinner at which the other emissaries "had a kind of triumph" over him because of Taylor's victory. Embarrassed by the other diplomats' sarcastic comments, Donelson blamed Cass's defeat on the Polk administration's insistence on initiating the war with Mexico. "We ought to have waited for an attack from Mexico, compelled Congress to adopt the war, and kept the President on the defensive," he wrote, noting that, in fact, that was the position the administration had held while he was chargé in Texas.[6]

Donelson had not always been so unhappy about the progress of the war. In the past, he had expressed the view that the war was necessary to preserve slavery and expand white supremacy. When Calhoun sent Donelson his speech opposing American involvement on the Yucatan Peninsula, the minister replied that "the institution of slavery[,] if abandoned in the Tropical regions[,] will leave the Anglo Saxon as incapable there of maintaining his true character as it has left the Spaniard in Mexico." Donelson remarked that the "only inquiry is whether it is better for humanity that that portion of the world should relapse into a savage negro & Indian state, or be gradually improved by permitting the white man to continue the civilization

5. AJD to JB, 26 November 1848, JBP; and JB to AJD, 8 January, 18 February 1849, in St. George L. Sioussat, ed., "Selected Letters, 1846–1856, from the Donelson Papers," *Tennessee Historical Magazine* 3 (1917): 263–4, 264–5.

6. AJD to JB, 21 February 1847, 1 August, 26 November, 14 December 1848, JBP; AJD to JB, 12 June 1848, in Despatches, vol. 4, DSA; AJD to JB, 25 September 1848, in Despatches, vol. 1, DSA; and Holman Hamilton, "Election of 1848," in *History of American Presidential Elections*, 4 vols., ed. Arthur M. Schlesinger and Fred L. Israel (New York: Chelsea House, 1971), 2:865–96.

which he is capable of enforcing as a legitimate superior of the negroe or Indian."[7]

The seizure of the slavery-in-the-territories issue by northern abolitionist and antislavery groups angered Donelson. If Thomas Jefferson were "now alive," he informed Calhoun, "he would see that the free soil party[,] instead of proposing to relieve the burdens of slavery, aimed to punish the white man in the South for having done what is his duty under the circumstances of his situation." The self-righteous claims by northern Free-Soilers, such as Van Buren, that they were helping both African Americans and whites rang hollow to Donelson: "They have only banished the black man from their Territory. . . . How many are the blacks who are to enjoy the benefit of the free soil. . . . Does not everybody know that the North western [*sic*] Territory contains comparatively no blacks, and never will? Is not therefore the practical effect of all such legislation an idle boast, not benefitting the black race but punishing the white man who has had the humanity to protect it[?]" Donelson's time in Germany had "satisfied" him "that this institution of ours called slavery, has had an agency in shaping our institutions which few of us in the South even sufficiently appreciate":

> The presence of the black race in the United States enabled the white man to treat as his equal all his own race. A basis was thus formed for liberty as broad as the population; and hence popular sovereignty was a reality, not a fiction. The absence of such a basis in Europe is the secret of the failure of all its attempts to found popular institutions. . . . This is only saying that in my judgement, if slavery be an evil as recognized by us in the South, it is one which has been sent by Providence, and our Northern friends ought long ago to have learned that their remedies for it, even if successful, would only doom them as well as ourselves to dangers far more threatening to our common liberty and prosperity.

Having said all of that, Donelson bitterly concluded that "the *Wilmot Proviso* is the invisible penalty of the Mexican War—a war which has given us

7. AJD to JCC, 3 March, 8 July 1848, in Clyde N. Wilson, Shirley Bright Cook, and Alexander Moore, *The Papers of John C. Calhoun*, vol. 25, *1847–1848* (Columbia: University of South Carolina Press, 1999), 221–3, 572–4.

a country that is unfit for slave labor and that will be a burden to the Union for the next 100 years." It further "supplied [Taylor] with a *Union* question which will reelect him just as nullification did Genl[.] Jackson."[8]

Donelson faced a perplexing problem. He did not like Taylor's ascension to the presidency or his association with those opposed to slavery, but this was the man who would determine his future. Taylor could recall him once he took office, which meant that he would lose his minister's post and any chance that Congress would grant him his requested outfit. This would probably ruin Donelson financially. If he remained in Germany, on the other hand, he was more likely to receive his raise and the additional compensation. Donelson's course, then, was clear. He had to convince Taylor to keep him as minister.

Donelson set out to do just that when he wrote the president-elect an ingratiating letter in February 1849. "I am unwilling to thwart any principle or measure of your administration should such require the office I hold to be filled by another individual," he began, and would "with great cheerfulness remain" in his present position, noting that his familiarity with German officials and politics made it easier for him to stay rather than be replaced by a "stranger, however superior he might be in other qualifications." Donelson also emphasized the "favorable" climate for finalizing a commercial treaty, undoubtedly hoping to predispose Taylor into giving him the authority Polk had withheld. He concluded with a masterful, if deceptive, flourish: "When I parted with you at the Island of St. Joseph[,] I could not forsee [*sic*] the dangers which were soon to cover you with glory, but I never had a doubt that if you were ordered to the enemie's country[,] your success would be complete and brilliant. And I did not hesitate to express the prediction even before you crossed the Rio Grande that the people would make you President." Donelson mailed the letter and hoped for the best.[9]

Just a few weeks later, John C. Calhoun wrote Donelson that he believed Taylor was "kindly disposed" toward keeping him in Germany. Calhoun may have been correct, but Polk made sure that it was in a different capacity. Before leaving office, he appointed Edward A. Hannegan, former U.S. senator from

8. AJD to JCC, 27 September 1848, in Boucher and Brooks, *Correspondence Addressed to JCC,* 475–7; and AJD to JB, 14 December 1848, 21 July 1849, JBP.

9. AJD to Zachary Taylor, 15 February 1849, in Despatches, vol. 5, DSA.

Indiana, as minister to Prussia, leaving Donelson only the Frankfurt ministership. John M. Clayton, the incoming secretary of state, informed Donelson of the change and instructed him to travel to Frankfurt, where Gales Seaton would serve as the legation's secretary. Clayton assured the American minister of his and Taylor's appreciation for his "abilities and patriotism," but he denied Donelson's request for negotiating powers and ordered him to cease all discussion of a commercial treaty with Prussian officials or face recall. Clayton delivered a final blow when he notified Donelson that he would not receive additional compensation for his mission and warned him not to surpass his allowed withdrawals. Polk and Buchanan had apparently advised Clayton to keep a close eye on the minister in Germany.[10]

Although he was at the time unaware of Clayton's patronizing despatches, which did not arrive until late May, Donelson reacted strongly to news of Hannegan's appointment, his first clue of the change coming from German newspapers. He angrily dashed off a despatch to Clayton criticizing the splitting of the German missions. By appointing Hannegan as its Prussian minister, Donelson scrawled, the United States risked accrediting him to a government that might not possess diplomatic autonomy when he arrived. At the same time, the State Department ordered Donelson to go to Frankfurt and serve as minister to a government "not knowing whether it will be in existence, or if it is, what will be its functions." In closing, Donelson insisted that he was making his criticism out of "a sense of public duty" in order to "correct . . . a mistake, in regard to our diplomatic course."[11]

Receiving no immediate answer to his protest, Donelson attacked Buchanan, the person he considered the source of his problems, chastising him for the loss of the Berlin mission. "Our true policy was to let things stand as they are until the question of a German Federal Union was settled," Donelson remarked. As for his request for an additional outfit, "I thought I was entitled to an outfit because of the new responsibility and expense thrown upon me," he grumbled. "It would have been better for the President to have let the affair remain as it is, than to bear the responsibility of creating a useless mission. . . . I cannot conceive how the President could suppose

10. JCC to AJD, 23 March 1849, in Sioussat, "Selected Letters, 1846–1856," 265–6; and JMC to AJD, 19 March 1849 (two despatches), in Diplomatic Instructions, DSA.

11. AJD to JMC, 29 March 1849, in Despatches, vol. 5, DSA.

he was befriending me by sending a man to take my place. . . . It was better to leave me in the hands of Genl[.] Taylor who if he removes me will do so without having the trouble to choose between Berlin and Frankfurt."[12]

At first, Buchanan ignored Donelson's complaints. When he expressed the same sentiments to one of Buchanan's friends, however, the former secretary of state defended himself and Polk, who had died shortly after leaving office. "You may rest assured that whatever may be the result," Buchanan told the minister, "neither the late lamented President nor myself is to blame. He was sincerely and devotedly your friend and chose Frankfurt for you; because he believed this choice would best promote your interest." Donelson had convinced Polk that German unification was imminent, he continued, so the president had chosen Frankfurt to benefit, not punish, him. "Of one thing you may rest assured," Buchanan patiently explained, "you had not two better friends in the United States than the late President and myself." The two men would reconcile later that summer, but Donelson, as he had with Van Buren, was alienating himself from a very important figure in the Democratic party.[13]

Oblivious to his own ill-conceived behavior, Donelson watched the German unification movement decline. Friedrich Wilhelm's cabinet dissolved the Prussian Diet in early December 1848, and shortly thereafter, the king established a constitution that granted German citizens basic civil rights, including freedom of religion and assembly, and placed legislative power under the shared control of the king and a bicameral assembly, the lower chamber of which was elected by "universal and direct suffrage." There was, however, no renouncement of the monarch's divine right, no foundation of the government on the people's sovereignty, and no relinquishment of military authority to the legislature. In Frankfurt, the provisional government struggled to maintain its legitimacy after the outbreak of violence in September 1848. To keep unification a viable choice, in March 1849, the Frankfurt Parliament narrowly voted to establish a hereditary emperorship and ask Friedrich Wilhelm IV to accept the position.[14]

12. AJD to JB, 11 March 1849, JBP.

13. JB to AJD, 29 June 1849, in Sioussat, "Selected Letters, 1846–1856," 266–7; and AJD to JB, 21 July 1849, JBP.

14. Holborn, *History of Modern Germany,* 69–79; Nipperdey, *Germany from Napoleon to Bismarck,* 563–4; and Eyck, *Frankfurt Parliament,* 341–3, 346–62, 369–77.

Donelson, who had rebuffed requests from the provisional government and his own government to return to Frankfurt, observed these changes from Berlin. He depended upon newspaper reports and diplomatic gossip to compose his despatches, which delayed his recognition that the Frankfurt Parliament was losing political strength. Donelson's sanguine reports about unification's inevitability and the triumph of republican ideology were also self-serving, however. Pessimistic news about Germany's progress would only diminish his justification for holding dual missions and their hoped-for pecuniary benefits.[15]

In late March 1849, shortly after the Polk administration gave way to Taylor and the Whigs, a glimmer of hope for German unification appeared. A delegation from the Frankfurt Parliament traveled to Berlin and offered Friedrich Wilhelm IV an appointment as hereditary emperor. When the Prussian monarch refused to accept a crown offered "from the gutter," the Parliament disintegrated, and with it went any chance of unification. After first moving to Stuttgart, then to Gotha, a small remnant of the assembly attempted to salvage something from their efforts. They passed resolutions urging the German states to accept their constitution establishing a German empire, with or without Friedrich Wilhelm IV as its emperor. With German monarchs reasserting their absolutist prerogatives and the people apathetic because of repeated failures, the Frankfurt moderates failed to generate any support and simply disappeared.[16]

The loss of support for German unification surprised Donelson. He reported at first that the Prussian king, hoping to retain his traditional rights, openly opposed the idea of emperorship. When Friedrich Wilhelm IV rejected the position, Donelson still believed that the Prussian monarch and the provisional government would somehow reach a compromise. In late April 1849, however, he admitted that he was unsure which direction the German states would take. In May, shortly before the Frankfurt Parliament disbanded, Donelson informed Clayton that he finally was going to

15. AJD to JB, 8–9, 13 October 1848, in Despatches, vol. 1, DSA; AJD to JB, 21, 23, 26–8 October, 4, 9–11, 13, 18, 22–4 November, 1–3, 6, 14–6, 19, 25 December 1848, 1–2, 7, 15, 19 January, 1–2, 3, 16–9, 26 February, 1, 11, 16, 20, 28 March 1849, Arnold Duckwitz to AJD, 27 October 1848 (copy), AJD to Arnold Duckwitz, 31 October 1848 (copy), memorandum by Theodore Fay on Prussian assembly's meeting, 17 November 1848, Charles Graebe to [AJD], 27 March 1849, in Despatches, vol. 5, DSA; and Eyck, *Frankfurt Parliament,* 345–6.

16. Eyck, *Frankfurt Parliament,* 382–7; Carr, *History of Germany,* 71; and Ramm, *Germany,* 246.

Frankfurt. He had only stayed away, he claimed, to keep from offending Prussia by leaving the Berlin legation vacant and ignoring Friedrich Wilhelm IV's government, which he thought was the most important in Germany.[17]

Donelson's excuses rang hollow. He had stubbornly interfered in German affairs, without orders, for his entire mission, but now he shrank from following the administration's instructions. Buchanan had directed him to travel between the two cities in July 1848, during the most important period for the success of the Parliament, and Donelson had simply ignored him. He had spent less than two complete months in Frankfurt in 1848 and had not returned there since October. It was an "extremely delicate" situation, as Donelson observed, but he had disobeyed direct orders, not only for the reasons that he gave but also because, by his own admission, decreased travel saved him money. He probably could not have changed any of the events in Frankfurt, but his voluntary absence served as a disturbing reminder that, as in the past, his commitment to his post often depended largely upon his disposition and personal interests, not on the larger benefit to the United States.[18]

By the time Donelson finally arrived in Frankfurt, on 14 May 1849, he discovered a city in chaos. The chances of success for the Frankfurt Parliament, he found, were fading quickly. The presence of thousands of troops along the road he traveled between Berlin and Frankfurt and popular revolts in Baden and Bavaria indicated to him the likelihood of civil war. The attitude of the German people also revealed the Parliament's fading power. "The great majority of the population in all the German States [now] prefer monarchy to republicanism," he observed. Those who still supported a German federal republic or even a constitutional monarchy faced "immense standing armies" who were ready "to shoot down all that desire" a change in government. Parliament's collapse only reinforced his despondency.[19]

Donelson's stay in Frankfurt lasted less than two weeks. Upon returning to Berlin, he at last received Clayton's March despatches informing him of Hannegan's appointment. The American minister sold his furniture and re-

17. AJD to JB, 16, 20, 28 March 1849, AJD to JMC, 3, 5–8, 16, 17, 25, 27 April, 1, 7, 8, 9 May 1849, Charles Graebe to [AJD], 27 March 1849, in Despatches, vol. 5, DSA.

18. AJD to JB, 16 February 1849, AJD to JMC, 25 April 1849, in Despatches, vol. 5, DSA.

19. Theodore Fay to JMC, 12, 19 May 1849, in Despatches, vol. 5, DSA; and AJD to JMC, 16, 17–9 May 1849, in Despatches, vol. 1, DSA.

linquished his apartment lease, and when the former Indiana senator proved tardy in reaching Berlin, Donelson was forced to seek lodging in a local hotel. This only increased his expenses and his worries. Realizing that the Taylor administration had a low opinion of his mission, he defended his conduct in relation to the Frankfurt government and unceremoniously deflected criticism onto Ambrose Dudley Mann, the U.S. minister at Hanover who was presently in Frankfurt as an unofficial observer.[20]

In early June 1849, as the unification movement folded, Donelson resumed his complaints. "Nothing is said in the despatch of the outfit which I much [*sic*] think will be allowed to me, notwithstanding it may seem an undue compensation to those who have never resided with a numerous family in such a capital as this," he pronounced. He had lost money on the sale of his Berlin furniture and would have to find money to furnish another dwelling in Frankfurt or live at a public hotel. He also objected to the precarious position in which the Polk and Taylor administrations had placed him with Hannegan's appointment. Finances never seemed to leave his mind.[21]

The gradual realization that the German unification movement had failed only frustrated Donelson even more. The opportunity to modify the political system had passed. "The failure of all the Constituent Assemblies in the German states, and above all the present condition of the National Assembly, expelled as a public enemy from Stuttgart," he noted, "is a proof that Republicanism is not the want of the German people, and is not the means by which they can attain at present a higher state of liberty and prosperity." Those who supported continued reform fought for a hopeless cause, in Donelson's opinion.[22]

Even after he and his family arrived in Frankfurt on 17 June to take up their permanent residence, Donelson remained unhappy. The onset of the hot summer season led to the exodus of many of the political leaders from Frankfurt to the baths, but Donelson, with cries of poverty, stayed behind to try to preserve what relations remained between the United States and the provisional government. He watched the civil wars that were underway in various German states and Prussian provinces and notified the Taylor

20. AJD to JMC, 24 May 1849, in Despatches, vol. 5, DSA.

21. AJD to JMC, 3 June 1849 and 4 June 1849, in ibid.

22. AJD to JMC, 8–9 June 1849, in ibid.; and AJD to JMC, 22 June, 8 July 1849, Despatches, vol. 1, DSA.

administration about the potential for European war over Denmark and Hungary. Donelson seemed resigned to unification's failure.[23]

President Taylor and Secretary of State Clayton realized from Donelson's despatches and other European diplomats' reports that the opportunity for German unification was swiftly passing. Clayton wrote Donelson in early July 1849 with new instructions. The changing political climate required "abundant caution and consummate prudence on the part of the diplomatic representatives of the United States," they read. Clayton ordered Donelson not to engage in any negotiations with the provisional government. "Your position," he directed, "will . . . be only that of a silent and vigilant sentinel." If the Frankfurt government did not make progress toward unification before the summer was out, the Taylor administration would recall him. A little over a week later, however, Clayton also informed Donelson that Congress had approved an additional outfit of nine thousand dollars for his mission.[24]

Disenchanted with the course of events in Germany and no doubt perceiving that his time there was nearing its end, Donelson requested permission on 20 August 1849 to "take one of the steamers and run over to the United States" for an eight- or nine-week leave of absence. He wanted to spend approximately two weeks in Washington discussing the administration's future course toward Germany, then use the rest of his time to settle the private business that once again demanded his attention. Donelson reminded Clayton that every American diplomat in Europe took vacations without orders and that Henry Wheaton, his predecessor, had actually spent half of his time in Paris. His request, he believed, was perfectly reasonable.[25]

Meanwhile, events were already moving toward Donelson's recall. In July, Hannegan requested his withdrawal from the Prussian mission. Clayton told him that the president would appoint a replacement and ordered Hannegan to return to the United States. Replacing him with Donelson,

23. AJD to JMC, 9, 15 June 1849, in Despatches, vol. 5, DSA; AJD to JMC, 17–9 May, 18 June 1849, in Despatches, vol. 1, DSA; and Arthur J. May, "Contemporary American Opinion of the Mid-Century Revolutions in Central Europe" (Ph.D. diss., University of Pennsylvania, 1927), 32–3.

24. JMC to AJD, 8 July 1849, in Diplomatic Instructions, DSA.

25. AJD to JMC, 12, 20 August 1849, in Despatches, vol. 1, DSA.

who had the necessary experience, would have been the logical choice, but it never appeared to enter Taylor's mind. The Tennessean's incessant complaints, though they had slowed after his move to Frankfurt, his desire for a leave of absence, and the failure of the German unification movement gave the Taylor administration sufficient reasons to abandon the German mission and rid itself of a malcontent. In September, Clayton informed Donelson that the president was recalling him; he thanked him for "the ability and faithfulness with which you have discharged the arduous and delicate duties which your mission imposed upon you."[26]

The news did not shock Donelson; in fact, it probably came as a relief. Except for his salary, he saw few reasons to remain in Germany. In early September, he had still expressed hope that German unification would succeed. The day before Clayton wrote his orders recalling him, however, the minister had reversed his mood. "It is painful to look upon this beautiful region of Germany, surrendering itself calmly to military force, and whilst talking about free constitutions permitting itself to be as effectually enslaved as if it was under the former French occupation," he observed. "Nothing is seen but the display of arms and munitions of war. From the Baltic to the Italian seas demagogic folly has paved the way for despotic vengeance." The republican impulse had fallen prey to the vagaries of tyrannical monarchism, and in his limited role, Donelson had been unable to sustain it.[27]

Upon receiving notification of his recall on 10 October, Donelson spent most of his time preparing the transfer of the legation's documents, sending his family to Paris to await his arrival, and attempting to meet with German government officials to announce his departure. When he had completed the necessary arrangements, Donelson departed, leaving Gales Seaton as the United States' confidential agent in Frankfurt.[28]

Donelson traveled to Paris, where he and his family took a steamer to Southampton, then boarded the *Hermann* for the United States. The long trip provided him with sufficient time to ponder his forty-month tenure in

26. JMC to Edward A. Hannegan, 8 August, 11 November 1849, JMC to AJD, 18 September 1849, in Diplomatic Instructions, DSA.

27. AJD to JMC, 2, 17 September 1849, in Despatches, vol. 1, DSA

28. AJD to JMC, 30 October, 2 November 1849, AJD's address to Archduke Johann, n.d. [2 November 1849], Archduke Johann's reply to AJD's address, n.d. [2 November 1849], in Despatches, vol. 1, DSA.

Germany and his accomplishments. He had sent the State Department accurate reports of events in Germany, giving the administration sufficient basis upon which to make decisions affecting international relations in Europe. That, however, was his only identifiable success.[29]

Donelson's failures were more numerous. He had not accomplished two diplomatic goals that had emerged: obtaining a commercial treaty with the Zollverein and realizing the establishment of a German federal republic. He also must have recognized that his persistent complaints and demands had alienated him from important politicians in both political parties, leaving him few options when he returned to public life. Additionally, Donelson had not accumulated enough money from his salary and outfits to pay off his creditors. The costly and extravagant lifestyle at the court of Berlin had sapped his intended savings, leaving him no closer than ever to obtaining financial independence. Donelson's ambition and finances had distracted him, and he had abandoned his duties at crucial times. All of these failures seemed to reveal a man overwhelmed by the tasks placed before him.

29. JMC to Gales Seaton, 1 October 1849, in Diplomatic Instructions, DSA; Gales Seaton to JMC, 30 October 1849, in Despatches, vol. 1, DSA; and AJD to Jackson Donelson, 3 February 1850, DTL.

Part 4

ASSUMING THE MANTLE

Now was the time. "Mr. Chairman, may I speak?" Without waiting for Georgia's Charles McDonald to acknowledge him, Donelson faced the delegates, some of whom were heckling him. Others shouted for silence so that the Tennessean could speak his piece. "I can keep quiet no longer," Donelson bellowed over the noise. "The state of Tennessee, home to Old Hickory, demands to be heard! South Carolina has been heard; Alabama has been heard; now, it is our turn!" The raucous din increased, as Chairman McDonald pounded his gavel for order. "Major Donelson, you had your chance to speak. The debate is over."[1]

1. *Republican Banner and Nashville Whig,* 19, 20 November 1850; and *Nashville Daily Union,* 19 November 1850.

16

"If Slavery Be an Evil . . . It Is One Which Has Been Sent by Providence"

On their way back from Germany, the Donelson family stopped first in Washington, allowing the returning minister to brief the administration on his mission. From there, they traveled to Tulip Grove, arriving on 10 January 1850. Tennessee had experienced both tremendous change and significant continuity during the Donelsons' absence. Economic prosperity and war had changed the nature of the state's politics. Instead of fighting over the reasons for the economic depression, which had receded by 1845, Democrats and Whigs clashed over the Polk administration's prosecution of the Mexican-American War. Democrats had hoped that one byproduct of the war would be more political patronage for their party, but Whigs gained the most benefit during the mid-to-late 1840s. The war enabled them to attack Polk and Tennessee's Democratic party for a multitude of problems and win control of the state's governorship and general assembly in 1847. During the 1848 presidential election, however, Democrats used the slavery issue to present themselves as the defenders of southern rights, a campaign theme that brought them significant victories in the 1849 state elections.[1]

The Mexican-American War, with its acquisition of additional territory, intensified emotional discussion of the slavery issue. Even before the war's end, northerners and southerners had divided over the introduction of the Wilmot Proviso, proposed in August 1846, which would have prohibited slavery in any Mexican territory acquired as a result of the war. The provision, which failed to pass into law, temporarily split the Democratic party into sectional factions and demonstrated the seriousness with which both the North and the South viewed slavery's extension.

1. Satterfield, "Moderate Nationalist Jacksonian," 420; and Atkins, *Parties, Politics, and Sectional Conflict*, 142–62.

The debate over slavery continued in the 1848 presidential election. Democrat Lewis Cass ran on a platform of "popular sovereignty," a policy that would allow a territory's residents to decide whether to allow slavery. Meanwhile, Whig candidate Zachary Taylor adapted his campaign to both northern and southern voters, alternately emphasizing both his neutrality toward, and his support of, slavery. Both major parties hoped their candidate had the answer to the problem, but the Free-Soil party, with Martin Van Buren heading its ticket, wanted to make slavery the campaign's principal issue. This group of abolitionists, antislavery Whigs, northern Democrats, and members of the Liberty party failed to win a substantial number of votes, but its development, based almost exclusively upon opposition to slavery's extension into the territories, increased sectional acrimony. The discovery of gold in California and the accompanying calls for that territory's inclusion as a state in the Union only added to the sectional tension and forced politicians from both sections to address their constituents' concerns.[2]

For many Americans, the issue was not simply slavery or its extension into the territories; it was the future of the nation. Northerners sought to restrain a southern society that in their view was based on the minority rule of a small group of elite planters and predicated on the enslavement of another class of people. As the institution gave southerners unequal political and economic advantages, some northerners believed it imperative to protect the nation from the "slavepower" conspiracy that they thought threatened the Republic. Southerners, on the other hand, defended what they saw as their constitutional right to expand as essential in maintaining equality with the northern states. To them, slavery served to remind them that their republican liberty could be taken away. White southerners might have argued over the elite status and political power that slave owners possessed, but they could all agree that banning territorial slavery constituted a threat to the very foundation of their society.[3]

The winter of 1848–49 proved pivotal in galvanizing the southern defense of slavery's extension into the territories. In the House of Represen-

2. The account of sectional politics given here is based on David Potter, *The Impending Crisis, 1848–1861*, ed. and completed by Don E. Fehrenbacher (New York: Harper and Row, 1976), 18–89; and James McPherson, *Battle Cry of Freedom: The Civil War Era* (New York: Ballantine Books, 1989), 60–4.

3. Holt, *Political Crisis*, 49–66.

tatives, northern politicians introduced bills proposing slavery's abolishment in the District of Columbia and linking the Wilmot Proviso to the admission of the California and New Mexico territories as states. Sixty-nine angry southern congressmen, Whigs and Democrats, met on 22 December 1848 and debated how best to counter their opponents. They appointed a committee, which included John C. Calhoun, to draw up an address outlining their grievances. Before the South Carolina senator could compose the address, however, the House retracted its support of the bill abolishing slavery in the District of Columbia. Nevertheless, Calhoun continued his work. When completed, the "Address of the Southern Congressmen" portrayed in bitter and exaggerated language a northern conspiracy bent on reducing white southerners to slavery by emancipating slaves and elevating them above their former masters. This diatribe garnered only 48 signatures from the 121 southerners in Congress, a disappointing failure resulting from partisan loyalty, suspicion of Calhoun's motives, and the Whigs' retreat from pressing abolitionism in the District. It served notice, however, that southerners were watching the North's actions carefully for signs of hostility.[4]

President Taylor's decisions upon taking office seemed to verify the South's suspicions. Taylor, a Louisiana slaveholder whom southern slaveholders considered one of their own, seemingly ignored their concerns by selecting Senator William H. Seward of New York, an ardent antislavery advocate, as his top adviser. The president also admitted publicly and privately that he would not oppose the Wilmot Proviso and assured northerners that slavery would not find a place in the territories. More important, Taylor sought to admit California and New Mexico as free states without having them pass through the territorial stage, a move that infuriated southerners who wanted to maintain that interim period with its guarantee that the residents could not dispense immediately with slavery.[5]

Throughout 1849, southerners decried the actions of Taylor and northern congressmen. The most notable response, however, came in October at

4. Potter, *Impending Crisis,* 83–6; and Niven, *JCC,* 323–7.

5. K. Jack Bauer, *Zachary Taylor: Soldier, Planter, Statesman of the Old Southwest* (Baton Rouge: Louisiana State University Press, 1985), 290–6; Elbert B. Smith, *The Presidencies of Zachary Taylor and Millard Fillmore* (Lawrence: University Press of Kansas, 1988), 59–63; and Potter, *Impending Crisis,* 86–8.

Jackson, Mississippi, where delegates from across that state, plus a few "observers" from other southern states, particularly South Carolina, met and debated what course to take. The Mississippi convention passed resolutions adamantly opposing any interference with slavery. To solidify southern unity in the face of these dangers, the delegates called for a southern convention to meet in Nashville, Tennessee, the next summer to discuss measures of resistance, up to and including secession.[6]

As the winter of 1849–50 progressed, it appeared that the Nashville Convention would be a momentous meeting. In December 1849, the House convened and fought through sixty-three partisan ballots to elect Georgia's Howell Cobb as its speaker. President Taylor issued his first annual message shortly thereafter, in which he repeated his intention to admit California and New Mexico immediately as states. His admonition to avoid sectionally-divisive topics went unnoticed, as abolitionists denounced slavery and "fire-eaters," or extreme states' rightists from the South, berated their opponents and threatened secession. Meanwhile, southern senators and representatives introduced legislation that strengthened the federal Fugitive Slave Law, proposed the admittance of the Mormon "state" of Deseret, and advised dividing Texas into two slave states, among other disputed subjects.[7]

As congressmen bickered over the nation's future and southerners discussed how best to represent their states in Nashville, Donelson was trying to discern how to keep himself afloat financially. He returned to Tulip Grove to find the house in bad shape but other matters not as bad as he had thought. Daniel was still recommending that his brother would do well to sell off some of his property, but Donelson believed that he could "discharge all my obligations without any sale of property should the price of cotton continue good for two years." Of greater concern to him seemed to be Jackson's safety (his oldest son was serving as an army engineer in the West) and Elizabeth's health during her pregnancy, which produced their fourth (and Donelson's eighth) child, Catherine, in February 1850.[8]

6. Thelma Jennings, *The Nashville Convention: Southern Movement for Unity, 1848–1850* (Memphis, Tenn.: Memphis State University Press, 1980), 17–40.

7. Potter, *Impending Crisis,* 90; Bauer, *Zachary Taylor,* 297–300; and Holman Hamilton, *Prologue to Conflict: The Crisis and Compromise of 1850* (Lexington: University of Kentucky Press, 1964), 43–52.

8. DSD to Jackson Donelson, 14 January 1850, BDP; and AJD to Jackson Donelson, 3 February, 25 April 1850, DTL.

Donelson could not avoid politics, though; it was in his blood. His immediate reaction to the calling of the Nashville Convention and the events precipitating it is unknown. As a planter dependent on slave labor for his financial well-being, however, and as a man who had spoken consistently in support of the Union, it is certain that he had been forced to reconcile the two seemingly conflicting principles. In 1850, he owned sixty-six slaves on twelve hundred acres in Tennessee and an uncertain number of slaves on his Mississippi plantation. Owning slaves was a normal part of Donelson's life and livelihood, and like many wealthy southerners, he had developed a belief system about slavery and the Union with which he felt comfortable.[9]

In sum, Donelson believed that African Americans were an inferior people destined by God to be enslaved by whites, that their enslavement was necessary to preserve the republican principles on which the United States had been founded, that the sanctity of the Union was paramount so long as slavery was protected, that secession was a choice of last resort for the southern states should the national government threaten the existence of slavery, and that it was the duty of all Americans, both northern and southern, to avoid rhetoric and activity that would lead to the dissolution of the nation. Donelson's views marked him as a moderate along the southern political spectrum, between those who advocated for secession at any slight against slavery and those who argued that secession was not an option no matter the circumstances.

Circumstances in Washington were also pushing other Americans to define their positions on the future of both slavery and the Union. On 29 January 1850, Henry Clay introduced a series of eight legislative measures intended to satisfy both North and South on three general issues: slavery in the territories, slavery in the nation's capital, and the Fugitive Slave Law. Clay intended by his compromise measures to end the bitter debates in Congress and save the nation from possible military conflict, just as he had done in 1820 and 1833. Northern supporters applauded his efforts, but southerners blasted Clay's proposals as yielding too much of substance to the North and

9. Jennings, *Nashville Convention,* 237; U.S. Census Office, *Seventh Census of the United States: 1850* (Washington, D.C.: GPO, 1853); and U.S. Census Office, *Seventh Census of the United States: 1850. Slave Inhabitants* (Washington, D.C.: GPO, 1853). Census data and other evidence indicating the size of, and number of slaves on, the Chickasaw County plantation has proven elusive.

providing only a theoretical victory for the South. In both congressional chambers, southerners took turns dissecting Clay's measures and finding them wanting in recognizing the South's rights. The South's self-designated spokesman, John C. Calhoun, who was near death, recommended a constitutional amendment guaranteeing a political balance between free and slave states. Daniel Webster responded by conceding many of the South's complaints but declaring that the "peaceable secession" some southerners advocated was impossible. He also reminded the delegates who planned to attend the Nashville Convention that they would meet near the home and grave of Andrew Jackson, who, if alive, would have opposed any attempt to dismember the Union he had fought to protect.[10]

Across the South, many politicians and laymen alike responded favorably to Webster's speech and criticized Calhoun's intransigence over slavery. Nevertheless, they continued planning to meet in Nashville in June. States' rights representatives from South Carolina, Mississippi, and other states, such as Virginia, agitated zealously for the assembly in order to discuss secession plans. Most of the other states decided to send delegates to Tennessee's capital in order to moderate the antagonistic calls of the radicals and to secure some agreement on the South's future goals.[11]

In Tennessee, preparations for the meeting had begun in late 1849. Sentiment in the state, although unenthusiastic, favored sending moderate delegates to the convention. Initially, both Whigs and Democrats espoused the convention, but by February 1850, the Democrats were virtually alone in their support. The *Nashville Daily Union,* the state's leading Democratic newspaper, criticized Whigs for undermining the southern meeting. They were afraid to settle the slavery dispute because it would mean the end of their party, editor E. G. Eastman declared. When a group of Philadelphians passed a resolution asking the people of Tennessee to avoid "the disgrace of a *second* HARTFORD CONVENTION, by preventing any band of conspirators from holding their treasonable assemblages upon the soil of Tennessee," the *Daily Union* retorted that the Whigs, by their "insults and aggressions," had

10. Hamilton, *Prologue to Conflict,* 53–65; Remini, *Henry Clay,* 730–9; Holt, *American Whig Party,* 476–81; Niven, *JCC,* 339–41; and Robert V. Remini, *Daniel Webster: The Man and His Time* (New York: W. W. Norton, 1997), 668–73.

11. Jennings, *Nashville Convention,* 51–6, 81–3, 57–79, 97–103.

forced the necessity of a southern convention upon them. Tennessee would "yield up every thing but her honor and her vital interests to preserve the Union," Eastman added.[12]

The fervor of partisan press coverage, however, failed to excite Tennesseans, and Whig opposition made the Democrats' task harder. Illustrating the state's partisanship, the general assembly failed to authorize the selection of delegates. Various counties, located mostly in Middle Tennessee, held meetings anyway and chose their own representatives, although many of these gatherings were held only a month before the convention's scheduled opening. Out of 101 delegates, only 8 came from outside of Middle Tennessee, where the Democratic party was strongest, with 29 or 30, including Donelson, selected from Davidson County, Nashville's home. At age fifty, Donelson exceeded the median age of the Tennessee delegates by three years and was one of the most educated attendees from the state. With sixty-six slaves and ownership of twelve hundred acres, valued at forty-seven thousand dollars, he was the tenth-wealthiest state delegate in terms of property value, the eighth-largest slave owner, and the fourth-largest property owner in acreage. He was also one of the few Tennessee delegates known outside of the state.[13]

Donelson was a prime participant in the movement to elect Davidson County's delegates. On 13 April 1850, an invitation went out under his signature, and that of other leading Democrats, asking individuals interested in attending the Nashville Convention to assemble on the first Monday in May. When the meeting convened on 7 May, its attendees chose Donelson as their president. As part of his duties, Donelson gave a speech summarizing his stance. "As I understand our position," he said, "our chief wish should be to have the freesoilers and abolitionists disarmed—disarmed not so much by our sectional opposition to them, as by the action of the sound portion of the American people without reference to Geographical lines, and by our union with the true friends of the constitution in the north, the east, and the west, as well as the south." Donelson, mindful of his close association with

12. Ibid., 77–8; *Nashville Daily Union,* 24 February, 6 March 1850; and Atkins, *Parties, Politics, and Sectional Conflict,* 163–6.

13. Jennings, *Nashville Convention,* 78, 94–7, 130–3, 233–50 (Appendix B); Atkins, *Parties, Politics, and Sectional Conflict,* 166–7; and *Nashville Daily Union,* 7 May 1850.

northern politicians, denied that they intended to "interfere with slavery as it was regulated by the framers of the constitution." He believed northerners understood that "neither their true interests nor those of their country can be advanced by any imitation of the conduct of foreign nations," such as Great Britain, toward slavery. Donelson praised the "temperance and dignity" of his fellow Davidson Countians and concluded with a republican flourish that recalled the failed German revolutions: "If we continue united in the bond of national affection with the members of our great confederacy, the influence of our theory that the people are capable of self government will soon become so great in Europe that the people will there too be able to build with it barricades which no despot can overthrow." [14]

Following Donelson's speech, the Democrats present quickly attempted to select delegates, but the attending Whigs, unaffected by his discourse, blocked these efforts and passed resolutions opposing the delegates' election. In a desperate move to save the day, Donelson adjourned the meeting and then reconvened it. It now consisted mostly of Democrats, as many of the dissenting Whigs had departed in triumph at their apparent victory. During this "rump" session, the attendees chose the county's delegates to the Nashville Convention and outlined their course in relation to the June meeting. They agreed on several resolutions: Congress had a duty to protect private property, including slaves; Congress possessed "no power" to regulate slavery in the United States or its territories; California should only be admitted as a free state if the rest of the Mexican Cession was organized under the authority of popular sovereignty; and the Free-Soil party, by opposing the advice of the nation's founding fathers, was anathema to the Constitution's foundational principles. A consistent theme in their resolutions was commitment to the Union and the Constitution, as illustrated by the adoption of Jackson's famous phrase from the 1832–33 Nullification Crisis, "Our federal Union must be preserved," undoubtedly suggested by Donelson.[15]

14. *Nashville Daily Union,* 13 April, 7 May, 26 September 1850; *Republican Banner and Nashville Whig,* 7 May 1850; Jennings, *Nashville Convention,* 94–5; and St. George L. Sioussat, "Tennessee, the Compromise of 1850, and the Nashville Convention," *Mississippi Valley Historical Review* 2 (December 1915): 323–4.

15. *Nashville Daily Union,* 13 April, 7 May 1850; *Republican Banner and Nashville Whig,* 7 May 1850; *Washington Daily Union,* 5 June 1851; Jennings, *Nashville Convention,* 94–5; and Sioussat, "Tennessee, the Compromise of 1850," 323–4.

The movements in Tennessee and across the South occurred as Congress continued to debate Clay's proposals. Suggestions for improvement by Whig senator John Bell of Tennessee and Senator Henry S. Foote of Mississippi failed to elicit much support, but Foote did convince the Senate to appoint a select committee of thirteen to debate the propositions and possibly combine them into one bill. He reasoned that, by placing the eight measures into one "omnibus" bill, both northerners and southerners would have to vote for the proposals they disliked in order to pass those they favored. After initially opposing the modification, Clay threw his support behind it and chaired the Committee of Thirteen charged with shepherding the bill through the Senate. After much discussion, on 8 May, the Kentuckian presented the omnibus bill, with only minor changes to the fugitive slave provision. Debate began immediately, and it was in this atmosphere that Nashville Convention delegates assembled at McKendree Methodist Church on Monday, 3 June 1850.[16]

Donelson later told how his decision to attend the Nashville Convention had come from "the hope that the patriotic exertions of Congress towards the adjustment of the slavery question might be aided." His old colleague, Cave Johnson, encouraged him to use his influence to calm emotions. The nation stood to benefit or lose from the proceedings in Nashville, he reminded Donelson, but the actions of Tennessee's Democratic delegates could very well determine the future of their party in the state for years to come. "Use your influence, which I know is great with the *excitable* masses that will be there[,] to keep them cool & prevent as far as possible any harsh expressions which may serve the Whigs for food in our next campaign," Johnson advised. Fresh from observing Europe's revolutions and grounded in republican commitment to the Union and the Constitution, Donelson made his way from Tulip Grove to downtown Nashville to take his place as a moderate voice.[17]

With Whig judge William L. Sharkey of Mississippi presiding, the delegates immediately set to work. Throughout the first week, representatives

16. Remini, *Henry Clay*, 739–46; Hamilton, *Prologue to Conflict*, 62; Joseph H. Parks, "John Bell and the Compromise of 1850," *Journal of Southern History* 9 (August 1943): 328–56; Potter, *Impending Crisis*, 103–4; Holt, *Political Crisis*, 85–6; and Jennings, *Nashville Convention*, 135–7.

17. Jennings, *Nashville Convention*, 132–3; Cave Johnson to AJD, 10 May 1850, DLC; and *Washington Daily Union*, 5 June 1851.

from several states presented resolutions recommending secession and revolution, as well as patience with the current compromise discussions taking place in Washington. On Saturday, the resolutions committee submitted for the delegates' approval thirteen resolutions and an address to the southern people. A. O. P. Nicholson, a Tennessean who served on the resolutions committee, reported that a minority of the committee approved of the resolutions but expressed concern with the tone of the address. Motions to table both the resolutions and address carried, and the convention adjourned its first week's proceedings.[18]

When the delegates reconvened the following Monday, they unanimously approved the proposed thirteen resolutions in slightly modified form. The resolutions denied congressional authority to interfere with territorial slavery and asserted the southern states' prerogative to ignore any law that denied slaveholders the right to own slaves in those areas. As an "extreme concession," they indicated the convention's willingness to accept the extension of the Missouri Compromise line to the Pacific Ocean. Other resolutions concerned the proposed division of Texas and challenged the authority of Congress to control slavery anywhere and in any form, including in the internal slave trade. Although he made no public statement, Donelson undoubtedly agreed with the spirit and substance of many of the declarations contained in these resolutions, as they coincided with his previously stated beliefs.[19]

Where the resolutions met with general approbation, the resolutions committee's address, written by Robert Barnwell Rhett of South Carolina, caused considerable discussion. Rhett chastised the South for allowing the North to abolish slavery incrementally and reminded its citizens that they could freely relinquish their liberty as easily as northerners could forcibly take it from them. He declared the compromise measures currently before Congress tantamount to southern capitulation but conceded that the South would accept the extension of the Missouri Compromise line as a final and definitive solution. Because most of the delegates supported the negotiations taking place in Congress, Gideon J. Pillow, Tennessee's representative

18. Jennings, *Nashville Convention,* 137–46.

19. Ibid., 146–7; and "Resolutions of the Nashville Convention," in Commager, *Documents of American History,* 324–5.

on the resolutions committee, suggested, with his delegation's support, an amended address to temper Rhett's address. Considerable debate ensued, but Pillow's amendments stood. After agreeing to reconvene in Nashville six weeks after Congress adjourned, the convention closed.[20]

Donelson's total silence in this first meeting probably surprised observers. His only recorded comment came secondhand, when Cave Johnson informed James Buchanan that Donelson had declared the "distracting questions . . . settled, and . . . the Republic . . . safe." Other Tennesseans, including Pillow, Thomas Claiborne, and William H. Polk, the former president's brother, took the floor and argued for their opinions, but not Donelson. For a man intimately involved with the Jackson administration and well acquainted with its guiding principles, Donelson should have been one of the convention's leaders. He had played a prominent role in the Davidson County meeting preceding the convention, but upon its commencement, he disappeared. Donelson possibly worked within the Tennessee delegation to temper its private debates and public pronouncements, but it appears that the state's representatives had determined beforehand to take a moderate stance.[21]

Donelson's reticence may have been another instance of his continued lack of leadership during key moments. His failure to assert his opinions was reminiscent of past episodes during the 1844 election, in Texas, and in Germany, when he receded into the background during important periods of decision. When it came time for Jackson's political heir and favorite ward to make a difference, to invoke the name of his esteemed uncle and save the nation from possible disunion, he sat silently with his delegation instead of leading the charge against the fire-eaters. Jackson undoubtedly would have shaken his head in disappointment.

Donelson left the first session of the Nashville Convention confident that Congress would heed the warning signs emanating from the South and permanently settle the slavery issue. The Taylor administration, however, displeased by Clay's usurpation of its own compromise efforts, ignored the

20. Jennings, *Nashville Convention*, 147–54; and William C. Davis, *Rhett: The Turbulent Life and Times of a Fire-Eater* (Columbia: University of South Carolina Press, 2001), 273–6.

21. Cave Johnson to James Buchanan, 30 March 1851, JBP; and *Nashville Daily Union*, 26 September 1850.

convention's proceedings. Seeking to act definitively, Taylor encouraged New Mexico's residents to ratify a state constitution outlawing slavery, which they did, and vowed to accept it over southern protest. The New Mexico imbroglio, combined with Taylor's and northern and southern extremists' opposition to the omnibus bill, appeared certain to doom all compromise efforts.[22]

Then everything changed. On 9 July, President Taylor died of acute gastroenteritis, and Vice-President Millard Fillmore took over the executive office. The new president, a former Anti-Mason from Buffalo, New York, had risen in the ranks of his state's Whig party to become the vice-presidential nominee in the 1848 election. Like most nineteenth-century vice-presidents, he had little influence over the president, his position further weakened by the presence of Seward, who was Fillmore's bitter opponent in New York. With Taylor dead, however, Fillmore's assumption of office immediately changed the complexion of the compromise movement. Seward's strident antislavery influence and the administration's hard-line tactics disappeared, replaced by the moderating tone of a man who had spent months in the Senate listening to arguments for and against compromise. The Union was now undoubtedly in better hands.[23]

Fillmore signified the administration's change in direction by immediately replacing staunch antislavery men in the cabinet with like-minded moderates, such as Webster, John J. Crittenden of Kentucky, and William Alexander Graham of North Carolina; later selections for the remaining posts continued that inclination. These initial appointments signaled to the public Fillmore's intention to pursue compromise. Webster's final speech as a senator before assuming his new position as secretary of state, in which he advised passage of the omnibus bill in separate parts if Congress would not pass it in bulk, and the president's announcement that he would accept "any constitutional measure passed by Congress," only served to re-

22. McPherson, *Battle Cry of Freedom,* 74; Potter, *Impending Crisis,* 106–7; Bauer, *Zachary Taylor,* 302–10; Mark J. Stegmaier, *Texas, New Mexico, and the Compromise of 1850: Boundary Dispute and Sectional Crisis* (Kent, Ohio: Kent State University Press, 1996), 115–33, 152–61; Hamilton, *Prologue to Conflict,* 98–106; and Remini, *Henry Clay,* 751–2.

23. McPherson, *Battle Cry of Freedom,* 74–5; Smith, *Presidencies,* 43–7, 156–8, 164–9; and Robert J. Rayback, *Millard Fillmore: Biography of a President* (Buffalo, N.Y.: Buffalo Historical Society, 1959), 185–91, 194–6, 199–205, 214, 224, 236–7.

mind Americans that a major change in administration policy had taken place.[24]

Despite Fillmore's support, the Senate defeated a watered-down omnibus bill on 31 July. His compromise reduced to nothing, the sickly Clay departed for a vacation. Fortunately, Stephen A. Douglas, the Democratic senator from Illinois, intervened and saved the compromise measures. Determined to see the compromise passed, he used sectional factions to guide Clay's measures individually through the House and rally support for them in the Senate. California would become a free state, while popular sovereignty would govern the New Mexico and Utah Territories. The Fugitive Slave Law was strengthened, but the District of Columbia's slave trade was prohibited. The Compromise of 1850, as it became known, had finally been reached.[25]

Reaction to the compromise varied. Many northerners and southerners celebrated it as a "final settlement" of the slavery issue. Extremists in both sections, however, found little satisfaction in it. For northern abolitionists, the Fugitive Slave Law was an odious price to pay for keeping the rebellious southern states in the Union, while southern fire-eaters feared the loss of sectional balance in the Senate and the possible failure of northern states to enforce the Fugitive Slave Law. The compromise held significant consequences for the South and the second meeting of the Nashville Convention. States' rights politicians from Mississippi, Alabama, Georgia, and South Carolina, who had agitated most strongly against Clay's proposals during the June meeting in Nashville, declared the compromise unsatisfactory and called for united southern action, meaning secession. Moderates in these states and across the upper South largely accepted the compromise legislation, but only because of the North's guaranteed enforcement of the Fugitive Slave Law.[26]

In Donelson's home state, the compromise met with general approbation. The Whig party lauded the settlement but warned that southern extremists

24. Rayback, *Millard Fillmore,* 240–6; Remini, *Henry Clay,* 752–3; Remini, *Daniel Webster,* 683–5, 687; Hamilton, *Prologue to Conflict,* 107–8; and McPherson, *Battle Cry of Freedom,* 74–5.

25. Hamilton, *Prologue to Conflict,* 109–14, 133–65; Remini, *Henry Clay,* 754–7; Smith, *Presidencies,* 180–1; Potter, *Impending Crisis,* 107–20; and McPherson, *Battle Cry of Freedom,* 75.

26. Hamilton, *Prologue to Conflict,* 166–8; Potter, *Impending Crisis,* 122–5; and Jennings, *Nashville Convention,* 174–85.

inside and outside Tennessee would not accept it. The state's Democratic party, meanwhile, found itself divided. Moderates applauded the compromise as indicative of the cooperative spirit then prevailing, but states' rightists denounced it as merely acquiescence to northern tyranny. Cave Johnson, writing James Buchanan shortly before the November meeting of southern delegates in Nashville, assured the Pennsylvanian of Tennessee's support for the compromise but warned that the people of his state expected strict enforcement of the Fugitive Slave Law. All sides in Tennessee and the South awaited the convening of the southern delegates in Nashville on 11 November 1850, anxious to settle conclusively the region's response to the many issues that had caused such dissension.[27]

The Nashville Convention's second meeting differed greatly from the first gathering. Only fifty-eight delegates from seven states made the trip to Nashville, and fewer than two-thirds of that number were present at the first meeting. Representatives from Mississippi, Alabama, Georgia, and South Carolina comprised the majority of the delegates, with Tennessee contributing fourteen members, Florida four, and Virginia only one. Many of the moderates from the June meeting, satisfied with the compromise passed by Congress, stayed away, leaving the makeup of the convention delegates tilted heavily in favor of the fire-eaters. Tennessee's delegation, which included Donelson, Pillow, Nicholson, Aaron V. Brown, and William H. Polk, embodied the moderate voice at the convention.[28]

Gathering at the Christian Church just down the street from its original meeting place, the convention opened its proceedings with many of the delegates still absent due to travel problems. The convention's designated chair, Charles J. McDonald of Georgia, delivered an address that indicated the initial anticompromise tenor of the meeting. He accused Congress of ignoring the June gathering in Nashville, denounced the compromise legislation, and warned southerners to be prepared to preserve their rights through force if necessary. The arrival of the absent delegates in time for Wednesday's morning session only increased talk of secession. Alabama's Clement C. Clay Sr.,

27. Jennings, *Nashville Convention*, 185–6; Atkins, *Parties, Politics, and Sectional Conflict*, 169–70; and Sioussat, "Tennessee, the Compromise of 1850," 343.

28. Jennings, *Nashville Convention*, 188–9, 253–4 (Appendix D); and *Republican Banner and Nashville Whig*, 15 November 1850.

who had been present since Monday, had waited for the appearance of the missing delegates to announce his stand. He asserted a state's constitutional right of secession and called for the formation of a southern congress modeled on the Nashville Convention. In such a body, southerners could meet regularly, compare their grievances, and decide appropriate response to northern actions. Delegates from Florida, Georgia, and Mississippi argued in the same vein.[29]

The Tennessee delegation finally received the opportunity to present its viewpoint on Thursday afternoon. Pillow, who was serving as chair of the credentials committee during this session, introduced resolutions reflecting the majority opinion of his state's representatives. Acknowledging that the compromise legislation "falls short of that measure of justice to which the South in our opinion was fairly entitled," the first resolution nevertheless pledged the convention to "abide by them with all that fidelity which has distinguished the South on all former occasions." This promise, however, depended upon the North's strict adherence to the legislation. By accepting the compromise, which some southerners considered a final settlement, northerners had agreed not to interfere with slavery. If the North broke the agreement, then the Tennessee delegation urged the southern states to engage in commercial non-intercourse, and, if necessary, to assemble a southern convention "with full power and authority to do any thing and every thing which the peace, safety, and honor of the South may demand."[30]

Finally breaking his silence, Donelson submitted his own minority resolutions, which were slightly more tempered. His first resolution encouraged the southern people and states "to acquiesce in the laws recently passed by Congress as a compromise of the differences of opinion growing out of the subject of slavery." The second resolution promised that the convention would not "anticipate a course of action on the part of Congress or of any of the sovereign States that are parties to the federal compact, which will justify extreme measures in preserving the terms of that compact." Third, Donelson proposed that "the forbearance manifested by the people of the

29. Jennings, *Nashville Convention,* 192–4; *Nashville Daily Union,* 12 November 1850; and *Republican Banner and Nashville Whig,* 13, 14, 15 November 1850.

30. Jennings, *Nashville Convention,* 194–5; *Republican Banner and Nashville Whig,* 15 November 1850; and *Nashville Daily Union,* 15 November 1850.

South, during the recent crisis, is the best pledge which they can give of their determination to maintain the Federal Constitution as long as it is administered in good faith." If Congress failed to execute its laws regarding slavery as guaranteed in the compromise, however, the South would unite with a "spirit of patriotic resistance." Finally, he reminded both southerners and northerners that the "motto of the Southern States is perpetuity to the Union and to the constitution, and . . . these States will look to resistance, open and undisguised resistance, as a revolutionary remedy only when such an interpretation of the federal compact is enforced as will place them on an unequal footing as members of the confederacy, and will make the federal government the instrument of intolerable tyranny and oppression."[31]

With these resolutions, Donelson clearly indicated his position. He would do everything in his power to maintain the recent compromise, but he also pledged his support for the South. His resolutions failed to elicit support among the delegates. One of his fellow Tennesseans, Thomas Claiborne, criticized Donelson's statement as the work of "hireling presses and juggling politicians" bereft of "the right understanding of their rights." Langdon Cheves of South Carolina, a rabid states' rightist, countered Donelson's moderate tone by introducing a short resolution that proclaimed "secession by the joint action of the slaveholding States is the only efficient remedy for the aggravated wrongs which they now endure and the enormous evils which threaten them in the future from the usurped and now unrestricted power of the federal government." He then launched into a three-hour speech that expanded upon the secession theme, listed the North's transgressions, and recommended the appropriate southern response. When Cheves finished, the convention adjourned for the evening.[32]

Thursday's proceedings left Donelson frustrated. The Friday and Saturday sessions only increased his annoyance. On Friday, speeches by Georgia's

31. Jennings, *Nashville Convention,* 194–5; *Republican Banner and Nashville Whig,* 15 November 1850; and *Nashville Daily Union,* 22 November 1850. While I believe that Donelson's time in Europe had shown him the dangers of revolution, based on the available evidence, I am not as convinced as Timothy M. Roberts that he used his experience as minister to the Frankfurt provisional government to influence the convention delegates. See his article, "'Revolutions Have Become the Bloody Toy of the Multitude': European Revolutions, the South, and the Crisis of 1850," *Journal of the Early Republic* 25 (Summer 2005): 280.

32. Jennings, *Nashville Convention,* 195–6; and *Republican Banner and Nashville Whig,* 15 November 1850.

Jacob G. McWhertor and Tennessee's Claiborne paradoxically advocated both secession and continued support for the Union, while on Saturday, the resolutions committee, of which Aaron V. Brown and A. O. P. Nicholson were members, submitted to the delegates a set of resolutions modeled on those introduced by Clement C. Clay Jr. of Alabama. After Brown offered a minority report for the Tennessee delegation, the Mississippi representatives registered their objections to Clay's resolutions as well. Agreeing to discuss the situation over the weekend, the convention recessed. It appeared that its members were set to accept disunionist resolutions when they reconvened following the Sabbath break.[33]

When the convention reassembled on Monday morning, the fire-eaters moved to secure passage of their platform. The resolutions committee submitted for approval a preamble to the resolutions, based on a plan by the Alabama delegation, that defended the South's racist society and implicitly advocated secession if the North tried to limit slavery's expansion. It accused the northern states of seeking to abolish "our relations of master and slave," a bond "marked by such distinctions of color, and physical and moral qualities, as forever forbid their living together on terms of social and political equality." Any attempt to sever those ties "must end in convulsion, and the entire ruin of one or both races," the preamble predicted. Admitting that the delegates had "no powers that are binding upon the states we represent," the committee nevertheless justified its stance as necessary to preserve "our rights—our independence—the peace and existence of our families." The resolutions that followed the preamble were modeled closely on those introduced by the Mississippi delegation. They asserted the compact theory of government, denounced the compromise passed by Congress, recommended the abstention of southern states from national party conventions, and proposed the organization of a southern convention possessing appropriate representation and adequate authority to defend the region against northern usurpation of its constitutional rights. The result was more tempered than the fire-eaters had hoped for, but they had made their point.[34]

33. Jennings, *Nashville Convention,* 196; and *Republican Banner and Nashville Whig,* 18 November 1850.

34. Jennings, *Nashville Convention,* 196–7; *Republican Banner and Nashville Whig,* 19 November 1850; and *Nashville Daily Union,* 19 November 1850.

The announcement of the preamble and resolutions elicited a heated response from the Tennessee delegation. Both Brown and Nicholson indicated their desire to speak on the floor, but in a questionable parliamentary move, the chair ruled the debate finished. The two Tennesseans accepted the decision, promising to provide the public with their views, but, at this point, Donelson finally made an assertive move. He stood up and demanded the floor. "*I pronounce the attempt to cut off debate by the application of the Previous Question, as* UNWORTHY OF THIS CONVENTION: *and I wish to* PROTEST *against its* UNHALLOWED PURPOSES," Donelson shouted. Others had had their chance; now it was his turn to speak for the minority who opposed the convention's proposed public address. McDonald, president of the convention, ruled Donelson out of order, whereupon the Tennessean asked for a reading of the committee's report. The chair took a voice vote from each delegation, and the results showed the Tennessee delegation as the only one opposing the recommended preamble and resolutions.[35]

After the delegations' votes were taken and the report adopted, Donelson, still determined to speak, again demanded the floor. Although the Tennessee delegation had voted to oppose the report, he had purposely voted in favor of it in order to "record his protest against the unhallowed purposes of the Convention." By voting in the majority, he believed that he had obtained the right to speak, even if in opposition. Taking a cue from the chair, Donelson was using a questionable parliamentary move to gain the floor. "Great confusion here ensued," according to one reporter, as the delegates loudly debated whether Donelson's maneuver was acceptable. President McDonald again ruled him out of order and, giving the excuse that a funeral was scheduled in the church that afternoon, adjourned the convention.[36]

The convention may have ended, but Donelson was not finished. The following Saturday, a group of Davidson County Unionists from both parties, led by Donelson and several others, met in Nashville. Donelson was a member of the resolutions committee, which composed nine resolutions passed by the assembly. The resolutions, reminiscent of those introduced

35. Jennings, *Nashville Convention,* 197; *Republican Banner and Nashville Whig,* 19, 20 November 1850; and *Nashville Daily Union,* 19 November 1850.

36. Jennings, *Nashville Convention,* 197; *Republican Banner and Nashville Whig,* 19 November 1850; and *Nashville Daily Union,* 19 November 1850.

by Donelson during the Nashville Convention, "recognize[d] attachment to the Union, and unhesitating submission to constitutional laws as the primary duty of all good citizens." They accepted the Constitution as the nation's ultimate authority, acknowledged the supremacy of Congress and the Supreme Court over the states, and denounced "the attempt of certain fanatics and designing politicians" to subvert their power. Any state's attempt to secede or "dissolve the federal compact," the resolutions continued, contravened the Constitution and would cause "anarchy, confusion and endless civil strife and bloodshed." The North possessed important obligations, they maintained. The abrogation of the federal Fugitive Slave Law by northern abolitionists and the agitation of the slavery issue by northern mobs were "destructive of the best interests of our country and . . . will paralize [*sic*] all our energies, and lead to a total alienation of one section of the Union from the other" if not discontinued. The attendees also approved a resolution supporting the right of the people, "whenever they shall be palpably, intolerably and unconstitutionally oppressed, to throw off the chains that oppress them and resist the action of the Government," but they denied the necessity of convening a southern congress at the present time. Finally, the meeting's members approved a resolution endorsing the 1850 compromise.[37]

With the resolutions passed, the crowd began calling for Donelson to speak. He had prepared a speech to give at the Nashville Convention, but when that meeting had closed without the opportunity to present it, he had lengthened it in preparation for the Union assembly. He rose from his seat on the platform and launched into a long exposition on the true motives of the "secession party" attending the Nashville Convention, his own reasons for attending, and a defense of the Constitution and the Union. Invoking the names of the nation's founders and his uncle, Donelson dismantled the fire-eaters' arguments. The founders' success proved "an influence almost divine belongs to the simple words of some men whose life has been hallowed by great sacrifices in the cause of liberty. They are like lamps that we hang up in our halls," he argued. "Light them, and all that around is seen and understood." Just as Jackson's steadfast opposition to nullification had caused "the despots of Europe to feel that the principle of popular government" had

37. *Nashville Daily Union,* 19, 25, 26 November 1850; and *Republican Banner and Nashville Whig,* 19, 25 November 1850.

prevailed, so too must Tennesseans and southerners oppose the darkness contained in the secessionists' arguments, Donelson insisted.[38]

"Democracy" was the watchword Donelson invoked as the hallmark of American political life and the path to avoiding disunion. "Demagogues may cry that the constitution has been violated, but the true democracy of America, instead of flying to arms, will read again the great lessons taught by those who framed the Constitution," he reasoned. "The true democracy will defend the legacy left them by the patriots of the revolution. The true democracy will never permit the doctrine of secession to undermine the empire of reason and law, which are provided by the constitution, and to substitute that which will be gained by the sword." What did Donelson mean by democracy? "I use the term democracy, gentlemen, as denoting a principle rather than a party. I have reference [*sic*] to that principle which derives power, political power, from the people—that principle which pervades all the institutions of America, State and Federal, and which is recognized by every patriot in the land whatever may be or may have been his party name," he explained. "If this principle is to be maintained . . . it can only be done by the preservation of our constitution." Allowing a single state or several states to secede, Donelson added, would "destroy this constitution and American glory and fame [would] sink[,] never to rise again."[39]

Despite his unionist themes, Donelson admitted that secession, horrible as the thought was to him, might one day take place if slavery were abolished. When it did, though, he believed there would be "revolution" and a reshaping of the U.S. government: "The sword then becomes the arbiter." No one could predict how such a revolution would conclude, but Donelson warned that ancient and modern history taught that "the objects of war are generally lost by the efforts of war." Secession, then, should be avoided if possible; southerners would not find their answer in that course of action.[40]

As he closed his speech, Donelson related a story concerning the 1844 Democratic National Convention that he believed demonstrated the significance of putting principle above both men and party. Undecided about who he should support as the Democratic presidential nominee, Donelson

38. *Nashville Daily Union*, 22, 25, 26 November 1850.

39. *Nashville Daily Union*, 26 November 1850.

40. Ibid.

recalled, he approached Jackson and relayed his concerns about alienating his friend, Martin Van Buren, and agitating the Texas issue, which undoubtedly would excite the slavery question. His uncle, "with warmth and earnestness," told Donelson that he had to adhere to his principles above any other consideration. "If he [Van Buren] is against Texas," Jackson advised, "I give up my friend and go for my country." He also encouraged Donelson to honor his conscience above his fears about slavery. "If at any given moment we are deterred from the adoption of a measure, not because the measure is wrong, but because others at a future day may be less mindful of their duty than they ought to be," the General remarked, "what would become of the country[?] Let us do our duty to-day, [and] tomorrow will take care of itself." Jackson's lesson, according to Donelson, was "that he lost sight of personal considerations, no matter how tender or how strong, if they conflicted with the paramount claims of his country and the preservation of its institutions." In light of his uncle's comments, Donelson believed Jackson, if alive, would now embrace Henry Clay, his sworn enemy of two decades, and congratulate him for trying to preserve the Union through his compromise measures. Donelson assured the audience that he felt the same.[41]

Donelson's position illustrated the dilemma faced by all slave-owning southern moderates: could they continue defending the Union if they would be forced to abolish slavery? However much they intellectually and ideologically supported liberty, white male slave owners usually only sought and defended liberty for themselves, not for those with minority status, such as slaves, women, and propertyless white males. Supporting the Union if it would cost them the institution that served as the foundation of their own economic and political welfare was problematic and, for some, unthinkable. Like many southern slave owners, Donelson would continue to grapple in the 1850s with an important choice: a potential Union without slavery or slavery without the Union. As the political lines hardened, it became more difficult to take the middle ground.

41. Ibid.

17

“The Constitution . . . Shall Be My Guide”

In addition to posing unsettling questions about the future of slavery and the Union, the year 1850 presented another, more familiar dilemma for Donelson: he was moving further into debt. Economic expediency once again led him to accept a government position, this time as editor of the *Washington Union,* a Democratic newspaper in the nation’s capital. During his thirteen-month tenure as the organ’s editor, from April 1851 to May 1852, Donelson, through his avowed platform based on the Constitution and the Union, attempted to steer the Democratic party toward moderation and away from the secessionist impulse that was becoming more prevalent within the party. The anticipated pecuniary windfall from the position never materialized, however, leaving Donelson in worse financial shape than when he took the post. More important, his moderate editorial tone and apparent greed in obtaining congressional patronage alienated him from many Democratic leaders, ultimately causing him to abandon the party of Andrew Jackson, Martin Van Buren, and James K. Polk.

Donelson’s economic woes, which had caused him such consternation while he served as minister in Germany, continued to increase upon his return to the United States. During the summer interregnum between the two meetings of the Nashville Convention, Donelson received confirmation that Congress had retroactively approved his requested outfit as minister to Frankfurt. But the departing secretary of state, John M. Clayton, refused to authorize Donelson’s reimbursement request of $2,250 for expenses incurred during his trips between Berlin and Frankfurt in 1848 and 1849, saying the $9,000 diplomatic outfit sufficiently covered his expenditures. Donelson also received a terse note from John H. Eaton, who berated him for not paying his debt of $570, despite his “repeated promises.” “When you left here [Washington, D.C.],” Eaton reminded him, “you assured me, that in ten days after reaching home, you would reply,” but “up to this time no compliance has been made." He demanded that Donelson pay him $500 "in *reasonable* time," or he would take him to court.[1]

Donelson had apparently learned nothing from his past experiences. Just as he had ignored Martin Van Buren's pleas for payment, Donelson continued to disregard Eaton's threats of litigation. Others might have considered his conduct at the very least rude, if not dishonorable, especially when he spent part of his early 1851 trip to the North purchasing a "first-class" carriage to send to Tennessee. According to one historian's estimate, Donelson's total debt in 1851 amounted to "more than $40,000," a significant sum for one whose cumulative wealth the previous year totaled only $47,000. With a family that had grown by two with the birth of William Alexander in January 1849 and Catherine in February 1850, and the continued schooling of four of the six older children, Donelson's family-related expenses devoured much of his annual income. His precarious situation explains why, when members of the Democratic party approached him with a proposed government position as editor of the *Washington Union,* he accepted the post.[2]

The *Washington Union* had replaced Francis P. Blair's *Globe* in 1845 as the official organ of the Polk administration and now served as the Democratic party's major newspaper. During the 1850 compromise negotiations, *Globe* editor Thomas Ritchie had espoused Henry Clay's peaceable settlement, infuriating the southern states' rights wing of the Democratic party. At the same time, northern Democrats believed him too closely allied with southern interests. Using the excuse that Ritchie was too old and opinionated to serve as party editor and that accusations of corruption were hindering his credibility, a number of nationally known Democrats, including Lewis Cass and Stephen A. Douglas, forced his resignation. They chose Donelson, who happened to be in Washington settling his accounts with the Department of State, as Ritchie's replacement. Expecting him to be a malleable mouthpiece, they approached him during his visit and asked him to accept the editorial position.[3]

1. JMC to S. Pleasanton, 18 July 1850, JHE to AJD, 30 November 1850, DLC.

2. AJD to ERD, 7 March 1851, DLC; and Satterfield, "Moderate Nationalist Jacksonian," 428. These numbers do not include his Mississippi plantation.

3. Roy Franklin Nichols, *The Democratic Machine, 1850–1854* (New York: Longman, Green, 1923), 32–4; Charles H. Ambler, *Thomas Ritchie: A Study in Virginia Politics* (Richmond, Va.: Bell Book and Sta-

Donelson was not immediately convinced of the necessity or wisdom of taking the job. The editorship did not promise much profit, and Donelson told his wife he preferred to pursue "the old business of cotton and corn." To convince him to take the post, party leaders made two promises. They agreed to find someone else to provide the necessary capital to purchase the newspaper from Ritchie, alleviating Donelson of the necessity of going further into debt, and they assured him that Congress would pass legislation giving the *Union* a printing contract for the 1850 census returns, an agreement that would provide the newspaper's editor and proprietor between one hundred and two hundred thousand dollars. With these financial inducements before him, in March 1851, Donelson put aside any compunction and agreed to accept the position.[4]

The transaction's details took over a month to finalize. For the proprietorship, which required a minimum capital investment of ten thousand dollars, Donelson approached John C. Rives and Francis P. Blair, but they turned him down. He eventually received financial backing from Robert J. Armstrong, his old newspaper associate from Tennessee. The official sale of the newspaper took place on 11 March, but not without some bitterness on Ritchie's part. He, along with Donelson, Armstrong, Mississippi senator Henry S. Foote, and Washington, D.C., banker William W. Corcoran, met at Washington's National Hotel on the evening of the eleventh to complete the deal. Shortly before the meeting began, however, Ritchie sent Corcoran a note sharply criticizing Donelson and Armstrong. "Can you see Donelson—and get him to come to a close in this harrassing [*sic*] negotiation[?]" he asked. "This thing almost bores me, as much as it does you—and it is almost time to end it. . . . They want to see the types, presses, etc—as if they knew any thing about such things—or as if types and presses were the principal considerations, independently of the *portion* of the press, which, after all, is the 'great' matter—along with the benefit which it [*sic*] comes along with it." Despite Ritchie's criticism of the Tennesseans' newspaper acumen and a last-minute proposal by another unnamed party to purchase

---

tionery, 1913), 278–88; and William Ernest Smith, *The Francis Preston Blair Family in Politics,* 2 vols. (New York: Macmillan, 1933), 1:269–70.

4. AJD to ERD, 24 February, 7 March 1851, DLC; Smith, *Francis Preston Blair Family,* 270; and Nichols, *Democratic Machine,* 33–4.

the *Union,* the two sides reached an agreement, and Armstrong acquired the newspaper for twenty thousand dollars.[5]

Initial reaction to Donelson's appointment as editor of the *Washington Union* was mixed. Some politicians, such as Buchanan, who had encouraged and advised Donelson on the newspaper, were favorable. "With Donelson," Buchanan declared, "I am both personally & politically satisfied." By his very name, he noted, Donelson possessed the emotional influence and political "prestige" of Andrew Jackson's memory, which would serve as an important reminder of Old Hickory's pro-Union stance and perhaps heal the rifts in the Democratic party. In addition, he was "a shrewd man & able writer," but, Buchanan predicted, Donelson would have a difficult time turning a large profit. Reports circulated that Illinois Democrat Stephen A. Douglas also supported Donelson. Others were not as confident about Donelson's chances of uniting the Democratic party and the South. Cave Johnson questioned "whether Donelson & Armstrong will conciliate the fire-eaters." Robert M. T. Hunter, a Virginia Democrat and supporter of southern rights, possessed little faith in Donelson, while Democratic newspapermen Francis Blair and John Rives were suspicious of the influence that potential Democratic presidential contender Lewis Cass had over him. Blair also questioned Donelson's motives. The Tennessean's financial woes were common knowledge in Washington, and it seemed to Blair that Donelson was looking for financial relief more than he was hoping to defend the party's principles.[6]

With such controversy swirling around him, Donelson began preparing his journalistic platform. He first consulted several prominent Democratic leaders, including New York's presidential hopeful, William L. Marcy, and asked for their counsel on what direction he should take. James Buchanan offered the only substantive advice. After congratulating Donelson on his new position as party spokesman and expressing his hopes that "it may prove a source of profit to yourself as well as a means of restoring harmony

5. Smith, *Francis Preston Blair Family,* 270; Nichols, *Democratic Machine,* 33–4; FPB to MVB, 10, 15 March 1851, VBL; and AJD to William W. Corcoran, 11 March 1851, Thomas Ritchie to William W. Corcoran, 12 [11] March 1851, William W. Corcoran Papers, Library of Congress.

6. JB to Cave Johnson, 22 March 1851, Cave Johnson to JB, 30 March 1851, JBP; FPB to MVB, 10, 15 March 1851, FPB to John Van Buren, 24 March 1851, VBL; and Robert M. T. Hunter to George N. Sanders, 27 March 1851, in Charles H. Ambler, ed., *Correspondence of Robert M. T. Hunter, 1826–1876,* in *Annual Report of the American Historical Association for the Year 1916,* 2 vols. (Washington, D.C.: GPO, 1918), 2:126.

and strength" to the Democratic party, Buchanan made a number of suggestions. First, the *Union* should "adopt the Virginia Resolutions," a set of declarations made by the Virginia legislature promoting the 1850 compromise as a final settlement of the slavery question and calling for South Carolinians and other southerners to cease agitating for secession. Winning the next presidential election, Buchanan emphatically stated, depended upon reconciling the states' rights and Union wings of the Democratic party. Second, Donelson had to call for the faithful execution of the Fugitive Slave Law. Next, he needed to support publicly a higher revenue tariff than the one already in place. Finally, Buchanan recommended that the prospectus oppose "a general [but not specific] system of internal Improvements." Concerning Democratic candidates in the next election , Donelson "[knew] both Cass and [Levi] Woodbury as well as any man," Buchanan remarked, "and you know that they are both deficient in moral firmness and in other qualities necessary to constitute great *practical* Statesmen."[7]

Buchanan warned Donelson, however, that the prospectus was his to construct, and he should follow his own principles in composing it, especially since the *Union* would influence Democrats in the next presidential election: "If our [the party's members] views should happen to differ[,] you might excite the jealousy of the one whose opinions were disregarded." Cass was a strong supporter of the compromise, and if Donelson did not handle the issue "with the greatest discretion," supporting the candidate from Michigan would "inevitably prevent the reunion of the party in the South." As for Woodbury, Buchanan predicted that Donelson would "not be able to extract much from" him. The editor, therefore, "had better pursue [his] own independent course." Buchanan paternalistically offered his services "as a warm personal and political friend anxious for your success" to examine Donelson's prospectus and make "no suggestion which I shall not honestly believe to be for your own advantage as well as that of the great party with which we are now identified." Any meeting would, of course, have to be made secretly to avoid "exciting unfounded suspicions."[8]

7. JB to AJD, 27 February 1851, DLC; AJD to William L. Marcy, 15 March 1851, William L. Marcy Papers, Library of Congress (hereafter cited as Marcy Papers); JB to AJD, 20 March 1851, in Sioussat, "Selected Letters, 1846–1856," 268–9; and Arthur C. Cole, *The Whig Party in the South* (Washington, D.C.: American Historical Association, 1914), 191–2.

8. JB to AJD, 20 March 1851, in Sioussat, "Selected Letters, 1846–1856," 268–9.

Bearing that advice in mind, Donelson took over the *Union*'s columns on Wednesday, 16 April 1851, and announced his prospectus one week later. His first editorial was strongly Democratic in principle, but he also wanted it to go beyond a statement of principles. He wanted Democrats to know that he would serve as no man's political lackey. Donelson opened with the admission that he was embarking on a job without "training" or "familiar acquaintance"; nevertheless, he vowed to direct the newspaper objectively. "This paper, whilst under my control," the new editor declared, "will never become the organ of any combination of aspiring individuals, banded together to promote their own selfish or ambitious purposes." It would also not become the mouthpiece of any one individual and would only sustain the Democratic party when it pursued "truly national measures by constitutional and just means." Donelson called for Americans to support the 1850 compromise and moderate their views on slavery but also demand enforcement of the Fugitive Slave Law. He additionally proclaimed his support of a low tariff for revenue purposes and a limit to general internal improvements. His prospectus was not out of line with the principles of most Democrats, which Buchanan had summarized in his recommendations.[9]

Donelson's opening editorial and prospectus emphasized the principles he held dear. As did many Americans of the time, he turned to lessons from the American Revolution to better understand the problems between North and South. In the 1760s and 1770s, the colonies and Great Britain grew apart because of Parliament's repressive acts, and that rift led to war. Just as Americans and the British once enjoyed a close relationship and then split acrimoniously, Donelson suggested, the United States faced the same outcome unless the North and the South worked to reconcile their differences over slavery. The best way to defuse the situation was to remove slavery as a divisive issue. To do so, the South had to abide by the Compromise of 1850 and the North had to enforce the Fugitive Slave Law. Otherwise, he concluded, "the preservation of the Union will become an impossibility."[10]

Donelson viewed himself as the party's spokesman for moderation. "The Constitution as administered and expounded by Washington, and the authority of those great minds which afterwards effected the civil revolution of

9. *Washington Daily Union,* 16, 23 April 1851; and AJD to JB, 15 April 1851, JBP.

10. *Washington Daily Union,* 16 April 1851.

1800, shall be my guide," he stressed, "on the one hand in insisting on the love of the Union, and the avoidance of whatever can tend to the alienation of one portion of the people from another; and, on the other, in guarding against the dangers of consolidation." Donelson urged both northern and southern Democrats to pursue compromise. Extremists were attacking "the cause of popular self-government," he declared, and Democrats of both regions needed to "pause, and unite once more with their true friends to strengthen the party which has never failed heretofore, with constitutional means, to foil all serious assaults upon the rights of the people and the States." Ever the moderate, Donelson also made it clear that he had little patience for extreme arguments. Whether the issue was secession advocated by his fellow southerners or abolition by northerners, the *Union*'s editor would brook no toleration for the radicalism that threatened to divide the nation. He intended to rely only on republican principles and institutions, values he believed were sufficient to resolve any dilemma that the nation or one of its regions faced.[11]

Realizing that southerners would question his commitment to slavery and states' rights, Donelson endeavored to clarify his stance on those issues in his second editorial, "Our Position as a Citizen of the South." Having been "familiar from our infancy . . . with the institution of slavery," Donelson declared himself a southerner "for weal or for wo[e]." "Not that we would characterize the institution of slavery as a blessing," he admitted, "but such is the mysterious connexion with which Providence binds man to the institutions under which he is born." Slavery, he argued, was far superior to the industrial factories of the North, because it "postpones the corruptions that are incident to the states of civilization in which human beings sink nearly to the level of the machines with which they earn a scanty subsistence." Slavery had played an important role in the nation's founding, encouraging "the diversification of our interests" and causing southerners to limit the power of the federal government. "It is better to improve and expand our blessings by strengthening the basis of existing relations," he remarked, "than by changes which can never be incorporated into our system without alienating its parts. Let us, then, all resolve . . . that the constitution

11. Ibid.

is our unchangeable hope and guide," he concluded, and slavery a permanent southern institution.[12]

Donelson's initial editorials left Democrats divided over their effectiveness. Archibald Campbell Jr., one of William L. Marcy's strongest supporters, liked Donelson's editorials. "It is truly refreshing to read his good manly sense after being deluged so long with the twaddle of the amiable but *shallow* old man Ritchie," he proclaimed. Other leading Democrats, including Buchanan, Cass, and Franklin Pierce of New Hampshire, added their approbation of his editorial voice. Some Democrats expressed reservations, however. Robert Tyler, son of the former Virginia president, criticized the *Union*'s inclusion of an article from the *Philadelphia Statesman,* a "vile and contemptible" newspaper controlled by the "greatest vagabonds and rascals" who were opposed to Buchanan's presidential candidacy. Donelson had to know, Tyler chided, that Pennsylvania's support was crucial to the Democratic party's victory in the next presidential election. Its success could not afford "any faltering or hesitation, or any tamporising with Traitors, Schemers, or men of doubtful politics." Francis P. Blair was lukewarm toward Donelson's editorials, believing that the Tennessean was missing an opportunity to "[consolidate] . . . the strength that his uncle wielded" during his administrations.[13]

Donelson was not oblivious to such criticism. He informed Elizabeth that "*false friends*" constantly approached him, "men that calculated to use me, and are not a little mortified to find that I can think for myself." Yet he remained undeterred. By the end of his first week at his new post, he informed his son Jackson that the newspaper was already making a profit, enough to enable his family to move to Washington. Within the month, though, Donelson noted to his wife that he was barely able to pay the five hundred dollars in weekly expenses that the newspaper regularly accrued, but he would press on. "My patronage is better in the West and in the mid-

12. *Washington Daily Union,* 17 April 1851.

13. A[rchibald] Campbell to William L. Marcy, 26 April 1851, Marcy Papers; Ivor Debenham Spencer, *The Victor and the Spoils: A Life of William L. Marcy* (Providence, R.I.: Brown University Press, 1959), 195; William L. Marcy to AJD, 7 May 1851, James B. Bowlin to AJD, 5 May 1851, Richard K. Meade to AJD, 7 May 1851, Lewis Cass to AJD, 16 May 1851, JB to AJD, 16 June 1851, Robert Tyler to AJD, 4 May 1851, in Sioussat, "Selected Letters, 1846–1856," 274–6, 271–4, 276–8, 278–9, 279–80, 270–1; FPB to MVB, 30 April, 14 May 1851, VBL; and Benjamin C. Howard to AJD, 19 May 1851, Franklin Pierce to AJD, 30 May 1851, AJD to ERD, 16 May 1851, DLC.

dle states than in the South," he told her. "The democratic party is scattered and broken down in many places. It can be rallied and will elect the next President. . . . To be instrumental in that is my work here."[14]

Donelson could take heart that some recognized and applauded his attempt to present a Unionist editorial voice. Prominent national newspapers representing both parties announced their support for the new editor. The Democratic *Boston Post* told its readers that Thomas Ritchie's "mantle is worthily worn by his successor . . . [and] the Union has still to pilot it a firm, skilful and judicious hand." Even the Whig organ in Washington, the *National Intelligencer,* conceded that Donelson was "upon the paramount questions of the day, imbued with sentiments of genuine patriotism" and his principles were "far above any mere party plans or dogmas."[15]

Donelson churned out editorials for the *Union*'s readers six times a week, usually writing them late at night. (During his time as editor, the *Washington Daily Union* did not publish on Mondays or on the day following federal holidays.) He also oversaw publication of semiweekly and weekly editions when Congress was not in session and a triweekly edition that replaced the semiweekly issue when Congress was meeting. Donelson described the daily grind of writing editorials as "more laborious than chopping with an axe." He had correspondents scattered throughout the United States and in Europe, individuals such as Theodore Fay, who had served as the legation secretary in Berlin throughout Donelson's tenure there. During these first months, however, his only editorial assistance came from Robert Armstrong, his financial backer; Charles Eames, former editor of the *Nashville Union,* who joined the *Washington Union*'s staff in August 1851 as an additional writer; and a man named Overton, not identified further except as one of Ritchie's former employees who was often inebriated.[16]

During Donelson's first few months as editor, he carried on numerous running disputes with the *Washington Republic,* the Fillmore administration's official organ, and the *Southern Press,* a Washington newspaper estab-

14. AJD to [Jackson Donelson], 20 April 1851, AJD to ERD, 11, 16 May 1851, DLC.

15. *Boston Post,* 7 June 1851, in *Washington Daily Union,* 10 June 1851; and *National Intelligencer* (Washington, D.C.), 17 April 1851, in *Republican Banner and Nashville Whig,* 24 April 1851.

16. AJD to ERD, 11, 16 May 1851, Theodore Fay to AJD, 24 May 1851 (fragment), Benjamin C. Howard to AJD, 19 May 1851, DLC; FPB to MVB, 30 April 1851, VBL; and *Washington Daily Union,* 6 July, 20, 26 August 1851.

lished by southern fire-eaters. Donelson also attacked the alleged corruption pervading the Whig party and paid close attention to events in his home state of Tennessee. Slavery received the most thorough treatment, though. Donelson presented himself as a southern supporter of the institution. He repeatedly argued that, in order for the 1850 compromise to work, the federal government had to enforce the Fugitive Slave Law. It was incomprehensible, Donelson argued, for the United States to return fugitives to foreign nations when requested but not to send back runaway slaves to southern slave owners. Slavery was not just a legal right, Donelson reiterated, but a natural condition. Employing biblical arguments, he explained to his readers that God had cursed the ancestors of African slaves during Noah's time, causing them to become subordinate to other "civilizations." The South, by maintaining slavery, was fulfilling "the precepts of religion," helping the "negroe [*sic*] . . . savage, helpless, and inferior," to become more enlightened. In Donelson's opinion, the southern states had worked "to improve the condition of the negro . . . in the great work of republican civilization."[17]

At the same time, Donelson emphasized the necessity of moderation in maintaining the nation's republican ideology and institutions. His most forceful and grandiose statement of this principle came in July 1851, when the Fourth of July holiday inspired him to publish a lesson on the importance of the United States in the eyes of the world. "The stately fabric of a free government, and the cheering spectacle of a prosperous and powerful people," he began, "vindicate before the world the eminent supremacy of republican institutions." As Americans celebrated their independence, "dangerous and designing men have shut their eyes on the past, and forgotten the lessons taught by the revolution. . . . Factionists have kindled the fires of sectional strife, reckless of the consequences which may follow. . . . Misguided men, dead to every patriotic impulse, and mindful only of personal aggrandizement, have attempted to depart from the safe example of our fathers, and to turn the government from its legitimate course." Americans, he wrote, had forgotten from where their freedom came: "Custom has made us callous." If sectionalists persisted in pressing their "insane" claims, he predicted that civil war would come. "It would be an announcement of the

17. *Washington Daily Union,* 18, 19, 20, 25, 26, 30 April, 4, 9, 13, 15 May, 10, 14, 17, 24, 25, 26, 28 June, 2, 3, 6 July 1851.

triumph of tyranny in the Old World—the beginning of a saturnalia in the New World. . . . Standing armies and ruinous military establishments will consume the substance of the people." Donelson believed, however, that Providence would intervene and that the American people would remain "firmly united by the remembrance of a common ancestry, and bound together by the thrilling memories of a glorious past."[18]

Having presented this strong declaration of his principles, Donelson left Washington for a much-deserved vacation to Tennessee. Congress was in recess, and his presence was not imperative for a few weeks. One impetus for the trip was political. Tennessee Whigs and Democrats had been engaged in a fierce election campaign, and he wanted to observe the final days before the state elections and perhaps assist the Democratic candidates. Incumbent Democratic governor William Trousdale had received Donelson's endorsement in April 1851 as the best choice for preserving "the old principles of republican democracy" against Whig gubernatorial nominee William B. Campbell. Donelson had also launched sarcastic barbs at the foremost Tennessee Whig, John Bell. Bell had regularly cried "*dictation*" against Andrew Jackson and the Democratic party; now, Donelson observed, Tennessee Whigs pronounced their platform "the *old* Jacksonian doctrine," a position Donelson labeled "inconsistency and folly." Donelson was disappointed to find that the Whigs carried the day overwhelmingly in the elections, a victory that he blamed on the "stupidity of those high in position who sympathize with nullification."[19]

Donelson's trip proved unsatisfactory in another way. Another purpose for traveling to Tennessee had been to ascertain the chances of bringing his family to Washington. He decided against the move, explaining that he did not want to expose his family to the hardship of travel until the weather cooled. When he returned to the nation's capital alone on 20 August 1851, Donelson assured his wife that their separation would only last a little while longer; until it ended, however, he asked her to "pick up energy and resolution and assist me by the assurance that you acquiesce in the enterprise and will not complain."[20]

18. *Washington Daily Union,* 4 July 1851.

19. *Washington Daily Union,* 25 April, 7 May, 17, 18, 19, 20 June, 6 July, 20 August 1851; AJD to Jackson Donelson, 16 May 1851, JDC; and Atkins, *Parties, Politics, and Sectional Conflict,* 175–80.

20. *Washington Daily Union,* 20 August 1851; and AJD to ERD, 23 August 1851, DLC.

Upon his return to Washington, Donelson faced the same old problems. He needed to maintain close ties with prominent leaders of the Democratic party, but appeasing all of its factions was a difficult, if not impossible, task. Warning of the consequences to come if the sections continued their divisive ways was not popular. Much of the South in particular was in no mood for moderation, and each day brought increased tensions. Though Donelson attempted to stand as a rock of moderation, isolating himself from his party would only damage his opportunities for securing government contracts as the *Union*'s editor or obtaining a future political appointment. "The whole success of my movement depends on the support which may be given me by Congress," Donelson told his wife, "and this would not be doubtful if it were not for difficulties which may be thrown in my way by those calling themselves democrats who are not so."[21]

Disapproval of the party's Washington organ had been increasing even before Donelson took his leave of absence in the summer of 1851. Archibald Campbell Jr., who in April had been a Donelson supporter, had changed his mind by late May. He criticized the editor's seemingly endless "small discussions with the [Washington] Republic" and failed to appreciate Donelson's political stance. "He harps on Washington[,] Jefferson & Jackson—a new combination it seems to me[, as] I never before knew that Genl Wash[ington] was considered a democrat." Others, such as Francis P. Blair and Philip Clayton, second auditor of the U.S. Treasury, found similar fault with Donelson's editorship.[22]

To solidify his place within the Democratic party, Donelson increased his attacks on the Whigs, reserving his most biting and inflammatory condemnation for their support of the burgeoning northern abolitionist movement. On 11 September 1851, a group of free blacks in Christiana, Pennsylvania, shot and killed a Maryland slave owner who was attempting to recapture one of his runaway slaves. Many of the participants in the killing, including two Quakers who had tried to mediate the dispute, were arrested and charged with treason against the federal government. The Christiana "riot," as it was

21. AJD to ERD, 23 August 1851, DLC.

22. [Archibald] Campbell to William L. Marcy, 25 May 1851, Marcy Papers; FPB to MVB, 17 June 1851, VBL; and Philip Clayton to Howell Cobb, 28 June 1852 [1851], in Ulrich B. Phillips, ed., *Correspondence of Robert Toombs, Alexander H. Stephens, and Howell Cobb,* in *Annual Report of the American Historical Association for the Year 1911,* 2 vols. (Washington, D.C.: GPO, 1913), 2:303–4.

called, provided Donelson a platform from which to criticize abolitionists, antislaveryites, and Free-Soilers and their failure to enforce the Fugitive Slave Law. He claimed that his condemnation originated not from partisanship but from a desire to oppose "*organized abolitionist treason and murder.*" The Christiana "murder," as the *Union* labeled it, occurred because of the "fanaticism" of Whig abolitionists in the Pennsylvania government and simply affirmed the "sad and sickening state of things" when ambitious men decided to subvert the Constitution to please their own political purposes.[23]

Still, Donelson's editorials kept coming back to the same theme: the Union was paramount. The continued agitation for secession by states' rights advocates particularly galled him. Donelson acknowledged the right of secession only as a last resort against "oppression and tyranny" when all other avenues for redress had failed. And in such an instance, he argued, secession was more rightfully labeled "revolution." Seceding "to destroy at pleasure" the federal compact that the Constitution had established was, Donelson claimed, an absurdity at odds with the republican system. From his vantage point, fire-eaters' charges that the 1850 compromise constituted "intolerable oppression" blasphemed the intentions of Jefferson and other supporters of the idea of states' rights and secession. By denying the primacy of the Constitution and the laws of the land, Donelson believed southern secessionists were just as guilty as northern abolitionists of placing the nation in danger of dissolution over slavery.[24]

In the middle of attacking what he perceived as threats to the nation's future, Donelson left Washington on another vacation. He had finally decided to bring his family to live with him. After initially asking his oldest son, Jackson, to escort them, Donelson changed his mind and set out in November 1851 to accompany them himself. He made an obligatory stop at his Chickasaw plantation, where he discovered the crops were in worse shape than he expected and found an unpaid debt of five hundred dollars plus interest. Donelson asked Jackson to pay off the note and promised to

23. *Washington Daily Union,* 23, 25, 27 August, 4, 5, 6, 10, 14, 16, 17, 18, 19, 21 September, 9, 16, 21 October 1851, 20 February 1852; Smith, *Presidencies,* 213–4; and Thomas P. Slaughter, *Bloody Dawn: The Christiana Riot and Racial Violence in the Antebellum North* (New York: Oxford University Press, 1991).

24. *Washington Daily Union,* 22, 29 August, 2, 7, 9, 24, 25 September, 3, 5 October, 18, 21 December 1851, 4, 6, 23 January, 13 February, 11 May 1852.

refund his son the money in the future. Donelson then traveled to Nashville, where he collected his family and took them to Washington.[25]

Back at his editorial post in late 1851, Donelson discovered that his efforts to produce unity were failing. Members of his own party were working to force him out as the *Union*'s editor. They justified this action for several reasons: Donelson's refusal to support a definite Democratic nominee for the 1852 presidential election, his alleged affiliation with a scandal involving steamship subsidies, and the failure of Congress to pass legislation granting the *Union* the 1850 census printing contract.

From the first rumor that Donelson would replace Ritchie at the helm of the *Union,* many Democrats believed that the new editor, despite his claims of neutrality, had already committed himself to a nominee for the 1852 election. Donelson's attempts to set up a newspaper in New York led to charges that William Marcy and the New York Hunker faction of the Democratic party were controlling him. The mention of Lewis Cass as a potential presidential candidate in the *Union*'s columns was cause for condemnation from some corners of the party. Edward W. Hubard, one of Robert M. T. Hunter's associates, feared that Donelson was under Cass's influence. "The [*Washington Union*] was clearly for Cass from the start," he observed. "He [Cass] would establish the inquisition if the Union would suggest it, or the alien and sedition laws. Should he be elected[,] the country might look out for the most high handed measures, all proved by the editor of the Union to be in accordance with the doctrines of Jefferson, Madison, and Jackson. May the Lord deliver our party from the hands of the quacks of Tennessee and Michigan." When Donelson also presented James Buchanan, Stephen Douglas, and Sam Houston as possible candidates for the party's nomination, supporters and opponents of these individuals counted the number and length of articles on each potential nominee and speculated on their meaning. Donelson, in fact, did not publicly support a candidate. He clung fiercely to the slogan "Principles and not men," and if he privately favored a particular nominee, neither his correspondence nor the *Union*'s columns revealed his preference.[26]

25. AJD to ERD, 14 September 1851, AJD to [Jackson Donelson], 12 October, 5, 13, 30 November 1851, JDC.

26. Nichols, *Democratic Machine,* 35; Smith, *Francis Preston Blair Family,* 1:270; Larry Gara, *The Presidency of Franklin Pierce* (Lawrence: University Press of Kansas, 1991), 23; M. R. Werner, *Tammany Hall*

So-called southern Unionists were surprisingly vocal in their opposition to him. Alexander H. Stephens, a Unionist Democrat from Georgia, criticized Donelson for being "a man of expedients [*sic*]" who was "for bolstering up and using palliatives. He is neither for North or South, but out and out for *Democracy* and nothing else." Robert Toombs, another Unionist Democrat from Georgia, criticized Donelson's moderation as dangerous to the South. It appeared that he could please none of the Democratic factions: fireeaters hated him for lambasting their advocacy of secession, Unionists criticized him for trying to preserve the Democratic party in all of its disparate elements, northern Democrats were upset with his alleged favoritism of southern candidates, and southern Democrats condemned his attempts to mediate the various factions' differences at the expense of the region's prominence.[27]

With criticism against the editor mounting, party leaders in Congress launched two lines of attack to force Donelson's retirement. Donelson had, after all, taken the job to make money that he desperately needed. Democratic leaders knew his situation, of course, and used his precarious financial position to oust him. On 9 December 1851, Senator Jesse Bright of Indiana introduced a resolution authorizing Congress to negotiate a census printing contract with Donelson and Armstrong. The Joint Committee on Printing reported the resolution back to the Senate for debate on 6 January 1852. The resolution immediately bogged down in mundane discussion over which chamber should negotiate the contract with the *Union*'s proprietors and whether or not the contract should go to Donelson and Armstrong or to the lowest bidder. There were also intimations that the entire bidding

(Garden City, N.Y.: Doubleday, Doran, 1928), 70; Spencer, *Victor and the Spoils,* 194; [Archibald] Campbell to William L. Marcy, 26 April, 25 May 1851, AJD to William L. Marcy, 26 April 1851, John A. Thomas to William L. Marcy, 26 June 1851, Charles Eames to William L. Marcy, 14 September, 11, 23 November 1851, Marcy Papers; William L. Marcy to AJD, 7 May 1851, in Sioussat, "Selected Letters, 1846–1856," 274–6; Herbert D. A. Donovan, *The Barnburners: A Study of the Internal Movements in the Political History of New York State and of the Resulting Changes in Political Affiliation, 1830–1852* (New York: New York University Press, 1925), 110–20; AJD to Howell Cobb, 22, 26 October 1851, in Phillips, *Correspondence* 2:262–3, 264; Edward W. Hubard to Robert M. T. Hunter, 8 May 1852, in Ambler, *Correspondence of Robert M. T. Hunter,* 141–2; and Friend, *SH,* 283.

27. Alexander H. Stephens to Howell Cobb, 26 November 1851, Robert Toombs to Howell Cobb, 2 January 1851 [1852], in Phillips, *Correspondence* 2:265–67, 218–20; Allan Nevins, *Ordeal of the Union: Fruits of Manifest Destiny, 1847–1852* (New York: Scribner's, 1947), 357–8, 375–6; Philip Clayton to Howell Cobb, 25 August 1852 [1851], in Phillips, *Correspondence* 2:317; and *Washington Daily Union,* 20, 21, 23, 27 January, 3, 22, 28 February, 5 March 1852.

process was corrupt and smacked of political "favoritism." When debate resumed on 12 January, opponents of the resolution attacked the necessity of a speedy passage. "Surely the worthy and highly-respectable gentlemen, who are the proprietors of the *Union,* are not in a state of starvation," one senator facetiously said. Why not allow printers to bid for the job, as was customary, the resolution's opponents inquired, instead of risking the possibility that Donelson and Armstrong would try to bilk the government out of a substantial amount of money?[28]

When it came time for the House to vote on the resolution, its members tabled the measure indefinitely by a vote of 134 to 51. Of the 185 representatives voting on whether to table this House resolution, Democrats held a 100 to 75 advantage over Whigs, with the balance being made up of 3 Free-Soilers, 6 southern Unionists, and 1 representative with an unclear party affiliation. Not surprisingly, Whigs voted unanimously in favor of setting aside the measure. What sealed the resolution's fate were the votes of twenty-four southern Democrats and Unionists, largely from the Deep South states of Louisiana, Alabama, Georgia, and South Carolina. After some debate, the Senate followed the House lead by a vote of 28 to 16. These congressional moves effectively ended any hope that Donelson had for making a substantial profit at the *Union.* Donelson advised his wife that "the influence of the *seceding* gentlemen is every where [*sic*] against me, not openly, but more effectively in the dark. Men that you would not suspect are at the bottom of it."[29]

As if denying the *Union* the promised congressional printing contract were not enough, Democrats further accused Donelson and Armstrong of trying to obtain steamship mail subsidies, government money used to support private entrepreneurs who promised to deliver mail to California and across the Atlantic. Democrats who advocated limited government support of private enterprise attacked Armstrong because his son-in-law, Arnold Harris, was a steamship subsidies lobbyist to Congress and castigated Donelson because he portrayed himself as a strict constructionist

28. *Journal of the Senate,* 32d Cong., 1st sess., 41; *Congressional Globe,* 32d Cong., 1st sess., 203–7, 245–51, 259–66; Mark W. Summers, *The Plundering Generation: Corruption and the Crisis of the Union, 1849–1861* (New York: Oxford University Press, 1987), 44–5; and Nichols, *Democratic Machine,* 35–6.

29. *Journal of the Senate,* 32d Cong., 1st sess., 41; *Congressional Globe,* 32d Cong., 1st sess., 203–7, 245–51, 259–66; Summers, *Plundering Generation,* 44–5; Nichols, *Democratic Machine,* 35–6; and AJD to ERD, 6 October 1851, DLC.

Democrat as long as it did not affect his pocketbook. There is no evidence that Donelson was connected to Harris's lobbying, but his cautious approval of the subsidies idea in a March 1852 editorial provided his opponents with enough ammunition to label him corrupt.[30]

The accusation, then, was corruption, but everyone involved knew what the real issue was. Just like his editorial predecessor, Donelson had offended numerous factions within the Democratic party, and they were determined to force his ouster by any means possible. Donelson attempted to defend himself in the *Union*'s columns, but he finally gave in on 12 May 1852, when he informed the newspaper's subscribers that he was resigning. He assured his readers that he had "endeavored faithfully to maintain the old and settled principles of the democratic party." In truth, however, his expectation of establishing the *Washington Union* as a "rallying point" for the party had been unsuccessful. The newspaper's failure to receive the census printing had made it "more than my pecuniary means could bear to remain here with no prospect of remuneration for my services," Donelson informed his son, Jackson.[31]

Donelson was bitter. He had been the victim of the "baneful influence of the presidential schemers," he told Howell Cobb. "Free-soil and secession are allowed to play what [pranks?] they please, because leading men standing on our platform are unwilling to provoke their wrath." To his son, he confided that at "a proper time the public will be informed more particularly than would be now useful, of the character of the opposition which has been made to my political views." An 18 May editorial in the opposition newspaper, the *Republican Banner and Nashville Whig*, which criticized the Democratic leadership's treatment of Donelson and his principles, undoubtedly lifted his spirits, although he would have been chagrined by the glee with which A. W. Venable reported his editorial demise to Buchanan.[32]

30. Summers, *Plundering Generation*, 44, 103–6; Nichols, *Democratic Machine*, 35; FPB to MVB, 15 March 1851, VBL; JB to Cave Johnson, 22 March 1851, JBP; and *Washington Daily Union*, 26 March 1852.

31. Albert G. Brown to Jefferson Davis, 1 May 1852, in Lynda Lasswell Crist, Mary Seaton Dix, and Richard E. Beringer, eds., *The Papers of Jefferson Davis*, vol. 4, *1849–1852* (Baton Rouge: Louisiana State University Press, 1983), 255–8; *Washington Daily Union*, 28 January, 1 February, 15, 16, 17, 18, 20, 22, 24, 25 April, 12 May 1852; and AJD to Jackson Donelson, 12 May 1852, AJD to ERD, 6 October 1851, DLC.

32. AJD to Howell Cobb, 10 [12] May 1852, in Phillips, *Correspondence* 2:294–5; *Republican Banner and Nashville Whig*, 18 May 1852; and A. W. Venable to JB, 19 May 1852, JBP.

Donelson was not quite ready, however, to give up hope of either regaining the *Union*'s editorship or obtaining some other patronage. He had always trusted the government to provide for him. It was especially important now that something substantial come his way, because his financial situation was critical. By taking the editorial position, Donelson had expected the "prospect of making far more for you and my dear children than I could do in twenty years at my farm," he had written his wife in October 1851. A set of other unfortunate circumstances had deflated his optimism. A fire at his Mississippi plantation in the early fall of 1851 cost him three hundred dollars. His family was so strapped for cash in October that Donelson advised Elizabeth to sell cotton bales as the need for money arose. He hoped that by moving his family to Washington in December 1851, he would save some money, but his expensive tastes, predicated on the promised printing contract, led him to choose a large home in Washington that overextended his income. The biggest blow came in early 1852, when Tulip Grove was placed on the auction block to pay his many debts. Only the help of Donelson's brother-in-law and cousin, William, kept him from losing the property.[33]

To add yet another financial burden, Donelson's oldest daughter decided to marry. Mary Emily Donelson was, by her own admission, a "very disobedient & disrespectful daughter," one who apparently had caused her father not a little grief. One story about her, which has proven impossible to verify, was that she fell in love with William H. Polk, brother of the recently deceased president. For some unexplained reason, Donelson opposed the match, but Mary defied his wishes and agreed to elope. Happening to see the couple on their way to find a minister, Donelson stopped the carriage in which they were riding and had words with both his daughter and her fiancé. A short time later, on 27 May 1852, Mary married John A. Wilcox, a veteran of the Mexican-American War who was serving as a Democratic congressman from Mississippi.[34]

33. AJD to ERD, 6, 26 October 1851, DLC; and Satterfield, "Moderate Nationalist Jacksonian," 462.

34. MED to AJD, 22 October 1851, JAW to MED, n.d. [1852], AJD to Jackson Donelson, 17 May, 22 June 1852, Jackson Donelson to MED, 20 May 1852, unattributed newspaper article, n.d., DLC; and "John A. Wilcox," in *Biographical Directory of the United States Congress, 1774–1989* (Washington, D.C.: GPO, 1989), 2050.

Thus Donelson had good reason to support the Democratic National Convention candidate: he needed party patronage to pay for these many expenses, despite his adamant claims to the contrary. Fortunately for him, the Democrats chose a candidate he deemed acceptable. Meeting in Baltimore in early June, the delegates, on the forty-ninth ballot, nominated Franklin Pierce of New Hampshire for the presidency, ahead of the more prominent Cass, Buchanan, Marcy, Douglas, and William O. Butler of Kentucky. Pierce, a former U.S. congressman and brigadier general during the Mexican-American War, had initially been reluctant to allow his friends to introduce his name into the contest, but he eventually acquiesced. His supporters' strategy—to wait until the balloting appeared deadlocked and then submit him as the only one who could "unite the party and win the election"—proved successful. Pierce supported the 1850 compromise, which pleased Donelson, while the party platform proclaimed an end to discussion of the slavery issue. After the criticism he had received at the Nashville Convention and as *Washington Union* editor, Donelson was especially gratified that the resolution he had "submitted to the Nashville Convention, as a substitute for the inflammatory and dangerous action recommended by that body, was substantially the very resolution" that the Democratic convention delegates adopted regarding the 1850 compromise.[35]

Donelson had every reason to support Pierce. He was, as contemporaries and historians alike noted, "everything to everybody." To Donelson, Pierce represented the victory of his efforts at the *Union.* He had urged Democrats to cease fighting over the 1850 compromise and accept its tenets, whatever qualms they possessed. Donelson had also been satisfied in his one past encounter with Pierce in May 1851, when the New Hampshire Democrat had applauded his editorial tenure at the *Union.* "There is a great battle before us," Pierce had written Donelson, "a battle for the Union—a battle for the ascendancy of the principles, the maintenance of which so nobly signalized the administration of Gen. Jackson. The tone, vigor, and statesmanlike grasp which you have brought to the columns of the *Union* are not merely important, they are absolutely indispensible [*sic*] at this crisis." Just in case Pierce had forgotten his compliments, Donelson sent him a reminder in

35. Bain, *Convention Decisions,* 44–7; Gara, *Presidency of Franklin Pierce,* 29–36; and Manuscript page, n.d. [1852], DLC.

July 1852 and lauded his support for the 1850 compromise. Pierce was a Constitution man, Donelson believed, one who would "be reproached with no sectionalism." "I trust the impulse which has been given to sound, patriotic, and national views by your nomination," he told Pierce, "will force all extremists to their proper level, and leave you, as Genl. Jackson was, free to pursue the dictates of a policy which looks alone to our progress as one people, and which guards alike the interests of the states and the powers of the Federal Government."[36]

Donelson insisted that his support of Pierce was purely ideological. When radical threats of secession and abolitionism threatened the spirit of compromise, he argued, the country needed a noncompromising leader with the fortitude to withstand such intimidation and hold the agreements together. Donelson believed that Pierce was just such a man, but that was only part of the reason for his support of the New Hampshire politician. The Democratic nominee approved of his course as *Union* editor, and Donelson, without needing or receiving encouragement, seemingly assumed that if he were elected, then Pierce would reward him for his sacrifices. His election would allow Donelson to exact revenge on his Democratic enemies and give him the monetary rewards he thought he deserved.

Returning to Tennessee in the summer of 1852, Donelson began campaigning for Pierce. On at least two occasions, he made public speeches against the Whig nominee, Gen. Winfield Scott, and for Pierce. At a Nashville gathering in September, Donelson explained his dismissal from the *Union* and his reasons for supporting Pierce. Rumors that party leaders had forced him out because of his backing of the 1850 compromise were unfounded, he explained, as were allegations "that the old Jeffersonian and Jacksonian doctrines are no longer the tests of Democracy." He admitted that some disgruntled Democrats had orchestrated his dismissal, but the Baltimore convention's candidate and platform demonstrated that the party as a whole "endorse[d] the course of the [Washington] Union" under his direction. During the proceedings of the Nashville Convention, "we recognised the necessity of adhering to the great principles which had been illustrated by Washington and the Fathers of the Republic,"

36. Gara, *Presidency of Franklin Pierce,* 35; Franklin Pierce to AJD, 30 May 1851, DLC; and AJD to Franklin Pierce, 26 July 1852, Franklin Pierce Papers, Library of Congress.

Donelson reminded the crowd, and that was the Democratic party's present creed.[37]

The presidential election was a Pyrrhic victory for Donelson. Pierce won the presidency by a large electoral majority (254–42) but by only a small popular count (1.6 million to Scott's 1.4 million). Donelson and other Tennessee Democrats were deeply disappointed in their state's voters, as Tennessee was one of only four states to give its electoral votes to Scott, although by a mere 1,300 votes. The Whigs had successfully convinced enough Tennesseans that the Democratic party's combination of Free-Soilers and nullifiers was more dangerous to the nation's republican future than northern abolitionists in their own party. Donelson expected to alleviate this defeat in his home state with a reappointment to the *Washington Union* or another lucrative position in the Pierce administration, but the president ignored him. Pierce instead seemed to reward every group but the moderates, and in trying to please the extremists, he eventually appeased no one, especially Donelson. It seemed that his time at the *Union* had made him a pariah in Jackson's party.[38]

Pierce's failure to advance his fortunes must have struck a familiar and unpleasant chord with Donelson. In his mind, the Democratic party had repaid him for many sacrifices at the head of the *Union* by chasing him out of Washington without the promised financial incentives. When Donelson had turned his political acumen to winning the election for the Democratic nominee, Pierce, the victorious candidate, a man who had once congratulated him for his ideological stance, failed to acknowledge his efforts with a compensatory appointment. At the end of 1852, Donelson considered himself politically and financially bankrupt, and based on later comments he made, he blamed Pierce and the Democratic party for his quandary.

37. Speech by AJD (at Nashville, Tennessee), n.d. [September 1852], Andrew Ewing to AJD, 3 September 1852, DLC; and Gara, *Presidency of Franklin Pierce,* 36–7. A speech at McNairy County, Tennessee, echoed these same themes. See speech by AJD (at McNairy County, Tennessee), n.d. [29 September 1852], Democratic corresponding committee of McNairy County to AJD, 14 September 1852, DLC.

38. Gara, *Presidency of Franklin Pierce,* 37–47; Roy F. Nichols and Jeannette Nichols, "Election of 1852," in *History of American Presidential Elections,* 4 vols., ed. Arthur M. Schlesinger and Fred L. Israel (New York: Chelsea House, 1971), 2:948–49; Atkins, *Parties, Politics, and Sectional Conflict,* 182–4; and Peter Wallner, *Franklin Pierce: New Hampshire's Favorite Son* (Concord, N.H.: Plaidswede Press, 2004), 235–40, 243, 245–48.

18

"Andrew Jackson, with the Donelson Annexed"

From late 1852 to early 1855, Donelson focused on "the cares and vexations incident to the return to a farmer[']s life." The Tulip Grove plantation was producing well, he informed his oldest son, despite the sickness that had stricken his slaves and others in the neighborhood. The news from his plantation in Chickasaw County, Mississippi, was just as satisfactory. Donelson predicted that in two years, he would be completely free of debt and able to take care of his wife and children for the rest of their lives. His confidence was such that he rejected an offer to sell the Mississippi plantation. But later that year, when it became clear that the crops would fail, Donelson changed his mind. He sold the Chickasaw County land and slaves but still found himself saddled with a three-thousand-dollar debt from shipping his cotton to market. As if that news were not bad enough, Donelson learned from his attorney (and former political foe), John H. Eaton, that, along with Eaton's fees, he owed the Treasury Department a small sum of money from his time as minister in Germany. In addition, he learned that his second oldest son, John, was wasting money by not applying himself to his studies at Yale College.[1]

With so much attention once again focused on his financial affairs, Donelson gave scant consideration to politics. His former legation secretary, Theodore Fay, asked Donelson to persuade the Pierce administration to appoint him as full minister to Berlin, but Fay's request went unmet. Donelson's son-in-law, John A. Wilcox, also solicited his assistance in finding a government position, but after meeting with Pierce and William L.

1. AJD to [Jackson Donelson], 9 September 1852, AJD to ERD, 10 October 1853, JDC; and J. M. Coffman to AJD, 4 December 1852, n.d. [1853], AJD to Jackson Donelson, 8 January 1853, B. H. Shepherd and A. J. Shepherd to AJD, 28 January 1853, W. F. Dowd to AJD, 14 November 1853, Bartlett Sims to AJD, 16 November 1853, JHE to AJD, 25 December 1853, Gray A. Chandler to AJD, 29 December 1853, DLC.

Marcy in May 1853, Donelson advised the Mississippi representative to seek reelection instead of accepting the inferior posts that the president wanted to give him. Donelson even tried to convince his son, Jackson, to turn down an offer to survey western lands for a possible railroad route and instead accept an engineering position in Tennessee. His efforts to dissuade Jackson from embarking on the journey ultimately failed, allowing the younger Donelson to become embroiled in a controversy with Isaac I. Stevens, governor of the Washington Territory, and Secretary of War Jefferson Davis.[2]

Donelson made clear his reasons for retreating from the political scene. Wilcox's request for his father-in-law's influence in procuring a government position "will not do him much good," Donelson confided to his son. Pierce's rumored cabinet appointments, which included Davis, William L. Marcy, and Caleb Cushing, attempted to please "the good will of the seceders and abolitionists," and it would be "better for a young man not to be considered as identified with the process of amalgamation now so fashionable," he concluded. To his wife, Donelson observed that he saw "nothing but intrigue, bargain and corruption" in Washington under Pierce's administration. "They turn out democrats and put in Whigs by mistake, being anxious chiefly for the glory of saying we are now at the helm and will have our fun when we get at the table of the spoils." In January 1853, Donelson still "hope[d] for the best and trust[ed] that the day has not yet come when Democracy will take leave of the good old doctrines it defended in the days of Jefferson and Jackson." By June of that same year, however, he informed Elizabeth that he had declined to give a speech in favor of "one of [Henry S.] Foote's appointments," the same Mississippi Unionist he had supported vociferously during his time as editor of the *Washington Union.* Wilcox's defeat in the fall elections, once considered a safe victory, simply confirmed in Donelson's mind the decline of the nation.[3]

2. [Laura Fay] to AJD, 7 (fragment), 13 December 1852, AJD to Jackson Donelson, 8 January 1853, AJD to ERD, 9 May, 22 June 1853, MED to JAW, 27 May 1853, DLC; JAW to AJD, 12 December 1852, AJD to [Jackson Donelson], 26 April 1853, AJD to ERD, 10 October 1853, JDC; and Lynda Lasswell Crist and Mary Seaton Dix, eds., *The Papers of Jefferson Davis,* vol. 5, *1853–1855* (Baton Rouge: Louisiana State University Press, 1985), 26, 189–90.

3. AJD to Jackson Donelson, 8 January 1853, AJD to ERD, 9 May, 22 June 1853, DLC; AJD to ERD, 10 October 1853, JDC; and Gara, *Presidency of Franklin Pierce,* 44–7.

The year 1854 proved pivotal in convincing Donelson, already disillusioned by the Democratic party's treatment of him at the *Union,* to leave its fold permanently. In May, Congress passed, and President Pierce signed, the Kansas-Nebraska Act. Senator Stephen A. Douglas of Illinois, the expansionist Democrat who had helped bring about the 1850 compromise, was the main proponent of the 1854 legislation. His desire to establish Manifest Destiny in the western territories led him to introduce a bill that would allow the Nebraska territory to organize and apply for statehood. When southern senators balked at his legislation, Douglas added provisions to gain their support. He proposed amendments allowing popular sovereignty in the new western states and repealing the Missouri Compromise's ban on slavery north of the 36°30' line in the Louisiana Purchase. Pierce and most of his cabinet initially refused to support the Douglas legislation because it annulled a compromise that had overcome sectional strife for three decades. Under pressure from Douglas and other supporters, however, Pierce relented in order to maintain his support in the South. When Congress voted on the Kansas-Nebraska Act, the vote split along sectional, not party, lines. With this legislative vote, the Whig party, barely alive by this time, effectively died, leaving a political void for a new party to fill.[4]

The American party, also known as the Know-Nothings, stood poised to fill that void. The party actually began as the Order of the Star Spangled Banner, a fraternal organization in New York during the late 1840s. This group refused to accept any member who was not an American by birth and a Protestant by choice and charged its members to keep its meetings and very existence secret. In the early 1850s, this order and other nativist organizations began to increase their membership. As rising numbers of Irish and Germans left the depressed social and economic conditions in their countries for the renowned prosperity of the United States, opposition to their entrance into the work force and political arena led more and more Americans to join nativist organizations. By 1854, the Order of the Star Spangled Banner became political when the Order of United Americans, an older nativist organization also founded in New York, absorbed its membership.

4. McPherson, *Battle Cry of Freedom,* 117–26.

This new nativist organization grew and expanded into other states, both North and South. Following passage of the Kansas-Nebraska Act in 1854, its membership and influence increased dramatically, as disgruntled Whigs sought a new outlet for political expression. That same year, the National Council of the Know-Nothings promulgated a national constitution and better organized the group, a move that allowed the organization to become an efficient political machine capable of electing politicians who supported its nativist and anti-Catholic beliefs.[5]

The Know-Nothing's ideology appealed to many voters. The party supported an explicit creed that emphasized the democratic foundation of Protestant Christianity, denounced the Catholic Church as anathema to democracy, decried that church's alleged political power, and considered the current political parties and their politicians corrupt and antirepublican. Catholicism, Know-Nothings insisted, was a foreign evil that threatened the religious fabric of the United States, and they singled out the pope as a menace. When Pierce selected James Campbell, a Catholic, as his postmaster general, and Archbishop Gaetano Bedini visited the United States to discuss the ownership and supervision of church property, Know-Nothings warned that a papal conspiracy was underway to establish a Catholic-led government. Such belief prodded many Americans to join the Know-Nothing party. If this new political party was for the Union and the Republic, it would obviously support the fight against the allegedly evil pope and his Catholic minions.[6]

There were, however, distinctions between the northern and southern wings of the organization. Northern Know-Nothings differed from their southern counterparts in opposing intemperance and, especially, slavery's

5. Tyler Anbinder, *Nativism and Slavery: The Northern Know Nothings and the Politics of the 1850s* (New York: Oxford University Press, 1992), 13, 15–22, 47–8. While recognizing the distinction between the Know-Nothing organization and the American party, which came later, I have chosen, for variety's sake, to use the two most common names for the movement interchangeably.

6. Harry J. Carman and Reinhard H. Luthin, "Some Aspects of the Know-Nothing Movement Reconsidered," *South Atlantic Quarterly* 39 (April 1940): 216; Richard Hofstadter, *The Paranoid Style in American Politics and Other Essays* (New York: Random House, 1952; Vintage Books, 1967), 3–40; David Brion Davis, "Some Themes of Counter-Subversion: An Analysis of Anti-Masonic, Anti-Catholic, and Anti-Mormon Literature," *Mississippi Valley Historical Review* 47 (September 1960): 205–24; and A. Cheree Carlson, "The Rhetoric of the Know-Nothing Party: Nativism as a Response to the Rhetorical Situation," *Southern Communication Journal* 54 (Summer 1989): 364–83.

extension. The two factions also viewed immigrants differently. Abolitionists and antislaveryites believed Catholic immigrants supported slavery, a conviction allegedly substantiated during the Kansas-Nebraska bill debate, when Catholics and naturalized immigrants were, at best, neutral toward the Free-Soil movement in the North. In fact, antislavery northerners found a corollary between the South's use of forced labor and the Catholic Church's autocratic behavior. In the South, the movement attracted adherents, mostly Whigs, as an alternative to the Democratic party. Like many northerners, southerner slaveholders saw the recent immigrants as a danger, but for different reasons. The newly arrived foreigners had no concept of slavery's benefits or the need for its continuation in the South, the argument went. This line of reasoning held that the new immigrants, most of whom resided in northern states, would fail to understand the southern slaveholder's fidelity to slavery and would vote against the institution once given suffrage. Thus immigrants, especially Catholics, were enemies of both regions.[7]

Donelson found the Know-Nothings appealing for several reasons. Their conspiratorial view of American politics, which identified Catholics, immigrants, and corrupt politicians as the source of the nation's many problems, fit his own republican ideology, one he believed the Democratic party had abandoned. This combination of antirepublican elements threatened to subvert the nation's very existence by fomenting sectionalism through the slavery issue, corrupting the political process through illicit and exorbitant patronage, and allowing demagogic politicians to deny the will of the people. To Donelson, a man committed to the maintenance of the Constitution and the preservation of the Union, the Know-Nothings, not the Democrats, represented the best chance to save the nation from internal collapse.[8]

7. Anbinder, *Nativism and Slavery,* chap. 5; Carman and Luthin, "Know-Nothing Movement," 221–2; William G. Bean, "An Aspect of Know Nothingism—The Immigrant and Slavery," *South Atlantic Quarterly* 23 (October 1924): 321–30; idem, "Puritan Versus Celt," *New England Quarterly* 7 (March 1934): 70–89; Avery O. Craven, *The Growth of Southern Nationalism, 1848–1861* (Baton Rouge: Louisiana State University Press and the Littlefield Fund for Southern History, University of Texas, 1953), 238–9; Holt, *Political Crisis,* 165–6; W. Darrell Overdyke, *The Know-Nothing Party in the South* (Baton Rouge: Louisiana State University Press, 1950), 16–33, 45–56; and Jean H. Baker, *Ambivalent Americans: The Know-Nothing Party in Maryland* (Baltimore: Johns Hopkins University Press, 1977).

8. Anbinder, *Nativism and Slavery,* 118–26; Holt, *Political Crisis,* 162–8; and John David Bladek, "America for Americans: The Southern Know Nothing Party and the Politics of Nativism, 1854–1856" (Ph.D. diss., University of Washington, 1998), chap. 2.

Donelson also had little compunction about the Know-Nothings' nativist and anti-Catholic views. During his time as minister in Germany, he had clearly stated his own negative opinion of Europeans and their institutions, immigrants, the pope, and Catholicism. Writing to James K. Polk in 1848, he had observed that the "free soil movement is the most dangerous one made against the harmony of our Union. Assisted by the Foreign vote which will hereafter be increased by the process of imigration [*sic*] from Europe[,] it may be considered a trial for us almost as dangerous as the socialism of Europe to her peace and tranquility." In an 1848 letter to John C. Calhoun, Donelson had decried the Mexican War because "it increases the immigration from Europe which itself is a danger—it multiplies our points of contact with Foreigners." As for the pope and Catholicism, Donelson had been even more critical. "The Pope as an organ of reform or of civil liberty is an absurdity," he had declared. "His power is indissolubly allied to the principle of despotism and will be the last to admit the doctrine in which we have based our institutions. I think the civilization of Africa by means of our colonization society is far more practicable than the regeneration of that portion of Europe which is under the influence of catholicism, as long as the infallibility of the Pope is maintained." Donelson's comments, which reflected the racism and religious prejudice of the antebellum period, indicated that his time in Germany had convinced him that Europeans and Catholics endangered the United States because both groups failed to recognize the superiority and inviolability of America's republican system.[9]

More important, the American party also offered an opportunity for Donelson to save his political career and exact revenge upon the party that had turned against him. Like many who migrated to the Know-Nothings, Donelson was a second-rank politician who found it difficult to compete with the party's leading politicians. Joining them gave him a fresh start and the chance to parlay his significant political experience into a high-ranking leadership role. Donelson's actions as a Know-Nothing also made it abundantly clear that he continued to resent his treatment at the hands of the Democrats. As one historian has noted, his membership in the party

9. AJD to JKP, 30 October 1848, JKP; AJD to JCC, 27 September 1848, in Boucher and Brooks, *Correspondence Addressed to JCC*, 475–7; and AJD to JB, 21 July 1849, JBP.

allowed him to oppose all of his enemies: "free-soilers, foreigners, Catholics, and Pierce."[10]

Exactly when Donelson joined the Know-Nothings is uncertain, although it was probably in late 1854 or early 1855. The movement's membership in Tennessee exploded during the fall elections of 1854, as their candidates won elections in several major cities in the state. "Parson" William G. Brownlow, an East Tennessee Whig and newspaper editor, had acknowledged the burgeoning nativist movement in the northern states as early as 1853, and by January 1855 he counted 150 Know-Nothing councils in Tennessee, a number that increased to 500 by July 1855 and 675 in October 1855. It appears that despite denials by their newspapers, former Whigs, such as John Bell, William B. Campbell, and Neill S. Brown, comprised a majority of the Know-Nothings, although many, such as Bell, never officially joined a council. As a former Democrat, then, Donelson was representative of the exceptional Know-Nothing.[11]

Having chosen his new party affiliation, Donelson enthusiastically entered the battle against the Democrats. The first public acknowledgment of a break with his former party appeared during the 1855 gubernatorial race between the incumbent, Democrat Andrew Johnson, and Donelson's brother-in-law, Meredith P. Gentry, who initially ran without a party label but eventually declared his allegiance to the Know-Nothings. In an 1855 letter published in response to inquiries from across the nation about his opinion of Johnson's nomination, Donelson blasted the "new school of Democrats" supporting "the treachery and imbecility of Mr. Pierce and his Cabinet." Governor Johnson was part of that "new school," he wrote, and mirrored the northern abolitionists in his refusal to support the 1850 compromise. Donelson could only conclude that Johnson agreed with the "higher-lawism" and "fanaticism" of prominent abolitionists, William H. Seward and Joshua Giddings. "This trickery and humbuggery belong not to the creed of the old[-]fashioned Tennessee Democrat," Donelson

10. Michael F. Holt, "The Politics of Impatience: The Origins of Know Nothingism," *Journal of American History* 60 (September 1973): 319–20; and Satterfield, "Moderate Nationalist Jacksonian," 478–9.

11. Sister Mary de Lourdes Gohmann, *Political Nativism in Tennessee to 1860* (Washington, D.C.: Catholic University of America, 1938), 83–9; Atkins, *Parties, Politics, and Sectional Conflict*, 196–9; *Republican Banner and Nashville Whig*, 18 July, 9 October 1854, 26 January 1855; and Satterfield, "Moderate Nationalist Jacksonian," 478.

remonstrated, those who had "follow[ed] in the footsteps of Washington, Jefferson, Madison, and Jackson" and fought against nullification in every form. As for Pierce, the president sought "to fill the most elevated and responsible national trusts" with "individuals the most prominent in adherence to this Treason" of nullification.[12]

Such rhetoric was intended to galvanize support for the American party, which, despite its electoral success in New England the previous fall, was facing increasing disunity on the national level. This division became apparent at the national meeting, which met in Philadelphia in mid-June 1855. The American National Council (the party's national organizing committee) introduced a platform setting the party's agenda for next year's national elections. Section 12, the resolution dealing with slavery, drew the most debate. Two blocs of delegates submitted reports on the section. One group, representing southern interests, introduced a proslavery report that supported repealing the Missouri Compromise and called for the protection of slavery in the territories, the states, and the District of Columbia. The other group, made up of delegates from northern states, offered an antislavery report that urged the continued acceptance of the Missouri Compromise. In the end, the council accepted the proslavery report, which became part of the party platform and caused many northern delegates to leave the meeting. In reality, neither southerners nor northerners in the American party were happy with the national platform. Northern members wanted the restoration of the Missouri Compromise and, in some cases, the abolition of slavery. Southern Know-Nothings desired a stronger proslavery stance, although they were satisfied with the platform's denial of Congress' constitutional right to regulate the territories, which had the same effect as protecting slavery there.[13]

12. Atkins, *Parties, Politics, and Sectional Conflict,* 200–3; Gohmann, *Political Nativism in Tennessee,* 92–106; *Nashville Daily Union and American,* 15 February 1855; *Washington Daily American Organ,* 19 February, 29 May 1855; *Republican Banner and Nashville Whig,* 5 May 1855; and AJD to [Allen A. Hall], editor of the *Republican Banner and Nashville Whig,* 24 May 1855, AJD to [E. G. Eastman], 22 May 1855, in *Republican Banner and Nashville Whig,* 25 May 1855.

13. *Washington Daily American Organ,* 16, 20, 22 June 1855; *Washington Daily Union,* 15, 22, 27 June 1855; *Republican Banner and Nashville Whig,* 14, 20, 21 June 1855; Overdyke, *Know-Nothing Party,* 128–33; Anbinder, *Nativism and Slavery,* 162–74; and American (Know-Nothing) party platform of 1855, 5–16 June 1855, in Michael F. Holt, "The Antimasonic and Know Nothing Parties," in *History of United States Political Parties,* 4 vols., ed. Arthur Schlesinger (New York: Chelsea House, 1973), 1:607, 701–5, 708–11.

Hoping to parlay his name into influence, Tennessee Know-Nothings had asked Donelson to attend the party's national meeting as an unofficial observer. His presence reportedly bolstered the delegates' enthusiasm, especially after the northern delegates departed. The committee in charge asked Donelson to speak, which he was unable to do because of his hoarse throat. He did, however, write out his speech, which the party's leaders published and distributed to the delegates. Donelson began by recalling Andrew Jackson's defense of the nation against nullification. He then turned his rhetorical cannons on Pierce and his administration, insisting that, in trying to please both southern nullifiers and northern abolitionists, the president had lost control of his administration. Pierce's appointments were "marked by an open contempt for his profession as a friend of the doctrines of the Democratic party," he claimed. William L. Marcy, Jefferson Davis, Caleb Cushing—all were men who placed their ambitions and disunionist policies above the people's will and the nation's good. As for Catholics, Donelson asserted that the Know-Nothing party had the right to defend the United States from those allied with "a system dangerous to liberty and subversive of the constitution." On the all-important question of slavery, he regretted that "the folly and recklessness of Mr. Pierce and his cabinet" had led Congress to pass the Kansas-Nebraska Act, but it was now law and must be followed. Slavery, Donelson declared, was a local issue, protected by the Constitution, and should be left alone; otherwise, northern and southern "nullifiers" would continue to "attempt to convert sectional jealousy into a permanent source of political power." He concluded by warning Pierce and his supporters that "the people are rallying, as in the days of old, to the preservation of the true principles of the constitution," and their cry, as well as his, would be, "*Our Federal Union—it must and shall be preserved [and] Americans shall rule America.*"[14]

For a man so committed to the Union, Donelson seemed oblivious to the divisiveness of the platform just passed by his new party. He may have been satisfied that the party membership had reached a compromise, one that also happened to support his own interests as a slaveholder, or maybe he was content to blame Pierce and his old Democratic comrades for increasing the

14. *Washington Daily American Organ,* 29 May 1855; *Republican Banner and Nashville Whig,* 26 June 1855; and Atkins, *Parties, Politics, and Sectional Conflict,* 197.

vituperative atmosphere of sectional acrimony. It may also have been that his hatred of the Democratic party blinded him to the reality that the Know-Nothings were already imploding over the slavery issue.

Whatever the case, Donelson's speech in Philadelphia elicited stinging responses from Democratic circles, and they gave even less attention to ideological arguments than their target. A. O. P. Nicholson, his former Tennessee ally and now editor of the *Washington Union,* criticized him harshly. He pointed out that Donelson was trying especially hard to emphasize his association with Jackson, even referring to himself as Andrew Jackson Donelson and not simply Andrew J. Donelson, as he had always done before. He was, after all, Jackson's nephew only by marriage, Nicholson reminded his readers. The connection with Jackson made almost as much sense as Donelson's speech, the editor continued, in which he claimed that the Democratic party had deserted him, not vice versa. "That might satisfy a man of elastic conscience, notwithstanding he saw all of his old associates standing together as compactly on their old platform as ever," Nicholson sneered, "but it fails to explain the singular fact that the old whigs now constitute his associates—the men against whom he had fulminated so many democratic thunderbolts." Donelson's attacks on Pierce rang false as well, he thought. "It is enough to say that if Mr. Pierce had been more lucky in one or two appointments[,] the speech would never have been made," Nicholson sarcastically concluded.[15]

Other criticism soon followed. The *Washington Union* published comments by John C. Rives, editor of the *Washington Globe,* in which the Virginian dismissed Donelson's implicit claim that he was a blood relative of Jackson and his incorrect characterization of George Washington as more favorably disposed to native-born Americans than foreigners. Privately, Cave Johnson confided to Francis P. Blair that Donelson's "defection will not probably lose us a vote" in the Tennessee elections, but it was proving "a source of deep mortification to the friends of the old chief [Jackson]."[16]

Donelson refused to let the criticism from former colleagues deter him from campaigning in Tennessee for the Know-Nothings. Following his re-

15. *Washington Daily Union,* 22, 23 June 1855.

16. *Washington Daily Union,* 28 June 1855; and Cave Johnson to FPB, 2 July 1855, Francis P. Blair–John C. Rives Papers, Library of Congress.

turn from Philadelphia, he gave speeches across the state, defending himself and his party's principles at each stop. The themes in his speeches closely followed those of his New York address, but Donelson began to stress more strongly the corruption of the Pierce administration and the Democratic party. "My speeches expose me to much abuse and calumny," Donelson informed his wife, but "I shall persevere in the cause of truth, and omit nothing in my power to prostrate the party which is upholding Pierce and his cabinet." The party faithful rewarded him at a Davidson County Know-Nothing meeting on 4 July 1855, electing Donelson president of the gathering and ratifying the platform adopted by the national convention.[17]

One of Donelson's campaign stops "exposed" him to more than just "abuse and calumny." On 16 July, he shared a platform in Columbia with Gideon J. Pillow, the staunch Democratic friend of the deceased James K. Polk and former delegate, along with Donelson, to the 1844 Democratic National Convention. Near the end of Donelson's speech, he averred that Pillow "*had* denounced the members of the Nashville Convention as traitors to their country." Pillow leapt to his feet, calling Donelson a liar and denying that he had ever made any such comment publicly or privately. Donelson, angered by Pillow's reaction, pronounced him "an impertinent fool," to which Pillow replied, "You are a liar—a scoundrel and a traitor to your party and your country." The two men exchanged more insults and then came to blows as each man attempted to bludgeon the other with a stick. Donelson received the worst of the altercation, and Pillow was left to finish his speech to "deafening applause."[18]

The violent confrontation in Columbia was, thankfully for Donelson, not usual. The mistreatment that he normally received was verbal. At the same Columbia meeting where Pillow and Donelson scuffled, Andrew Ewing criticized the Know-Nothing's speech as "one of the wildest, strangest and *maddest* harangues that we have ever heard," noting that Donelson was

17. Gohmann, *Political Nativism in Tennessee,* 112; *Republican Banner and Nashville Whig,* 4, 6, 8, 11, 18, 21, 24, 25, 29 July, 1 August 1855; drafts of AJD's speeches, n.d. [1855], DLC; diary entry, 4 July 1855, in Herschel Gower and Jack Allen, eds., *Pen and Sword: The Life and Journals of Randal W. McGavock* (Nashville: Tennessee Historical Commission, 1960), 336–7; and AJD to ERD, 23 July 1855, DLC.

18. Nathaniel Cheairs Hughes Jr. and Roy P. Stonesifer, *The Life and Wars of Gideon J. Pillow* (Chapel Hill: University of North Carolina Press, 1993), 140; and *Columbia (Tenn.) Democratic Herald,* 21 July 1855.

"deranged and incurably crazed upon the [Pierce] administration's want of judgment and patriotism in failing to enlist *his* services in the management of the count[r]y's affairs." "From the vindictive and personal character of Major Donelson's remarks," Ewing remarked, "it is evident, that his present course is prompted more by feelings of revenge for some imagined wrong than by the pure and holy patriotism which he would have the world believe burns in his breast." Ewing also evaluated Donelson's use of his uncle's name. "He labors under the worse hallucination of supposing that the mantle of Jackson has fallen upon his shoulders, and that he could do whatever old Hickory accomplished," he observed. "In his blind furor and unpardonable self-importance, the Maj[or] evidently forgets that" whatever Jackson's fondness for him, "it was utterly impossible for him to cram *his brains* into another man's head, and that his pretensions, in this particular, will but serve to remind the world of the *ass* that covered himself with the *lion's* skin."[19]

Ewing's vilifying speech made public what others, probably even Jackson, had realized years ago. Donelson had always presented himself as Jackson's political heir, but he was not cut from the same cloth. His ideological convictions were sincere, but he simply did not possess the political skills and abilities of his uncle. Donelson, in fact, had repeatedly shown he could not be trusted to finish the tasks the party assigned to him and that money and praise meant more to him than ideology. His accomplishments seemed to happen in spite, not because, of him. His record during Jackson's administrations, in Tennessee politics, as a diplomat in Texas and Germany, and as the *Washington Union*'s editor indicated to everyone around Donelson that he shared only a name with his uncle. Ewing was only expressing what Democrats had whispered for years—Andrew Jackson Donelson was no Andrew Jackson.

Ewing's criticism stung Donelson, but he persevered in working for the American party, especially after it gained a majority in the Tennessee state legislature and elected five of the state's ten congressmen. He attended a meeting in Nashville immediately following the state elections and responded positively to requests for speaking engagements from Know-Nothings in other states. Donelson continued to attack Pierce for "professing the Union

19. *Columbia (Tenn.) Democratic Herald*, 21 July 1855; and *Republican Banner and Nashville Whig*, 11 July 1855.

doctrine of Jackson" but remaining "the instrument of the Abolitionist and Nullifier," and he persisted in his claims that the Know-Nothing's "leading principle [was] the suppression of slavery agitation and opposition to whatever tends to weaken the bonds of our beloved Union." As a reward for his endeavors, the Tennessee Know-Nothings selected him a delegate to the national American Party Convention, set to meet in Philadelphia in February 1856.[20]

The delegates who attended the American party's 1856 convention needed committed leaders such as Donelson. While the party appeared to be making gains in Tennessee, in Congress, and across the nation, its prospects were actually mixed. Following the June 1855 debacle in Philadelphia, at which the northern and southern delegates split over the slavery issue, the Know-Nothings disappointed supporters by running poorly in the fall elections in Ohio and Pennsylvania, although they fared well in New York and Massachusetts. In Congress, the party was able to elect Nathaniel P. Banks Jr. of Massachusetts Speaker of the House, but the unprecedented balloting needed to elect Banks, a nominal Know-Nothing at best, illustrated the American party's division. This obvious rift threatened the party's dominance in several northern states and boded ill for their prospects in the upcoming presidential election.[21]

When the Know-Nothings met in Philadelphia in February, then, one of their goals was to nominate a ticket and compose a platform that would heal the divisions within their party and unify the two regions. Achieving that aim proved difficult. Even before the meeting officially opened, the party's National Council debated replacing the 1855 platform's contentious statement on slavery with a new one, which said simply that "as regards the subject of Slavery, we abide by the principles and provisions of the Constitution

20. Overdyke, *Know-Nothing Party,* 107–11; Atkins, *Parties, Politics, and Sectional Conflict,* 205; *Republican Banner and Nashville Whig,* 4, 5, 7, 12, 17, 23, 26, 28 August, 3, 11, October, and 6 December 1855; *Nashville Daily Union and American,* 4 August, 12, 14 October 1855; and R. M. Williamson to AJD, 20 October [1855], Invitation of American Mass Meeting of Louisville to AJD, 3 November 1855, AJD to [American Mass Meeting of Louisville], 19 November 1855 (draft), DLC.

21. Craven, *Growth of Southern Nationalism,* 239–40; Anbinder, *Nativism and Slavery,* 174–202; Holt, "Antimasonic and Know Nothing Parties," 612–3; Ray Allen Billington, *The Protestant Crusade, 1800–1860: A Study of the Origins of American Nativism* (New York: Macmillan, 1938; Chicago: Quadrangle Books, 1964), 407–17; *Republican Banner and Nashville Whig,* 11 December 1855; *Washington Daily American Organ,* 8, 14 January, 4 February 1856; and *Nashville Daily Union and American,* 12 February 1856.

of the United States, yielding no more and claiming no less." Northern delegates embraced the new statement, but southerners opposed it, believing it too conciliatory to the antislavery delegates. The resolution passed by a 104 to 65 vote, with most of the southern delegates voting against it. Under pressure from southern delegates, who were threatening to leave the convention and the party, the next day the council introduced a different platform that varied very little from the one chosen in 1855. Its members disposed of the resolution adopted just the previous day and replaced it with one that avoided any mention of slavery and instead supported the "maintenance and enforcement of all laws constitutionally enacted until said laws shall be repealed, or shall be declared null and void by competent judicial authority." Having started with a moderate proslavery plank, the American party moved to a neutral declaration of obedience to the laws of the land. The council accepted this statement and the rest of the platform by a vote of 108 to 77.[22]

Donelson, along with most of the other Tennessee delegates, did not arrive in time to hear much of the debate that resulted in a platform silent on the slavery issue. Many of them had attended the Tennessee state convention, held just over a week before the national convention, and thus were late in arriving at Philadelphia. Tennessee had only five delegates on the second day, but by the final day, Donelson and six others were present. He and a majority of the Tennessee delegation voted to accept the compromise platform.[23]

When the American Party Convention officially opened on 22 February, the controversy continued. Disputes over the recognition of competing state delegations and the milquetoast resolution ignoring slavery led to heated exchanges. The delegates debated adjourning to restore calm, but

22. Overdyke, *Know-Nothing Party,* 134–6; Anbinder, *Nativism and Slavery,* 206–7; Records of the American (Know Nothing) National Council meeting, 18–21 February 1856, in Holt, "Antimasonic and Know Nothing Parties," 714–21; *Washington Daily American Organ,* 19, 20 February 1856; and William E. Gienapp, *The Origins of the Republican Party, 1852–1856* (New York: Oxford University Press, 1987), 251–64.

23. Anbinder, *Nativism and Slavery,* 206–7; *Washington Daily American Organ,* 21 February 1856; *Republican Banner and Nashville Whig,* 13, 14, 27, 28 February 1856; and Records of the American (Know-Nothing) National Council meeting, 18–21 February 1856, in Holt, "Antimasonic and Know Nothing Parties," 721.

the motion failed because some of the leaders thought that the emerging Republican party, already in session at its own nominating convention in Pittsburgh, was engineering the dissension. Four days into the convention, the leadership finally brought a motion to the floor that launched the nomination process, and several New England, mid-Atlantic, and western delegations, hoping to force further discussion of the platform, left the convention in protest. With 179 of 241 on the first ballot, the delegates chose former president Millard Fillmore as the American party's 1856 presidential candidate. Fillmore, who won out over Sam Houston, George Law, and Kenneth Rayner, had provided a firm and steady hand during the 1850 compromise debates, and delegates hoped that his strong commitment to the Constitution and the Union would appeal to voters tired of sectional squabbling.[24]

The convention then proceeded to choose Donelson, with 181 of 209 votes, over Rayner, Percy Walker, and two other nominees as the party's vice-presidential nominee. In words reminiscent of his uncle's before the 1824 election, Donelson stated that "he had not sought the nomination, and he would not decline it." He declared that the Democratic party, determined to encourage sectionalism, had deserted him, not vice versa. In response to a question about which party Andrew Jackson would choose if he were still living, Donelson assured the Know-Nothing delegates that his uncle, as well as Henry Clay and Daniel Webster, would all have preferred the American party. This speech satisfied the delegates, most of whom were former Whigs, and they adjourned with high expectations for the coming campaign.[25]

Privately, Donelson expressed confidence that the party needed his participation. "You will see that I am on the ticket for the vice Presidency," he wrote Elizabeth, "a position that I could not have declined without breaking up the party." Donelson was less sure about his running mate. "The nomination of Fillmore was against the sense of a large portion of our friends in New York, but I hope [it] will work out right," he declared. Characteristically,

24. Anbinder, *Nativism and Slavery,* 202, 208–9; Carman and Luthin, "Know-Nothing Movement," 226–7; Records of the American (Know-Nothing) National Council meeting, 18–21 February 1856, in Holt, "Antimasonic and Know Nothing Parties," 722–32; and *Republican Banner and Nashville Whig,* 4 March 1856.

25. Anbinder, *Nativism and Slavery,* 209; Records of the American (Know-Nothing) National Council meeting, 18–21 February 1856, in Holt, "Antimasonic and Know Nothing Parties," 722–32; and *Republican Banner and Nashville Whig,* 4 March 1856.

Donelson seemed more concerned about his financial standing at the time than the upcoming campaign. Although he promised financial help to his oldest son, Jackson, then considering marriage, he warned him that he would not have enough money until Fillmore's election provided him with a more profitable position. While to outsiders it appeared that he remained in the North to make speeches and meet supporters, Donelson was actually arranging for a loan of ten thousand dollars, apparently to pay the Tulip Grove mortgage. His financial reputation was so bad that he feared the bank would require Elizabeth's signature on the mortgage as a guarantee. Even at this point in his political career, Donelson could not escape his poor financial decisions.[26]

The Know-Nothings intended their nominations to appeal to both sections. Fillmore represented a faction of former northern Whigs, while Donelson embodied the southern Unionist Democratic wing. Neither man fully met the expectations of the more conservative, pro-nativist, anti-Catholic core of the American party, but both were flexible enough to appeal to all constituencies. Many loyal Know-Nothing members and newspapers across the United States, including those in Tennessee, enthusiastically greeted news of the party's nominations. Vespasian Ellis, editor of the *Washington Daily American Organ,* highlighted Donelson's contribution to the ticket. "He is no mere party tool, grown in the hot-bed of corruption and demagoguism, and moulded into a statesman by political machinery," he observed, seemingly ignorant of Donelson's many years of service in the Democratic party.[27]

Some Know-Nothings, however, were not impressed with either nomination, especially Donelson's. Kenneth Rayner, a prominent North Carolina Know-Nothing who had lost nomination bids both to Fillmore and Donelson at the national convention, only reluctantly supported the ticket. Privately, a bitter Sam Houston denounced Donelson for misleading him

26. AJD to ERD, 27 February 1856, AJD to [Jackson Donelson], 20 May 1856, DLC; and AJD to Jackson Donelson, 18 March, 3, 8 April 1856, JDC.

27. Anbinder, *Nativism and Slavery,* 209–12; Atkins, *Parties, Politics, and Sectional Conflict,* 206; Gohmann, *Political Nativism in Tennessee,* 132; Bladek, "America for Americans," chap. 6; Horatio Seymour to Jackson Donelson, 28 February 1856, in Sioussat, "Selected Letters, 1846–1856," 285–6; *Republican Banner and Nashville Whig,* 28, 29 February, 5, 6, 11, 12, 16, 29 March 1856; and *Washington Daily American Organ,* 26, 28, 29 February, 1 March 1856.

regarding the presidential nomination, which Houston thought belonged to him. Donelson, he told a friend, had plotted to place Fillmore at the top of the ticket to ensure his own selection as the vice-presidential nominee because "he thought the mantle of Gen. Jackson rested upon him, which with his own position would carry the Ticket, for he thinks *well of himself*." When Donelson visited Houston on his way home and asked the Texan not to hurt the American party's cause, his old ally considered telling him that "dead Ducks need no killing!" Another Know-Nothing listed Donelson's two major deficiencies: "He has so many political sins to answer for to the Whigs, and the democrats look on him as a traitor."[28]

Democrats, indeed, viewed Donelson as a turncoat, even more so than before, and they took particular delight in attacking him. A. O. P. Nicholson continued to use the *Washington Union* against its former editor. He especially criticized Donelson's hypocrisy concerning immigration and Fillmore. While editor of the *Union* in 1851 and 1852, Nicholson pointed out, Donelson had supported European immigration into the United States and had practically gushed over famed Hungarian revolutionary Louis Kossuth. As for Fillmore, the former president had been the subject of much criticism from Donelson's pen; and now, Nicholson asked incredulously, Donelson considered him reformed enough to join on a political ticket? Taking his cue from Tennessee Democrats, Nicholson also gleefully latched onto the American party's emphasis on Donelson's affiliation with Jackson. It was nothing more than a ploy to use the name of "Andrew Jackson, with the Donelson Annexed," he informed his readers.[29]

In Tennessee, Democratic critics of the American ticket dismissed the Know-Nothing threat. Nashville Democrat Randal McGavock called the party and its ticket "weak," while Governor Andrew Johnson declared the Fillmore-Donelson pairing "the dead deadest ticket ever presented in good earnest to the people of Tennessee." Democrats constantly reminded

28. Anbinder, *Nativism and Slavery*, 209–12; Gregg Cantrell, *Kenneth and John B. Rayner and the Limits of Southern Dissent* (Urbana: University of Illinois Press, 1993), 107–9; idem, "Southerner and Nativist: Kenneth Rayner and the Ideology of 'Americanism,'" *North Carolina Historical Review* 68 (April 1992): 141; SH to Ana S. Stephens, 22 March 1856, in Williams and Barker, *Writings of SH* 6:299–300; Friend, *SH*, 245, 294–5; and Atkins, *Parties, Politics, and Sectional Conflict*, 206.

29. *Washington Daily Union*, 5, 13, 14 March 1856; and *Nashville Daily Union and American*, 6 March 1856.

their fellow Tennesseans of Donelson's former opposition to Fillmore, his desertion of the party, and his tiring references to the memory of Jackson. One Democratic-controlled Nashville paper derisively chided Donelson for being "afflicted with the chronic idea that the nation can never pay off her obligations to himself for the accidental relations to his illustrious patron [Jackson]." William G. Brownlow wrote Donelson in April 1856 that the Democrats in "this end of the state, as yet, . . . have had but little to say against Fillmore, but they are very abusive of you."[30]

One Tennessean even privately accused Donelson of wanton drunkenness. Cave Johnson, who was always quick to dismiss Donelson's importance to the Know-Nothing campaign, told Buchanan that his former friend "drinks too much. . . . He does not hesitate to speak publicly of you both, when drinking, as damned scoundrels, corrupt knaves, &c. &c." Johnson also reported that Donelson was very vocal in his public criticism of Buchanan, pontificating "in the lowest & most vulgar language when drinking which is nearly always the condition in which he is found." He admitted that he had never observed these outbursts personally but had depended on "reliable gentlemen" for the information because Donelson "never comes near me."[31]

Democratic criticism did not seem to bother Donelson much, but the lack of support from his own family members pained him deeply. His brother, Daniel S. Donelson, remained a staunch Democrat and was very critical of his defection to the Know-Nothings. More public, however, was the estrangement between Andrew Jackson Jr. and Donelson, the roots of which dated back at least to the early 1840s. Andrew Jr. was even more financially incompetent than his more famous cousin; by 1855, he had

30. Diary entry, 26 February 1856, in Gower and Allen, *Pen and Sword,* 354; Andrew Johnson to A. O. P. Nicholson, 27 June 1856, Andrew Johnson's speech to Nashville Democrats, 15 July 1856, in Leroy P. Graf, Ralph W. Haskins, and Patricia P. Clark, eds., *The Papers of Andrew Johnson,* vol. 2, *1852–1857* (Knoxville: University of Tennessee Press, 1970), 387–90, 395–436; Gohmann, *Political Nativism in Tennessee,* 132–3; *Nashville Daily Union and American,* 6 March, 2, 3 August 1856; and William G. Brownlow to AJD, 24 May 1856, in Sioussat, "Selected Letters, 1846–1856," 286–7.

31. Cave Johnson to JB, 24 August, 5 October 1856, JBP. I am indebted to Doug Spence for pointing out these references to Donelson's alleged drunkenness. I am not as convinced as he that Johnson was telling the truth, however, as Johnson's information was gleaned second hand and served a political purpose that surely the Democrats would have exploited if true, especially considering the Know-Nothings' affiliation with the temperance movement.

managed to turn the $100,000 of wealth that Andrew Jackson had left him into $150,000 of debt. The following year, he sold the Hermitage and five hundred acres of the surrounding property to the state of Tennessee for $50,000. This sale peeved Donelson, who likely blamed his own pecuniary problems in part on his uncle's preference for Andrew Jr. in his final will. Donelson also expressed displeasure with his cousin's questionable disposal of Jackson's papers, leading Andrew Jr. to defend publicly both his sale of the Hermitage and his distribution of his father's papers to Amos Kendall and Francis P. Blair. Andrew Jr., on the other hand, seemed especially annoyed with Donelson's failure to correct supporters who mistakenly referred to him as Jackson's son. The family squabble became political news and led several members of Donelson's immediate and extended family to ostracize him. "There is a plentiful supply of malignant gossip and scandal [in the family] to take the place of reason and common sense," he informed his son Jackson.[32]

To Donelson's credit, he ignored many of these distractions and worked hard to achieve victory in the fall election. His supporters produced a biographical sketch emphasizing his relationship to Jackson and his friendliness toward Fillmore. Donelson actually proved more visible than Fillmore, who, ironically, was in Europe visiting the pope when the nativist, anti-Catholic party nominated him as its presidential candidate. Donelson bore the burden of campaigning for the American party, giving speeches and answering letters of inquiry about his principles. As the summer progressed into fall, Donelson's speeches and letters relied less often on nativist and religious arguments and more on the threat that slavery and sectionalism posed for the nation. As he wrote one supporter, "The evil of the day is sectionalism, and the country can find no repose until this dangerous spirit is rebuked by the voice of the people, animated as they were in the days of Washington, by a holy love for the Union, and determined to withhold their confidence from those who do not regard its preservation as the paramount object of

32. Gohmann, *Political Nativism in Tennessee*, 139–40; diary entry, 5 October 1856, in Gower and Allen, *Pen and Sword*, 434–5; Galloway, "AJ, Jr.," pt. 2, 327–38; AJ Jr. to [?], 4 July 1856, AJD to Jackson Donelson, 3, 27 September 1856, DLC; J. C. Gaines to AJ Jr., 13 August 1855, Andrew Jackson III to Sarah Jackson, 24 March 1856, AJ Jr. to Sarah Jackson, 16 May 1856, AJ Jr. to WBL, 24 June 1856, AJ Jr. to Jefferson Davis, 20 June 1856, Sarah Jackson to Andrew Jackson III, 17 September 1856, Ladies' Hermitage Association, Nashville, Tenn.

their lives." Donelson was depending upon the will of the people to save the nation, and, as always, he considered himself their spokesman.[33]

Therein lay much of the problem for Donelson, Fillmore, and the Know-Nothings. The "sack" of Lawrence, Kansas, by proslavery zealots and the caning of Massachusetts senator Charles Sumner by South Carolina representative Preston Brooks, both occurring in May 1856, highlighted to voters the seriousness of sectionalism and the slavery agitation. By emphasizing these very dangers, the Know-Nothings may have reminded their fellow countrymen of the nation's grave political and social atmosphere and accentuated their own party's weaknesses. They employed arguments calling for the protection of the Union from sectionalism, but by doing so, they abandoned the very issues that had gained them so much success in 1854 and 1855—longer naturalization periods, mandatory Bible reading in schools, prohibition of church property ownership by priests, and opposition to corruption in the major political parties. The election results would prove the ineffectiveness of this change in campaign strategy.[34]

The national Democratic and Republican conventions that met in June produced further problems for the Know-Nothings. The Democrats nominated James Buchanan, giving their party an esteemed, if bland, candidate. Their platform outlined the usual Democratic tenets of limited government and a low tariff, while denying Congress' right to interfere with slavery. When the Republicans met shortly thereafter, they chose John C. Frémont, who, while the youngest and least experienced politically of the Republican candidates, possessed two strengths: a dramatic military career in the West

33. *Nashville American Banner,* 19 April 1856; Anbinder, *Nativism and Slavery,* 211–2; Frank H. Severance, ed., *Millard Fillmore Papers,* 2 vols. (Buffalo, N.Y.: Buffalo and Erie County Historical Society, 1975), 2:3; *Republican Banner and Nashville Whig,* 9, 12, 16, 18 March 1856; AJD to [American party meeting at Baltimore], 5 March 1856, in *Republican Banner and Nashville Whig,* 12 March 1856; AJD to [American party meeting at Philadelphia], 30 March 1856, in *Washington Daily American Organ,* 15 April 1856; AJD to [American party state convention of Georgia], 17 July 1856, in *Washington Daily American Organ,* 30 July 1856; AJD to Edward Bates, 30 September 1856, in *Washington Daily American Organ,* 7 October 1856; and J. J. Marlett to AJD, 10 July 1856, Simeon Baldwin to AJD, [25?] July 1856, [Notifying Committee of American party meeting in New York] to AJD, 25 July 1856, AJD to Simeon Baldwin, 3 August 1856 (copy), AJD to [unknown], 27 October 1856 (copy of fragment), DLC. Several of Donelson's undated 1856 speeches reiterate the same themes.

34. Potter, *Impending Crisis,* 208–11; Holt, *Political Crisis,* 194–6; and Anbinder, *Nativism and Slavery,* 214–5, 220–6.

and political flexibility. Republicans adopted a free-soil platform advocating Congress' authority to regulate slavery in U.S. territories. Voters, then, possessed a clear choice: a known commodity, the Democratic party and its eventual nominee, James Buchanan; an unknown factor, John C. Frémont and the Republican party, which to southerners seemed intent on eradicating slavery; and a questionable organization, the American party, which was trying to represent both northern and southern moderates but appeared incapable of pleasing either.[35]

Northern defections from the American party, in fact, resulted in the formation of the North Americans, a faction that nominated its own presidential candidate, Nathaniel P. Banks, who then declined the nomination and threw his support to Frémont. This maneuver revealed the lack of understanding among northern Know-Nothings that the party was dedicated to antislavery goals while also shaking southern Know-Nothing confidence that the party was truly intent on maintaining the status quo regarding slavery. Fillmore's obvious Whiggish predilections and Donelson's reputation as a Unionist Democrat who opposed extremism failed to help the Know-Nothing cause. The party's division over the slavery issue took away votes from their candidates, weakened the party in the eyes of many voters, and cost Fillmore and Donelson momentum leading up to the election.[36]

Nevertheless, the Know-Nothing nominees waged a valiant rhetorical war. When Fillmore finally returned to the United States in June 1856, he joined Donelson in condemning both the Republican and Democratic parties as threats to the Union. He particularly castigated the Republicans. "We see a political party presenting candidates for the Presidency and Vice-Presidency, selected for the first time from the free States alone, with the avowed purpose of electing those candidates by suffrages of one part of the Union only, to rule over the whole United States," he warned one New York audience.[37]

Donelson, for his part, concentrated his attacks on the Democrats. He told Fillmore that "my idea throughout the canvass has been that it was

35. Bain, *Convention Decisions,* 52–60; and Gienapp, *Origins of Republican Party,* 307–46.

36. Anbinder, *Nativism and Slavery,* 209–19, 233; Holt, "Antimasonic and Know Nothing Parties," 613–6; and Rayback, *Millard Fillmore,* 404–5.

37. Speech of MF (at Brooklyn, New York), 24 June 1856, speech of MF (at Albany, New York), 26 June 1856, in Severance, *MF Papers* 2:11–3, 2:20–1.

our policy first to kill off Buchanan." "I consider him worse than Pierce," Donelson wrote his oldest son that fall, "because he has more talents and less principle. . . . If the argument by which the South hopes to elect him is worth any thing, it secures the election of Fremont. But it is fallacious, and means nothing but a combination of a few discontents to keep up the slavery agitation in order that they may ride into power and distribute the spoils." Donelson repeatedly emphasized a crucial Know-Nothing campaign theme: the Democrats and Buchanan were using the slavery issue for their own personal ambitions and political gains. He assured supporters that American voters would choose men full of compromise, integrity, and union, such as Fillmore and himself, and eschew corrupt, greedy men such as Buchanan and extreme radical abolitionists such as Frémont.[38]

Both Fillmore and Donelson were confident that the American party would win in the fall elections. In July, Fillmore reported to Donelson that New York Democrats were "deserting Mr. Buchanan by scores and hundreds every where [*sic*]." By late September, Donelson informed his son that Fillmore confidently expected New York's support, and the party could also count on the voters in Kentucky, Tennessee, Louisiana, Maryland, and California. He concluded that "should the Oct. elections in Penn. show that Buchanan is in a minority in that state, it then becomes probable that the South will go in a body for Fillmore." Two weeks later, Donelson received another optimistic letter from Fillmore. "Every thing looks encouraging in this State," he wrote from New York. "The Americans and Whigs unite cordially and even enthusiastically in support of our tickets, all of which thus far have been quite satisfactory."[39]

Fillmore and Donelson were being overly optimistic. When the Pennsylvania and Indiana state election returns became public, the Democrats had won, virtually assuring the support of those crucial states in November's national election. The Know-Nothings had withheld enough votes from the Republican candidates to ensure their defeat, but they had been

38. AJD to MF, 2 October 1856, quoted in Gienapp, *Origins of the Republican Party,* 409; and AJD to H. V. M. Miller, 17 July 1856, AJD to Simeon Baldwin, 3 August 1856 (copy), AJD to Jackson Donelson, 27 September 1856, speeches of AJD, n.d. [1856], DLC.

39. MF to AJD, 10 July 1856, AJD to Jackson Donelson, 27 September 1856, in Sioussat, "Selected Letters, 1846–1856," 289, 289–90; AJD to MF, 26 July, 18 August 1856, Millard Fillmore Papers, State University of New York, Oswego (hereafter cited as Fillmore Papers); and MF to AJD, 9 October 1856, DLC.

unable to gather enough votes to win themselves. Donelson particularly denounced the Pennsylvania result. "Throughout this contest I have considered Mr. Buchanan as the real foe we had to contend with," he remarked to a supporter. "In my judgement therefore our friends have made a great mistake" by allowing the Democrats to win Indiana and Pennsylvania. Donelson's letters to Fillmore were filled with contempt for Buchanan, "the real enemy" who was "identified with all that is corrupt in the country."[40]

Prospects for an American victory in Tennessee's November election were also declining. During the summer, "Parson" Brownlow had predicted great success, but his enthusiasm waned as it became clear that moderate Democrats and former Whigs were flocking to Buchanan as the only hope of preserving southern rights. As late as September, Donelson believed "the American ticket is the strongest in this state," but even by that time, there had been a decisive shift toward Buchanan, as the Kentucky, North Carolina, and Missouri state elections in August demonstrated. The decision by John Bell and other former Whigs to endorse the Fillmore-Donelson ticket and Donelson's attempt to discredit his former business associate, Democrat John Catron, who was now sitting on the United States Supreme Court, failed to inject life into the American party.[41]

The results of the presidential contest demonstrated the failure of the Know-Nothing movement. Buchanan won the popular vote, with 1.8 million votes, to Frémont's 1.4 million and Fillmore's approximately 870,000. The electoral vote was even more convincingly in Buchanan's favor: 174 votes for the Democratic candidate, with Frémont securing 114 votes and Fillmore only 8. Many northern Know-Nothings supported the Republican party, while their party's southern wing supported Buchanan. Fillmore received most of popular votes in the border states of Delaware, Kentucky,

40. Anbinder, *Nativism and Slavery,* 238–42; Gienapp, *Origins of Republican Party,* 394–405; Philip Shriver Klein, *President James Buchanan: A Biography* (University Park: Pennsylvania State University Press, 1962), 259–60; AJD to [unknown], 27 October 1856 (copy of fragment), DLC; and AJD to MF, 25, 29 October 1856, Fillmore Papers.

41. Atkins, *Parties, Politics, and Sectional Conflict,* 206–12; AJD to [Jackson Donelson], 3 September 1856, DLC; William G. Brownlow to AJD, 18 March, 18 April, 24 May, 12 June 1856, Meredith P. Gentry to AJD, 12 June 1856, FPB to AJD, 26 October 1856, in Sioussat, "Selected Letters, 1846–1856," 286, 286–7, 287–8, 288, 288–89, 291; Anbinder, *Nativism and Slavery,* 237; Gohmann, *Political Nativism in Tennessee,* 140; and *Nashville Daily Union and American,* 23 September 1856.

Missouri, and Tennessee and had substantial support in Louisiana, Alabama, and Florida. Maryland, however, was his only electoral victory. The only saving grace for the American party was the realization that a shift of only 8,016 popular votes in Kentucky, Tennessee, and Louisiana would have left Buchanan without an electoral majority and would have forced the House of Representatives to choose the next president.[42]

The election results, especially those in his home state, disappointed Donelson, whose own moderate stance on slavery helped seal his party's fate. Tennessee voters had given Buchanan a nearly seventy-five-hundred-vote majority in the state's election. Despite the backhanded compliments paid by the editor of the Democratic *Nashville Daily Union and American*—that while he had "little use" for Donelson as a politician, Fillmore had been the ticket's "dead weight" in Tennessee and the South—Donelson had to realize that his political career was, if not over, perilously close to extinction. Still, he told his wife in March 1857, after conversing with Stephen A. Adams, U.S. senator from Mississippi, "I [rejoice] that my connection with the corruptions of the Democratic party, ceased when it did. It is better to be situated as I am than to have any share in the honors of a party that can boast of nothing but treachery to the great interests of the country."[43]

The Know-Nothing party swiftly declined in numbers and influence, but its leaders scheduled another national convention at Louisville, Kentucky, in June 1857. Donelson apparently did not participate in the reorganization of the Tennessee Know-Nothings, which saw them officially fuse with the former Whig party, but he did send a letter to the national convention that indicated his continued support for their cause against the "*sham Democracy.*" The arguments he had once used against Pierce he now turned against Buchanan. The president's cabinet, which included Tennessean Aaron V. Brown as postmaster general, was "a coalition of the most discordant elements." Donelson encouraged the attending delegates to "hold up to public scorn this shameful feature of party degeneracy and corruption. Let us con-

42. McPherson, *Battle Cry of Freedom*, 157; Roy F. Nichols and Philip S. Klein, "Election of 1856," *History of American Presidential Elections*, 4 vols., ed. Arthur M. Schlesinger and Fred L. Israel (New York: Chelsea House, 1971), 2:1032; Rayback, *Millard Fillmore*, 413–4; and Anbinder, *Nativism and Slavery*, 237–8.

43. Gohmann, *Political Nativism in Tennessee*, 141; *Nashville Daily Union and American*, 16 November 1856; AJD to ERD, 14 March 1857, DLC; and Atkins, *Parties, Politics, and Sectional Conflict*, 212–3.

stantly contrast it with the ennobling examples left us by the early founders of the Republic." He left the party members with an important question to ponder: "Are Americans to be still proscribed for daring to uphold the doctrines of Washington, Jefferson, Madison, and Jackson, and for repeating their admonitions against the dangers of foreign influence and the counsels of those demagogues who would lessen the attachment of the people to the Constitution and the Union?"[44]

The American party suffered significant defeats in 1857, but the worst blow for Donelson came in Tennessee. Southern rights Democrat Isham G. Harris defeated American party candidate Robert S. Hatton for the governor's chair by over eleven thousand votes, and Democrats won seven of the ten congressional seats and a majority of twenty-two in the state legislature. After the elections, Democratic legislators selected Nicholson, whose term would begin in 1859, and Andrew Johnson as U.S. senators; neither man was a favorite of Donelson. The Know-Nothing movement in Tennessee, like the national party, was dead, and so, it seemed, was Donelson's political future.[45]

44. Anbinder, *Nativism and Slavery,* 246–8; Gohmann, *Political Nativism in Tennessee,* 144; Mary E. R. Campbell, *The Attitude of Tennesseans toward the Union, 1847–1861* (New York: Vantage Press, 1961), 90; *Republican Banner and Nashville Whig,* 2, 7 May 1857; AJD to B. Duncan, 26 May 1857, in *Republican Banner and Nashville Whig,* 9 June 1857; and Elbert B. Smith, *The Presidency of James Buchanan* (Lawrence: University Press of Kansas, 1975), 17–22.

45. Atkins, *Parties, Politics, and Sectional Conflict,* 212; Gohmann, *Political Nativism in Tennessee,* 144–53; and Campbell, *Attitude of Tennesseans,* 90–1.

19

"A Fratricidal Contest"

Following the 1856 election, Donelson spent the next few years once again occupied in efforts to salvage his financial situation. In early 1857, he purchased 1,579 acres of land in the Australia Landing/Duncan community of Bolivar County, Mississippi, which is located in the delta region of the state southwest of Memphis. Situated on the east bank of the Hushpuckena River, this plantation reportedly cost Donelson $46,358, an enormous sum of money considering his financial travails. Donelson, however, was committed to making a living as a planter, traveling between his Tulip Grove and Bolivar County plantations throughout 1857. He informed Elizabeth in February of that year that he wanted to buy more land in Mississippi, where the cotton prices were better than in the Nashville area. At the same time, however, Donelson noted that because he had waited a month to sell his cotton, prices had dropped and cost him several thousand dollars in profit. While away from Nashville, he sent his wife numerous suggestions for managing Tulip Grove in his absence, but he made it clear that he placed great confidence in her "good management" skills, even telling her to give their Nashville overseer "all the aid you can in hiring hands."[1]

The life of the planter, as Donelson discovered, was not always pleasant or easy. For one thing, slaves were sometimes not as submissive as he would have liked. In June 1857, he reported to Elizabeth that one of his slaves, a man named Payman, had assaulted the overseer at the Bolivar County plantation when the latter "corrected" the former's pregnant wife by whipping her. "Payman slipped up behind him [the overseer] and struck him in the head

1. Loyce Braswell Miles, "Duncan, Mississippi: The Origins and Survival of a Town," *Journal of the Bolivar County Historical Society* 5–7 (March 1983): 13; Wirt A. Williams, ed., *History of Bolivar County, Mississippi* (Jackson, Miss.: Hederman Brothers, 1948), 137; AJD to ERD, 26 January, 11, 13, 19 February, 8 June 1857, JDC; and AJD to ERD, 14 March 1857, DLC.

several blows leaving him senseless on the ground," Donelson recounted. The overseer was slowly recovering from the assault, but Payman had run away. The overseer's "accident," as Donelson described it, had caused the other slaves to slow down their work, and he was having considerable difficulty keeping them under his control. "The negroes have a plenty [*sic*] to eat and to wear. They have coffee and molasses, and vegetables of every description, yet they are not satisfied," he remarked incredulously, "and I fear that I shall find some of them in the woods in a few days." The problem, according to Donelson, was that in Mississippi, "they miss the groggeries in our neighborhood, and have no chance to steal." Overall, he concluded, "the amount of land necessary to make it [his plantation] profitable, and the difficulty of managing the negroes, are quite discouraging." Later that fall, he observed to his wife that "the negroes have improved a little, but they take fresh chills nearly as fast as I send them to the field." These illnesses may have been real, as Donelson supposed, or, more likely, they were another indication of indirect rebellion.[2]

Donelson also discovered that national economic cycles and past indebtedness made plantation life difficult to manage. Pressured to pay his personal debts and state property taxes, which by his account were enormous, in early 1857, Donelson placed his Tulip Grove plantation on the market. He eventually found a buyer in April 1858 in the person of Mark R. Cockrill, a successful wool producer, who purchased Donelson's 1,063 acres for $53,000. In addition to paying his many debts, Donelson also hoped to use the profit from the sale of the Tulip Grove land to finance his Mississippi plantation. After finalizing the sale, Donelson moved his family (which had increased by two with the births of Lewis Randolph in 1855 and Rosa Elizabeth in 1858) to Memphis, where Elizabeth and the children stayed while he traveled between the city and his Bolivar County plantation.[3]

It must have struck Donelson at some point that he was leaving behind the mansion, the land, and the area that had been his connection to Jackson since birth. While he had traveled extensively throughout his life and lived infrequently at Tulip Grove since its construction, it had served as an

2. AJD to ERD, 7, 9 June, 17 October, 21 November 1857, JDC.

3. Sarah Jackson to Andrew Jackson III, 16 January 1857, 15 April 1858, courtesy of the Ladies' Hermitage Association, Nashville, Tenn.; and Lawrence, "Tulip Grove," 16.

anchor for his life. The friction between Donelson and Andrew Jackson Jr. undoubtedly made the decision easier, as did the growing animosity between the Donelson brothers. Following the 1857 state elections in Tennessee, a letter to the editor of the *Nashville Union and American* suggested that Daniel S. Donelson be made speaker of the state house. This endorsement elicited a heated response from the opposition newspaper, the *Nashville Patriot.* An anonymous editorial denounced "Gen. Donelson" as a nullifier and a member of the "sham democracy." There was little doubt that the editorial's author was either Andrew J. Donelson or someone who had talked extensively with him. Over the next month, several letters and editorials appeared in both newspapers. The substance of the argument was whether Daniel Donelson could rightly claim the mantle of Andrew Jackson and the Democratic party when he had indicated his support of the South Carolina nullification movement in 1832–33. To his credit, once he determined that Andrew was behind the public attack, Daniel refused to engage in "a fratricidal contest" and allowed the squabble to die.[4]

Why Andrew Donelson chose to attack his brother publicly was no mystery; he was frustrated by his own political decline and jealous that Daniel seemed to be succeeding. In addition, his brother was claiming their uncle's legacy, and Donelson had demonstrated repeatedly that he was extremely protective of Jackson's memory, which he believed legitimized his own political choices. Having alienated himself from family and friends in Nashville, it simply made sense to leave the area and start fresh in a new place, which Donelson chose to do in moving to Memphis.

The Panic of 1857 was proving wrong Donelson's optimism about success in Mississippi, though. He had wanted to keep his land because of its potential profitability, believing that its value would soon exceed $50.00 per acre. While selling the Tulip Grove land in April 1858, Donelson also explored the possibility of doing the same with his Australia plantation, "one of the best in the South," but he abandoned the idea when it became apparent he could not find a buyer willing to pay the requested price of $40.00 per acre. (Donelson was probably too optimistic in his appraisal, as the average value of an acre of Bolivar County land in 1860 was only $29.03.) The Panic of 1857 was

4. *Nashville Daily Union and American,* 29 August, 8 September, 3 October 1857; and *Nashville Patriot,* 3 September, 2, 5 October 1857.

causing Donelson so many problems that he bemoaned his inability even to send his new granddaughter, Mary Rachel Wilcox, a present.[5]

By 1859, the nation was recovering economically, and Donelson's financial prospects looked brighter. The price of cotton, which had dropped as low as ten cents per pound in 1857, rebounded dramatically, offering him an opportunity not only to pay off his debts but also potentially to turn a profit. Donelson had to make many repairs and improvements on his Bolivar County plantation that he had previously delayed because of the lack of funds, but with his slaves free from illness (or less prone to resistance), he predicted success where before he had only envisaged failure. It seemed that he was correct in his optimistic assessment. By 1860, Donelson could boast of owning fourteen slaves in Shelby County, Tennessee, and eighty-four more on his Bolivar County plantation; while the total value of his personal and real estate property was two hundred thousand dollars.[6]

Donelson did experience some adversity that year, however. In October, his oldest son, Jackson, died of an unnamed disease. Jackson had followed in his father's footsteps by becoming a successful army engineer. After assisting with the survey of western lands for the Pacific Railroad, Jackson had returned to West Point as an instructor. When Secretary of War John B. Floyd ordered Jackson to Utah, where he expected to see military service against the Mormons, Donelson advised him to "hunt out a wife, and leave Utah and Buchanan to take care of themselves. The idea of sending Engineers to fight Brigham Young is ridiculous." There is some debate about whether Jackson even made it to Utah; in any case, he died after an extended illness in Memphis in October 1859. As with his mother's death two years earlier,

5. AJD to ERD, 19, 24, 30 January, 4 February 1858, 6 May [1858], AJD to [John Donelson], 24 November 1858, JDC; and Anna Alice Kamper, "A Social and Economic History of Ante-Bellum Bolivar County, Mississippi" (master's thesis, University of Alabama, 1942), 50–51.

6. James L. Huston, *The Panic of 1857 and the Coming of the Civil War* (Baton Rouge: Louisiana State University Press, 1987), 33–4, 211–2; AJD to ERD, 4 February 1858, 6 November 1859, AJD to John Donelson, 7 September 1859, JDC; Smith, *Presidency of JB*, 65–8; United States Census Office, *Eighth Census of the United States: 1860* (Washington, D.C.: GPO, 1864); and United States Census Office, *Eighth Census of the United States: 1860. Slave Inhabitants* (Washington, D.C.: GPO, 1864). William K. Scarborough's claim that Donelson owned forty-six slaves in Lafourche Parish, Louisiana, in 1860 is incorrect. The Donelson listed was a nine-year-old boy in the household of A. Louise Donelson. See William K. Scarborough, *Masters of the Big House: Elite Slaveholders of the Mid-Nineteenth-Century South* (Baton Rouge: Louisiana State University Press, 2003), 280.

Donelson did not leave a record of his reaction to his son's death, but it must have been painful to see his hopes for a successful legacy diminished.[7]

Donelson was not one to let grieving consume him when politics called him back to the public stage. His failed vice-presidential bid on the 1856 American ticket and the subsequent collapse of the Know-Nothings had seemingly marked the end of his political activities. Since the unsuccessful 1856 election, he had appeared at a notable public function only once, in January 1859, when the city of Memphis dedicated a bust of Andrew Jackson. Donelson was also approaching his sixtieth birthday, and a younger generation was fast eclipsing him and those in his cohort who remained interested in politics. The formation of Tennessee's Opposition party, composed of former Whigs and Know-Nothings, however, beckoned him from his retirement. This new fusion party sought to wrest control of the state from the Democratic party in the 1859 elections. Its candidates ran on a platform blaming the Democrats for the Panic of 1857, which produced mixed results. Opposition gubernatorial candidate John Netherland failed to defeat Democratic incumbent Isham G. Harris, but the party cut in half the Democrats' majority in the Tennessee General Assembly. More important, the Opposition party prevailed in seven of the eight congressional district races in which it ran a candidate. Although John Bell, who had been forced into retirement from the Senate by the Democrats following the 1857 elections, did not actively participate in the campaign, Opposition members were already mentioning him as a possible presidential candidate in the 1860 election.[8]

Donelson's support for the Opposition party, which was common knowledge among his political associates, stemmed from several sources. He naturally gravitated toward any party that opposed the Democrats, and he found in the Opposition party many old acquaintances from his Know-Nothing days. The platform of the new party, which opposed "further agitation of the slavery question," sectional jealousies, the "dissolution of the Union," and parties and leaders that sustained these problems, also appealed to him.

7. Satterfield, "Moderate Nationalist Jacksonian," 536; AJD to John Donelson, 7 September 1859, JDC; and newspaper obituary, n.d., DLC.

8. *Republican Banner and Nashville Whig,* 19 December 1858, 12, 21 January, 30 March, 9 August 1859; Atkins, *Parties, Politics, and Sectional Conflict,* 216–7; Campbell, *Attitude of Tennesseans,* 90–5; Parks, *John Bell,* 339, 342–3; and John Burgess Stabler, "A History of the Constitutional Union Party: A Tragic Failure" (Ph.D. diss., Columbia University, 1954), 155–72.

Bell and the Opposition party's advocacy of these issues undoubtedly made Donelson's decision easier.[9]

In late 1859 and early 1860, when Bell supporters in Pennsylvania and Tennessee formally nominated him as their candidate for the 1860 presidential election, Donelson gave his first recorded public endorsement of Bell and the Opposition, or Constitutional Union, party. In a letter to fellow Memphis resident Jere Clemens meant for publication, he expressed his regrets that, because of "private business," he could not attend the state's February convention of the party as an official delegate. Nevertheless, he promised to support Bell if "a majority of the people" in the party selected him as their candidate. Once one of his fiercest critics, Donelson now described his former political foe as "one of the ablest statesmen and purest patriots that the country ever produced." Bell aside, Donelson found many positives in the party. "To reinstate the doctrines of Washington, Jefferson, Madison, and Jackson, and to heal the dissensions which have grown out of the influence of sectional men and sectional measures" appeared to Donelson the leading principles of the party, and these measures, he remarked, he could wholeheartedly support. Using the rhetoric he had employed against the Democratic party for several years, Donelson also took the opportunity to blast his former political associates, especially President Buchanan, for encouraging sectionalism, which had recently resulted in John Brown's raid at Harpers Ferry, Virginia. Such violence had been "fostered by demagogues for the sake of the offices gained by deceiving the honest yeomanry of the land. That the result should be corruption, imbecility, and unfaithfulness, in the Executive Department, was inevitable."[10]

The delegates who attended the February 1860 convention of the Tennessee Opposition party approved resolutions supporting the Constitution, opposing the continued slavery debate, and endorsing Bell as their candidate. They also selected Donelson as one of three delegates from West

9. *Republican Banner and Nashville Whig,* 6 April 1859; AJD to B. Duncan, 26 May 1857, in *Republican Banner and Nashville Whig,* 9 June 1857; Gohmann, *Political Nativism in Tennessee,* 148–52; Atkins, *Parties, Politics, and Sectional Conflict,* 216–7; Parks, *John Bell,* 315–6; and *Washington Daily Union,* 2, 14 March 1852.

10. *Republican Banner and Nashville Whig,* 12, 13 January 1860; AJD to Jere Clemens, 16 February 1859, in *Republican Banner and Nashville Whig,* 21 February 1860; Atkins, *Parties, Politics, and Sectional Conflict,* 225–7; and Parks, *John Bell,* 344–7.

Tennessee to the national convention. When the Constitutional Union National Convention met in Baltimore in May, its delegates chose Donelson to sit on the committee on permanent organization, where he helped select Washington Hunt of New York as permanent presiding officer. "There was never an assemblage more respected than ours in point of numbers, character and fame," Donelson reported to his wife. The real business, of course, was finding a viable ticket and a suitable platform. Bell, Sam Houston of Texas, and John J. Crittenden of Kentucky were the leading choices for the presidential nomination, although Crittenden had clearly stated his disinclination to accept any nomination. Once the balloting began, it was a race between Bell and Houston that quickly turned into a victory for the Tennessean. Edward Everett of Massachusetts reluctantly accepted the vice-presidential nomination. For their platform, the delegates pledged only "to recognize no political principle other than the Constitution of the Country, the Union of the States and the Enforcement of the Laws," the slogan that gave the national party its name.[11]

Donelson had voted with the other eleven Tennessee delegates to nominate Bell, but reports circulated that the Tennessee delegation had only intended to vote for Bell on the first ballot, then had meant to give its votes to Houston. Bell, in fact, believed that very thing. Donelson may have been one of those who "wavered," as Bell observed, after the first ballot had been taken on 9 May. Donelson wrote Elizabeth that Houston "was evidently our strongest man for the race," and another delegate, A. M. Gentry of Texas, later indicated that Donelson thought Houston would be the stronger candidate in Tennessee. Still, whatever private concerns Donelson may have had about Bell, he voted with his fellow delegates to give the Tennessean his state's unanimous endorsement. Donelson would do whatever necessary to see "the sham Democracy go down with all its iniquities."[12]

11. Parks, *John Bell,* 348–52; Campbell, *Attitude of Tennesseans,* 107–15, 119–20; Atkins, *Parties, Politics, and Sectional Conflict,* 225–6; Elting Morison, "Election of 1860," in *History of American Presidential Elections,* 4 vols., ed. Arthur M. Schlesinger and Fred L. Israel (New York: Chelsea House, 1971), 2:1113–4; *Republican Banner and Nashville Whig,* 26 February, 11, 12, 15 May 1860; Stabler, "History of the Constitutional Union Party," 353–5, 441–70; and John V. Mering, "The Slave-State Constitutional Unionists and the Politics of Consensus," *Journal of Southern History* 43 (August 1977): 395–410.

12. AJD to ERD, 11 May 1860, DLC; *Republican Banner and Nashville Whig,* 15 May 1860; Parks, *John Bell,* 348–52; and Stabler, "History of the Constitutional Union Party," 528.

As he had once done for the Democrats and the Know-Nothings, Donelson turned to speechmaking to make the case for the Constitutional Union ticket. At meetings in Baltimore and Memphis, he described Bell, Everett, and their supporters as "men who derived their political faith from the Fathers of the Revolution—from the great minds which founded and reformed our system—from the examples of such men as Washington, Jefferson, Madison, and Jackson." "These great patriots," he reminded the crowds, "rebuked successfully the spirit of disunion . . . by invoking the spirit of the Constitution, the Union, and the Laws, as the source of all our national greatness, and the highest guarantee we possess for the maintenance of our civil and religious liberties." He disingenuously defended Bell as an opponent not of Jackson but only of Martin Van Buren. Donelson concluded with calls for voters to "rally around the standard with glad enthusiasm in such a manner as would spread terror in the ranks [of those] whose chief aim it was to dissolve the Union." If voters elected Bell and Everett, he argued, "the country will be restored to its ancient traqnquility [*sic*]. The laws will be enforced. All sectional controversy will cease, and the prosperity and welfare of the people will be secured."[13]

By the end of June 1860, the other two major political parties had selected their candidate. The Democratic National Convention, which met in Charleston, South Carolina, in April 1860, was initially unable to nominate a candidate. After several southern state delegations walked out in a dispute over the platform and the remaining delegates failed to find a two-thirds majority for Stephen A. Douglas, the convention adjourned. When the Democrats reconvened in Baltimore in June, southern delegations again left after an intense argument over the seating of competing pro- and anti-Douglas delegations. The remaining attendees declared Douglas their unanimous choice, hoping his candidacy would bridge the gap between northern and southern Democrats. Meanwhile, the disgruntled southern delegates met and nominated Buchanan's vice-president, John C. Breckenridge of Kentucky, as their presidential candidate and adopted a platform calling for Congress to protect territorial slavery. The Republicans, in contrast, looked

13. Speech of AJD (at Baltimore), May 1860, quoted in Satterfield, "Moderate Nationalist Jacksonian," 541–2; and speech of AJD (at Memphis), 4 June 1860, in *Republican Banner and Nashville Whig*, 8 June 1860.

for a moderate candidate to unite the North, the only region they had a realistic chance of winning. After considering William Seward of New York and Edward Bates of Missouri, the convention chose Abraham Lincoln of Illinois, a relatively inexperienced national politician who had made a name for himself in the 1858 state elections by touring Illinois to debate Douglas. Confident they could carry the New England states, Republican leaders hoped Lincoln could help them win Illinois and other moderate states.[14]

The Bell-Everett ticket, then, faced formidable but not insurmountable competition. The Democratic party weakened itself by splitting and nominating two sectional candidates, while the Republicans seemed intent on winning only the northern free states. Just as with the Know-Nothings in 1856, there was a chance that American voters, worried by the increasingly acrimonious rhetoric coming from the South, would decide to support a party dedicated to defending the Constitution, preserving the Union, and enforcing the existing laws regarding slavery. Once again, such optimistic predictions of success for the moderate party in the election proved false. Lincoln carried the day with 180 electoral votes (all from northern states, California, and Oregon) and nearly 1.9 million votes. Breckenridge ran second with 72 electoral and 848,000 popular votes from mostly southern states, while Douglas had a larger popular tally (almost 1.4 million) but a smaller electoral total (12). Bell ran strongly in the border states, winning the 39 electoral votes of Tennessee, Kentucky, and Virginia but only 593,000 popular votes. Moderate political voices had once again failed to carry the day; it appeared that a new generation of politicians was replacing the stodgy, dated candidates of the Constitutional Union party.[15]

Donelson's immediate reaction to Lincoln's election went unrecorded. He was back in Mississippi, working to get his crops to market. He had another child, Andrew Jackson, born in January 1860, for which to provide, and his second-oldest daughter, Rachel Jackson, had married William B. Knox on 18 November. Both events added to Donelson's expenses. When

14. Potter, *Impending Crisis,* 407–16, 418–30.

15. Ibid., 417, 442–5; Morison, "Election of 1860," 2:1116–7; Stabler, "History of the Constitutional Union Party," 591–9; and Peter Knupfer, "James Buchanan, the Election of 1860, and the Demise of Jacksonian Politics," in *James Buchanan and the Political Crisis of the 1850s,* ed. Michael J. Birkner (Selinsgrove, Pa.: Susquehanna University Press, 1996), 146–70.

South Carolina voted to secede from the United States on 20 December, however, he attended a meeting of West Tennesseans in Memphis at which they passed resolutions calling for a southern convention. The convention's purpose would be to air the southern states' concerns and find a path that would protect both slavery and the Union without resorting to revolution or violence. The South's, and Tennessee's, moderation depended, of course, on the absence of the federal government's coercion.[16]

The idea of a southern Constitutional Union convention failed to elicit much support in Tennessee or elsewhere. Still, as Mississippi, Florida, Alabama, Georgia, Louisiana, and Texas all seceded and formed the Confederate States of America, Tennessee held firmly to its position as a part of both the United States and the South. Southern rights Democrats, however, including Governor Isham G. Harris, were openly pushing for Tennessee's secession. Hoping to prevent that result, Unionist legislators called for elections on 9 February 1861 to consider whether to hold a convention to vote on secession and elect delegates. Donelson declined to play any part in a proposed convention, but as a member of a group of Shelby County Unionists, he signed an address to West Tennesseans that contained language very reminiscent of his earlier speeches. It called for the state's voters to assist in "the preservation of the Union" by "saving the Republic . . . vindicated by Clay, Webster, and Jackson" as opposed "to one *to be built* by the leader of disunion [Governor Isham G. Harris], who would drag us out of this Union, and 'precipitate us into revolution.'" He also reportedly stated that "if the Rebellion was carried out, and a civil war broke out," then he would be "bound by interest to follow the fortunes of the South, but that the South must be overcome and the Rebellion would be the overthrow of Slavery on the American continent."[17]

16. AJD to Martin Donelson, 6 December 1860, JDC; Potter, *Impending Crisis,* 489–505; Atkins, *Parties, Politics, and Sectional Conflict,* 228–33; and Satterfield, "Moderate Nationalist Jacksonian," 544.

17. Potter, *Impending Crisis,* 505–13; Campbell, *Attitude of Tennesseans,* 136–58; Atkins, *Parties, Politics, and Sectional Conflict,* 233–40; Satterfield, "Moderate Nationalist Jacksonian," 544–5; *Nashville Republican Banner,* 22 January 1861; AJD to Editor, 19 January 1861, in *Memphis Bulletin,* n.d.; AJD to Editor, 15 March [1861], in *Nashville Union and American,* n.d., DLC; Mary R. Campbell, "The Significance of the Unionist Victory in the Election of February 9, 1861 in Tennessee," *East Tennessee Historical Society's Publications* 14 (1942): 11–30; A. Clark Denson to Andrew Johnson, 2 July 1862, in Leroy P. Graf, Ralph W. Haskins, and Patricia P. Clark, eds., *The Papers of Andrew Johnson,* vol. 5, *1861–1862* (Knoxville: University of Tennessee Press, 1979), 527–9.

Tennessee voters heeded the call and voted decisively against holding a convention (69,691 to 57,798) and overwhelmingly in favor of Unionist delegates (88,803 to 24,749) should the convention vote pass. West Tennesseans, however, ignored Donelson's request by approving by a large margin the call for a convention (23,052 to 8,488). They did, however, follow the other two grand divisions of the state in voting for Unionist delegates (21,091 to 9,344). As one historian of Tennessee politics correctly surmises, "While slavery was an accepted institution and southern rights did appear endangered, most voters as yet saw no reason to destroy the Union." [18]

Once South Carolina troops fired on Fort Sumter and Lincoln issued a call for seventy-five thousand militia troops from those states still in the Union to resist this insurrection, however, Unionism lost support in Tennessee. Donelson reported to his daughter Mary that in Memphis, "every thing here is preparation for war." He informed her and another daughter, Rachel, that two of their brothers, John and Daniel, were stationed in the same regiment at Randolph, Virginia, and that he himself had joined the home guard "to protect the families who may be left without defence." Donelson condemned President Lincoln, who "assume[d] the right to subjugate us, and his leading newspapers threaten[ed] us with extermination if we do not yield to his demands." The day he had predicted for so long had finally come. Extremists in both sections had finally used sectionalism to split the United States. "You know how earnestly I have endeavored to avert the calamities which have come upon us," he reminded Mary. "But it has all been in vain. Sectional animosity has at last destroyed the Union, and no alternative is left the patriot but the assertion of the rights which belong to a free people. When the invader comes[,] we must meet him as we did the British in the Revolutionary War." Donelson warned her to "prepare . . . for the trials to which you may be subjected by the folly of those Demagogues who have brought the present ruin upon the country." [19]

18. Atkins, *Parties, Politics, and Sectional Conflict,* 240–7.

19. Ibid., 242–53; J. Milton Henry, "The Revolution in Tennessee, February, 1861, to June, 1861," *THQ* 18 (June 1959): 99–119; Charles L. Lufkin, "Secession and Coercion in Tennessee, the Spring of 1861," *THQ* 50 (Summer 1991): 98–109; and AJD to MED, 24 May 1861, DLC. Unbeknown to Donelson, one R. W. Latham had recommended that Lincoln make the Tennessean a member of his new cabinet; despite later recollections by MED, Lincoln never seriously considered Donelson for any government position. See R. W. Latham to Abraham Lincoln, 8 November 1860, Abraham Lincoln Papers, Library of Congress, Washington, D.C.; and Reminiscence by MED, n.d., DLC.

Elizabeth also denounced the war in a public letter to Gen. Winfield Scott. Perhaps written with her husband's help, her correspondence, published in a Memphis newspaper and distributed throughout the South, regarded the elderly general "as the only man in the country who can arrest the civil war now begun." Like Donelson, Elizabeth blamed Lincoln "the usurper and his Abolition band" for "desecrate[ing] the honored place once filled by our Washington, Jefferson and Jackson." She asked Scott to tell "the North, you shall not shed your brother's blood. The sons of Tennessee and the South have buckled on their armor, and are ready for the fight. We will fight this battle, every man, woman and child, to the last cent in our pockets and the last drop of blood in our veins."[20]

As Donelson foresaw in his letter to Mary and as Elizabeth warned General Scott, on 8 June 1861, sixteen years to the day after Andrew Jackson's death, Tennesseans overwhelmingly approved secession (102,172 to 47,238), although the total vote was smaller than that taken in February. The only substantial opposition came from the East Tennessee counties. Popular ratification of secession only confirmed what was already occurring. In late April and early May, the general assembly authorized Governor Isham G. Harris to begin preparations for entering the Confederacy, which he promptly did by creating a provisional army and signing a defense alliance with the Confederate States. With the people approving the action, Tennessee became a part of the Confederate States of America. The home of Jackson, Polk, and Donelson was now a participant in a revolution against the Republic they had fought so hard to maintain.[21]

As news of Tennessee's secession spread, northerners who remembered Donelson assumed he supported secession. The *New York Daily Times* reported that he was "in the ranks of the rebellion, fighting against 'our glorious Union!' Among 'domestic traitors,' battling for the overthrow of 'the constitutional rights of our country,' through the destruction of the Constitution itself." Donelson, along with other Shelby County Unionists, publicly stated his "fealty ALONE" to his home state, and his private comments clearly indicate his belief that Tennessee and other southern states were participating in a revolution against the "usurper" Lincoln and "his Abolition band."

20. ERD to Winfield Scott, quoted in *Memphis Bulletin*, 29 April 1861.

21. Phillip Shaw Paludan, *The Presidency of Abraham Lincoln* (Lawrence: University Press of Kansas, 1994), 57–70; and Potter, *Impending Crisis*, 564–5, 567–83.

As he told Mary in September 1861, "We have no alternative but to establish our independence. If Lincoln were to succeed, the south would be ruined. He justifies measures that are at war with all our ideas of a constitutional Government. He must therefore be whipped, and I hope that all my friends will help do it."[22]

Civil War Memphis proved to be a difficult place to live for all of its residents, including the Donelson family. In early 1862, troops from both sides moved into position for the battle that would take place near the Shiloh church. Donelson reported on 22 March that the city "was all in a state of confusion, amounting almost to despair." Reports from Middle Tennessee were just as alarming. "Andy Johnson is at Nashville as provisional Governor and is clothed with military power to crush the rebellion," he informed Elizabeth. Donelson's brother, Daniel, was fighting as a brigadier general in the Confederate army, but his Sumner County property was in danger of being confiscated, while his wife, Margaret, and their children had fled the area looking for "some place of safety." Donelson's main concern, however, was West Tennessee, where his family lived, and West Mississippi, where his plantation was located. With armies moving all around the city, he believed that "the fate of Memphis will be settled in a few days," although he thought, incorrectly, that an attack on Island No. 10 on the Mississippi River was more likely than action near Corinth.[23]

When Memphis fell under Union control in early June 1862, Federal officials and troops treated Donelson "with courtesy," which Elizabeth attributed to his public statements before the war opposing secession and supporting the Union. "He talks to the *Federals* and *Southerners just* as he has done for *30* years, regardless [of] *who* it pleases or *displeases*," she wrote their son John. Neither he nor Elizabeth mention in their letters whether Donelson took the oath of allegiance required while Ulysses S. Grant commanded the city in June and July 1862. Once William T. Sherman succeeded

22. Satterfield, "Moderate Nationalist Jacksonian," 546; *New York Daily Times,* n.d., quoted in Frank Moore, comp., *The Rebellion Record,* 12 vols. (New York: G. P. Putnam, 1862–68), 1:138; AJD to MED, 28 September 1861, ERD to Winfield Scott, 29 April 1861, in *Memphis Bulletin,* n.d., DLC.

23. Joseph H. Parks, "Memphis under Military Rule, 1862 to 1865," *East Tennessee Historical Society's Publications* 14 (1942): 31–58; idem, "A Confederate Trade Center under Federal Occupation: Memphis, 1862–1865," *Journal of Southern History* 7 (August 1941): 289–314; AJD to ERD, 22 March 1861 [1862], DLC; and McPherson, *Battle Cry of Freedom,* 405–14.

Grant's command in Memphis, conditions and morale in the city improved, except among the staunchest Confederates.[24]

Donelson's support for the Confederate States, however, failed to keep them from arresting him in August 1862. According to Elizabeth's account, Confederate sympathizers in Memphis followed her husband around, "making notes of his remarks." Apparently dissatisfied with what Donelson had to say, they arrested him, presumably somewhere outside of the Union-held city, and forced him to "ride on horseback in the heat and dust of summer, first to Prentiss, then to Grenada, Jackson, and Vicksburg." When he finally reached Vicksburg, Gen. Earl Van Dorn "pronounced the charges against him 'frivolous'" and released him. Making his way back to Memphis, Donelson set out for his Australia plantation; Elizabeth worried that he would be unable to return to Memphis anytime soon: "*Both parties* require those passing the lines to take the oath of Allegiance, and it is said that the Confederates will not grant papers on any condition." To Elizabeth's surprise, however, Donelson appeared in Memphis just two days after her pessimistic letter.[25]

Throughout the war, Donelson enjoyed a friendly relationship with the United States and its military representatives, whereas his association with the Confederate States deteriorated. The Union soldiers allowed him to move with impunity between Memphis and his Bolivar County plantation, although there were times when he had to ask Union officers for permission to travel. On one occasion in late 1862, Donelson mentioned his displeasure with "Lincolnites" who visited his slaves and likely gave them news of the impending Emancipation Proclamation. In January 1865, as the war neared an end, he complained that Union soldiers and refugees, both black and white, were tearing down fences and "interfer[ing] with our comforts" and would leave the South "desolated." Otherwise, his complaints about the Federal military occupation of his state and region were few.[26]

24. Parks, "Memphis under Military Rule," 31–41; ERD to John Donelson, 2 December 1862, JDC; and John F. Marszalek, *Sherman: A Soldier's Passion for Order* (New York: Free Press, 1993; New York: Vintage Books, 1994), 188–201.

25. ERD to John Donelson, 2 December 1862, JDC.

26. AJD to ERD, 22 March 1861 [1862], AJD to Stephen A. Hurlbut, 29 May 1863, AJD to MED, 27 August 1864, [6?] January 1865, DLC; and ERD to John Donelson, 2 December 1862, AJD to John Donelson, 4 December 1862, AJD to ERD, 17 [?] 1863, JDC.

Donelson saved his harshest comments for Confederate soldiers and their government. He particularly hated the Confederate policy of burning cotton and taking farm animals to keep them from Union troops. Both acts were common occurrences that compelled him to hide his cotton bales in order to salvage something for the market. "The cotton burning demoralizes every thing," he told his wife in 1863, and in 1864, he complained to his oldest daughter, that the "Confederates have injured me more than the Yankees, by burning my cotton and pressing my stock." Donelson's frustration with the Confederate government increased as the war progressed. "The foolish policy of the Confederate Govt in burning cotton and destroying our stock in the bottom has damaged me immensely," he declared. "I have lost by this policy more than 300 bales of cotton and all the Negroes which they pressed from me under the pretences of carrying provisions to Vicksburgh." "In the bottom," or in the Mississippi Delta region, Confederate "bushwhackers and Guerillas [argue] that it is better to destroy crops than to let the Yankees get them. They are very willing themselves to take the cotton and trade it for supplies," Donelson bitterly grumbled, "but seem to forget that the families who are dependent for their support upon this cotton ought to have the benefit of it."[27]

Donelson obviously resented the effect of Confederate policy on his economic potential. He had struggled to make ends meet for years while working for the Democratic party and the U.S. government, usually advocating limited government. Now, the Confederacy, supposedly premised on states' rights and decentralized government, was placing obstacles in front of his attempts at "farming," as he called it. Donelson's complaints, however, did not mesh with reality. The Civil War years were, in fact, some of his most profitable. Ironically, concerns about moving his crops, especially cotton, to market disappeared as the war lengthened. Early in 1864, he believed that cotton prices, which were at sixty cents per pound, would net him a profit of ten thousand dollars. In August 1864, he confidently predicted that, if he could keep the Confederates from destroying his cotton crop, it would "make me as much money as I want." It is unclear whether or not Donelson

27. AJD to MED, 27 August 1864, [6?] January 1865, DLC; AJD to John Donelson, 4 December 1862, AJD to ERD, 17 [?] 1863, JDC; and Stephen V. Ash, *When the Yankees Came: Conflict and Chaos in the Occupied South, 1861–1865* (Chapel Hill: University of North Carolina Press, 1995), 17.

made the profit that he expected, but either way, he still owed enormous debts.[28]

Donelson, fortunately, received an unexpected windfall from an unfortunate circumstance. His brother-in-law and cousin, William Donelson, died in November 1864, leaving Donelson and Elizabeth a "life estate" and their son, William Alexander, part of his property. William Donelson's estate, worth ninety thousand dollars on the eve of the war, had declined in value because of the loss of slaves, but it was still worth enough to bolster his brother-in-law's own precarious finances and led one newspaper mistakenly to announce that Donelson was moving back to Nashville.[29]

The Civil War, then, proved to be an economic boon for Donelson, but it was also a time of great loss in other, more personal, ways. Just months after Tennessee seceded, his daughter, three-year-old Rosa, died. His estranged brother, Confederate brigadier general Daniel Donelson, died near Knoxville in April 1863. In September of that year, Donelson's son, John, was killed at the Battle of Chickamauga, after having fought at Shiloh and suffering a wound at Murfreesboro. (Andrew Jackson Jr.'s son, Samuel, also died after being wounded at Chickamauga.) Five months later, his son-in-law, John Wilcox, died in Richmond, Virginia, of a heart condition. The biggest blow, however, came in January 1864, when Donelson's son Daniel, a Confederate soldier, was murdered in De Soto County, Mississippi, while on furlough, allegedly for his horse and boots. The murderer, apparently a Confederate soldier or bushwhacker, left Daniel's body on the side of the road, where it lay for three months before Donelson learned of his death and traveled from nearby Memphis to recover it. Donelson tried unsuccessfully to find and prosecute Daniel's murderer, but the case was apparently never solved. These personal losses, added to the economic difficulties military directives caused for him, resulted in Donelson blaming the Confederate government for many of his problems. "How fleeting is life—how

28. AJD to MED, 28 September 1861, 27 August 1864, [6?] January 1865, AJD to ERD, 22 March 1861 [1862], AJD to H. Windly, 8 April 1865, DLC; and AJD to John Donelson, 4 December 1862, AJD to ERD, 17 [?] 1863, 23 March 1864, AJD to A. W. [William Alexander] Donelson, 13 August 1864, JDC.

29. G. W. Curry to AJD, 20 November 1864, JDC; Leroy P. Graf, Ralph W. Haskins, and Patricia P. Clark, eds., *The Papers of Andrew Johnson,* vol. 6, *1862–1864* (Knoxville: University of Tennessee Press, 1983), 193; AJD to MED, [6?] January 1865, promissory note from AJD and ERD to Harry Smith, [?] May 1865, DLC; and *Nashville Dispatch,* 21 January 1865.

vain is the glory which comes from men," he told Mary as he informed her of her brother's murder.[30]

As the war progressed and Donelson's personal losses mounted, he became more critical of the conflict that he had worked so hard to prevent. He lamented the war's effect on slavery, which he expected would end regardless of the war's result. More important, Donelson commented privately on the war's effect on the states, northern and southern, and proclaimed publicly the necessity of restoring the former Republic. "If the evil could fall upon the two factions which have brought their country to this extremity," he told his son, John, in 1862, "it would be some consolation to us, but unfortunately the ruin which is overtaking us, falls alike upon the innocent and the guilty."[31]

In a letter to a member of the Confederate Congress in the fall of 1863, which did not become public until April 1865, Donelson commented on the war and offered suggestions for its end. The Confederacy had to realize that the war was not winnable, he told the unnamed congressman. He suggested that the "extermination" of millions cease and called for "*a return to the Constitution as we received it from our Fathers.*" Donelson proposed that the Confederacy try for peace "on honorable terms" and "an adequate assurance that the Southern States can occupy their old *status.*" The abolitionists and secessionists, or "exterminationists," especially Confederate president Jefferson Davis, were to blame for the present state of war, he observed. If the people would find another issue about which to fight instead of slavery, Donelson believed that it was not "*too late to retrace steps that lead to destruction. It is never too late to declare that we were satisfied with the Government made by Washington, Madison and Jefferson, and that we are still willing to live under it, if it can be administered in good faith.*" "Let those who brought on the revolution and staked their political fortunes on the doctrines of secession and abolition share the blame of heresies so directly opposed to the

30. Moore, *Rebellion Record* 6:38, 64; AJD to MED, 28 September 1861, 27 August 1864, [6?] January 1865, John Donelson to ERD, 2 February 1863, newspaper obituaries of John S. Donelson, n.d., newspaper obituaries of John A. Wilcox, n.d., Affidavit by S. W. White, 16 July 1864, DLC; ERD to John Donelson, 2 December 1862, AJD to John Donelson, 4 December 1862, ERD to AJD, [9?] October 1863, AJD to A. W. [William Alexander] Donelson, 13 August 1864, JDC; and Galloway, "AJ, Jr.," pt. 2, 342.

31. AJD to John Donelson, 4 December 1862, JDC; and AJD to MED, 27 August 1864, AJD to H. Windly, 8 April 1865, DLC.

spirit of our institutions," he proclaimed, "but let the people be free once more to try the virtues of the ballot-box and unfettered discussion."[32]

Donelson's assessment of the war and the possibility of peace in 1863 were, of course, naïve. By that time, the end of slavery had become a goal of the Lincoln administration, and a return to the days when North and South lived in harmony with African Americans in legal bondage was impossible. Still, Donelson's comments clearly indicate that, however unsophisticated his plan for peace was, he remained confident that appeals to the nation's republican past would save the nation from what he had foreseen at the beginning of the war: "bankruptcy and ruin upon both sections . . . [and] the sacrifice of the flower of our population."[33]

Donelson also found it necessary to defend his conduct during the war. Some individuals had charged him with betraying his principles by becoming a rabid secessionist; others had accused him of conveying contraband for the United States. "I have been represented as lately a member of the Confederate Congress, an active secessionist . . . [and] a refugee to the Federal lines seeking the protection of the Amnesty Oath of President Lincoln," he informed readers of the *Memphis Argus*. "All such statements are unfounded and unjust." Federal troops had allowed him to travel freely to his Bolivar County plantation and "to purchase and transport such articles of necessity as would enable me to support the negroes who chose to remain with me." Lest anyone forget who he was, Donelson reminded southerners that his "creed was formed in the school of President Jackson, whose confidence I possessed up to the time of his death."[34]

As the war drew to a close, Donelson had to adjust to Tennessee's new political and social atmosphere. Andrew Johnson had led the state as military governor since March 1862, and it was under his leadership that a convention of Unionist delegates met in Nashville in January 1865 to organize a reconstructed government. The convention delegates passed a state constitutional amendment abolishing slavery and resolutions rescinding the state's secession and calling for new elections for governor and the general

32. *Memphis Argus*, 4 April 1865. The unnamed Confederate congressman was likely Henry S. Foote (Satterfield, "Moderate Nationalist Jacksonian," 549).

33. AJD to MED, 24 August 1861, DLC.

34. AJD to Editor, 5 February 1865, in *Memphis Argus*, n.d., DLC.

assembly. In February 1865, eligible Tennesseans (meaning only those who had voted in the 1864 presidential election) voted in favor of the amendment and resolutions. A month later, the electorate chose Donelson's former Know-Nothing ally, William G. Brownlow, as governor and installed a legislature composed almost exclusively of radical Unionists, who opposed slavery. Johnson, who had been elected vice-president on Lincoln's ticket in 1864, moved to Washington in April to begin his term in office and became president soon after when John Wilkes Booth assassinated Lincoln.[35]

Donelson apparently approved of many of the social and political changes in Tennessee and the nation. His 1863 letter to an anonymous Confederate congressman appeared in early April 1865, the very day the new legislature took office. Perhaps he hoped to use its publication to calm the animosity felt by many Confederates, especially in West Tennessee, toward the radical Unionists, as the outcome of the war was becoming a foregone conclusion. In September, he gave his public support to President Johnson, who appeared to represent to many white southerners a milder form of Reconstruction. Donelson also publicly stated his satisfaction with the Freedmen's Bureau, but in 1866, according to one historian, he ignored attempts by conservative Unionists to use his name in support of their campaign to attract black voters; it turned out that they did not need his endorsement.[36]

Donelson's final political foray centered on the issue of African American suffrage, a subject about which he gave ambivalent signs. In 1867, he was elected as a delegate to a meeting of Davidson County Conservatives, where he became one of three vice-presidents of the Conservative state convention. This convention's leaders met to select candidates to run against the Radicals, especially Governor Brownlow, in the state's August elections. The

35. Hans Trefousse, *Andrew Johnson: A Biography* (New York: W. W. Norton, 1989), 152–75; and Paul H. Bergeron, Stephen V. Ash, and Jeanette Keith, *Tennesseans and Their History* (Knoxville: University of Tennessee Press, 1999), 150–1.

36. *Memphis Argus,* 4 April 1865; *Nashville Republican Banner,* 5 September 1865, quoted in Satterfield, *Jackson's Confidant,* 190; Satterfield, "Moderate Nationalist Jacksonian," 553; Davidson M. Leatherman to Andrew Johnson, 10 December 1865, in Paul H. Bergeron, ed., *The Papers of Andrew Johnson,* vol. 9, *September 1865–January 1866* (Knoxville: University of Tennessee Press, 1991), 9:501–2; AJD to the editor, *Augusta (Ga.) Weekly Constitutionalist,* 20 September 1865, in E. Merton Coulter, *The South During Reconstruction, 1865–1877* (Baton Rouge: Louisiana State University Press and the Littlefield Fund for Southern History of the University of Texas, 1947), 78; and Eric Foner, *Reconstruction: America's Unfinished Revolution, 1863–1877* (New York: Harper and Row, 1988), 270–1.

Conservatives' speeches seemingly indicated that they supported black suffrage, which they actually opposed, and the restoration of republican government, of which Donelson undoubtedly approved. Conservatives lost the fall elections by large margins. The following year, Donelson found himself elected as a representative to the Conservatives' Davidson County convention, but he apparently did not attend, objecting to their continued emphasis on enfranchising and courting black voters. In 1869, after watching Mississippi's "negroe loving democracy" put African Americans in office, he told Elizabeth that it was "terrible to contemplate the future if what is called democracy in the south succeeds in giving office and power to the negroe." His comments demonstrated an unwillingness to accept a society that allowed racial equality.[37]

That was not surprising, since they were spoken by a man who had lived the vast majority of his life defending and depending upon slavery. Donelson found the transition from slave labor to free labor difficult to accept, not only politically but personally. With two farms to maintain (one in Mississippi, one in Tennessee), realizing a profit in what was a difficult period for any southern farmer to grow crops, while also paying former slaves wages, stretched Donelson's finances to their limits. His oldest living son, Martin, a graduate of Washington University in St. Louis, Missouri, and the Kentucky Military Institute, lived in nearby Duncan, Mississippi, and attempted to help his busy father, who traveled among Bolivar County, Nashville, and Memphis. Donelson often complained to Martin and Elizabeth that African American workers on the Mississippi plantation were troublesome. Local whites, including one man who was hired to oversee the farm's operation, "put it into their head that something is due to them for service in past years." "They would steal all that we have if not watched," he assured Elizabeth. Still, their discontent threatened to impede Donelson's attempts at farming, so he was forced to "deal liberally" with them.[38]

Donelson often vacillated, sometimes from one week to the next, over whether his ventures would be a success or a failure. His crops, which

37. *Nashville Republican Banner,* 2, 17 April 1867, 2 June 1868; Bergeron, Ash, and Keith, *Tennesseans,* 161–6, 174–6; and AJD to ERD, 11 September 1869, DLC.

38. AJD to [?], 13 December [1865?], AJD to ERD, 11 September 1869, DLC; AJD to Martin Donelson, 12 December 1868, 10 March, 1 April 1869, Martin Donelson to AJD, 2 January 1869, DTL; and AJD to ERD, 22 December 1868, 18 February, 19, 21 June, 6 August 1869, 13 September 1870, JDC.

included corn, potatoes, wheat, and cotton, seemed to net him little profit. By 1870, his debts were at least ten thousand dollars and were probably more, while the value of his real and personal estates was only fourteen thousand dollars. With his African American help expressing their dissatisfaction, Donelson considered employing immigrant Chinese workers, who would work at a cheaper rate, or even renting out his land to former slaves. As if that were not enough, he also continued to experience personal heartbreak, as his eighteen-year-old daughter, Catherine (nicknamed Katie), "young, beautiful, bright, and accomplished," died in 1868 from inflammation of the brain.[39]

Depression over his circumstances eventually brought suicidal thoughts to Donelson's mind. In June 1869, he wrote Elizabeth that while walking along a bayou near their Mississippi farm, "I felt that a slip into the water might not prove a great calamity if I rose no more from its depths." He was able to shake off his depression by reminding himself that he could still prove "useful to you & the dear children." He was not able, however, to avoid reminding both himself and Elizabeth that their future depended upon remedying poor decisions he had made. "Think of nothing but economy and making something," he wrote her several months later. "We are too poor to think of anything but making enough to pay for past follies."[40]

The anxiety of worrying about mistakes made finally taxed Donelson's health beyond its limitations. On the afternoon of 25 June 1871, he became ill and left his Bolivar County plantation for Memphis to receive medical treatment. He arrived by steamship, and his condition was such that Elizabeth and Martin, who accompanied him on the trip, had him carried directly to the Peabody Hotel, where he had often stayed on his visits to the city. The next evening, at 8:30 P.M., Donelson died. The funeral took place on 27 June at the hotel, and he was buried at Elmwood Cemetery. Memphis and Nashville newspapers hailed him as "a citizen distinguished for his tal-

39. AJD to [Martin Donelson and William Alexander Donelson], 24 May 1867, AJD to Martin Donelson, 24 November, 6, 12, 14, 15, 18 December 1868, 2 January, 10 March, 1, 26 April 1869, 16 August 1870, Martin Donelson to AJD, 20 January 1869, DTL; AJD to ERD, 22 December 1868, 18 February, 19, 21 June, 16 July, 6, 22, 23 August, 3, 4 September 1869, JDC; and funeral announcement for Katie Donelson, 15 August 1868, AJD to [Martin Donelson?], 15 July 1869, AJD to ERD, 11 September 1869, DLC.

40. AJD to ERD, 19 June 1869, JDC.

ent" and "one of the most devoted adherents to the cause of the American Union."[41]

Donelson's life ended as he had always lived it—in debt. Creditors forced Elizabeth, who died only two months later, to vacate the Bolivar County plantation in order to sell it; her late husband had left twenty-six thousand dollars in debts that needed paying. At the time of his death, Donelson was still battling the financial demons that had shadowed him all his adult life.[42]

41. William C. Miller to G. W. Curry, 26 June 1871, DLC; *Memphis Daily Appeal,* 27 June 1871; and *Nashville Republican Banner,* 27, 28, 30 June 1871.

42. James C. Cobb, *The Most Southern Place on Earth: The Mississippi Delta and the Roots of Regional Identity* (New York: Oxford University Press, 1992), 75.

CONCLUSION

If one visits Andrew Jackson's home today, docents laud the president's democratic tendencies, admire his courage, point out his modest wealth, and concede his status as a slave owner. Rarely mentioned is the presence of a house called Tulip Grove, which sits on a small hill not far from the Hermitage. For financial reasons, it is open only on special occasions and is largely ignored by the public.

Much like his house, Donelson's life has also been ignored. It certainly has not received the attention of one who was "intimately connected" with many of the most significant events of nineteenth-century America. He was part of an advisory body to a president who oversaw the development of a more democratic, although still imperfect, political process. Donelson fought fiercely for the preservation of the Union, from the Nullification Crisis through the Civil War, basing his arguments on the foundation of republican principles outlined by the founding generation and modified to fit a United States influenced by the market revolution. Like Andrew Jackson, James Madison, and others, he believed that territorial expansion was necessary to preserve the Republic, so going to Texas to advocate for its annexation was not only a financial and political decision but also one based on ideological principle. Paradoxically, the same ideological principles that convinced Donelson to defend the Republic also led him to justify the existence of slavery, for both himself and his nation.

Donelson had been able to play an important role, either directly or indirectly, in these events because of his association with Andrew Jackson, which opened the door to opportunities that other young men did not encounter. Following his uncle's example, Donelson came to embody what it meant to be a southern gentleman of the time: virtuous, ambitious, and honorable. With confidence in his nephew's character, Jackson early on gave him every chance to succeed, and, in many ways, it appeared that Donelson took advantage of that relationship. His political career was extraordinary; he served as presidential advisor, chargé d'affaires, minister plenipotentiary, editor of a national newspaper, and vice-presidential candidate. He was a nephew of whom Jackson could be proud.

But for all of his accomplishments, Donelson remained largely in the background, working as a minor politician. It seemed that circumstances overwhelmed him, that he did not always understand what he was facing. In fact, he often seemed a step behind, lacking the political sagacity necessary to shape, rather than be shaped by, the momentous events with which he was involved. Often, when Donelson experienced adversity, he became depressed, caustic, and brooding and alternated between blaming others for his problems and castigating himself for poor decisions. These responses were not conducive to inspiring confidence in his skills and talents, of which he actually possessed not a little. Instead, Donelson alienated himself from old friends and new allies, then complained when others pointed out his shortcomings.

It appears that Donelson understood, but found it difficult to accept, what Jackson had come to realize during the Eaton affair: he did not have a firm understanding of the political world. Before the Eaton affair, Donelson was confident, self-assured, and focused. He knew his uncle's expectations and lived up to them as best as he could. After the Eaton affair, Donelson was insecure, self-doubting, and unsure about how to prove himself to Jackson. As he grew older, particularly after the Old Hero died, Donelson became obsessed with convincing himself and others that Jackson had anointed him as his political successor. He was certain that one day others would acknowledge that he was talented and deserved recognition for his loyalty and service to his uncle, his party, and his nation. Surely, that time for recognition has come, even if it also requires acknowledgment of Donelson's many shortcomings.

BIBLIOGRAPHY

MANUSCRIPT COLLECTIONS

HISTORICAL SOCIETY OF PENNSYLVANIA. PHILADELPHIA.

James Buchanan Papers

JAMES D. HOSKINS LIBRARY, UNIVERSITY OF TENNESSEE. KNOXVILLE.

Andrew Jackson Donelson Papers

Tennessee Documentary Project

JOINT UNIVERSITY LIBRARIES. NASHVILLE, TENN.

Andrew Jackson–Jackson Donelson Collection

LADIES' HERMITAGE ASSOCIATION. NASHVILLE, TENN.

Jackson-Donelson Family Papers

LIBRARY OF CONGRESS. WASHINGTON, D.C.

Francis P. Blair–John C. Rives Papers

William W. Corcoran Papers

Andrew Jackson Donelson Papers

Andrew Jackson Papers

Abraham Lincoln Papers

William L. Marcy Papers

Franklin Pierce Papers

James K. Polk Papers

William C. Rives Papers

Nicholas P. Trist Papers

Martin Van Buren Papers

Martin Van Buren Papers, Chadwyck-Healey Collection

Levi Woodbury Papers

MILWAUKEE COUNTY HISTORICAL SOCIETY. MILWAUKEE, WISC.

Arthur Holbrook Collection

SCHOLARLY RESOURCES. WILMINGTON, DEL.

Andrew Jackson Papers

STATE UNIVERSITY OF NEW YORK. OSWEGO.

Millard Fillmore Papers

TENNESSEE STATE LIBRARY AND ARCHIVES. NASHVILLE.

Andrew Jackson Donelson Papers

Bettie M. Donelson Papers

Robert Dyas Collection

NEWSPAPERS

Columbia (Tenn.) Democratic Herald, 1855.

Memphis Argus, 1865.

Memphis Bulletin, 1861.

Memphis Daily Appeal, 1871.

Nashville American Banner, 1856.

Nashville Daily Union, 1850.

Nashville Daily Union and American, 1855–57.

Nashville Dispatch, 1865.

Nashville Patriot, 1857.

Nashville Republican, 1835.

Nashville Republican Banner, 1843–71.

Nashville Union, 1835–44.

Nashville Union and American, 1861.

National Banner and Nashville Whig, 1835–36.

Republican Banner and Nashville Whig, 1850–60.

Washington Daily American Organ, 1855–56.

Washington Daily Union, 1846–56.

Washington Globe, 1833–37.

GOVERNMENT DOCUMENTS

DEPARTMENT OF STATE ARCHIVES, NATIONAL ARCHIVES II, COLLEGE PARK, MD.

Despatches from United States Ministers to the German States and Germany. Federal Government of Germany. Vol. 1.

Despatches from United States Ministers to the German States and Germany. Prussia. Vol. 4.

Despatches from United States Ministers to the German States and Germany. Prussia. Vol. 5.

Diplomatic Instructions. German States. Vol. 14.

LIBRARY OF CONGRESS, WASHINGTON, D.C.

U.S. Congress. *Congressional Globe.* 32d Cong. 1st sess.

———. *Journal of the House of Representatives.* 32d Cong. 1st sess.

———. *Journal of the Senate.* 32d Cong. 1st sess.

———. *Senate Executive Journal.* 32d Congress. 1st Session.

UNITED STATES CENSUS OFFICE, WASHINGTON, D.C.

Seventh Census of the United States: 1850. Washington, D.C.: GPO, 1853.

Seventh Census of the United States: 1850. Slave Inhabitants. Washington, D.C.: GPO, 1853.

Eighth Census of the United States: 1860. Washington, D.C.: GPO, 1864.

Eighth Census of the United States: 1860. Slave Inhabitants. Washington, D.C.: GPO, 1864.

PUBLISHED CORRESPONDENCE, MEMOIRS, AND DIARIES

Ambler, Charles H., ed. *Correspondence of Robert M. T. Hunter, 1826–1876.* In *Annual Report of the American Historical Association for the Year 1916,* vol 2. Washington, D.C.: GPO, 1918.

Barker, Eugene C., ed. *The Writings of Sam Houston.* 8 vols. Austin: University of Texas Press, 1938–43.

Barker, Nancy N., ed. *The French Legation in Texas.* 2 vols. Austin, Tex.: State Historical Association, 1971–3.

Bassett, John Spencer, and J. Franklin Jameson, eds. *Correspondence of Andrew Jackson.* 7 vols. Washington, D.C.: Carnegie Institute of Washington, 1926–35.

Benton, Thomas Hart. *Thirty Year's View; or, A History of the Workings of the American Government for Thirty Years, from 1820 to 1850.* 2 vols. New York: D. Appleton, 1857.

Bergeron, Paul H., ed. *The Papers of Andrew Johnson.* Vol. 9, *September 1865-January 1866.* Knoxville: University of Tennessee Press, 1991.

Boucher, Chauncey S., and Robert P. Brooks, eds. *Correspondence Addressed to John C. Calhoun, 1837–1849.* In *Annual Report of the American Historical Association for the Year 1929.* Washington, D.C.: GPO, 1930.

Commager, Henry Steele, ed. *Documents of American History.* 5th ed. New York: Appleton-Century-Crofts, 1949.

Crist, Lynda Lasswell, and Mary Seaton Dix, eds. *The Papers of Jefferson Davis.* Vol. 5, *1853–1855.* Baton Rouge: Louisiana State University Press, 1985.

Crist, Lynda Lasswell, Mary Seaton Dix, and Richard E. Beringer, eds. *The Papers of Jefferson Davis.* Vol. 4, *1849–1852.* Baton Rouge: Louisiana State University Press, 1983.

Cunningham, Noble, Jr. *The Presidency of James Monroe.* Lawrence: University Press of Kansas, 1995.

Cutler, Wayne, and James P. Cooper Jr., eds. *Correspondence of James K. Polk.* Vol. 7, *January–August 1844.* Nashville: Vanderbilt University Press, 1989.

Cutler, Wayne, and Robert G. Hall II, eds. *Correspondence of James K. Polk.* Vol. 9, *January–June 1845.* Knoxville: University of Tennessee Press, 1996.

Cutler, Wayne, Robert G. Hall II, and Jayne C. DeFiore, eds. *Correspondence of James K. Polk.* Vol. 8, *September–December 1844.* Knoxville: University of Tennessee Press, 1993.

Cutler, Wayne, and Carese M. Parker, eds. *Correspondence of James K. Polk.* Vol. 6, *1842–1843.* Nashville: Vanderbilt University Press, 1983.

Cutler, Wayne, Earl J. Smith, and Carese M. Parker, eds. *Correspondence of James K. Polk.* Vol. 5, *1839–1841.* Nashville: Vanderbilt University Press, 1979.

Duane, William J. *Narrative and Correspondence Concerning the Removal of the Deposits and Occurrences Connected Therewith.* New York: Burt Franklin, [1838].

Eaton, Margaret. *The Autobiography of Peggy Eaton.* New York: Scribner's, 1932.

Fitzpatrick, John C., ed. *The Autobiography of Martin Van Buren.* In *Annual Report of the American Historical Association for the Year 1918,* vol. 2. Washington, D.C.: GPO, 1920.

Freehling, William W., ed. *The Nullification Era: A Documentary Record.* New York: Harper and Row, 1967.

Garrison, George P., ed. *Diplomatic Correspondence of the Republic of Texas.* In *Annual Report of the American Historical Association for the Year of 1907,* vol. 2, pt. 1. Washington, D.C.: GPO, 1908.

———. *Diplomatic Correspondence of the Republic of Texas.* In *Annual Report of the American Historical Association for the Year of 1908,* vol. 2, pts. 1 and 2. Washington, D.C.: GPO, 1911.

Gower, Herschel, and Jack Allen, eds. *Pen and Sword: The Life and Journals of Randal W. McGavock.* Nashville: Tennessee Historical Commission, 1960.

Graf, Leroy P., Ralph W. Haskins, and Patricia P. Clark, eds. *The Papers of Andrew Johnson.* Vol. 2, *1852–1857.* Knoxville: University of Tennessee Press, 1970.

———. *The Papers of Andrew Johnson.* Vol. 5, *1861–1862.* Knoxville: University of Tennessee Press, 1979.

———. *The Papers of Andrew Johnson.* Vol. 6, *1862–1864.* Knoxville: University of Tennessee Press, 1983.

Hemphill, W. Edwin, ed. *The Papers of John C. Calhoun.* Vol. 4, *1819–1820.* Columbia: University of South Carolina Press for the South Caroliniana Society, 1969.

———. *The Papers of John C. Calhoun.* Vol. 5, *1820–1821.* Columbia: University of South Carolina Press for the South Caroliniana Society, 1971.

———. *The Papers of John C. Calhoun.* Vol. 6, *1821–1822.* Columbia: University of South Carolina Press for the South Caroliniana Society, 1972.

Howe, M. A. De Wolfe. *The Life and Letters of George Bancroft.* 2 vols. Port Washington, N.Y.: Kennikat Press, 1971.

Jameson, J. Franklin, ed. *Correspondence of John C. Calhoun.* In *Annual Report of the American Historical Association for the Year 1899,* vol. 2. Washington: GPO, 1900.

Jones, Anson. *Memoranda and Official Correspondence Relating to the Republic of Texas, Its History and Annexation.* New York: D. Appleton, 1859; New York: Arno Press, 1973.

Manning, William R., ed. *Diplomatic Correspondence of the United States: Inter-American Affairs: 1831–1860.* 12 vols. Washington, D.C.: Carnegie Endowment for International Peace, 1935.

McGrane, Reginald, ed. *The Correspondence of Nicholas Biddle Dealing with National Affairs, 1807–1844.* Boston: Houghton Mifflin, 1919.

Moore, Frank. *The Rebellion Record.* 6 vols. New York: G. P. Putnam, 1861–66.

Moore, John Bassett, ed. *The Works of James Buchanan.* 8 vols. Philadelphia: J. B. Lippincott, 1909.

Moser, Harold D., David R. Hoth, Sharon Macpherson, and John H. Reinhold, eds. *The Papers of Andrew Jackson.* Vol. 3, *1814–1815.* Knoxville: University of Tennessee Press, 1991.

Moser, Harold D., and J. Clint Clifft, eds. *The Papers of Andrew Jackson.* Vol. 6, *1825–1828.* Knoxville: University of Tennessee Press, 2002.

Moser, Harold D., David R. Hoth, and George H. Hoemann, eds. *The Papers of Andrew Jackson.* Vol. 4, *1816–1820.* Knoxville: University of Tennessee Press, 1994.

———. *The Papers of Andrew Jackson.* Vol. 5, *1821–1824.* Knoxville: University of Tennessee Press, 1996.

Moser, Harold D., Sharon Macpherson, and Charles F. Bryan Jr., eds. *The Papers of Andrew Jackson.* Vol. 2, *1804–1813.* Knoxville: University of Tennessee Press, 1984.

Phillips, Ulrich B., ed. *Correspondence of Robert Toombs, Alexander H. Stephens, and*

Howell Cobb. In *Annual Report of the American Historical Association for the Year 1911,* vol. 2. Washington, D.C.: GPO, 1913.

Quaife, Milo M., ed. *The Diary of James K. Polk During His Presidency, 1845 to 1849.* 4 vols. Chicago: A. C. McClung, 1910.

Richardson, James D., ed. *The Messages and Papers of the Presidents, 1789–1897.* 10 vols. Washington, D.C.: GPO, 1896–99.

Severance, Frank H., ed. *Millard Fillmore Papers.* 2 vols. Buffalo, N.Y.: Buffalo and Erie County Historical Society, 1975.

Sioussat, St. George L., ed. "Diaries of S. H. Laughlin of Tennessee, 1840, 1843." *Tennessee Historical Magazine* 2 (1916): 43–85.

———. "Letters of James K. Polk to Andrew J. Donelson, 1843–1848." *Tennessee Historical Magazine* 3 (1917): 51–73.

———. "Selected Letters, 1844–1845, from the Donelson Papers." *Tennessee Historical Magazine* 3 (1917): 134–62.

———. "Selected Letters, 1846–1856, from the Donelson Papers." *Tennessee Historical Magazine* 3 (1917): 257–91.

Smith, Margaret Bayard. *The First Forty Years of Washington Society.* Edited by Gaillard Hunt. New York: Scribner's, 1906.

Smith, Sam B., and Harriet Chappell Owsley, eds. *The Papers of Andrew Jackson.* Vol. 1, *1770–1803.* Knoxville: University of Tennessee Press, 1980.

Tyler, Samuel, ed. *Memoir of Roger Brooke Taney, LL.D., Chief Justice of the Supreme Court of the United States.* Baltimore: J. Murphy, 1872.

Wallace, Sarah Agnes, ed. "Opening Days of Jackson's Presidency as Seen in Private Letters." *Tennessee Historical Quarterly* 9 (December 1950): 367–71.

Weaver, Herbert, and Paul Bergeron, eds. *Correspondence of James K. Polk.* Vol. 2, *1833–1834.* Nashville: Vanderbilt University Press, 1972.

Weaver, Herbert, and Wayne Cutler, eds. *Correspondence of James K. Polk.* Vol. 4, *1837–1838.* Nashville: Vanderbilt University Press, 1977.

Weaver, Herbert, and Kermit L. Hall, eds. *Correspondence of James K. Polk.* Vol. 3, *1835–1836.* Nashville: Vanderbilt University Press, 1975.

Wilcox, Mary E. D. *Christmas under Three Flags.* Washington, D.C.: Neale, 1900.

Williams, Amelia W., and Eugene C. Barker, eds. *The Writings of Sam Houston.* 8 vols. Austin: University of Texas Press, 1938–43.

Wilson, Clyde N., Shirley Bright Cook, and Alexander Moore, eds. *The Papers of John C. Calhoun.* Vol. 20, *1844.* Columbia: University of South Carolina Press, 1991.

———. *The Papers of John C. Calhoun.* Vol. 21, *1845.* Columbia: University of South Carolina Press, 1993.

———. *The Papers of John C. Calhoun*. Vol. 25, *1847–1848*. Columbia: University of South Carolina Press, 1999.

SECONDARY SOURCES: BOOKS

Adams, Ephraim D. *British Interests and Activities in Texas, 1838–1846*. Gloucester, Mass.: P. Smith, 1963.

Allgor, Catherine. *Parlor Politics: In Which the Ladies of Washington Help Build a City and a New Government*. Charlottesville: University Press of Virginia, 2000.

Ambler, Charles H. *Thomas Ritchie: A Study in Virginia Politics*. Richmond, Va.: Bell Book and Stationery, 1913.

Ambrose, Stephen E. *Duty, Honor, Country: A History of West Point*. Baltimore: Johns Hopkins University Press, 1966.

Ammon, Harry. *James Monroe: The Quest for National Identity*. New York: McGraw-Hill, 1971.

Anbinder, Tyler. *Nativism and Slavery: The Northern Know Nothings and the Politics of the 1850s*. New York: Oxford University Press, 1992.

Andrew, Rod, Jr. *Long Gray Lines: The Southern Military School Tradition, 1839–1915*. Chapel Hill: University of North Carolina Press, 2001.

Ash, Stephen V. *When the Yankees Came: Conflict and Chaos in the Occupied South, 1861–1865*. Chapel Hill: University of North Carolina Press, 1995.

Atkins, Jonathan M. *Parties, Politics, and the Sectional Conflict in Tennessee, 1832–1861*. Knoxville: University of Tennessee Press, 1997.

Bain, Richard C. *Convention Decisions and Voting Records*. Washington, D.C.: Brookings Institution, 1960.

Baker, Elizabeth F. *Henry Wheaton: 1785–1848*. Philadelphia: University of Pennsylvania Press, 1937.

Baker, Jean H. *Ambivalent Americans: The Know-Nothing Party in Maryland*. Baltimore: Johns Hopkins University Press, 1977.

Bardaglio, Peter W. *Reconstructing the Household: Families, Sex, and the Law in the Nineteenth-Century South*. Chapel Hill: University of North Carolina Press, 1995.

Bartlett, Irving H. *John C. Calhoun: A Biography*. New York: W. W. Norton, 1994.

Bauer, K. Jack. *Zachary Taylor: Soldier, Planter, Statesman of the Old Southwest*. Baton Rouge: Louisiana State University Press, 1985.

Belohlavek, John M. *George Mifflin Dallas, Jacksonian Patrician*. University Park: Pennsylvania State University Press, 1977.

———. *"Let the Eagle Soar!": The Foreign Policy of Andrew Jackson.* Lincoln: University of Nebraska Press, 1985.

Bergeron, Paul H. *Antebellum Politics in Tennessee.* Lexington: University Press of Kentucky, 1982.

———. *The Presidency of James K. Polk.* Lawrence: University Press of Kansas, 1987.

Bergeron, Paul H., Stephen V. Ash, and Jeanette Keith. *Tennesseans and Their History.* Knoxville: University of Tennessee Press, 1999.

Billington, Ray Allen. *The Protestant Crusade, 1800–1860: A Study of the Origins of American Nativism.* New York: Macmillan, 1938; Chicago: Quadrangle Books, 1964.

Booraem, Hendrik. *Young Hickory: The Making of Andrew Jackson.* Dallas: Taylor, 2001.

Bridges, Peter. *Pen of Fire: John Moncure Daniel.* Kent, Ohio: Kent State University Press, 2002.

Bruce, Dickson D., Jr. *Violence and Culture in the Antebellum South.* Austin: University of Texas Press, 1979.

Burke, Pauline Wilcox. *Emily Donelson of Tennessee.* 2 vols. Richmond, Va.: Garrett and Massee, 1941.

———. *Emily Donelson of Tennessee.* Edited by Jonathan M. Atkins. Knoxville: University of Tennessee Press, 2001.

Burstein, Andrew. *The Passions of Andrew Jackson.* New York: Knopf, 2003.

Campbell, Mary E. R. *The Attitude of Tennesseans toward the Union, 1847–1861.* New York: Vantage Press, 1961.

Cantrell, Gregg. *Kenneth and John B. Rayner and the Limits of Southern Dissent.* Urbana: University of Illinois Press, 1993.

Carr, William. *A History of Germany, 1815–1945.* New York: St. Martin's Press, 1969.

Censer, Jane Turner. *North Carolina Planters and Their Children, 1800–1860.* Baton Rouge: Louisiana State University Press, 1984.

Cobb, James C. *The Most Southern Place on Earth: The Mississippi Delta and the Roots of Regional Identity.* New York: Oxford University Press, 1992.

Cole, Arthur C. *The Whig Party in the South.* Washington, D.C.: American Historical Association, 1914.

Cole, Donald B. *A Jackson Man: Amos Kendall and the Rise of American Democracy.* Baton Rouge: Louisiana State University Press, 2004.

———. *Martin Van Buren and the American Political System.* Princeton, N.J.: Princeton University Press, 1984.

———. *The Presidency of Andrew Jackson.* Lawrence: University Press of Kansas, 1993.

Cooper, William J. *The South and the Politics of Slavery, 1828–1856.* Baton Rouge: Louisiana State University Press, 1978.

Coulter, E. Merton. *The South During Reconstruction, 1865–1877.* Baton Rouge: Louisiana State University Press and the Littlefield Fund for Southern History of the University of Texas, 1947.

Craven, Avery O. *The Growth of Southern Nationalism, 1848–1861.* Baton Rouge: Louisiana State University Press and the Littlefield Fund for Southern History of the University of Texas, 1953.

Curtis, James C. *Andrew Jackson and the Search for Vindication.* Boston: HarperCollins, 1976.

———. *The Fox at Bay: Martin Van Buren and the Presidency, 1837–1841.* Lexington: University Press of Kentucky, 1970.

Daniels, Jonathan. *The Randolphs of Virginia.* Garden City, N.Y.: Doubleday, 1972.

Davis, William C. *Rhett: The Turbulent Life and Times of a Fire-Eater.* Columbia: University of South Carolina Press, 2001.

Donovan, Herbert D. A. *The Barnburners: A Study of the Internal Movements in the Political History of New York State and of the Resulting Changes in Political Affiliation, 1830–1852.* New York: New York University Press, 1925.

Durham, Walter T. *Daniel Smith: Frontier Statesman.* Gallatin, Tenn.: Sumner County Library Board, 1976.

Ellis, Richard E. *The Union at Risk: Jacksonian Democracy, States' Rights, and the Nullification Crisis.* New York: Oxford University Press, 1987.

Eyck, Frank. *The Frankfurt Parliament, 1848–49.* New York: St. Martin's Press, 1968.

Feldberg, Michael. *The Turbulent Era: Riot and Disorder in Jacksonian America.* New York: Oxford University Press, 1980.

Fleming, Thomas J. *West Point: The Men and Times of the United States Military Academy.* New York: William Morrow, 1969.

Foner, Eric. *Reconstruction: America's Unfinished Revolution, 1863–1877.* New York: Harper and Row, 1988.

Fowler, Dorothy G. *The Cabinet Politician: The Postmasters General, 1829–1909.* New York: Columbia University Press, 1943.

Fox-Genovese, Elizabeth. *Within the Plantation Household: Black and White Women of the Old South.* Chapel Hill. University of North Carolina Press, 1988.

Freehling, William W. *Prelude to Civil War: The Nullification Controversy in South Carolina, 1816–1836.* New York: Harper and Row, 1966.

———. *The Road to Disunion.* Vol. 1, *Secessionists at Bay, 1776–1854.* New York: Oxford University Press, 1990.

Friend, Llerena. *Sam Houston: The Great Designer.* Austin: University of Texas Press, 1954.

Gara, Larry. *The Presidency of Franklin Pierce.* Lawrence: University Press of Kansas, 1991.

Gienapp, William E. *The Origins of the Republican Party, 1852–1856.* New York: Oxford University Press, 1987.

Glover, Lorri. *All Our Relations: Blood Ties and Emotional Bonds among the Early South Carolina Gentry.* Baltimore: Johns Hopkins University Press, 2000.

Gohmann, Sister Mary de Lourdes. *Political Nativism in Tennessee to 1860.* Washington, D.C.: Catholic University of America, 1938.

Goodstein, Anita Shafer. *Nashville, 1780–1860: From Frontier to City.* Gainesville: University Press of Florida, 1989.

Greenberg, Kenneth S. *Honor and Slavery: Lies, Duels, Noses, Masks, Dressing as a Woman, Gifts, Strangers, Humanitarianism, Death, Slave Rebellions, the Proslavery Argument, Baseball, Hunting, and Gambling in the Old South.* Princeton, N.J.: Princeton University Press, 1996.

Haley, James L. *Sam Houston.* Norman: University of Oklahoma Press, 2002.

Hamerow, Theodore S. *Restoration, Revolution, Reaction: Economics and Politics in Germany, 1815–1870.* Princeton, N.J.: Princeton University Press, 1958.

Hamilton, Holman. *Prologue to Conflict: The Crisis and Compromise of 1850.* Lexington: University of Kentucky Press, 1964.

Hammond, Bray. *Banks and Politics in America: From the Revolution to the Civil War.* Princeton, N.J.: Princeton University Press, 1957.

Haynes, Sam W. *James K. Polk and the Expansionist Impulse.* New York: Longman, 1997.

Henderson, William Otto. *The Zollverein.* London: Frank Cass, 1959.

Hietala, Thomas R. *Manifest Design: Anxious Aggrandizement in Late Jacksonian America.* Ithaca, N.Y.: Cornell University Press, 1985.

Hofstadter, Richard. *The Paranoid Style in American Politics and Other Essays.* New York: Random House, 1952; Vintage Books, 1967.

Holborn, Hajo. *A History of Modern Germany, 1840–1945.* New York: Knopf, 1969.

Holt, Michael F. *The Political Crisis of the 1850s.* New York: John Wiley, 1978; W. W. Norton, 1983.

———. *The Rise and Fall of the American Whig Party: Jacksonian Politics and the Onset of the Civil War.* New York: Oxford University Press, 1999.

Hughes, Nathaniel Cheairs, Jr., and Roy P. Stonesifer. *The Life and Wars of Gideon J. Pillow.* Chapel Hill: University of North Carolina Press, 1993.

Hunt, Charles H. *Life of Edward Livingston.* New York: D. Appleton, 1864.

Huston, James L. *The Panic of 1857 and the Coming of the Civil War.* Baton Rouge: Louisiana State University Press, 1987.

Jabour, Anya. *Marriage in the Early Republic: Elizabeth and William Wirt and the Companionate Ideal.* Baltimore: Johns Hopkins University Press, 1998.

James, Marquis. *Portrait of a President.* Indianapolis: Bobbs-Merrill, 1937.

Jennings, Thelma. *The Nashville Convention: Southern Movement for Unity, 1848–1850.* Memphis, Tenn.: Memphis State University Press, 1980.

Jones, Peter. *The 1848 Revolutions.* Harlow, U.K.: Longman Group, 1991; New York: Addison Wesley Longman, 1998.

Kerber, Linda K. *Women of the Republic: Intellect and Ideology in Revolutionary America.* Chapel Hill: University of North Carolina Press for the Institute of Early American History and Culture, 1980.

Klein, Philip Shriver. *President James Buchanan: A Biography.* University Park: Pennsylvania State University Press, 1962.

Larkin, Jack. *The Reshaping of Everyday Life, 1790–1840.* New York: Harper and Row, 1988.

Latner, Richard B. *The Presidency of Andrew Jackson: White House Politics, 1829–1837.* Athens: University of Georgia Press, 1979.

Marszalek, John F. *The Petticoat Affair: Manners, Mutiny, and Sex in Andrew Jackson's White House.* New York: Free Press, 1997.

———. *Sherman: A Soldier's Passion for Order.* New York: Free Press, 1993; Vintage Books, 1994.

McCormac, Eugene I. *James K. Polk: A Political Biography.* Berkeley and Los Angeles: University of California Press, 1922.

McCormick, Richard P. *The Second American Party System: Party Formation in the Jacksonian Era.* Chapel Hill: University of North Carolina Press, 1966.

McCoy, Charles A. *Polk and the Presidency.* Austin: University of Texas Press, 1960.

McCoy, Drew R. *The Elusive Republic: Political Economy in Jeffersonian America.* Chapel Hill: University of North Carolina Press for the Institute of Early American History and Culture, 1980.

McCurry, Stephanie. *Masters of Small Worlds: Yeoman Households, Gender Relations, and the Political Culture of the Antebellum South Carolina Low Country.* New York: Oxford University Press, 1995.

McPherson, James M. *Battle Cry of Freedom: The Civil War Era.* New York: Ballantine Books, 1989.

Mooney, Chase C. *Slavery in Tennessee.* Bloomington: Indiana University Press, 1957.

Nevins, Allan. *Ordeal of the Union: Fruits of Manifest Destiny, 1847–1852.* New York: Scribner's, 1947.

Nichols, Roy F. *The Democratic Machine, 1850–1854.* New York: Longman, Green, 1923.

———. *Franklin Pierce: Young Hickory of the Granite Hills.* Philadelphia: University of Pennsylvania Press, 1931.

Nipperdey, Thomas. *Germany from Napoleon to Bismarck, 1800–1866.* Translated by Daniel Nolan. Princeton, N.J.: Princeton University Press, 1996.

Niven, John C. *John C. Calhoun and the Price of Union: A Biography.* Baton Rouge: Louisiana State University Press, 1988.

———. *Martin Van Buren: The Romantic Age of American Politics.* New York: Oxford University Press, 1983.

Norton, Mary Beth. *Liberty's Daughters: The Revolutionary Experience of American Women, 1750–1800.* New York: Little, Brown, 1980.

Oakes, James. *The Ruling Race: A History of American Slaveholders.* New York: Knopf, 1982; New York: Vintage, 1983.

Ohrt, Wallace. *Defiant Peacemaker: Nicholas Trist in the Mexican War.* College Station: Texas A&M University Press, 1997.

Overdyke, W. Darrell. *The Know-Nothing Party in the South.* Baton Rouge: Louisiana State University Press, 1950.

Owsley, Frank L., Jr., and Gene A. Smith. *Filibusters and Expansionists: Jeffersonian Manifest Destiny, 1800–1821.* Tuscaloosa: University of Alabama Press, 1997.

Paludan, Phillip Shaw. *The Presidency of Abraham Lincoln.* Lawrence: University Press of Kansas, 1994.

Parks, Joseph H. *Felix Grundy: Champion of Democracy.* Baton Rouge: Louisiana State University Press, 1940.

———. *John Bell of Tennessee.* Baton Rouge: Louisiana State University Press, 1950.

Parish, Peter J. *Slavery: History and Historians.* Boulder, Colo.: Westview, 1989.

Parton, James. *Life of Andrew Jackson.* 3 vols. New York: Mason Brothers, 1861.

Peter, Robert, and Johanna Peter. *Transylvania University: Its Origin, Rise, Decline, and Fall.* Louisville: Filson Club Historical Society, 1896.

Peterson, Norma Lois. *The Presidencies of William Henry Harrison and John Tyler.* Lawrence: University Press of Kansas, 1989.

Pinson, Koppel S. *Modern Germany: Its History and Civilization.* New York: Macmillan, 1954.

Pletcher, David M. *The Diplomacy of Annexation: Texas, Oregon, and the Mexican War.* Columbia: University of Missouri Press, 1973.

Potter, David M. *The Impending Crisis, 1848–1861.* Edited and completed by Don E. Fehrenbacher. New York: Harper and Row, 1976.

Price, Glenn W. *Origins of the War with Mexico: The Polk-Stockton Intrigue.* Austin: University of Texas Press, 1967.

Ramm, Agatha. *Germany, 1789–1919: A Political History.* London: Methuen, 1967.

Ratner, Lorman. *Andrew Jackson and His Tennessee Lieutenants: A Study in Political Culture.* Westport, Conn.: Greenwood Press, 1997.

Rayback, Robert J. *Millard Fillmore: Biography of a President.* Buffalo, N.Y.: Buffalo Historical Society, 1959.

Reichard, Richard W. *Crippled from Birth: German Social Democracy, 1844–1870.* Ames: Iowa State University Press, 1969.

Register of Graduates and Former Cadets of the United States Military Academy. New York: West Point Alumni Foundation, 1953.

Remini, Robert V. *Andrew Jackson and the Bank War.* New York: W. W. Norton, 1967.

———. *Andrew Jackson and the Course of American Democracy, 1833–1845.* New York: Harper and Row, 1984.

———. *Andrew Jackson and the Course of American Empire, 1767–1821.* New York: Harper and Row, 1977.

———. *Andrew Jackson and the Course of American Freedom, 1822–1832.* New York: Harper and Row, 1981.

———. *Andrew Jackson and His Indian Wars.* New York: Viking Penguin, 2001.

———. *Daniel Webster: The Man and His Time.* New York: W. W. Norton, 1997.

———. *The Election of Andrew Jackson.* New York: J. B. Lippincott, 1963.

———. *Henry Clay: Statesman for the Union.* New York: W. W. Norton, 1991.

———. *The Legacy of Andrew Jackson: Essays on Democracy, Indian Removal, and Slavery.* Baton Rouge: Louisiana State University Press, 1988.

Richards, Leonard L. *"Gentlemen of Property and Standing": Anti-Abolition Mobs in Jacksonian America.* New York: Oxford University Press, 1970.

Satterfield, Robert B. *Andrew Jackson Donelson: Jackson's Confidant and Political Heir.* Bowling Green, Ky.: Hickory Tales, 2000.

Scarborough, William B. *Masters of the Big House: Elite Slaveholders of the Mid-Nineteenth-Century South.* Baton Rouge: Louisiana State University Press, 2003.

Sellers, Charles G., Jr. *James K. Polk, Continentalist: 1843–1846.* Princeton, N.J.: Princeton University Press, 1966.

———. *James K. Polk, Jacksonian: 1795–1843.* Princeton, N.J.: Princeton University Press, 1957.

Sheehan, James J. *German History, 1770–1866.* Oxford: Clarendon Press, 1989.

Silbey, Joel H. *Storm over Texas: The Annexation Controversy and the Road to the Civil War.* Oxford: Oxford University Press, 2005.

Williams, Wirt A., ed. *History of Bolivar County, Mississippi.* Jackson, Miss.: Hederman Brothers, 1948.

Slaughter, Thomas P. *Bloody Dawn: The Christiana Riot and Racial Violence in the Antebellum North.* New York: Oxford University Press, 1991.

Sloan, Herbert E. *Principle and Interest: Thomas Jefferson and the Problem of Debt.* Oxford: Oxford University Press, 1995.

Smith, Elbert B. *Francis Preston Blair.* New York: Free Press, 1980.

———. *Magnificent Missourian: The Life of Thomas Hart Benton.* Philadelphia: J. B. Lippincott, 1958.

———. *The Presidencies of Zachary Taylor and Millard Fillmore.* Lawrence: University Press of Kansas, 1988.

———. *The Presidency of James Buchanan.* Lawrence: University Press of Kansas, 1975.

Smith, Justin H. *The Annexation of Texas.* New York: Barnes and Noble, 1941.

Smith, William Ernest. *The Francis Preston Blair Family in Politics.* 2 vols. New York: Macmillan, 1933.

Spencer, Ivor Debenham. *The Victor and the Spoils: A Life of William L. Marcy.* Providence, R.I.: Brown University Press, 1959.

Stadelmann, Rudolph. *Social and Political History of the German 1848 Revolution.* 2d. ed. Translated by James G. Chastain. Athens: Ohio University Press, 1975.

Stearns, Peter N. *1848: The Revolutionary Tide in Europe.* New York: W. W. Norton, 1974.

Stegmaier, Mark J. *Texas, New Mexico, and the Compromise of 1850: Boundary Dispute and Sectional Crisis.* Kent, Ohio: Kent State University Press, 1996.

Stowe, Steven M. *Intimacy and Power in the Old South: Ritual in the Lives of the Planters.* Baltimore: Johns Hopkins University Press, 1987.

Summers, Mark W. *The Plundering Generation: Corruption and the Crisis of the Union, 1849–1861.* New York: Oxford University Press, 1987.

Swisher, Carl Brent. *Roger B. Taney.* New York: Macmillan, 1935.

Temin, Peter. *The Jacksonian Economy.* New York: W. W. Norton, 1969.

Trefousse, Hans L. *Andrew Johnson: A Biography.* New York: W. W. Norton, 1989.

Valentin, Veit. *1848: Chapters of German History.* London: George Allen and Unwin,

1940. Reprint, translated by Ethel Talbot Scheffauer, Hamden, Conn.: Archon Books, 1965.

Wallner, Peter. *Franklin Pierce: New Hampshire's Favorite Son.* Concord, N.H.: Plaidswede Press, 2004.

Watson, Harry L. *Liberty and Power: The Politics of Jacksonian America.* New York: Hill and Wang, 1990.

Werner, M. R. *Tammany Hall.* Garden City, N.Y.: Doubleday, Doran, 1928.

White, Leonard D. *The Jacksonians: A Study in Administrative History, 1829–1861.* New York: Macmillan, 1954.

Wilson, Major L. *The Presidency of Martin Van Buren.* Lawrence: University Press of Kansas, 1984.

Winders, Richard Bruce. *Crisis in the Southwest: The United States, Mexico, and the Struggle over Texas.* Wilmington, Del.: Scholary Resources, 2002.

Windrow, John E., ed. *Peabody and Alfred Leland Crabb: The Story of Peabody as Reflected in Selected Writings of Alfred Leland Crabb.* Nashville: Williams Press, 1977.

Wood, Gordon. *The Creation of the American Republic, 1776–1787.* Chapel Hill: University of North Carolina Press, 1969; New York: W. W. Norton, 1972.

Wyatt-Brown, Bertram. *Southern Honor: Ethics and Behavior in the Old South.* New York: Oxford University Press, 1982.

SECONDARY SOURCES: ARTICLES

Abernethy, Thomas P. "The Origin of the Whig Party in Tennessee." *Mississippi Valley Historical Review* 12 (March 1926): 504–22.

Atkins, Jonathan M. "The Presidential Candidacy of Hugh Lawson White in Tennessee, 1832–1836." *Journal of Southern History* 58 (February 1992): 27–56.

Barker, Eugene C. "The Annexation of Texas." *Southwestern Historical Quarterly* 50 (July 1946): 49–74.

Basch, Norma. "Equity vs. Equality: Emerging Concepts of Women's Political Status in the Age of Jackson." *Journal of the Early Republic* 3 (Fall 1983): 297–318.

Bean, William G. "An Aspect of Know Nothingism—The Immigrant and Slavery." *South Atlantic Quarterly* 23 (October 1924): 319–34.

———. "Puritan Versus Celt." *New England Quarterly* 7 (March 1934): 70–89.

Bergeron, Paul H. "James K. Polk and the Jacksonian Press in Tennessee." *Tennessee Historical Quarterly* 41 (Fall 1982): 257–77.

———. "Tennessee's Response to the Nullification Process." *Journal of Southern History* 39 (February 1973): 23–44.

Brown, Thomas. "From Old Hickory to Sly Fox: The Routinization of Charisma in the Early Democratic Party." *Journal of the Early Republic* 11 (Fall 1991): 339–70.

———. "The Miscegenation of Richard Mentor Johnson as an Issue in the National Election Campaign of 1835–1836." *Civil War History* 39 (March 1993): 5–30.

Bryan, Charles Faulkner, Jr. "The Prodigal Nephew: Andrew Jackson Donelson and the Eaton Affair." *East Tennessee Historical Society's Publications* 50 (1978): 92–112.

Campbell, Mary R. "The Significance of the Unionist Victory in the Election of February 9, 1861 in Tennessee." *East Tennessee Historical Society's Publications* 14 (1942): 11–30.

Cantrell, Greg. "Southerner and Nativist: Kenneth Rayner and the Ideology of 'Americanism.'" *North Carolina Historical Review* 68 (April 1992): 131–47.

Carlson, A. Cheree. "The Rhetoric of the Know-Nothing Party: Nativism as a Response to the Rhetorical Situation." *Southern Communication Journal* 54 (Summer 1989): 364–83.

Carman, Harry J., and Reinhard H. Luthin. "Some Aspects of the Know-Nothing Movement Reconsidered." *South Atlantic Quarterly* 39 (April 1940): 213–34.

Chambers, William N. "Election of 1840." In *History of American Presidential Elections,* edited by Arthur M. Schlesinger and Fred L. Israel, 1:643–90. New York: Chelsea House, 1971.

Crabb, Alfred L. "James Priestley, Pioneer School Master." *Tennessee Historical Quarterly* 12 (June 1953): 129–34.

Dahl, Curtis. "The Clergyman, the Hussy, and Old Hickory: Ezra Stiles Ely and the Peggy Eaton Affair." *Journal of Presbyterian History* 52 (Summer 1974): 137–55.

Davis, David Brion. "Some Themes of Counter-Subversion: An Analysis of Anti-Masonic, Anti-Catholic, and Anti-Mormon Literature." *Mississippi Valley Historical Review* 47 (September 1960): 205–24.

Doherty, Herbert J., Jr. "Andrew Jackson vs. the Spanish Governor." *Florida Historical Quarterly* 34 (October 1955): 142–58.

Edwards, Laura F. "Law, Domestic Violence, and the Limits of Patriarchal Authority in the Antebellum South." *Journal of Southern History* 65 (November 1999): 733–70.

Galloway, Linda Bennett. "Andrew Jackson, Jr." Pt. 2. *Tennessee Historical Quarterly* 9 (December 1950): 306–43.

Garrison, George P. "The First Stage of the Movement for the Annexation of Texas." *American Historical Review* 10 (October 1904): 72–96.

Grant, C. L. "The Public Career of Cave Johnson." *Tennessee Historical Quarterly* 10 (September 1951): 195–223.

Green, Fletcher M. "On Tour with President Jackson." *New England Quarterly* 36 (June 1963): 209–28.

Hamerow, Theodore S. "The Elections to the Frankfurt Parliament." *Journal of Modern History* 33 (March 1961): 15–32.

Hamilton, Holman. "Election of 1848." In *History of American Presidential Elections,* edited by Arthur M. Schlesinger and Fred L. Israel, 2:865–96. New York: Chelsea House, 1971.

Harlan, Louis R. "Public Career of William Berkeley Lewis." Pt. 1. *Tennessee Historical Quarterly* 7 (March 1948): 3–37.

———. "Public Career of William Berkeley Lewis." Pt. 2. *Tennessee Historical Quarterly* 7 (June 1948): 118–51.

Hay, Robert P. "The Case for Andrew Jackson in 1824: Eaton's *Wyoming Letters.*" *Tennessee Historical Quarterly* 29 (Summer 1970): 139–51.

———. "'The Presidential Question': Letters to Southern Editors, 1823–24." *Tennessee Historical Quarterly* 31 (Summer 1972): 170–86.

Henry, J. Milton. "The Revolution in Tennessee, February, 1861, to June, 1861." *Tennessee Historical Quarterly* 18 (June 1959): 99–119.

Holt, Michael F. "The Antimasonic and Know Nothing Parties." In *History of United States Political Parties,* edited by Arthur Schlesinger, 1:575–620. New York: Chelsea House, 1973.

———. "The Politics of Impatience: The Origins of Know Nothingism." *Journal of American History* 60 (September 1973): 309–31.

Hopkins, James F. "Election of 1824." In *History of American Presidential Elections,* edited by Arthur M. Schlesinger and Fred L. Israel, 1:349–81. New York: Chelsea House, 1971.

Huston, Reeve. "The 'Little Magician' After the Show: Martin Van Buren, Country Gentleman and Progressive Farmer, 1841–1862." *New York History* 85 (Spring 2004): 93–121.

Jaenicke, Douglas W. "The Jacksonian Integration of Parties into the Constitutional System." *Political Science Quarterly* 101 (Spring 1986): 85–108.

Knupfer, Peter. "James Buchanan, the Election of 1860, and the Demise of Jacksonian Politics." In *James Buchanan and the Political Crisis of the 1850s,* edited by Michael J. Birkner, 146–70. Selinsgrove, Pa.: Susquehanna University Press, 1996.

Kruman, Mark W. "The Second American Party System and the Transformation of Revolutionary Republicanism." *Journal of the Early Republic* 12 (Winter 1992): 509–37.

Latner, Richard B. "The Eaton Affair Reconsidered." *Tennessee Historical Quarterly* 36 (Fall 1977): 330–51.

———. "The Kitchen Cabinet and Andrew Jackson's Advisory System." *Journal of American History* 65 (September 1978): 367–88.

———. "The Nullification Crisis and Republican Subversion." *Journal of Southern History* 43 (February 1977): 19–38.

Lawrence, Stephen S. "Tulip Grove: Neighbor to the Hermitage." *Tennessee Historical Quarterly* 26 (Spring 1967): 3–22.

Longaker, Richard P. "Was Jackson's Kitchen Cabinet a Cabinet?" *Mississippi Valley Historical Quarterly* 44 (June 1957): 94–108.

Lowe, Gabriel L., Jr. "John Eaton, Jackson's Campaign Manager." *Tennessee Historical Quarterly* 11 (June 1952): 99–147.

Lufkin, Charles L. "Secession and Coercion in Tennessee, the Spring of 1861." *Tennessee Historical Quarterly* 50 (Summer 1991): 98–109.

Marshall, Lynn. "The Authorship of Jackson's Bank Veto Message." *Mississippi Valley Historical Review* 50 (December 1963): 466–77.

———. "The Strange Stillbirth of the Whig Party." *American Historical Review* 72 (January 1967): 445–68.

Mayo, Edward L. "Republicanism, Antipartyism, and Jacksonian Party Politics: A View from the Nation's Capital." *American Quarterly* 31 (Spring 1979): 3–20.

McCormick, Richard P. "Was There a 'Whig Strategy' in 1836?" *Journal of the Early Republic* 4 (Spring 1984): 47–70.

McFaul, John M. "Expediency vs. Morality: Jacksonian Politics and Slavery." *Journal of American History* 62 (June 1975): 24–39.

Mering, John V. "The Slave-State Constitutional Unionists and the Politics of Consensus." *Journal of Southern History* 43 (August 1977): 395–410.

Middleton, Annie. "Donelson's Mission to Texas in Behalf of Annexation." *Southwestern Historical Quarterly* 24 (April 1921): 247–91.

———. "The Texas Convention of 1845." *Southwestern Historical Quarterly* 25 (July 1921): 26–62.

Miles, Edwin A. "After John Marshall's Decision: *Worcester v. Georgia* and the Nullification Crisis." *Journal of Southern History* 39 (November 1973): 519–44.

———. "The First People's Inaugural—1829." *Tennessee Historical Quarterly* 37 (Fall 1978): 293–307.

Miles, Loyce Braswell. "Duncan, Mississippi: The Origins and Survival of a Town." *Journal of the Bolivar County Historical Society* 5–7 (March 1983): 11–57.

Moore, Powell. "The Political Background of the Revolt against Jackson in Tennessee." *East Tennessee Historical Society's Publications* 4 (1930): 45–66.

———. "The Revolt against Jackson in Tennessee, 1835–1836." *Journal of Southern History* 2 (August 1936): 335–59.

Morison, Elting. "Election of 1860." In *History of American Presidential Elections,* edited by Arthur M. Schlesinger and Fred L. Israel, 2:1097–1127. New York: Chelsea House, 1971.

Morrison, Michael A. "Martin Van Buren, the Democracy, and the Partisan Politics of Texas Annexation." *Journal of Southern History* 61 (November 1995): 695–724.

Murphy, James Edward. "Jackson and the Tennessee Opposition." *Tennessee Historical Quarterly* 30 (Spring 1971): 50–69.

Narrett, David E. "A Choice of Destiny: Immigration Policy, Slavery, and the Annexation of Texas." *Southwestern Historical Quarterly* 100 (January 1997): 270–302.

Nichols, Roy F., and Philip S. Klein. "Election of 1856." In *History of American Presidential Elections,* edited by Arthur M. Schlesinger and Fred L. Israel, 2:1007–45. New York: Chelsea House, 1971.

Nichols, Roy F., and Jeannette Nichols. "Election of 1852." In *History of American Presidential Elections,* edited by Arthur M. Schlesinger and Fred L. Israel, 2:921–50. New York: Chelsea House, 1971.

Owsley, Harriet Chappell. "Andrew Jackson and His Ward, Andrew Jackson Donelson." *Tennessee Historical Quarterly* 41 (Summer 1982): 124–39.

———. "The Marriage of Rachel Donelson." *Tennessee Historical Quarterly* 36 (Winter 1977): 479–92.

Parks, Joseph H. "A Confederate Trade Center under Federal Occupation: Memphis, 1862–1865." *Journal of Southern History* 7 (August 1941): 289–314.

———. "John Bell and the Compromise of 1850." *Journal of Southern History* 9 (August 1943): 328–56.

———. "Memphis under Military Rule, 1862 to 1865." *East Tennessee Historical Society's Publications* 14 (1942): 31–58.

Pukl, Joseph M., Jr. "James K. Polk's Congressional Campaigns, 1829–1833." *Tennessee Historical Quarterly* 40 (Winter 1981): 348–65.

———. "James K. Polk's Congressional Campaigns of 1835 and 1837." *Tennessee Historical Quarterly* 41 (Summer 1982): 105–23.

Remini, Robert V. "Election of 1832." In *History of American Presidential Elections,* edited by Arthur M. Schlesinger and Fred L. Israel, 1:495–516. New York: Chelsea House, 1971.

Roberts, Timothy M. "'Revolutions Have Become the Bloody Toy of the Multitude': European Revolutions, the South, and the Crisis of 1850." *Journal of the Early Republic* 25 (Summer 2005): 259–83.

Roeckell, Lelia M. "Bonds over Bondage: British Opposition to the Annexation of Texas." *Journal of the Early Republic* 19 (Summer 1999): 257–78.

Satterfield, Robert B. "The Uncertain Trumpet of the Tennessee Jacksonians." *Tennessee Historical Quarterly* 26 (Spring 1967): 79–96.

Scheiber, Harry N. "The Pet Banks in Jacksonian Politics and Finance, 1833–1841." *Journal of Economic History* 23 (June 1963): 196–214.

Schroeder, John H. "Annexation or Independence: The Texas Issue in American Politics, 1836–1845." *Southwestern Historical Quarterly* 89 (October 1985): 137–64.

Sellers, Charles G., Jr. "Election of 1844." In *History of American Presidential Elections,* edited by Arthur M. Schlesinger and Fred L. Israel, 1:745–861. New York: Chelsea House, 1971.

Shade, William G. "'The Most Delicate and Exciting Topics': Martin Van Buren, Slavery, and the Election of 1836." *Journal of the Early Republic* 18 (Fall 1998): 459–84.

Silbey, Joel H. "Election of 1836." In *History of American Presidential Elections,* edited by Arthur M. Schlesinger and Fred L. Israel, 1:577–600. New York: Chelsea House, 1971.

Sioussat, St. George L. "Tennessee, the Compromise of 1850, and the Nashville Convention." *Mississippi Valley Historical Review* 2 (December 1915): 313–47.

Spence, Richard Douglas. "John Donelson and the Opening of the Old Southwest." *Tennessee Historical Quarterly* 50 (Fall 1991): 157–72.

Thweatt, John H. "James Priestley, Classical Scholar of the Old South." *Tennessee Historical Quarterly* 39 (Winter 1980): 423–39.

Timberlake, Richard H., Jr. "The Specie Circular and Distribution of Surplus." *Journal of Political Economy* 68 (April 1960): 109–17.

———. "The Specie Circular and Sales of Public Lands: A Comment." *Journal of Economic History* 25 (September 1965): 414–6.

Wallace, Michael. "Changing Concepts of Party in the United States: New York, 1815–1828." *American Historical Review* 74 (December 1968): 453–91.

Williams, Frank W., Jr. "Samuel Hervey Laughlin, Polk's Political Handyman." *Tennessee Historical Quarterly* 24 (Winter 1965): 356–92.

Wilson, Major L. "The 'Country' versus the 'Court': A Republican Consensus and Party Debate in the Bank War." *Journal of the Early Republic* 15 (Winter 1995): 619–47.

Wood, Kirsten. "'One Woman So Dangerous to Public Morals': Gender and Power in the Eaton Affair." *Journal of the Early Republic* 17 (Summer 1997): 237–76.

Wyatt-Brown, Bertram. "Andrew Jackson's Honor." *Journal of the Early Republic* 17 (Spring 1997): 1–36.

THESES AND DISSERTATIONS

Bladek, John David. "America for Americans: The Southern Know Nothing Party and the Politics of Nativism, 1854–1856." Ph.D. diss., University of Washington, 1998.

Kamper, Anna Alice. "A Social and Economic History of Ante-Bellum Bolivar County, Mississippi." Master's thesis, University of Alabama, 1942.

May, Arthur J. "Contemporary American Opinion of the Mid-Century Revolutions in Central Europe." Ph.D. diss., University of Pennsylvania, 1927.

Pigott, Sister M. Perpetua. "Emily Donelson and the Eaton Affair." Master's thesis, Catholic University of America, 1948.

Pike, William Joseph. "The Public Life of Andrew Jackson Donelson." Master's thesis, Southwest Texas State University, 1988.

Satterfield, Robert B. "Andrew Jackson Donelson: A Moderate Nationalist Jacksonian." Ph.D. diss., Johns Hopkins University, 1961.

———. "The Early Public Career of Andrew Jackson Donelson, 1799–1846." Master's thesis, Vanderbilt University, 1948.

Stabler, John Burgess. "A History of the Constitutional Union Party: A Tragic Failure." Ph.D. diss., Columbia University, 1954.

Walters, Frederick Ray. "The Donelson Mission to the German Federal Government." Master's thesis, American University, 1964.

Woodard, David E. "Sectionalism, Politics, and Foreign Policy: Duff Green and Southern Economic and Political Expansion, 1825–1865." Ph.D. diss., University of Minnesota, 1996.

REFERENCE WORKS

Biographical Directory of the United States Congress, 1774–1989. Washington, D.C.: GPO, 1989.

West, Carroll Van, ed. *The Tennessee Encyclopedia of History and Culture.* Nashville: Rutledge Hill Press, 1998.

INDEX